# Democrats and the American Idea

# Democrats and the American Idea

## A Bicentennial Appraisal

Peter B. Kovler
Editor



Center for National Policy Press
Washington, D.C.

Distributed by
National Book Network
4720 Boston Way
Lanham, MD 20706

European Distribution by
Eurospan
3 Henrietta Street
London WC2E 8LU England


Printed in the United States of America
British Cataloging in Publication Information Available

**Library of Congress Cataloguing-in-Publication Data**

Democrats and the American Idea : a bicentennial appraisal
editor, Peter B. Kovler : afterword by Arthur M. Schlesinger, Jr.
p. cm.

1. Democratic Party (U.S.)—History. I. Kovler, Peter B.
JK2316.D46 1992
324.2736—DC20 92-31798

ISBN 0-944237-36-3 (cloth: alk paper)

All Center for National Policy Press books are produced on acid-free
paper which exceeds the minimum standards set by the National
Historical Publications and Records Commission

# Contents

**Part Four—The Rise and Decline of the New Deal Majority: 1930s-1990s**



**Part Five—Bicentennial Appraisals**

# Preface

The concept of "a vision" is now taking a sort of rhetorical center stage in our political theater. Those who wish to lead our country clash on the matter of who can see ahead, what they can see, and even how they see us getting there. I would contend—and it is my hope that our readers will agree—that it is equally essential to have a sense of where we have been. Without the perspective of memory, of a knowledge of the past, and the inspiration it can give us, our view ahead will be poorly grounded—leading to the folly that destroys all people who believe they are the first to undertake great efforts.

The underlying concept of this book is that memory of what has happened to and within the Democratic party can make current political practitioners a little more competent, even a little wiser. This idea is partially an adaptation of a process most prominently advocated by Richard Neustadt and Ernest May.[1] In brief, they assert the importance of a kind of applied history. One can use or misuse historical lessons, and the way we look at the particular lessons we choose to draw from the past will certainly influence how we look at current challenges. For the post-World War II generation now moving into positions of influence in both major political parties, this means that care must be taken in deciding which "historic events" of the nineteenth and twentieth centuries to deem relevant—and which to cast aside.

Making history seem significant to people who are—in Teddy Roosevelt's unmatchable phrase—"in the arena," is not an easy job. The lives of legislators and their assistants, journalists, administration officials, staffers of non-governmental organizations, and others in the world of politics move rapidly. Trying to persuade such people to stop a moment to reflect is a challenge.

But there are occasions which offer small but important opportunities in this sphere and one is an anniversary—in this case the 200th anniversary of the founding of the Democratic party in May of 1792. Over the years I have found that major anniversaries, or birthdays, have an interesting effect on people. Busy individuals who never exhibit any great interest in history are suddenly inordinately curious about the hows and whys of the past when they are reminded that the time period we're in is the anniversary of something enduring.

Beyond policy-makers, pundits, and politicians, our other audience for this book, we hope, will be students of politics and history and other citizens who still believe that politics does make a difference. Among the latter are many individuals whose day to day lives do not demand a knowledge of history. Nonetheless, we are predisposed to believe that a democracy is strengthened by an electorate which possesses historical memory. Luckily, current events have made the story of the Democratic party relevant to a much wider group of people than just "people in the arena." The few among us who still vividly recall the nation's emergence from the Great Depression, its victory in World War II, and the years of Democratic party dominance of national politics, remember a time when the Democrats were the party of new ideas, reform, and change. Many citizens who came of age during the late 1970s and the 1980s came to view the Republican party as the vehicle of new thinking. Now, with the economic good times and the ideological steam evaporating from the Reagan revolution, much of America is looking for a new engine of change. As the nation once more examines the Democratic party's credentials for national leadership, there is a curiosity about the party's origins and basic beliefs. In the case of this particular anniversary, I hope we have stumbled into one of the rare moments where retrospection is fully appreciated.

In putting this enterprise together we observed that whether the subject is strong central government, political economy, civil rights, inclusiveness, or bigotry, different authors presented dissimilar views on particular aspects of Democratic party history. But no matter which authors one may side with, what comes through finally is the adaptability of the party. Somehow, it has survived while most political organizations have died off.

A particularly enjoyable aspect of this project has been working with the contributors to this volume. Their enthusiasm has been infectious and their insights have been profound and provocative. In the initial phases of our project research we heard from more than a few academics that the field of American political history has suffered a loss of prestige in recent decades. If among some circles political history is considered to be in "decline," one certainly can not tell by the level of scholarship in the following pages. To all our contributors we offer our deepest thanks.

We are indebted to a number of scholars who provided us critical advice at all stages of this project. They include: Richard Baker, Carl Brauer, William Galston, Michael Holt, Seymour Martin Lipset, James

Patterson, Leo Ribuffo, and Raymond Smock. In addition, one of our contributors, Alonzo Hamby, deserves special thanks. He was an ongoing source of scholarly guidance and a valued sounding board.

The process of creating this book has brought surprises, most of them pleasant, although as with any intellectual enterprise, each day has brought ups and downs. For the many people involved in this effort, two symposia on the party's history, sponsored by the Center for National Policy (CNP), created the most excitement. It was a special privilege to listen to the many individuals who have devoted their lives to trying to understand when and how the Democratic party has been one of the great forces for good and when it has not lived up to its ideals.

For their time and energy, we would like to thank the participants in the symposia: Jean Baker, Sam Beer, former U.S. Representative John Brademas, U.S. Senator Bill Bradley, Alan Brinkley, Peter Brown, U.S. Representative Mike Espy, former U.S. Representative William Frenzel, Alonzo Hamby, former U.S. Senator Gary Hart, Allan Lichtman, former Secretary of State and CNP Chairman Edmund Muskie, Washington, D.C. Delegate Eleanor Holmes Norton, Kevin Phillips, Washington, D.C. Councilman John Ray, Robert Remini, Steve Roberts, U.S. Representative Tom Sawyer, Wendy Sherman, Ted Sorensen, Margaret Warner, Ben Wattenberg, and former U.N. Ambassador Andrew Young.

Other friends of the Center for National Policy assisted us by discussing the book concept, helped us identify potential contributors, read the manuscript, and offered their advice. They include David Bohmer, Joseph Crapa, Peter Edelman, Ralph Everett, Michael Levy, Eleanor Lewis, Mark Mellman, Stuart Rothenberg, and William Sweeney, Jr.

One of the primary reasons we proceeded with this project was the response generated by a letter we sent to the Center for National Policy Board of Directors and National Advisory Board. There was such enthusiasm to the idea of the book concept that we were reassured that we were on the right track. To the members of both Boards who took the time and effort to put their thoughts on paper, our thanks. Much of your advice has found its way into this final product.

I would be remiss without recognizing the Staff of the Center for National Policy staff: Laura Bowman, Michael Calabrese, Michael Petro, Rick Regan, Amy Weiss Tobe, and Holly Woodson, who gave their time and effort generously to this project.

Special thanks goes to CNP President Madeleine Albright, who perhaps as much as anyone understands the unique importance of the Democratic party and its durability to other nations, particularly newly emerging ones. CNP Vice President Mo Steinbruner managed the editorial process.

Veneta Worthington put in incredibly long hours preparing this volume for the typesetter. Sarah Orrick, a consultant to the Center, joined the project in its last two months as copy editor. Without Veneta's and Sarah's efforts we would have never made our tight deadlines.

The Center's two research assistants during the 1991-1992 time-frame, Brian Portnoy and Kelley Connolly, were persistent, thoughtful, and tireless in assembling background material and handling the logistics of manuscript review. My assistant over the past year, Pam Chesky, spent many hours at many libraries in this process and I am grateful to her for her time.

In a very real sense this book is the work of Ira Forman who coordinated the entire project, developing a list of authors, making judgments about scope, reviewing and helping to revise manuscripts, and generally taking responsibility for getting the job done. He is a valued colleague and a first rate student of political history and how it relates to current events. A special thanks also goes to Caryn Pass, Ira's wife, who gave up a vacation and her husband's time during the past year.

Finally, I am grateful to relatives. To Everett and Jon who played their part on the financial side. And, most of all, to Judy, Daniel, and Mark who have tolerated my endless tales about events of long ago.

Peter Kovler
August 1992
Washington, D.C.

1. Richard E. Neustadt and Ernest R. May, *Thinking in Time: The Uses of History for Decision Makers* (New York: The Free Press, 1986).

# Introduction

*Ira Forman*

> . . . I've seen th' dimmycratic party hangin' to th' ropes a score iv times. I've seen it dead an' burrid an' th' raypublicans kindly buildin' a monymint f'r it. . . . I've gone to sleep nights wondhrin' where I'd throw away me vote afther this an' whin I woke up there was that crazy-headed ol' loon iv a party with its hair sthreamin' in its eyes, an' an axe in its hand, chasin' raypulbicans into th' tall grass.
>
> Mr. Dooley (1901)[1]

The Democratic party's obituary has been penned a thousand times. Ninety years ago, when Finley Peter Dunne's fictional Irish saloon keeper, Mr. Dooley, was at the height of his popularity, the venerable party of Thomas Jefferson and Andrew Jackson succumbed to four straight Republican landslides. At the turn of the century, Democrats were as much of an oddity in large sections of the country as Socialists or Anarchists—and not the least bit more socially acceptable. During the 1860s the party's enemies hung the albatross of "treason" around its neck and the *New York Tribune* would describe it as "a myth, a reminiscence, a voice from the tomb, an ancient and fishlike smell."[2]

Yet, here we are, 200 years after Mr. Jefferson first mentioned his party in a letter to President George Washington,[3] and the oldest political party in the world still stalks the political landscape. It's like one of those old black and white Dracula movies—time and time again the (Republican) villagers defeat their deadly (Democratic) enemy but are unable to drive the stake through its heart.

As we approach another century, it's possible we are finally witnessing the end of the road for American political parties in general, and the Democratic party in particular. After all, Americans have come full circle in their attitudes toward political parties. Nearly all the founders originally cast a jaundiced eye toward parties. Even when the parties first formed in the 1790s, the leading political figures of the day only grudgingly accepted them, and then as necessary evils. Yet by the fifth decade of the nineteenth century Americans had adopted a worshipful attitude toward political parties. Indeed, it is hard for the late-twentieth century mind to comprehend the fervor with which Victorian-era Americans committed themselves to their beloved political parties. Party became, for the vast majority of white male Americans, an association every bit as precious as ethnicity, religion and nationalism. In the 1990s, the vast majority of American voters would subscribe to a notion that the founders would have fathomed but that our Victorian ancestors would have found incomprehensible, namely, "I vote the man, not the party." The American public's growing cynicism about politics has rubbed off on political parties and probably less than 30 percent of the current electorate are strong partisans.

So perhaps it soon will be time to consign the Democrats to the dustbin of history. Maybe, but it is the bias of those who worked on this volume that there is still life in this old party. Perhaps it's because without the glue of party to bind the legislative and executive branches, we foresee a gridlock of democracy. Or maybe it's because some of us are "romantics" who couldn't bear the thought of politics without the raucous, rowdy, party "which rayspictable people speak iv . . . in whipsers."[4] Most likely it's because the history of the Democratic party is inextricably intertwined with American uniqueness—with peculiarly American ideas—with the American Idea. Hence, the title of this book.

Americans sometimes overlook the uniqueness of the American experience with democracy: that we were the first modern democracy; that we are a multi-ethnic, multi-religious, multi-cultural society; that American individualism stands out in the world; that, in international affairs, Americans demand from their leaders policies that are not just advantageous to the nation but live up to national ideals. To scrutinize Democratic history is to be struck by how peculiarly American circumstances have been reflected in the ideology and the make-up of the Democrats from Jefferson's era to the present.

## MEMORY AND JUDGMENT

As Peter Kovler writes in the preface to this volume, memory—historical memory—is a tool which political practitioners should bring to their craft. One of the objectives of this book is to use the Democratic party as a lens to peer back into that memory.

The Democrats are a particularly good mirror to hold up to American history because the party coalesced within a few years of the ratification of the Constitution, and its members participated in nearly every political struggle in the republic's history. Moreover, the tensions that have characterized American politics for at least 200 years have all been reflected in ideological positions the party has adopted, rejected, or split over. Though particular issues changed from one era to another, though the ideological center of the party shifted over time, many of the same tensions that activated the Founding Fathers' generation still resonate in the party rhetoric of the 1990s.

Yet memory alone cannot serve as a good road map to the future. Judgment about the applicability of particular episodes of history to a set of current circumstances is also critical.

This book offers both memory and judgment.

In the first 12 chapters, American political historians lead the reader back through time to an America of earlier generations, to illustrate the Democratic party of the past—what its followers believed, how its leaders changed the party, how events affected its ideology and its electoral base, what type of Americans were Democrats, and why they were so fervid in their devotion to a political party. In short, these chapters address memory.

The final four chapters, along with Arthur Schlesinger, Jr.'s afterword, are an exercise in judgment. Each of the authors in these essays—two journalists, one political scientist, and one former Democratic senator—have called upon memory to give us alternative frameworks for making our own judgments about the Democratic party of the 1990s.

Inevitably, some will question why a specific author was included in, or excluded from, this volume. Others may wonder why a particular topic was or was not systematically examined. The answer to each of these questions would begin with an explanation of what this book is not. It is not a complete chronology. If one wishes to know what happened in Democratic party history in May 1847, or look up the results of the 1904 presidential race, there are other works to consult. Though we believe these essays offer a broad representation of party history, some years are covered in greater detail than others.

One should also point out that nineteenth century Democrats are examined more thoroughly here than Democrats of the twentieth century. There is only one essay, for example, covering the "golden era" of modern Democratic history, 1932-1964, while four chapters are devoted to the party of the mid-nineteenth century Democrats. This concentration on "ancient history" is purposeful. Many modern readers are undoubtedly familiar with Franklin D. Roosevelt, Harry S Truman, and John F. Kennedy. Yet, most know precious little about American politics prior to the New Deal, though the voices of Jefferson, Jackson, Stephen Douglas, Samuel Tilden and William Jennings Bryan speak of themes, if not issues, that still echo today.

Moreover, for a party which has averaged 43 percent of the vote in the five presidential elections prior to 1992, the story of the struggling Democrats of the Victorian era is more instructive than a chronicle of electoral success.

A few readers may challenge the premise that 1992 is the 200th anniversary of the Democratic party. This bicentennial assertion is based on the Democratic National Committee's decision to recognize 1792 as the date of the party's founding, which in turn is based on Jefferson's own reference to his party in May of that year. Some academics would argue that two distinct political parties did not materialize until the late 1790s when disagreements over foreign policy widened the split between the backers of the Adams Administration and Jefferson's followers. Others will contend that 1832, when Jackson's party held its first political convention, is the correct year of this institution's establishment. Some even cite 1840, when Jacksonians finally settled on the name "Democratic party," as the party's birth year.[5]

There are good reasons to pinpoint 1792 as the party's genesis—not the least of which is that the modern party itself chooses to recognize this date. Democratic leaders as far back as the 1830s and 1840s, such as Jackson and Martin Van Buren, traced their partisan ancestry back to Jefferson. Moreover, there is little doubt that some type of political organization was formed by Jefferson and James Madison in the early 1790s for there is solid evidence that as early as the year 1791, these two were laying the groundwork for the formation of a political following.[6]

Part of the difficulty today's reader encounters in trying to trace Democratic roots is the confusion over the name of the party. Jefferson's and Madison's followers originally adopted the name "Republican party," or sometimes "Democratic-Republican party." Scholars often refer to this party as the "Jeffersonian Republicans," in order to distinguish it from the modern G.O.P. In the 1820s this Jeffersonian party split into Democratic-Republican (led by Andrew Jackson) and National Republican (associated with Henry Clay and John Quincy Adams) factions. Most National Republicans became Whigs in the 1830s and by the 1840s Jacksonians were called simply Democrats.[7]

What is quite clear is that the modern Democratic party, unlike any other political party in existence, is lineally descended from the organized following that Jefferson and Madison established in the 1790s. Modern-day Republicans did not evolve from either of the two wings of the party which formed when the Jeffersonian party split in the 1820s. One wing, the Whigs, disappeared in the early 1850s and only the Democratic wing survives today.[8]

But in the final analysis, for the purposes of this work, it is not of fundamental importance whether one believes the Democratic party is 200,

195, or even 152 years old. Nor is it important that this volume does not devote the same degree of attention to each year or each era of Democratic party history. Our basic objective is to provide the reader a more complete understanding of the differences that distinguished the Democrats of one generation from another. For it is our hope that the readers of this work will gain from this presentation a more complete understanding of the growth and evolution of this party, that they will consider the appraisals at the back of this book, and ultimately, that they will draw their own judgments about the lessons to be learned.

This work is divided into five parts. Parts One to Four roughly correspond with the party systems typology developed by political scientist V. O. Key, Jr. and others.[9] Most scholars identify four or five separate periods of party competition—periods in which partisan voter preferences have been relatively stable from one election to another.[10] Part Five, Bicentennial Appraisals, is comprised of four essays which provide an analytical framework for the preceding history.

**Part One—Jeffersonian and Jacksonian Roots: 1790s-1840s.** This section explores the party's birth as the "Republican," or "Democratic-Republican," party in the 1790s and its evolution into modern form by the fourth and fifth decades of the century. One of the focuses of these chapters is the party's roots in "republican" ideology and how that doctrine dealt with issues of government, power, economic equity, democracy, and race. The two "partisan founders," Thomas Jefferson and Andrew Jackson, are the dominant personalities in these pages.

Two authors in this section, Harry Watson and Robert Remini, offer somewhat conflicting pictures of Jacksonian Democrats. Watson views Democratic racism in the early nineteenth century as more pronounced than Whig racism and regards it as a somewhat natural, if perverse, complement to the party's passion for white male equality. Remini does not see racism as being so central to the party's appeal. He believes that the Democrats of the era saw the issue in terms of property and constitutional rights, not moral rights. Moreover, he points out that Democrats charged that their Whig opponents were disingenuous in their publicly articulated concerns for blacks and Indians.

**Part Two—Democrats and the Civil War Legacy: 1840s-1890s.** This era is covered by four chapters, following Democrats from the break-up of their Whig opposition through the party's post-reconstruction return to electoral competitiveness in the 1880s and 1890s. One focus of this section is the ethnic and cultural roots of the Democratic coalition and the changes the coalition experienced as a result of rising nativism, expansion of slavery into the territories and, finally, the Civil War itself. A second topic is the development of a political culture that tightly bound Democrats to their party from the late 1830s until the end of the century. The section also returns to the economic views of Democrats and complexities surrounding race and party competition in nineteenth century America.

Robert Kelley writes in this section that the antebellum Democratic leadership was deeply committed to the laissez-faire economic policies of Adam Smith. He believes that, though fear of the new economic realities may have motivated some Democrats, the party as a whole was not against business growth but against both the inefficiency of government support for business and the danger of economic power controlling government power. This differs from Watson's view that Democrats were so fearful of the societal changes wrought by the "market revolution" that their primary concern was to stop the new economic development by cutting off its government support.

**Part Three — Democrats in a Republican Age: 1890s-1930s.** These three chapters cover the Democrats during their true nadir—from the "Democratic" depression of the 1890s to the Republican's own Great Depression. During a span of thirty-six years (1897-1933), the party was shut out of the White House in all but eight years, was a minority in the House of Representatives in all but ten years, and controlled the Senate for a mere four years. Yet, during this era both the philosophy and the coalition that would characterize the modern party began to take form. The central figures of the party in this period were Bryan and Woodrow Wilson. Both Bryan in defeat and Wilson in the presidency deserve substantial credit for transforming the party from the "conservative" institution of Cleveland's presidency into America's primary political vehicle for social and economic change.

**Part Four — The Rise and Decline of the New Deal Majority: 1930s-1990s.** The coalition that Franklin D. Roosevelt constructed enabled the Democrats to dominate America's political landscape—as they had from the time of Jefferson to the convulsions of the 1850s. This section examines how the diversity of this coalition influenced the development of the New Deal program and how repeal of the New Deal was precluded by the results of the 1948 election and the actions of the Truman administration. The section continues with a description of the similarity between Truman's coalition of 1948 and Kennedy's of 1960 and the development of Johnson's Great Society. The focus then shifts to an examination of the reasons for the collapse of the Democratic presidential majority in the 1970s and 1980s.

**Part Five — Bicentennial Appraisals.** The end of this volume consists of four essays, each of which assesses the Democratic past and provides a framework for evaluating this history's impact on the present and likely relevance to its future. E.J. Dionne finds his organizing principle in irony: the irony of a party of egalitarian ideas that once staunchly defended the institution of slavery; the irony of a party that celebrates diversity while trying to offer America a unifying, national vision.

Reform and hope are Gary Hart's themes. In citing Jefferson and Emerson he posits that there are always in democratic societies parties of change and reform and parties of the status quo. He suggests that it is the Democratic party's natural role to champion change through reform, in an effort to keep up with the ongoing process of societal transformation. The former Senator then offers a platform of reform that addresses the challenges of the 1990s.

Hanes Walton asks the reader to look at Democrats through the prism of the "American idea" of equality. Walton reminds us that while the concept of equality permeated the Founding Fathers' writings, its implementation in practice was dealt with as a political issue rather than a moral one when they drafted the Constitution and were confronted with the institution of slavery. Until the 1960s this failure to face the moral dimension of race was one of the great unsolved problems of the party. He describes how growing African American participation in the Democratic party has helped transform the institution in the twentieth century but has also had electoral consequences.

Michael Barone describes an old, boisterous, diverse party which, despite its age, maintains a "whiff of the rebel," "a slight flavor of rowdyism," and "a sense that there is something a bit raffish about being a Democrat." Barone sees in party history a tale of tensions. There are economic policy tensions over whether to advocate equity or growth; foreign policy tensions over internationalism and isolationism; and cultural tensions over whether to celebrate America or to maintain critical detachment toward it.

The final essay in this book is Arthur Schlesinger, Jr.'s "Afterword." At least since the publication of the landmark *Age of Jackson* in 1945, Professor Schlesinger has been in the forefront of the debate over the Democratic party's legacy. Here he argues that Democrats of the future must be true to their Jeffersonian, Jacksonian, Rooseveltian heritage and oppose attempts by private interests to turn government to their own selfish purposes. To reach these Jeffersonian objectives, he believes, the party must not only employ Hamiltonian methods but must also articulate a national message—one that transcends mere pandering to the assorted groups which comprise the Democratic coalition. If the party is true to its spirit, he says, it just might be around for another century or so.

## UNRAVELING THE HISTORICAL THREADS

No single metaphor, nor concise model accurately summarizes the full complexity of the chronicle of the Democrats found in these pages.

What can be pulled from the history is a series of ideas or themes which weave themselves throughout the party's history. Sometimes one is struck by the continuity of creed, at other times by a complete evolution in philosophy.

**How much government? For what ends?** As America has transformed itself from a east coast republic of four million "yeoman" farmers into a continent-wide superpower of 250 million mostly urban citizens, so too has the Democratic party evolved. Less than 100 years after Jefferson retired from the presidency and less than 60 years after Jackson's death, Mr. Dooley could already comment:

> 'Tis on'y the' part iv th' party that can't r-read that's thrue to th' principals iv Jefferson an' Jackson.[11]

Nowhere is the distance from Jefferson more apparent than in Democratic attitudes toward the role of government—and in particular the role of the federal government.

For one-half of the party's 200 years it was a force for minimal government, for another half the institution of activist government. Think for a moment of a timeline stretching from the 1790s on the left to the 1990s on the right. Now imagine the line as a sort of teeter-totter, with the exact mid-point of the board, the 1890s, the era of Cleveland, Bryan and the Populists. This is the point at which both sides of Democratic history are evenly balanced. To the left is the old Democracy of Jefferson, Jackson, Douglas, Tilden, and Cleveland, the Democracy of "a wise and frugal government." Precisely balanced to the right is the party which has believed in the positive potential of the federal government—the party of Bryan, Wilson, FDR, Truman, Kennedy, Johnson, and the party of today.

If the Democrats of 100 years ago executed a 180-degree turn with regard to their philosophy of the role of government, there was not a comparable change in their underlying objectives. This is reflected in the old adage that the party adopted Hamiltonian means to carry out Jeffersonian ends.

As Lance Banning and Watson assert in their chapters, the early party leadership was acutely sensitive to the fragility of the new American experiment. For these leaders, the greatest threat to a republic was the growth of economic and political inequities. From their reading of classical and English history, they reasoned that an activist federal government could only increase disparities in wealth and power and thus threaten republican institutions.

The power of this Jeffersonian argument was demonstrated by the fact that even during a time of rapid economic transformation in American society, mid-century and Gilded Age Democrats clung tenaciously to this view. Such an old Jeffersonian as President Grover Cleveland—even when faced with the depression of 1893— could not fathom the concept of a government activism that might rescue a floundering economy, because he was immersed in a world view that saw such a course as only serving the "very rich and powerful."

More than is often appreciated, William Jennings Bryan is a pivotal character in the Democratic epic. Today Bryan, if he is remembered at all, is recalled as an ardent supporter of prohibition and an opponent of the teaching of evolution. But this is only one side of "the Great Reformer." His was an age when increasing inequality of wealth and the dislocations of the industrial revolution were widely apparent. Under these circumstances he concluded that only one institution, the federal government, was capable of addressing the economic injustices rampant in his society. Both Robert Cherny and John Milton Cooper, Jr. demonstrate how Bryan held onto the Jeffersonian aversion to inequality and the "money power" as the root of twentieth century Democratic philosophy, but then, borrowing from the Populists, grafted on to that root the Federalist-Whig-Republican creed that an activist federal government was a legitimate means to serve his ends.

Adopting Hamiltonian means for Jeffersonian ends does not adequately encapsulate the full range of twentieth century Democratic goals. What is rarely noted is that once the door to activist government was flung open by Bryan, it became infinitely easier to add to the menu of party objectives. And after Bryan the party had a powerful and flexible tool to apply to the problems of an increasingly complex society.

At the point at which Bryan and his allies seized control of the party from the Cleveland wing, it was economic equity issues—free coinage of silver (to transfer wealth from Wall Street to the Great Plains) and trust-busting—and, to a lesser degree, institutional political reforms (an old Democratic tradition) that were at the heart of the Democrats' agenda for government. Wilson, whom Cooper describes as "Joshua" to Bryan's "Moses," in his first few years in office pushed an ambitious legislative agenda to carry out a Jeffersonian goal of battling economic inequity — lowering the tariff (to aid consumers), enacting a graduated income tax and passing anti-trust legislation. But Wilson's objectives represented one further step in expanding traditional Democratic principles. His support for large groups such as labor (eight-hour day legislation) and small business reflected a very un-Jeffersonian idea that group interests sometimes supersede individual liberty.

Roosevelt and Truman expanded considerably the definition of Democratic aims. Franklin Roosevelt was the antithesis of Grover Cleveland when it came to responding to economic crisis. In the 1930s he did not hesitate to employ unprecedented federal actions to solve the nation's economic woes. The Democratic party of Roosevelt, far more than even the G.O.P. of McKinley's era, was willing to place the responsibility for economic prosperity squarely on the shoulders of the federal government. When economic growth resumed in the period 1934 to 1937 the party of Roosevelt was also willing to appropriate the heretofore G.O.P.'s moniker of the "party of prosperity." As Alonzo Hamby points out in his chapter "The Democratic Moment," by the end of the Truman presidency the Democratic party was no longer driven simply by equity or even government stabilization of the economy. It was a party pledged to, and solidly identified with, economic growth. Truman, along with Kennedy, Johnson, and the Democratic leadership of the past twenty years, continued this process by adding such items as protection of civil rights and the environment to the Democratic menu of objectives. All of these Democratic initiatives did not merely require government action but they also embodied the concept that government action was to be invoked on behalf of a national interest—a distinctly Hamiltonian notion.

In the 100 years since Bryan's emergence, the party has indeed employed Hamiltonian methods to reach Jeffersonian objectives. Eighteenth and nineteenth century opposition to growing inequity remains at the core of twentieth century party goals. But by mid-twentieth century something fundamental had changed. The early Democrats nurtured a vision of a society in which good government was minimal government and the well-being of the nation was maximized by maximizing individual liberty. These Jeffersonian doctrines are not extinct in the Democratic party of the 1990s. In the realms of civil liberties, separation of church and state, and privacy rights, the Democrats have largely clung to these libertarian roots. But in other arenas Democrats no longer believe that individuals pursuing their own interests is in the best interests of the nation. Now Democrats often embrace the notion that group, community, or national interests take precedence over individual interests. Another way to describe this phenomenon is by saying that the Democratic party has adopted Hamiltonian means and, while it partially adopted Hamiltonian and Whig ends, remained true to Jeffersonian ends.

**A Democratic foreign policy.** On the face of it, there appears to be little commonality among the various foreign policies advocated by Democrats across the span of two centuries. For example, it is difficult to discern a consistency between James Polk's vision of Manifest Destiny, Bryan's anti-imperialism, Wilson's Fourteen Points, Truman's principles of containment, and Jimmy Carter's human rights policy. Certainly neither isolationism nor internationalism is a useful tool for categorization.

A closer look at our historical chapters does yield a thread of consistency. Democratic party foreign policy has been characterized generally by some degree of allegiance to specific principles of idealism—that is, the exportation of American notions of democracy, liberty, and equality. In contrast, the party's political opponents have more often adhered to policies characterized by a stricter adherence to principles of *Realpolitick* and national self-interest. Democrats traditionally have believed that the United States is different from other countries in the world, that it is not simply a self-interested player on the world stage, finely calculating each move to advance its own peculiar interests. America, in this view, is exceptional, it is the "shining city on a hill." Though the term is often used to describe other aspects of the American experience, "American exceptionalism," is a useful handle for this idealistic variant of international relations.

Still, this paradigm of Democratic foreign policy is not a perfect means of discriminating between Democratic and Republican approaches. One can find historical examples of Democrats who have assiduously practiced the art of *Realpolitick* in foreign affairs. Conversely, it was one Republican president, Abraham Lincoln, who declared his country the "last, best hope of earth,"[12] and another, Ronald Reagan, who borrowed the "city on a hill" imagery.[13] Yet this generalization is accurate often enough to be useful in assessing the Democratic past.

For example, Banning tells us that one of the crucial distinctions between Jeffersonian Republicans and Federalists was in foreign policy. Jefferson and his followers were sympathetic to republican France in its struggles with England, whereas the Federalists sided with England. Jeffersonian Republican attitudes toward these two global powers in the 1790s can be attributed partially to France's support for the colonies during the American Revolution, but mostly to the simple desire to support a sister republic.

The Manifest Destiny and Young America movements supported by antebellum Democrats were not merely ideological pretext for American expansion. As Jean Baker explains in "In Eclipse," Democrats like Stephen Douglas were generous with their financial and rhetorical support of the European republican revolutions of 1848. Reflecting this point of view, a *Democratic Review* article of 1839 stated that the mission of America was to spread throughout the world "freedom of conscience, freedom of person, freedom of trade and business pursuits, universality of freedom and equality."[14]

The anti-imperialism of Democrats in the Gilded Age and the Bryan era was imbued with some of the same principles. With westward, continental expansion complete and with Caribbean and Central American expansion less attractive to the southern wing of the party after the demise of slavery, Democrats in the fifty years after the Civil War opposed Republican attempts to expand U.S. possessions. This position was accompanied by the argument that the United States ought not to act like the European imperialist powers—that our strength in the world should be used to support local autonomy, not colonialism.

While the internationalism of Democratic foreign policy under Wilson manifested itself in increased American involvement abroad, its uncompromising idealism was a stark contrast to the fierce Republican nationalism of Theodore Roosevelt. Wilson's internationalism promoted a vision of a world dominated by American notions of democracy, self-determination and international cooperation to end the scourge of war.

More indelibly than Wilson, Franklin Roosevelt left his internationalist mark on the Democratic party and the nation. At the end of World War II, the United States was the world's unchallenged superpower, but one guided by the idealistic principles of Roosevelt's Four Freedoms—"a world founded upon . . . freedom of speech, freedom of religion, freedom from want and freedom from fear."[15]

The policy of containment of Soviet expansionism, constructed in the Truman administration, was also much more than a matter of attention to narrowly-defined American interests abroad. For Democratic leaders like Truman, Kennedy, and Johnson, it also encompassed the notion of "American exceptionalism"—that Americans would "pay any price, bear any burden, meet any hardship, support any friend, oppose any foe in order to assure the survival and success of liberty. . . ."[16]

The irony of Vietnam for the party was that this notion of American uniqueness came to motivate both Democratic hawks and Democratic doves. Many Democratic supporters of the Johnson administration who were weaned on the cold war were convinced that they were protecting a small nation's freedom from the onslaught of communist expansion. All but the most anti-American doves of the era were often harkening back, albeit unconsciously, to Bryan's argument that the United States should be better than other great powers; that it should refrain from destroying a tiny nation it was supposed to be saving. This debate between hawks and doves has continued within the party for the last twenty-five years. As recently as the Gulf War, the strains of American Exceptionalism could be heard in the rhetoric of many Democrats—both some who opposed immediate military action and some who supported it.

**Leadership Matters.** Few, if any, of the authors in this book would subscribe to a "great man" theory of history—to the simple notion that all history is shaped by the will of great leaders. Nevertheless, in reading these pages one can't escape the notion that, at least for Democrats, strong leadership has been most often associated with the party's ability to leave a lasting imprint on American society, as well as with its electoral victories.

In the 136 years since Democrats and Republicans began their competition for the presidency, eight individual Democrats have held the White

House for 52 years. By contrast, 17 individual Republicans have occupied the executive mansion for 80 years.[17] The Republican party has often won elections with candidates who ended up with historical reputations as weak chief executives—for example, Grant, Hayes, Harrison, Taft, and Harding. Few Democratic presidents in this period would be so judged.

Baker does point out in her chapter that mid-nineteenth century Democracy is not remembered for its strong leadership, but this was also a period in which the party's major accomplishment was mere survival. By contrast, the democratization of the republic in the early nineteenth century is not linked simply to the party but to President Jackson. The establishment of the party as the party of prosperity is attributed to F.D.R. The civil rights revolution is tied to Kennedy and Johnson. And it is not just presidents who have left their mark as leaders on the party and on American society. Bryan, a three-time presidential loser, is a central figure in transforming the party into an institution committed to the use of government as an instrument of economic and social reform. In the postwar era a presidential candidate like Robert Kennedy could inspire a whole generation of politically involved Americans to dream of a society less racially divided and of a nation imbued with a more communitarian spirit.

**Inclusion.** The final thread that winds its way through this book is the attractiveness of the Democratic party to society's outgroups. For unlike their Federalist, Whig, and even Republican opponents, the Democrats observed a faith that conferred equality on all white men. Throughout the nation's history the Democrats have demonstrated an eagerness to accept most groups at the outer edges of American society.

In the early 1800s, non-English settlers like the Scotch Presbyterians, the German Lutherans, or the Irish Catholics were welcomed in the home of Jefferson and Jackson. The party not only sought the votes of immigrants, religious minorities, and the poor, but offered these groups an equal share in the American dream. As a strong party ethos formed in the fourth and fifth decade of the nineteenth century, any white male who joined the Democratic brotherhood also became an American—a citizen the equal of any blue-blooded Boston Brahmin—at least in the creed of the Democracy.

This broad circle of equality, this wide-spread notion of inclusion, was a radical concept one hundred and sixty years ago. As one wave of outsiders assimilated in the larger society (and often then left the Democracy) another wave of even "stranger" outsiders took their place. Thus the Germans and the Irish of mid-century were followed by the southern and eastern Europeans of the 1880s to the 1920s. But as wide as the circle was drawn, it still excluded large categories of human beings—conflicting with the Declaration of Independence's statement that "all men are created equal." Like all political organizations of the last century, the Democrat party excluded women from its fraternal circle. More than their competitors, it must be acknowledged, Democrats excluded African Americans. As a number of our authors have noted, it is ironic that the party that championed the revolutionary notion of full equality of all white men could also form the bedrock of support for white supremacy.

Mr. Jefferson, in his *Notes on Virginia*, condemned slavery and wrote, "Indeed I tremble for my country when I reflect that God is just." He could well have substituted "party" for "country." From the vantage point of the last decade of the twentieth century, the party's extreme nineteenth century racism may overshadow its democratic, inclusionary ethic. Yet, in the end, this inclusionary ethic proved much more durable than the legacy of white supremacy.

In post-Cold War America, ethnic, religious, and even racial hierarchies have been diminished (if not abolished) to a degree that would have startled even the most "democratic" of our Jacksonian forbearers. Today, both parties are at least rhetorically wedded to the principles of equality of opportunity. Even the Republican party, with its roots among the Yankee aristocracy, actively recruits "ethnic" America—Hispanics, Asians, and eastern Europeans for example. One need look no further, however, than the faces on the floors of the two parties' conventions to understand that Jefferson's party remains the party of America's outsiders, the party of inclusion.

The story that unfolds in these pages is not a simple, well-ordered tale. But no one ever accused the Democratic party of being orderly. This is a party that remained true to many of its Jeffersonian goals. But it is also a party that radically altered its methods of achieving those goals and fundamentally changed its world view concerning the relationship between the individual and society. This is an institution that championed toleration for, and acceptance of, many of society's downtrodden, but was long saddled with the legacy of white racism. This is an organization of ofttimes idealistic Americans who over the years stood for territorial expansion and then anti-imperialism, isolationism and then internationalism.

But if two centuries of past history are not orderly, they are reflective. For the Democratic party of each generation mirrored America. Sometimes the mirror produced a faithful reflection and the party commanded a national majority. Other times, the glass was imperfect, the likeness a bit distorted, and the Democrats struggled at the polls. That's the history of the Democratic party—diverse, untidy, and a storehouse of images of a nation's ideals and imperfections.

# NOTES

1. Finley Peter Dunne, "Discusses Party Politics," in *Mr. Dooley: Now And Forever,* ed. Charles T. Cullen (Stanford, Calif.: Academic reprints, 1954), 169.

2. *New York Tribune*, April 3, 1868.

3. Thomas Jefferson, *Papers of Thomas Jefferson* 23 (Princeton: Princeton University Press, 1990): 537. This is a letter from Jefferson dated May 23, 1792. Jefferson states his opposition to the policies of Hamilton and critiques the Hamiltonian policies as a threat to the republic. In this letter, Jefferson for the first time refers to "The republican party. . . ."

4. Dunne, *Mr. Dooley*, 169.

5. For a defense of the 1830s or 1840s as the period of the party's founding see Bernard A. Weisberger, "The Lives of The Parties," *American Heritage*, vol. 43, no. 5 (September 1992), 48. See also a Statement of Administration Policy, March 17, 1992 in which the Bush Administration opposed S. 2047 which would have established a government commission to commemorate the bicentennial of the party.

6. Noble E. Cunningham, Jr., *The Life of Thomas Jefferson* (New York: Ballentine, 1987), 168-169. See also Stefan Lorant, *The Glorious Burden* (Lenox, Mass.: Authors Edition, 1976), 42.

7. For a further discussion of the use of the terms "Republican" and "Democratic-Republican" in referring to the party of Jefferson and Jackson, see the first paragraph and note 1 of Lance Banning's "The Jeffersonians: First Principles," in this volume. Another name for the Democratic party, "The Democracy," has fallen out of modern usage.

8. Another point of confusion over party names arises out of the loose Federalist/Antifederalist competition in the years leading up to the ratification of the Constitution. These factions of the 1780s could hardly be called political parties. The Antifederalists opposed the ratification of the Constitution in the late 1780s, while the supporters of ratification were called Federalists. The Jeffersonian Republicans are not descended from the Antifederalists even though their opponents in the next decade were called Federalists. Some former Antifederalists did become Jeffersonians Republicans in the 1790s but the party's leaders—Jefferson and Madison—had supported ratification of the Constitution years earlier.

9. V. O. Key, Jr., "A Theory of Critical Elections," *Journal of Politics* 17 (1955): 3-18. Scholars have identified certain turning points or realigning elections in American history—elections such as 1800, 1828, 1860, 1896, and 1932—or according to some, a number of realigning elections, such as 1932 and 1936. The first party system roughly corresponds with the weak party competition between the Democratic-Republicans and the Federalists (1792-1816). The second party system is associated with the formation of the Jacksonian Democrats and Whigs in the late 1820s and 1830s and lasted until the break-up of the Whigs after the 1852 election. Part One in this volume covers the events of the first and second party system. The period 1853-1893 is generally associated with a third party system which featured the emergence of the Republican party in the North and the dominance of the Democrats in the South—this era is covered in Part Two. The fourth party system, which is covered in Part Three, began with the depres-

sion of 1893 and lasted until the Great Depression of the 1930s and was a period of national Republican domination. The fifth party system, described in Part Four, established the New Deal Democratic majorities. Though New Deal voting patterns broke down on the presidential level in the late 1960s and early 1970s, Democratic party dominance continues at the congressional, state, and local level. There has been an ongoing debate among academics over whether critical election (or realignment) theory is still relevant to the political system of the 1990s where party identification is so atrophied.

10. There is some dispute over whether the party competition of the Jeffersonian Republicans and Federalists should be categorized as a true party system. See Ronald P. Formisano, "Federalists and Republicans: Parties, Yes—System, No," in *The Evolution of American Electoral Systems* (Westport, Conn.: Greenwood Press, 1981).

11. Dunne, *Mr. Dooley,* 165-166.

12. Abraham Lincoln's Second Annual Message to Congress, December 1, 1862, *Collected Works of Abraham Lincoln,* ed. Roy P. Basler (New Brunswick: Rutgers University Press, 1953), 518-537.

13. John Winthrop, "A Model of Christian Charity," 1630, *Familiar Quotations*, ed, John Bartlett (Boston: Little, Brown, 1980), 264.

14. "The Great Nation of Futurity," *Democratic Review* 6 (November 1939): 427. From Arthur M. Schlesinger, Jr., *Age of Jackson,* n. 11, (Boston: Little, Brown, 1945), 427.

15. Robert Dallek, *Franklin D. Roosevelt and American Foreign Policy 1932-1945* (New York: Oxford University Press, 1979) 256-258.

16. John F. Kennedy, Inaugural Address, in *Public Papers of the Presidents of the United States, John F. Kennedy* (Washington: Office of the Federal Register, 1962).

17. Andrew Johnson, a war Democrat who was elected Lincoln's Vice-President on the Union Party (Republican) ticket, is not counted as either a Democrat or a Republican for the purposes of this calculation.

PART ONE

# Jeffersonian and Jacksonian Roots

## 1790s–1840s

## Chapter 1

# The Jeffersonians: First Principles

*Lance Banning*

The Democratic Party—which, to the befuddlement of countless college freshmen, called itself "Republican" at first—emerged within three years of the adoption of the Constitution.[1] This was not coincidental. The Constitution marked, at once, a new beginning for the nation and a milestone in the revolutionary reconstruction which had started ten years before. In consequence, its launching led directly to the first and most ferocious party conflict in our annals. Supporters of the Constitution thought that it had saved the Union from the danger of a speedy dissolution and had armed that Union, after years of ineffectuality, with powers equal to its duties. At the same time, they were almost painfully aware that every measure of the infant federal government would set a precedent for everything to come, and that the Constitutional Convention had provided only a beginning toward a working federal system. Moreover, nearly half of those who voted on the question had opposed the Constitution, in many instances because they thought it inconsistent with the principles of 1776; and the division over the adoption of the Constitution had intensified a feeling, in its friends and foes alike, that human liberty itself might stand or fall on the decisions of the next few years.[2] The smallest actions had to be considered in an atmosphere that citizens, today, must struggle to imagine.

On the other hand, the present moment in world history may offer us an unexampled guide to understanding the conditions under which these founders went about their work. In 1789, Americans were still a revolutionary people, and the launching of the reconstructed federal government was not unlike the reconstructions going forward at this writing through the whole of Eastern Europe. As is true in Poland, Russia, or Rumania today, awesome consequences seemed to hinge on even small decisions—consequences that contemporaries thought could literally determine if the first great democratic Revolution would survive, consequences that would certainly decide what sort of nation the United States would be. The members of the first administration and the first new Congress were confronted first with the specific problems that had wrecked the old Confederation. But beyond those problems lay the shaping of the future; and among the leading framers of the Constitution—not to mention its opponents—there were radically contrasting visions of the sort of future the United States should have. Out of these divisions, the first political parties would emerge.

## FIRST PRINCIPLES

The argument began within the infant federal government itself, when Alexander Hamilton, the first Secretary of the Treasury, presented his proposals for the funding of the revolutionary debt. Including the arrears of interest, which had not been paid for years, the state and federal governments owed $80,000,000, mostly to domestic creditors who held the bonds and other promises that had financed the Revolution. Hamilton's *Report on Public Credit*, submitted to Congress on January 14, 1790, recommended that the federal government assume responsibility for the remaining obligations of the states as well as those of the Confederation Congress, and that it undertake to pay the whole, at full face value, to the current holders of the notes. Under the provisions of this plan, the old certificates of debt would be replaced by new ones paying lower interest. In exchange, the government would pledge specific revenues to steady payment of that interest, and the nation's public credit (its ability to borrow) would be instantly restored. With interest payments guaranteed, the bonds would hold their value on the private money markets, and retirement of the principal could be postponed until it was convenient for the government to act.[3]

The implications of this plan were grander than was evident upon its face, although the secretary said enough to trouble several members of the Congress. Dashing, arrogant, and absolutely brilliant—he was barely 35 but had ascended like a rocket through the Continental staff and into national politics, where he had played a central role in the adoption of the Constitution—Hamilton has been described as "the premiere state-builder in a generation of state-builders."[4] He faced toward the Atlantic and envisioned an arena of competing empires which America would have to enter much like any other state. In time, as he conceived it, the United States could take a brilliant part in this arena, and he meant to earn immortal fame as founder of its greatness. But for America to have this kind of future, Hamilton believed, it would be necessary first for it to have the economic and financial underpinnings for successful competition: institutions similar to those that had enabled tiny England to achieve the pinnacle of international prestige.[5] It would be necessary, too, for the United States to conscientiously avoid a confrontation with Great Britain, the single nation which (with its naval power) could threaten the United States in war, or through investments in the new republic's economic growth, could aid it most impressively toward greatness. Taking British institutions as a model, Hamilton was setting out to build a modern state, a nation able to compete with European empires on the Europeans' terms.[6]

Hamilton's design for national greatness may have been essentially complete when he delivered his first report, although the whole of it was not to be apparent for at least another year. With proper management, he realized, the heavy burden of the revolutionary debt could be transformed into a positive advantage for the country. Federal funding of states' as well as national obligations could accomplish more than the establishment of public credit: it could tie the economic interests of a vital segment of America's elite to the success of national institutions and create a counterbalance to the local loyalties that Hamilton perceived as potent dangers to the Union.[7] And even as it bound the monied interests to the central government's success, the funding program would erect a framework for the nation's future role in global competition, transforming governmental obligations into liquid capital, a currency supply, that could be multiplied by using the certificates of debt to back creation of a national bank. The bonds and banknotes could be used, in turn, to foster manufacturing and commerce, whose rapid growth would lay the groundwork for the nation's economic independence. Thus, the funding program was intended from the first to further major economic and political, as well as narrowly financial, goals.[8]

The trouble with this scheme, which Hamilton unveiled in a succession of reports, was that it aided certain citizens and regions more immediately than others. More than that, it deeply threatened other founders' visions of the sort of nation the United States should be.

Both problems were immediately apparent. In the House of Representatives, the funding program instantly aroused intense anxieties about corrupting links between the federal government and special interest factions. In many cases, current holders of the debt had purchased their certificates for fractions of their value, often from disbanding, unpaid revolutionary soldiers who had sold the government's uncertain promises for ready cash. Over time, the bonds had gravitated disproportionately into the hands of monied interests in the North and East. To pay the full face value to the present holders would entail a major shift of wealth from South to North, from West to East, and from the body of the people to a few rich men whose fortunes would expand dramatically as a result of federal largesse.[9] Moreover, federal assumption of the states' remaining debts would temporarily reward the states that had done least to pay their debts at the expense of those that had done most. In addition, by demanding that the federal government impose internal taxes, the financial plan would tilt the federal balance markedly toward greater central power—which, of course, was part of what the secretary *hoped* it would accomplish. All of this, some congressmen objected, was profoundly incompatible with harmony among the nation's sections, with republican morality, and with the relatively modest gap between the rich and poor that seemed essential to a healthy representative regime.[10]

Indeed, to Hamilton's alarm, James Madison, the major architect of constitutional reform and very much the "first man" in the Congress—Hamilton's collaborator in the classic exegesis of the Constitution and the draftsman of the Bill of Rights—soon assumed the leadership of this minority of critics.[11] Disgusted by the speculative orgy sparked by Hamilton's report,[12] revolted by the prospect that the victims of the government's original default would now be victimized again, and drawing back in horror from the notion that the country would "erect the monuments of her gratitude, not to those who saved her liberties, but to those who had enriched themselves in her funds," Madison insisted that the case was so extraordinary that it had to be decided "on the great and fundamental principles of justice."[13] As an alternative to Hamilton's proposals, Madison suggested paying present holders of the debt the highest value that securities had reached on private markets, but returning the remaining portion of the full face value of the bonds to the soldiers and other original owners.

Madison was easily defeated on his plan to discriminate between original and secondary holders, which many saw as such a violent breech of preexisting contracts as to absolutely wreck the nation's credit. But Madison was not so easily defeated on the issue of a federal assumption of the states' remaining debts. Over this, a bitter battle raged for months, provoking threats of an immediate disruption of the Union, until the Secretary of the Treasury appealed to Thomas Jefferson, who had returned from France to take up duties as the first Secretary of State, to help him end the crisis.[14] With Jefferson's assistance, Madison and Hamilton resolved the impasse in an after-dinner bargain. The resulting Compromise of 1790 modified the details of assumption and traded passage of the funding legislation for an act providing that the federal government would move in 1800 to a permanent location on the Potomac River.[15]

In 1791, however, Hamilton delivered his reports proposing the creation of a national bank and federal encouragement of native manufactures. Jefferson agreed with Madison that the incorporation of a bank was not within the powers granted by the Constitution—indeed, that the creation of a national monopoly of this or any other sort amounted to a usurpation of authority that could be likened to the parliamentary encroachments that had ended in the Revolution.[16] Increasingly, the two Virginians feared that Hamilton was following a course that could result in concentrated central power, domination of the South and West by the commercial and financial ppealed to merchants, artisans, and market farmers—and beyond those groups, to many who believed that ordered liberty was threatened by the adical contagion started by the Revolution.[23] As opponents of a grasping entral government, which seemed to shower favors on a few, the Republicans, by contrast, appealed to former Antifederalists who had insisted hat a distant central government would threaten popular control, to southrners who had suspected that the Constitution would result in domination y the North and East, and to the rising democratic sentiments of countess ordinary voters, who were often special targets for the Federalists' ontempt.

The two emerging parties plainly had their strongest bases in New ngland and the South, a consequence of their contrasting economic prorams. Nevertheless, the party battle also pitted centralists against the rincipled proponents of a strict construction of the Constitution, enemies f popular commotions against the champions of popular participation in olitical affairs, and advocates of governmental guidance of the nation's onomic growth against opponents of monopolies and privilege, who vored private actions and decisions. The controversy split the leading chitects of constitutional reform into two groups: those who had conuded from the lessons of the 1780s that liberty was most endangered by own excess—a group for whom the Constitution was an instrument for rning back the Revolution—and those who held, as did the two Virginis, that the Constitution was an instrument for shielding and extending volutionary gains.[24] The disagreement penetrated to the very essence of lliding visions of America itself.

Alexander Hamilton, like most Americans, believed that proper govments are founded on consent, and are created to protect the natural erties that citizens do not surrender when political societies are formed. t while he clearly planned to make the people prosperous and free, milton's concerns were focused tightly on the state, not upon the citns of whom the public is composed. Although he certainly believed that ryone would benefit in time from rapid economic growth, the secretary hasized the quick development of manufacturing and commerce, which e critical to the correction of a chronic deficit of payments, and dissed as selfish the inevitable complaints about the temporary sectional class inequities that would result.

Madison and Jefferson, by contrast, were committed to an image of ore responsive government supported by, and nurturing, a revolutionsocial order. Sound republics, they believed, must rest on relatively al, self-directing, independent citizens whose personal autonomy would e them capable of free political decisions and assure their vigilant, inuing participation in political affairs. The great co-architects of ersonian ideals were not the enemies of independent artisans and

East, subversion of the federal government's responsiveness tc
control, oppression of the agricultural majority of people, and—
a threat to the survival of democracy itself.[17]

Their reasoning requires some further explanation, but sho
difficult to grasp. Already troubled by the funding program's t
the nation's wealth from the productive to the non-productiv
Jefferson and Madison suspected that creation of a national ba
deepen the emerging chasm, permitting those who had already
from the secretary's program to enrich themselves again by tra
certificates for bank stock, which was guaranteed to earn substa
its.[18] Federal encouragement of manufacturing and comme
compound this problem, while the broad construction of the C
used to justify these programs would accelerate the shift of
the states to the central government and from the House of
tives to the federal executive. The economic program and
disregard for constitutional restraints both seemed to center
level and in governmental branches least responsive to the pe
same time, the financial program seemed to be creating in th
men and private citizens who were enriched by governmental
interest fundamentally at odds with that of the majority of pe
direct involvement in the nation's daily politics most Federa
obviously to dread. In fact, the more apparent it became that I
following a British model, the more opponents saw him as a
Walpole: as a minister who was subverting legislative inde
endangering the social fabric by creating a corrupted follo
gressmen and other citizens who lived off of the treasu
expense.[19] By the fall of 1791, Madison and Jefferson belie
ilton intended to "administer" the new republic toward a go
a society that would subvert the revolutionary dream.[20] Th
urged the revolutionary poet, Philip Freneau, to come to P
start a paper that would rouse the nation to the danger. D
unsigned essays in this *National Gazette*, Madison and oth
tematic ideology of opposition and called upon the voters
"Republican Interest" in the fall congressional elections.

The partisan division of the early 1790s can be analy
of ways. Like many of the conflicts in the old Confederat
pitted the New England states against Virginia and her neig
that benefitted from the funding program against those th
mercial areas against the planting regions and the small
1792, however, each of the emerging parties was beginni
own adherents in every section of the country, showing t
involved a great deal more than simple economic interes
of a strong new government and rapid economic growt

merchants, but they did oppose monopolies and other programs (like the national bank or Hamilton's Society for Establishing Useful Manufactures) which seemed to them to be creating classes who depended for their livelihoods on governmental privileges and payments. Beyond that, Madison and Jefferson resisted plans to force the country prematurely toward intensive economic change, for that could replicate the European factories and cities which divided workers from employers and confined "the lower orders" to a narrow, straitened, and dependent life that might be incompatible with freedom. The archetypal citizen, for the Virginians, was the independent farmer-owner, who produced necessities of life and who, by being free from personal dependence, would be free as well to vote or fight according to his own, autonomous desires.[25]

## THE FRENCH REVOLUTION

By the summer of 1792, when Hamilton decided to confront his critics by attacking Jefferson's connection with the *National Gazette*, the clashing groups within the federal government had hurled themselves into a full-fledged public war. In anonymous but hardly secret essays in the Philadelphia *Gazette of the United States*, Hamilton condemned his rival for provoking popular suspicions, blasted Jefferson's original ambivalence about the Constitution, and insisted that the opposition leader should resign his post if he could not support administration programs. Jefferson's supporters answered with defenses of his record and repeated accusations that Hamilton's economic program was deliberately designed to undermine the Constitution, build a native aristocracy, and gradually reintroduce hereditary rule. (Angered by the anti-democratic tone of high society in Philadelphia and by a growing disapproval of developments in France, Jefferson had accidentally contributed to the commotion in the press and, in the process, had supplanted Madison as the symbolic leader of the opposition. An enterpriser published as a preface to *The Rights of Man*—Thomas Paine's reply to Edmund Burke's *Reflections on the Revolution in France*—a private note in which the penman of the Revolution wrote that he was pleased that something would at last be said against "the political heresies which have sprung up among us.")[26] As the controversy spread from newspapers in Philadelphia to sheets throughout the country, citizens in every section were beginning to identify with one or the other of the two emerging parties.[27]

Still, as long as party conflict focused on the mysteries of Hamiltonian finance, great masses of the people were unmoved. The tiny federal government intruded little on their daily lives. George Washington was at its helm, prosperity was rising, and the implications of the economic program could be difficult to understand.

Soon, however, all of this would change. Great masses of the people were aroused. Indeed, they were aroused so strongly that the bitterness of the division has been equalled only once in American history—during the time that actually resulted in a civil war. By the later 1790s, crowds were fighting each other in the streets. Gentlemen eluded one another on the sidewalks to avoid the courtesy of tipping hats. Self-appointed agents spied on leaders of the opposition party, and a congressman was jailed for his political opinions. Party leaders on both sides considered a recourse to force.

All this happened when the clashing visions of the two emerging parties intermeshed with their colliding sympathies about the Revolution in France and with their different judgments of the country's interests as a neutral. From 1787 through 1792, Americans had followed the developments in France with general admiration. Most believed that Lafayette and other revolutionaries were inspired by the American example. Many hoped that liberty would spread from France to every part of Europe. Then the Revolution turned in much more radical directions. On February 1, 1793, 11 days after the execution of Louis XVI, the revolutionary French Republic declared war on Great Britain. On April 22, President Washington proclaimed that the United States would pursue a "friendly and impartial" conduct toward the warring powers. While almost no one wished to see the country get entangled in the war, great numbers were offended that America would not be able, at the least, to lean in the direction of republican France, with which America had a treaty of alliance since the Revolutionary War. On the other side, of course, large numbers of conservative Americans, who were increasingly alarmed about the violence in France, confiscations of aristocratic property, a very democratic constitution, and attacks upon the Church, believed that Washington was absolutely right.

The Proclamation of Neutrality divided ordinary citizens as no preceding policy had done, and the division deepened as the warring powers both began to prey on neutral shipping. As the greatest trading neutral of the time, America could not avoid entanglement in what was rapidly developing into a worldwide war; advocating different ideologies and different forms of government, the European powers were immersed in mortal combat, and each of them intended to deny the other the benefits of neutral commerce. Neither could Americans escape emotional involvement. Republican idealism and the memory of French assistance in the Revolution generated potent sympathies, on one side, for the French Republic. Others sympathized with England, the motherland of libertarian ideas, the most effective barrier to French expansion, and by far the most important trading partner of the new American Republic.

The European war divided citizens along the lines already marked by

offended by Jay's Treaty, the French announced that they would treat American ships "in the same manner as they suffer the English to treat them." Seizures followed, and the President responded, much as Washington had done in 1794, by recommending both negotiations and increased appropriations for defense. Adams chose John Marshall of Virginia, Charles C. Pinckney of South Carolina, and Elbridge Gerry of Massachusetts for a mission to resolve the crisis. The negotiations stalled when unofficial agents of the French foreign minister—referred to in American dispatches as X, Y, and Z—informed the American commissioners that nothing could be done until they paid a bribe to Talleyrand and agreed to a large American loan to the Republic.

In April 1798, goaded by Republicans in Congress, Adams released the papers revealing the XYZ Affair. Patriotic fury of a wholly unexampled nature swept the states from end to end; and on the crest of this hysteria, which swelled into a widespread fear of treasonable plots between the French and their Republican supporters, the Federalists embarked upon a naval war with France. They also seized the opportunity to launch a program of repression consciously intended to destroy domestic opposition to their programs. French and Irish immigrants supported the Republicans and favored France in its collision with Great Britain. In June and July, in the Alien Act, Congress extended to fourteen years the period of residence required for naturalization and gave the President the power to summarily deport any alien whose residence he deemed a threat to the United States. Then, in a direct blow to the opposition, Congress passed the Sedition Act, making it a criminal offense to incite opposition to the laws or to "write, print, utter, or publish . . . any false, scandalous, and malicious writing . . . against the government of the United States, or either house of the Congress of the United States, or the President of the United States with intent to defame them or to bring them . . . into disrepute."[33]

Enforced by a partisan judiciary, the Alien and Sedition Acts established a bloodless reign of terror in the country. Under the Sedition Act (or under the common law of seditious libel), every important Republican newspaper in the country was attacked. William Duane of the *Philadelphia Aurora* (which had replaced the *National Gazette* as the leading Republican sheet when the latter failed financially in 1793), Thomas Adams of the *Independent Chronicle* in Boston, and Republican pamphleteers such as Thomas Cooper and James Thompson Callender all faced prosecution. The *Time Piece* and the *Argus*, the only Republican newspapers in New York City, were forced out of business. Matthew Lyon of Vermont, a Republican congressman, was imprisoned for a publication incident to his reelection campaign in 1798. Men were prosecuted under the Sedition Act for offenses as diverse and as trivial as circulating a petition for its repeal, erecting a liberty pole, or expressing a drunken wish that a cannon ball had struck the President in his behind.

At first, Republicans were seriously disheartened. At the peak of the patriotic fever, several congressmen retreated to their states and left the Federalist majority to work its will. Jefferson and others who remained in Philadelphia were trailed by self-appointed spies, who hoped for proof of the leaders' French connections. In the elections of 1798, the Federalists made sizable gains. To the Republicans, the quasi-war with France, the Alien and Sedition Acts, and a measure authorizing the enlistment of a provisional army of 50,000 men, which could be mobilized in the event of an invasion, seemed abundant proof that the conspiracy against the country's liberty had burst into the open. A handful of Virginians talked about secession and about preparing to defend themselves against the federal army. Yet Jefferson and other party leaders never lost their faith in their ability to bring the people to their senses.

While Albert Gallatin and Edward Livingston opposed the crisis laws in Congress, insisting that the legislation was a patent violation of the First Amendment and a potent danger to the people's underlying right to criticize official acts and change their government through free elections, Jefferson and Madison decided to arouse the states. The two Virginians each prepared a secret draft of legislative resolutions condemning the Alien and Sedition Acts. Madison, who had decided not to stand for reelection to Congress in 1796, gave his draft to John Taylor of Caroline, Virginia's agricultural thinker and the Republican party's most influential pamphleteer. Jefferson slipped his to John Breckenridge of Kentucky. On November 16, 1798, Kentucky's legislature resolved that the repressive laws were unconstitutional, "void and of no force." On December 24, Virginia voted a similar condemnation and called upon the other states to join the protest.[34]

All the other states refused to join Virginia and Kentucky on a path that led, much later, to nullification and secession. Still, the resolutions served the party leaders' more immediate objectives. For two full years, Republicans condemned the Federalists' hostility to popular control, always with the election of 1800 firmly in their minds. Victims of the federal prosecutions were portrayed as martyrs. Wartime taxes made new friends. The federal tax on lands and houses met with organized resistance from some Pennsylvania Germans, although the trouble hardly justified the name of Fries's "Rebellion." In time, the opposition even found an accidental ally in the plump and self-important person of John Adams.

The President had lost his first enthusiasm for the quasi-war before the end of 1798. While he supported naval warfare with the armed French cruisers, the Hamiltonians within his party pressed continually for a larger army, partly for its value in intimidating the domestic opposition. Sharing some of the Republican suspicion of a "standing army," which was deeply rooted in American tradition, Adams liked the larger army even less when Washington compelled him to accept "that creole bastard," Hamilton himself, as second in command.[35] Meanwhile, there were growing indications that the French had seen the folly of their course and would receive a new American ambassador with the dignity befitting the representative of a sovereign republic.[36]

On February 18, 1799, without consulting with his cabinet or the Federalists in Congress, Adams nominated William Vans Murray, ambassador to the Netherlands, to make another effort to negotiate with France. Adams's message to the Congress was a bombshell, and in no great time, his conduct shattered Federalist cohesion. In the first place, the appointment of an envoy to the French Republic signalled that the crisis could be ended short of an extension of the war. The Federalists were left with swollen military forces, higher taxes, and an unrelenting effort to suppress the opposition at a time when it was clear that any danger of a French invasion (which was always slight) had passed. Public sentiment began to swing to the Republicans again. Moreover, the reversal of the public mood went forward as the Federalists divided in a bitter intraparty war. On May 6, 1800, Adams blasted Secretary of War James McHenry, who was in the President's office on some minor business, berating him for his subservience to Hamilton and forcing him to offer his resignation. Four days later, when Timothy Pickering refused to follow McHenry's example, Adams fired the Secretary of State. With the quasi-war concluding and the presidential contest drawing near, the split among the Federalists was open and complete.

In the election of 1800, the Federalists were too distracted by their own internal quarrel to manage their Republican opponents. Immersed in intraparty plots, Hamilton was outmaneuvered in New York by his despised opponent Aaron Burr, who ran a stronger slate of candidates, worked harder in the city's wards, and carried both the legislature and the state's electoral vote for the Republican alliance. (Here, as elsewhere, artisans and laborers who had supported constitutional reform had gradually deserted from the Federalist alliance as administration measures failed to offer some protection from imported British goods, and as the local Federalists displayed an arrogant contempt for ordinary voters.)[37] Republicans, of course, delighted in their foes' internal fight, insisting all the whi' 'hat the disputants were distinguished only by the Hamiltonians' subs to England. They even managed to secure the publication of pamphlet in which Hamilton came close to calling the Presi When the electoral votes were counted, Jefferson and B Adams's 65.

The Federalists made one last stand. In the lame

sion of the Federalist Fifth Congress, which was constitutionally required to break the awkward tie between the Republicans' first and second presidential choices, the Federalists held ranks through 35 ballots for Aaron Burr. Still, their unity and zest for party warfare had been badly shaken during the campaign, and they were never to control the national government again.

## THE JEFFERSONIANS IN POWER

Thomas Jefferson described the victory of 1800 as "as real a revolution in the principles of our government as that of 1776 was in its form."[38] Jefferson exaggerated, as was frequently his bent, and yet the comment also captured two important truths: the party battle of the first few years of the Republic was as fierce as any in our annals, flowing as it did from radically contrasting visions of the sort of nation the United States should be; and Jefferson's inauguration did initiate as sharp a change in governmental attitudes and policies as almost any party triumph one might name.

For twelve years after Washington's inauguration, the infant federal government had been directed by a Hamiltonian design for national greatness. It was a brilliant scheme, in service to a grand ambition, and it worked in much the way that Hamilton expected (although the plan for federal encouragement of native manufactures was never written into law). A clash with Britain was avoided during the 1790s, if only at the cost of a demeaning treaty and a naval war with France. The funding program and the national bank provided capital for economic growth and placed the government's finances on a solid institutional foundation. As Europe went to war, the new Republic prospered, and prosperity attached the people to the government's success. Nevertheless, in 1798 and 1799, the Federalists were swept up in a panic that endangered fundamental liberties as we have since defined them in the federal republic. In the end, although the Federalists believed that they were certainly the wisest and the best—"natural" social leaders whose positions, educations, and experience equipped them, and perhaps entitled them, to put a vigorous new government into effect—the Federalists were always far less confident of their abilities as politicians. They expected ordinary voters to be silent and submissive in the intervals between elections, and they could never trust that, even then, the people would defer to those best qualified to lead. The upshot was a devastating loss in 1800. The presidential contest was a close one, in part because so many states decided that electors would be chosen by the legislatures rather than the voters.[39] The popular elections were a very different story, with the Federalists losing 40 seats in Congress. For the first time, the Repub-
-s would easily control the Senate as well as the House. There would

be little to prevent them from pursuing the ideas they had developed in the years of opposition.

The victory of 1800, as the Jeffersonians perceived it, rescued the Republic from a counterrevolutionary plot. Nevertheless, a change of men was not enough without a change of governmental measures. Hamilton had looked toward the Atlantic and supported rapid economic growth, envisioning the quick emergence of an integrated state in which the rise of native manufactures would provide materials for export and a large domestic market for the country's agricultural producers. The Republicans, by contrast, were more concerned about the preservation of the relatively democratic distribution of the nation's wealth. While they had always advocated freeing oceanic commerce and providing foreign markets for the farmers, their ambitions for the nation focused much more on the West, where a republic resting on the sturdy stock of independent farmer-owners could be constantly revitalized as it expanded over space. Hamilton had been intent on the creation of a potent central state. Jefferson and his lieutenants—Madison at State and Albert Gallatin at Treasury—were dedicated to restricting federal action to the limited responsibilities envisioned at the government's creation, trusting that America would make its impact on the world by sheer example of its democratic institutions. Hamilton had seen the national debt as an advantage for the nation, because it could be used to back a stable currency supply. The Jeffersonians despised it. To their minds, the interest payments on the debt enriched a non-productive few and forged a dangerous, corrupting link between the federal executive and wealthy monied interests. They would not repudiate it, to be sure, any more than they would move immediately for revocation of the charter of the national bank. The public's contracts would be kept. But they were willing to subordinate much else to the retirement of the debt as quickly as existing contracts would permit, and they were bent on doing so without resorting to internal taxes, which were better left, in peacetime, to the states.

The Jeffersonians did not dismantle all their predecessors' work. With sound Republicans in power, they assumed, the country could be eased toward change; and it would change more certainly that way. But Jefferson proclaimed the party's dedication to a major change of course in his inaugural address, announcing his commitment to "a wise and frugal government which shall restrain men from injuring one another, shall leave them otherwise free to regulate their own pursuits of industry and i[...]-ment, and shall not take from the mouth of labor the bread it h[...] This kind of government, he hinted, would be guided by a se[...] profoundly different from the Federalist design: genuine [...] national subservience to Britain; rapid payment of th[...] withdrawal of the federal government from its involve[...]

tion's economic life; reliance on the state militia rather than a standing army; and a recognition that the states "in all their rights," were "the most competent administrations for our domestic concerns and the surest bulwark against anti-republican tendencies."[40]

Reform began in 1801 while Jefferson awaited the December meeting of the Seventh Congress, in which his party would control both houses. Presidential pardons went to the remaining victims of the Federalists' Sedition Act, which had been written to expire with Adams's administration.[41] A handful of the most committed Federalists were purged from federal office, and the President appointed only sound Republicans to fill these public trusts.[42] The evolution of a partisan appointments policy was not complete enough or quick enough to satisfy some members of the party, who argued that "no enemy to democratic government [should] be provided with the means to sap and destroy any of its principles nor to profit by a government to which they are hostile in theory and practice."[43] But even radicals were satisfied when Jefferson announced his program at the opening of Congress.[44] After a review of foreign policy and Indian affairs, he recommended the repeal of all internal taxes. "The remaining sources of revenue will be sufficient," he insisted,

> to provide for the support of government, to pay the interest on the public debts, and to discharge the principals in shorter periods than the laws or the general expectations had contemplated. . . . Sound principles will not justify our taxing the industry of our fellow citizens to accumulate treasure for wars we know not when, and which might not perhaps happen but from temptations offered by that treasure.

Public burdens, Jefferson admitted, could be lifted only if expenditures fell too. But there was room to wonder "whether offices or officers have not been multiplied unnecessarily." The army, for example, had been swollen far beyond the numbers necessary to defend the western posts, and there was no use for the surplus. "For defense against foreign invasion, their number is as nothing; nor is it conceived needful or safe that a standing army should be kept up in time of peace." The judiciary system, packed and altered by the Federalists at the conclusion of their reign, would naturally "present itself to the contemplation of Congress." And the laws concerning naturalization might again be liberalized.[45]

The Seventh Congress, voting usually on party lines, enacted everything that Jefferson had recommended. It also gave approval to a plan by Gallatin for the complete retirement of the public debt by 1817, despite the abolition of internal taxes. Indeed, the session seemed to Jefferson so [illegible] a start toward introducing proper principles that there was little left to recommend in 1802.[46] The effort of the next few years would be to keep the course already set.[47]

"The revolution of 1800," as Jefferson described it, was amazingly successful. To the Federalists' surprise, America did not collapse into disorder. No one's property was threatened by the mob.[48] Instead, the country prospered and expanded as it never had before. In 1804, the people showed their general approval, reelecting Jefferson by a margin of 162 electoral votes to just 14 for Charles C. Pinckney while increasing the Republican majority in Congress. By that time, the President had even shown that he would not permit fine points of principle to stand between his conduct and the public good. In 1803, he authorized the purchase of Louisiana from the French despite his doubts that strict construction of the Constitution authorized the act. The Louisiana Purchase doubled the size of the United States and seemed to promise that the republic of the Jeffersonian vision—the republic of independent, landowning farmers who seemed to be ideally suited for self-governance and freedom—could continue to expand as far into the future as the men of 1803 could see.

And yet, there was a weakness in this vision, which would plague the President and his successor through the next three terms. Alexander Hamilton had always argued that the world would not permit republican idealists to dream their dreams in peace. Other powers would prevent it. And, indeed, in 1803, France and Britain resumed their titanic war. In 1805, Napoleon destroyed the European coalition and became essentially unchallengeable by land, while British Admiral Horatio Lord Nelson shattered the French fleet at the Battle of Trafalgar. At this point, the two great powers, the tiger and the shark, resorted necessarily to economic warfare, especially to dedicated efforts to deny the other the advantages of neutral commerce. As the greatest trading neutral of the age, although a minor military power, the United States was caught between these giants. By 1807, they had seized some 1,500 U.S. ships, and there were few remaining ports to which Americans could sail without the threat of seizure by one or the other of the two warring powers. Moreover, in the summer of 1807, near the mouth of the Chesapeake Bay, the British frigate "Leopard" fired upon the American warship "Chesapeake," forced it to submit to search, and pressed four sailors into British service. For years, the British had been stopping merchant ships to search them for deserters, taking naturalized Americans of British birth, and sometimes seizing native-born Americans as well. The "Chesapeake" affair was nonetheless an outrage of a different sort. To fire upon a frigate was an act of war.

War was what the people called for in a fury reminiscent of the XYZ Affair ten years before. Especially in the American Northwest—in Indiana, Michigan, and Illinois, where British officials in Canada soon began to give assistance and encouragement to Tecumseh and the Prophet, Shawnee brothers who were trying to unite the western tribes against the advance of American settlement—the demand for war rose steadily from this point on. Yet Jefferson's administration was determined to confront the troubles in the way their principles required. Both war itself and all the normal preparations for a war—high taxes, swollen military forces, rising debts, and larger governmental powers—had always seemed a deadly peril for republics. Any of these measures would require a radical reversal of the course that the administration had been following since 1801.

In addition, Jefferson and Madison had long believed that the United States possessed a weapon that provided an alternative to war, a weapon that had proven its effectiveness during the long struggle preceding American Independence. That weapon was its trade. Most American exports, as they saw it, were necessities of life: raw materials and food on which the Europeans and their island colonies were vitally dependent. Most American imports, on the other hand, were "niceties" or "luxuries" that the United States could either do without or manufacture at a shop or household level on its own. Accordingly, in any confrontation with the Europeans (especially the British), the United States could force the enemy to terms by a denial of its commerce, and without the dangers to its government or social order that a war would necessarily entail.[49]

In 1807, Jefferson's administration answered French and British measures by placing a complete embargo on foreign trade.[50] The great embargo did impose some hardships on the Europeans. Unhappily, its consequences for America were even worse; it called for more self-sacrifice than many citizens were willing to display. All American sailings for foreign ports were halted for more than a year. The result was a depression that affected every section of the country, but was most severe in Federalist New England, whose economy was heavily dependent on its shipping. Resistance by New Englanders was fierce, and non-cooperation and illegal sailings could be countered only by enforcement measures so draconian that they endangered the Jeffersonians' reputation as defenders of civil rights.[51] The Federalists enjoyed a brief revival.

In short, the great embargo broke America before it broke the Europeans. To maintain the peace within America, the Jeffersonians—whose party vision did not change when Madison succeeded Jefferson in 1809—were forced to settle for less stringent measures. The embargo was replaced in 1809 with a measure confining nonintercourse to trade between America and the two belligerent powers, France or England.[52] In 1810, nonintercourse gave way in turn to a provision that restrictions would be reimposed on either European power if the other would respect America's neutral rights—a carrot rather than a stick. Napoleon, who realized that the removal of American restrictions could only aid the British, delivered an ambiguous announcement suggesting that he would exempt Americans from his Berlin and Milan Decrees against neutral vessels. Madison chose to interpret the announcement as fulfilling the American demands and called upon the British to repeal their Orders in Council. When the British government refused, he reimposed nonintercourse with Britain.

By the winter of 1811-1812, commercial warfare had been pressed, in one form or another, for a full four years. It had enraged the shipping center of New England and encouraged the resurgence of a party that the Jeffersonians regarded as a danger to democracy itself. The people were becoming restless under policies that damaged their own prosperity without compelling any change by Britain. The choice now seemed to lie between submission to the British and a war, and neither the people's sense of national honor nor the survival of the Republican party—a party that still believed that American liberty depended on its guidance—would permit submission. Thus, before the new Twelfth Congress met, Madison reluctantly decided on a war. In what was basically a party vote, a declaration passed the Congress on June 18, 1812.[53]

What followed was a tragedy of errors: thirty months of warfare during which it was uncertain whether the United States would manage to survive intact, followed by a peace that settled none of the essential issues over which the fighting had begun. After years of stubborn dedication to an anti-preparation ideology, America embarked on war with Britain with fourteen warships and a regular army of less than 7,000 well-trained men. It entered on the conflict so divided that New England governors refused to let the country's best militia march beyond the borders of their states, and wealthy Yankees stubbornly declined to lend financial aid. Not too surprisingly, the War of 1812 brought little glory, other than some striking victories by U.S. frigates in their single-ship engagements with the British and, of course, the smashing triumph at New Orleans, where Andrew Jackson crushed the last invasion two weeks after peace had been agreed upon at Ghent in Belgium on December 24, 1814.[54] But then, the War of 1812 had not been undertaken for the sake of national glory. It had been declared to demonstrate that a republican regime could safeguard national interests and defend the country's rights. And in the minds of those who fought it, although little had been gained, nothing had been lost in a collision with the greatest power on the earth. National honor had been satisfied. The Union had endured. Republicans had learned important lessons.

The War of 1812 had major consequences for the nation. In December 1814, as Jackson was preparing to defend New Orleans, a convention met at Hartford, Connecticut, to consider New England's grievances against the nation, which had crippled the administration's effort to conduct the war. The delegates demanded radical amendments to the Constitution to protect their region from the Jeffersonian majority in Washington, D.C., and threatened stronger actions if the changes were refused.[55] It was a classic case of dreadful timing. The manifesto from the gathering at Hartford reached the capital in close conjunction with the news of Jackson's dramatic victory at New Orleans. In consequence, New England's effort to extort concessions in the face of war appeared both foolish and disloyal. Lifted by the people's swelling pride, the Madison administration reached unprecedented heights of national prestige.[56] Simultaneously, the reputation of the Federalists was damaged beyond repair. Within four years of Madison's retirement, the triumph of the Jeffersonians was practically complete. With James Monroe's essentially unanimous election to a second term, the nation entered into a period of single-party rule.

As it did so, the Republicans adjusted to the lessons of the war and to the economic transformation it had fostered. Early in 1815, President Madison recommended a peacetime army of 20,000 men. In his last annual message, on December 5, 1815, the great co-architect of Jeffersonian ideals called also for a federal program of internal improvements, tariff protection for the infant industries that had sprung up during the war, and the creation of a new national bank (Congress having refused in 1811 to recharter the old Hamiltonian institution). All these measures were enacted by the Congress early in 1816, although the President refused to sign the bill for internal improvements until a constitutional amendment clearly authorized the federal government to act. Together, these initiatives amounted to another striking change of governmental course.

Madison's proposals, to be sure, were far from a complete surrender to the Federalists' ideas. The President still hoped that education, an enormous reservoir of western lands, and the continued leadership of the legitimate defenders of the people's Constitution would indefinitely postpone the civic evils he and Jefferson still feared. Like Jefferson, however, Madison had learned that "there exists both profligacy and power enough to exclude us from the field of interchange with other nations"; that Americans must either manufacture more of the necessities and niceties of life, accept "dependence on that foreign nation," or "be clothed in skins and . . . live like wild beasts in dens and caverns."[57] The policies of the Republican administrations—the war itself and many years of economic conflict with the British—had encouraged an explosive growth of native manufactures, which the President could not abandon at the peace. Meanwhile, as he saw it, Britain had been able to supply itself with raw materials and food from Canada and Latin America, which would continue to provide a rival source of the necessities on which commercial warfare hinged.[58] Accordingly, the aging founder hinted that the party's old ideas must now be blended with some fragments of the Hamiltonian design (although without the Hamiltonian monopolies or Federalist contempt for popular political participation). In the process, Madison legitimized the other side of a debate that had embroiled the nation since adoption of the Constitution.

The old debate did not abruptly reach a permanent conclusion. In 1819, a serious financial panic and a sectional collision over the admission of Missouri to the Union provoked new arguments about the country's economic transformation and the wisdom of the legislation of 1816. Soon, in the guise of Henry Clay's "American System," a Hamiltonian conception of a self-sufficient nation, where industrial development would build domestic markets for the farmers' surplus, and federal programs like the tariff and the bank would tie the country's sections into a harmonious whole, would revitalize the old disputes. Moreover, the United States has seldom had a less effective central government than during the years between 1820 and 1828, not least because the last of the Jeffersonian presidents, James Monroe and John Quincy Adams, did not believe in leading Congress, and Republicans did not believe in being led. Presidential leadership and presidential patronage still smelled too much of influence and corruption, as did blind allegiance to a party.[59] By the early 1820s, it was clear that the destruction of the Federalists had left Republicans too free to fight among themselves. But even as they did, the fundamental principles enunciated at the party's founding would endure as a foundation for the views of both the Democrats and Whigs, refurbished and revitalized to fit the different needs and different spirit of the age of Andrew Jackson.

## NOTES

1. Americans of the 1780s referred more often to their "republican" Revolution against aristocracy and monarchy than to "democracy," especially when they wanted to distinguish their representative forms of government from the direct democracies of ancient Greece. Nevertheless, "republican" and "democratic" were often used synonymously during these years, and by the late 1790s the progenitors of the modern party were sometimes called the Democratic-Republicans. Today's Republicans (the G.O.P.) did not appear until the 1850s and were not the lineal descendants of the Federalists of the early Republic.

2. See Lance Banning, "1787 and 1776: Patrick Henry, James Madison, the Constitution, and the Revolution," in *Toward a More Perfect Union: Six Essays on the Constitution*, ed. Neil L. York (Provo: Brigham Young University Press, 1988), 58-89 together with the secondary sources cited there.

3. E. James Ferguson, *The Power of the Purse: A History of American Public Finance, 1776-1790* (Chapel Hill: University of North Carolina Press, 1961), 292-96; Forrest McDonald, *Alexander Hamilton: A Biography* (New York: Norton, 1979), chap. 8; and Donald F. Swanson, *The Origins of Hamilton's Fiscal Policies* (Gainesville: University of Florida Press, 1963).

4. *The Federalist Papers*, ed. Isaac Kramnick (Harmondsworth, England: Penguin, 1987), 67. See, more fully, 67-75.

5. P. G. M. Dickson, *The Financial Revolution in England: A Study in the Development of Public Credit, 1688-1756* (New York: St. Martin's Press, 1967).

6. For Hamilton's life and vision see, especially, John C. Miller, *Alexander Hamilton: Portrait in Paradox* (New York: Harper & Row, 1959); McDonald, *Alexander Hamilton*; and Gerald Stourzh, *Alexander Hamilton and the Idea of Republican Government* (Stanford: Stanford University Press, 1970).

7. "If all the public creditors receive their dues from one source," Hamilton's Report observed, "their interests will be the same. And having the same interests, they will unite in support of the fiscal arrangements of government." *The Papers of Alexander Hamilton*, Harold C. Syrett et al., eds. 26 vols. (New York: Columbia University Press), 6:80-81.

8. In addition to the sources cited in notes 3 and 6 above, see Drew R. McCoy, *The Elusive Republic: Political Economy in Jeffersonian America* (Chapel Hill: University of North Carolina Press, 1980), 146-152; and Lance Banning, "Political Economy and the Creation of the Federal Republic," forthcoming in *The Possession of Freedom*, ed. David T. Konig, vol. 5 of *The Making of Modern Freedom* (Stanford: Stanford University Press, 1993).

9. Ferguson, *The Power of the Purse*, 329-330, calculates that funding raised the market value of the federal debt from about $5,000,000 in 1786 to nearly $42,000,000 (including the arrears of interest) in 1791. It multiplied the value of state certificates by similar proportions. In 1789 and 1790, North Carolina and South Carolina securities sold for ten to twenty cents on the dollar, Virginia securities for twenty to thirty cents. Sixty percent of Virginia's certificates and ninety percent of North Carolina's were in the hands of large secondary holders. See Whitney K. Bates, "Northern Speculators and Southern State Debts, 1790," *William and Mary Quarterly*, 3d ser., 19 (1962): 32-34, 39.

10. In these objections, congressmen were drawing on an old and very potent Anglo-American critique of the disastrous consequences of a funded debt and mercantilistic economics. The literature on the tremendous influence of this eighteenth century critique is now enormous. For an introduction, see Robert Shalhope, "Toward a Republican Synthesis: The Emergence of an Understanding of Republicanism in American Historiography," *William and Mary Quarterly*, 3d ser., 29 (1972): 49-80; Shalhope, "Republicanism and Early American Historiography," ibid., 39 (1982): 334-356; Peter S. Onuf, "Reflections on the Founding: Constitutional Historiography in Bicentennial Perspective," ibid., 45 (1989): 341-375; and Lance Banning, "The Republican Hypothesis: Retrospect and Prospect," forthcoming in American Antiquarian Society, *Proceedings* (Fall, 1992). The congressional debate on funding (February 1790) may be followed in *Annals of Congress*, 1:1180-1224, 1234-1239, 1248-1322; 2:1324-1354.

11. Irving Brant, *James Madison*, 6 vols. (Indianapolis: Bobbs-Merrill, 1941-1961); Ralph Ketcham, *James Madison: A Biography* (New York: Macmillan, 1971); and Jack N. Rakove, *James Madison and the Creation of the American Republic* (Glenview, Illinois: Scott, Foresman/Little, Brown, 1990).

12. Some congressmen and other insiders at New York hurried cash and agents to the farthest reaches of the Union to gobble up outstanding state certificates before their holders were aware of how much they would increase in value.

13. Speech of February 18, 1790, in *The Papers of James Madison*, William T. Hutchinson et al., eds. 17 vols. to date (Charlottesville: University Press of Virginia, 1962—)13:48-49.

14. Dumas Malone, *Jefferson and His Time*, 6 vols. (Boston: Little, Brown, 1948-1981); Merrill D. Peterson, *Thomas Jefferson and the New Nation: A Biography* (London: Oxford University Press, 1970).

15. The most recent discussion is Kenneth R. Bowling, "The Compromise of 1790," chap. 7 of *The Creation of Washington, D.C.: The Idea and Location of the American Capital* (Fairfax: George Mason University Press, 1991).

16. Madison's speech on the national bank, February 2, 1791, in Hutchinson, *The Papers of James Madison*, 13:373-381; Jefferson's "Opinion on the Constitutionality of a National Bank," February 15, 1791, in *The Works of Thomas Jefferson*, ed. Paul Leicester Ford, 12 vols. (New York: Putnam, 1904), 5:284-289.

17. Lance Banning, *The Jeffersonian Persuasion: Evolution of a Party Ideology* (Ithaca: Cornell University Press, 1978) traces the development of party thought.

18. Madison came as close to outrage as it was possible for him to do in response to the "scramble for . . . public plunder" attendant on the opening of the national bank, writing Jefferson that "My imagination will not attempt to set bounds to the daring depravity of the times. The stock-jobbers will become the pretorian band of the government, at once its tools and its tyrants; bribed by its largesses, and overawing it by clamors and combinations." Hutchinson, *Papers of Madison*, 14:43, 69.

19. Jefferson warned President Washington that Hamilton's program "flowed from principles adverse to liberty and was calculated to undermine and demolish the republic by creating an influence of his department over the members of the legislature. . . . to draw all the powers of government into the hands of the general legislature, to establish means for corrupting a sufficient corps in that legislature to . . . preponderate. . . , and to have that corps under the command of the Secretary of the Treasury for the purpose of subverting step by step the principles of the Constitution, which he has so often declared a thing of nothing which must be changed." Ford, *Works of Jefferson*, 7:138-139. Robert Walpole was prime minister of England in the second quarter of the eighteenth century and the classic villain of this well-established condemnation of the British system of administration and finance.

20. This characterization of Hamilton's course came in an interview with Madison by Nicholas P. Trist, September 27, 1834. But compare Jefferson's late-life discussion in his preface to the "Anas," *Works of Jefferson*, 1:167-183

21. Banning, *Jeffersonian Persuasion*, 153-155 and chap. 6.

22. Recent discussions of the configurations of the first party struggle include Richard Buel, Jr., *Securing the Revolution: Ideology in American Politics, 1789-1815* (Ithaca: Cornell University Press, 1972); David Hackett Fischer, *The Revolution of American Conservatism* (New York: Harper & Row, 1965), appendix 1; and Paul Goodman, "The First American Party System," in *The American Party Systems: Stages of Political Development*, eds. William Nesbit Chambers and Walter Dean Burnham (Oxford: Oxford University Press, 1967), 56-89. Among many state and local studies, two have been especially influential: Paul Goodman, *The Democratic-Republicans of Massachusetts* (Cambridge: Harvard University Press, 1964); and Alfred F. Young, *The Democratic Republicans of New York* (Chapel Hill: University of North Carolina Press, 1967).

23. See Gordon S. Wood, *The Radicalism of the American Revolution* (New York: Knopf, 1992); and—for the division between friends of liberty and friends of order—Thomas P. Slaughter, *The Whiskey Rebellion: Frontier Epilogue to the American Revolution* (New York: Oxford University Press, 1986).

24. See Banning, "1787 and 1776" for an argument that prevailing scholarly opinions do not properly distinguish Madison's objectives from those of other advocates of the Constitution and thus suggest that Madison shifted course in the years after 1789 more radically than was in fact the case.

25. Query xix of Jefferson's *Notes on the State of Virginia*, written in 1781-1782, is most often quoted: "Generally speaking, the proportion which the aggregate of other classes of citizens bears in any state to that of its husbandmen is the proportion of its unsound to its healthy parts. . . . While we have land to labor then, let us never wish to see our citizens occupied at a workbench or twirling a distaff. Carpenters, masons, smiths are wanted in husbandry; but for the general operations of manufacture, let our workshops remain in Europe. . . . The loss by the transportation of commodities across the Atlantic will be made up in happiness and permanence of government. The mobs of great cities add just so much to the support of pure government as sores do to the strength of the human body. It is the manners and spirit of a people which preserve a republic in vigor." But see also Madison's *National Gazette* essays on "Republican Distribution of Citizens" (March 3, 1792) and "Fashion" (March 20, 1792), written in response to Hamilton's report on manufactures and available in Hutchinson, *Papers of Madison,* 14: 244-246, 285-288. My discussion of Republican political economy prefers McCoy, *The Elusive Republic*, to Joyce Appleby, *Capitalism and a New Social Order: The Republican Vision of the 1790s* (New York: New York University Press, 1984), but draws on Appleby as well for its insistence on the forward-looking, revolutionary enterprise of freeing individuals from hierarchical restraints and creating a harmonious society of self-directing equals. For an argument that revolutionary (or Republican) demands for public virtue seldom sought a selfless, sacrificial dedication to a larger public good, but did expect a self-assertive, vigilant participation in a politics of equals, see Lance Banning, "Some Second Thoughts on Virtue and the Course of Revolutionary Thinking," in *Conceptual Change and the Constitution*, eds. Terence Ball and J. G. A. Pocock, (Lawrence: University Press of Kansas, 1988), 194-212. For the debate among historians about the character and sources of Republican ideas, see further Banning, "The Republican Hypothesis" and "Jeffersonian Ideology Revisited: Liberal and Classical Ideas in the New American Republic," *William and Mary Quarterly*, 3d ser., 43 (1986): 3-19, together with the sources cited in these essays.

26. Banning, *Jeffersonian Persuasion*, 154-155.

27. The progress of the party quarrel, with a special emphasis on the development of the Republicans' ideas, can be followed in Banning, *Jeffersonian Persuasion*. Other studies of the struggle's progress include Buel, *Securing the Revolution*; John C. Miller, *The Federalist Era, 1789-1801* (New York: Harper & Row, 1960); Joseph Charles, *The Origins of the American Party System: Three Essays* (New York: Harper & Row, 1961); and William Nesbit Chambers, *Political Parties in a New Nation* (New York: Oxford University Press, 1957). Noble E. Cunningham, *The Jeffersonian Republicans* (Chapel Hill: University of North

Carolina Press, 1957) remains the best study of the development of party machinery.

28. Harry Ammon, *The Genet Mission* (New York: Norton, 1973).

29. Eugene Perry Link, *Democratic-Republican Societies, 1790-1800* (New York: Columbia University Press, 1942).

30. Slaughter, *The Whiskey Rebellion.*

31. The most respected recent studies conclude that he did: Jerald A. Combs, *The Jay Treaty* (Berkeley: University of California Press, 1970); and Charles R. Ritcheson, *Aftermath of Revolution: British Policy toward the United States, 1783-1795* (Dallas: Southern Methodist University Press, 1969), chap. 16.

32. For the administration of John Adams, Stephen G. Kurtz, *The Presidency of John Adams: The Collapse of Federalism, 1795-1800* (Philadelphia: University of Pennsylvania Press, 1957); Manning J. Dauer, *The Adams Federalists* (Baltimore: The Johns Hopkins University Press, 1953); and Ralph A. Brown, *The Presidency of John Adams* (Lawrence: University Press of Kansas, 1975) should be added to the sources cited in note 27 above. Alexander DeConde, *The Quasi-War: The Politics and Diplomacy of the Undeclared War with France, 1797-1801* (New York: Scribner, 1966) is the best source for the diplomacy discussed below.

33. James Morton Smith, *Freedom's Fetters: The Alien and Sedition Laws and American Civil Liberties* (Ithaca: Cornell University Press, 1956); and John C. Miller, *Crisis in Freedom: The Alien and Sedition Acts* (Boston: Little, Brown, 1951).

34. Adrienne Koch and Harry Ammon, "The Virginia and Kentucky Resolutions: An Episode in Jefferson's and Madison's Defense of Civil Liberties," *William and Mary Quarterly*, 3d ser., 5 (1948): 145-176.

35. In retirement at Mt. Vernon, Washington agreed to assume active leadership of the enlarged and provisional armies only if they were required to take the field against invasion, joining with the cabinet to insist that Hamilton should head the list of major generals and thus assume effective leadership until that time. When Washington died on December 13, 1799, Hamilton, who had come to late-colonial New York from the West Indian island of Nevis and was the illegitimate son of an obscure member of a Scottish noble family, was officially in command.

36. Richard H. Kohn, *Eagle and Sword: The Beginnings of the Military Establishment in America* (New York: Free Press, 1975), chap. 12, is an excellent discussion of the pivotal role of the army question in Adams's decision. Contrast Jacob E. Cooke, "Country Above Party: John Adams and the 1799 Mission to France," in *Fame and the Founding Fathers*, ed. Edmund P. Willis, (Bethlehem, Pa.: Moravian College, 1967), 53-77.

37. Young, *The Democratic Republicans of New York*; John R. Nelson, "Alexander Hamilton and American Manufacturing: A Reexamination," *Journal of American History*, 65 (1979): 971-995.

38. Jefferson to Spencer Roane, September 6, 1819, in Ford, *Works of Jefferson*, 12:136.

39. Article II, Section 1 of the Constitution provides that presidential electors shall be chosen in such manner as the state legislatures direct. Until the age of Jackson, legislatures often chose the electors themselves. Constitutionally, they still could do so.

40. *Works of Jefferson*, 9:197-198.
41. When Congress met, the Federalists proposed renewal of the act, which was at least consistent with their claim that it was actually more liberal than the common law of libel. The Republicans defeated the proposal.
42. Noble E. Cunningham, *The Jeffersonian Republicans in Power: Party Operations, 1801-1809* (Chapel Hill: University of North Carolina Press, 1963), chap. 2 is a fine brief treatment of Jefferson's appointments policy. See also Carl E. Prince, "The Passing of the Aristocracy: Jefferson's Removal of the Federalists, 1801-1805," *Journal of American History*, 57 (1970):563-575.
43. William Duane in the *Philadelphia Aurora*, February 27, 1801.
44. Duane himself described the first annual message as "an epitome of republican principles applied to practical purposes," ibid., December 18, 1801.
45. Ford, *Works of Jefferson*, 9:341-342.
46. Jefferson to Dupont de Nemours, Jan. 18, 1802, Ford, *Works of Jefferson*, 9:343-344.
47. For these years, the classic history is Henry Adams, *History of the United States during the Administrations of Thomas Jefferson and James Madison*, 9 vols. (New York: Scribner, 1889-1890), although the reader should be wary of the biases of this descendant of John Adams. A briefer, modern overview is Marshall Smelser, *The Democratic Republic, 1801-1815* (New York: Harper & Row, 1968). See also Forrest McDonald, *The Presidency of Thomas Jefferson* (Lawrence: University Press of Kansas, 1976); Robert Allen Rutland, *The Presidency of James Madison* (Lawrence: University Press of Kansas, 1990); Noble E. Cunningham, *The Jeffersonian Republicans in Power: Party Operations, 1801-1809* (Chapel Hill: University of North Carolina Press, 1963); Cunningham, *The Process of Government under Jefferson* (Princeton: Princeton University Press, 1978); and Robert M. Johnstone, *Jefferson and the Presidency: Leadership in the Young Republic* (Ithaca: Cornell University Press, 1978).
48. These *were*, however, the very years when the contagious faith in liberty, equality, and the capacity of ordinary citizens to shape their own beliefs and institutions were transforming the religious as well as the political landscape, not the least by furious assaults on settled, well-paid clergy. See Nathan O. Hatch, *The Democratization of American Christianity* (New Haven: Yale University Press, 1989).
49. The best source for the Jeffersonian policy of commercial confrontation is McCoy, *The Elusive Republic*, chap. 9. See also Banning, "Political Economy and the Creation of the Federal Republic."
50. It does not seem certain that the President himself intended the embargo from the outset as a long-term alternative to war. But Secretary of State Madison probably did, and Jefferson himself was soon committed to that course. Gallatin did not agree. "In every point of view, privations, sufferings, revenue, effect on the enemy, politics at home, etc.," he told the President, "I prefer war to a permanent embargo." *The Writings of Gallatin*, ed. Henry Adams, 3 vols. (Philadelphia: Lippincott, 1879), 1:386. On these matters, see Burton Spivak, *Jefferson's English Crisis: Commerce, Embargo, and the Republican Revolution* (Charlottesville: University Press of Virginia, 1979).
51. *Jefferson and Civil Liberties: The Darker Side*, rev., ed. Leonard Levy (New York: Quadrangle Books, 1973).

52. The repeal occurred during the last days of Jefferson's administration and without the President's wholehearted approval. Jefferson virtually abdicated his leadership role once Madison had been elected, but he continued to believe that the experiment should be prolonged or abandoned only for a declaration of war.

53. Roger H. Brown, *The Republic in Peril: 1812* (New York: Columbia University Press, 1964).

54. Harry L. Coles, *The War of 1812* (Chicago: University of Chicago Press, 1965); J. C. A. Stagg, *Mr. Madison's War: Politics, Diplomacy, and Warfare in the Early American Republic, 1783-1830* (Princeton: Princeton University Press, 1983); and Donald R. Hickey, *The War of 1812: A Forgotten Conflict* (Urbana: University of Illinois Press, 1989).

55. James M. Banner, Jr., *To the Hartford Convention: The Federalists and the Origins of Party Politics in Massachusetts, 1789-1815* (New York: Knopf, 1970).

56. From his retirement, Adams wrote to Jefferson that "notwithstanding a thousand faults and blunders, [Madison's] administration has acquired more glory, and established more Union, than all three predecessors, Washington, Adams, and Jefferson put together" *The Adams-Jefferson Letters*, ed. Lester Cappon, 2 vols. (Chapel Hill: University of North Carolina Press, 1959), 2:508.

57. Jefferson to Benjamin Austin, January 9, 1819, *Works of Jefferson*, 2:502-505.

58. J. C. A. Stagg, "James Madison and the Coercion of Great Britain: Canada, the West Indies, and the War of 1812," *William and Mary Quarterly*, 3d ser., 38 (1981):3-34; Donald R. Hickey, "American Trade Restrictions during the War of 1812," *Journal of American History* 68 (1981): 517-538; and—more broadly—Steven Watts, *The Republic Reborn: War and the Making of Liberal America, 1790-1820* (Baltimore: The Johns Hopkins University Press, 1987).

59. James Sterling Young, *The Washington Community, 1800-1828* (New York: Columbia University Press, 1966) is still useful here. See also, Richard Hofstadter, *The Idea of a Party System:The Rise of Legitimate Opposition in the United States, 1780-1840* (Berkeley: University of California Press, 1969).

Chapter 2

# The Democratic Party in the Jacksonian Era

*Robert V. Remini*

The Democratic party of General Andrew Jackson began with a shout of moral outrage following the presidential election of 1824. "*The people* [have] *been cheated*," Old Hickory thundered to a crowd in Frankfort, Kentucky. "*Corruptions and intrigues at Washington . . . defeated the will of the people*."[1]

His intensely blue eyes smoked with anger. As he spoke he drew himself up to his full height of six feet. Commanding in appearance, cadaverously thin, with a long, sharp, lantern jaw and grey-white hair bristling with electricity and standing up from his head as though at attention, Andrew Jackson of Tennessee, Old Hickory, looked about as presidential as any man in the history of this country. He carried himself with military stiffness and instantly conveyed to all about him a sense of leadership and authority.

"We did all we could for you here," wailed one man, "but the rascals at Washington cheated you. . . ." The "rascals" had "stolen" the presidency, he said, stolen it from the man who had outpolled all the other candidates in the fall election, both in popular and electoral votes.

"Indeed, my old friend," responded Jackson, "there was *cheating*, and *corruption*, and *bribery* too."[2]

How had this happened? How had the political process seemingly failed? How was it possible in a free and republican society for the people to speak their will in a presidential election and have it totally ignored? Some later argued that the signs of this "catastrophe" could have been predicted. The early signs had appeared years before.

## THE ERA OF GOOD FEELINGS

The Republican party of Thomas Jefferson faced no political opposition on the national level following the War of 1812, and James Monroe, the Republican nominee in 1816, won the presidency with only token opposition. On the national level the old Federalist party of George Washington, Alexander Hamilton, and John Adams had begun its descent into political oblivion because of its association with the Hartford Convention in 1814 that many believed had barely skirted treason.[3] Thus, with only one viable national party in existence after the War of 1812, it was expected that political differences would cease, and that an era of harmony would ensue. Indeed, a Boston newspaper editor erroneously dubbed the eight years of the Monroe administration an "Era of Good Feelings."[4]

But political differences did not cease in the decade following the end of the war. As men of different and conflicting political persuasions crowded into the Republican party they began bickering with one another over such issues as the tariff, internal improvements, and a national bank, as well as the party's future direction. Central to their disputes was concern over the expanding powers of the central government and the scope of federal authority under the Constitution. "Conservative" Republicans preached fiscal and legislative restraint, reminding fellow Republicans that their party was committed to states' rights, and that those powers not specifically delegated by the Constitution to the central government were reserved to the states and the people. To document their case, they cited the Tenth Amendment to the Constitution, as well as the states' rights doctrines contained in the Kentucky and Virginia Resolutions written by Jefferson and Madison in 1798.

More "liberal" Republicans disagreed. They found nothing unconstitutional in utilizing the powers of the central government to advance the material well-being of the nation. They believed that espousing a national bank could hardly be faulted after the dire financial difficulties the nation had experienced during the War of 1812. After all, President James Madison, in one of his last official acts, had signed the bill that created the Second National Bank of the United States. And approving federally sponsored public works and enacting protective tariffs seemed equally legitimate. A market economy, triggered by the introduction of the Industrial Revolution, as well as massive changes in transportation and, a little later, communications, seemed to necessitate a more active role for the federal government. Henry Clay of Kentucky—"Harry of the West," as his admirers called him—argued this line of reasoning, expressing his ideas in a program he called the "American System." He especially sought higher tariff rates to safeguard infant American manufactures, along with the building of roads, canals, bridges, and turnpikes on a national scale.[5] But conservatives condemned such thinking as "heretical," a violation of everything Jeffersonian Republicanism represented, and a throwback to Federalist ideas.

These differences within the Republican party would sharply define political discourse for the next quarter century. They not only resonated throughout the Jacksonian era, they still resonate today, influencing both conservatives and liberals, modern-day Republicans and modern-day Democrats.

## THE ELECTION OF 1824-25

None of these controversial issues actually surfaced in any serious way during the presidential campaign of 1824.[6] Rather, the election revolved around a personal contest among several distinguished men from different sections of the country who represented the new generation of American statesmen, now that the Revolutionary generation had died or retired. For the most part, these Republicans accepted nominations for the presidency from their respective states; only one man, Secretary of the Treasury William H. Crawford of Georgia, received a nomination from a congressional caucus, the traditional method of nominating presidential candidates. The other candidates included Andrew Jackson of Tennessee, whose reputation and popularity rested almost solely on his great victory over the British at the Battle of New Orleans during the War of 1812; John Quincy Adams of Massachusetts, the distinguished diplomat and Secretary of State under President James Monroe; and Henry Clay of Kentucky, who was largely responsible for lifting the office of speaker of the House of Representatives to a level of importance and power second only to that of the president. A fifth candidate, the Secretary of War in Monroe's cabinet, John C. Calhoun of South Carolina, dropped out of the race when his northern support shifted to Jackson, choosing instead to run for the office of vice president, which he subsequently won without appreciable opposition.

Not surprisingly, because of the number of candidates in the contest, the fall election ended with no one winning the constitutionally mandated majority of electoral votes. However, Jackson had pluralities in both the popular vote and the electoral college.[7] According to the Twelfth Amendment to the Constitution, when no candidate receives a majority of electoral votes, the election goes to the House of Representatives, where a majority of states decide who will be the next president. Each state casts one vote for the candidate of its choice, as determined by a majority of its delegation, and only the three candidates with the highest number of electoral votes are considered. In the election of 1824, that stipulation automatically eliminated Henry Clay, which was unfortunate for him because, as Speaker of the House, he enjoyed enormous influence and power and no doubt would have been elected President. Instead he became, in effect, the "king-maker."

Early in 1825 Clay publicly announced his support of Adams. The two men entertained nearly identical ideas about the authority of the government to improve the condition of society, so their "coalition" might have been anticipated. Clay could expect Adams to submit his "American System" to Congress for implementation, something neither Jackson nor Crawford were likely to do, considering their conservative philosophies. But a rumor also circulated, almost at once, that Clay had promised to deliver sufficient votes in the House election to win the presidency for Adams, in return for which Clay would be appointed Secretary of State. Clay wanted this office because it traditionally led immediately to the presidency itself.[8]

## "THE CORRUPT BARGAIN"

On February 9, 1825, on the very first ballot, the members of the House of Representatives chose John Quincy Adams as the sixth president of the United States.[9] A few days later Adams announced that upon taking office on March 4, 1825, he would name Henry Clay as his Secretary of State.

"So you see," Jackson raged when he heard the news, "the Judas of the West has closed the contract and will receive the thirty pieces of silver. His end will be the same. Was there ever witnessed such a bare-faced corruption in any country before?"[10]

The cry "corrupt bargain" instantly echoed around the country. The "will of the people," expressed in the fall election, had been contemptuously cast aside by arrogant politicians in Washington. And Clay's actual appointment tended to confirm the earlier rumors of a bargain. Jackson spoke for many Americans when he later wrote: "Clay voted for Adams and made him President and Adams made Clay secretary of state. Is this not proof as strong as holy writ of the understanding and corrupt coalition between them."[11]

Indeed so, was the verdict of many voters. And the moral issue raised by this "criminal" act was as clear to them as "holy writ": the rights of the majority had been trampled and scorned by an elite few. Those committed to advancing special interests by federal action—Clay's "American System"—had overturned the results of the fall election. In that moment, not only had the principal issue for the presidential election of 1828 been defined, but actions and events began to take shape that would result in the emergence of a reorganized Democratic party.

## MARTIN VAN BUREN

Unquestionably, the most important person in the realignment of political forces following the House election in 1825 was the conservative

Republican Senator from New York, Martin Van Buren, a short, balding, elegantly dressed politician who was sometimes called the "Little Magician" or "Red Fox of Kinderhook" in recognition of his superb managerial and political skills. He had built an organization in New York called the Albany Regency to run the state in his absence. But make no mistake. This was no association of hack politicians out for plunder and power; it was a corps of intelligent and devoted Republican leaders in the state dedicated to preserving the principles of Jeffersonian Republicanism. For the most part, they advocated limited government, states' rights, and fiscal restraint by the central government.

During the years of Monroe's presidency, Van Buren had been deeply concerned about the direction of the party. He accused the administration of adopting a policy of "amalgamation," of seeking to integrate the Republican and Federalist parties. Monroe was guilty of disregarding or blurring the essential differences between the two parties, said Van Buren, and in effect, of destroying the two-party system. He called it "Monroe's fusion policy." And he condemned it. Van Buren and others believed that a two-party system was essential for stable government: one-party rule inevitably invited tyranny; multi-party rule invited chaos. The legitimacy of a "loyal" opposition was something Van Buren could understand and accept. Jackson, on the other hand, regarded opponents as personal enemies and treated them accordingly.

Van Buren felt that a great many Republicans shared his concerns and that, like him, they wanted "radical reform." What was needed, he wrote, was the restoration of the two-party system and the "general resuscitation of the old democratic party."[12]

## THE MAKING OF THE DEMOCRATIC PARTY

To achieve this restoration and resuscitation Van Buren decided to go over to General Jackson and support him for the presidency in 1828. The two men had met in the U.S. Senate and Van Buren had a fairly accurate sense of Old Hickory's political philosophy. "My political creed," Jackson admitted in 1826, "was formed in the old republican school." "The moment the Sovereignity [sic] of the Individual States, is overwhelmed by the General Government, we may bid adieu to our freedom."[13] Still, Van Buren did not hesitate to warn the General, after they had joined forces, against avowing "any opinion upon Constitutional questions at war with the doctrines of the Jeffersonian School."[14]

As his first step in the reorganization of the Republican party, Van Buren enlisted the support of the newly elected Vice President, John C.

Calhoun, who he knew opposed the Adams-Clay coalition. Van Buren spent the Christmas holidays of 1826 conferring with Calhoun. The two men agreed that if the presidency could be stolen to serve the interests of an elite, then liberty itself was in peril. They also noted with alarm that President Adams had lost no time in revealing his nefarious intentions; in his first message to Congress in December 1825, Adams had advocated a broad program of government-sponsored internal improvements, including roads, canals, harbor installations, bridges, and even an astronomical observatory, a national university, and other such "unrepublican" horrors. To make matters worse, Adams had urged immediate action on his proposals by admonishing Congress not to give the world the impression that "we are palsied by the will of our constituents."[15]

Indeed, "the will of our constituents" apparently meant nothing to Adams and his friends. Forget that will, he seemed to be saying. Do what has to be done to make this nation stronger and more prosperous. "For the fulfillment of those duties," said Adams in his message, "governments are invested with power, and to the attainment of the end—the progressive improvement of the condition of the governed—the exercise of delegated powers is a duty."[16]

Conservatives were horrified. Even Jefferson said that some of the proposals were unconstitutional, and Senator Thomas Hart Benton of Missouri later reflected that the message "went to the reconstruction of parties on the old line of strict . . . construction of the constitution."[17]

To reaffirm the principles of Jeffersonian Republicanism against this revival of Hamiltonian Federalism, Van Buren believed, required the defeat of Adams and the election of Jackson in 1828. Only then would the "will of our constituents" be restored to its rightful place in the political world. Only then would liberty and the rights of the people be reaffirmed. Van Buren and Calhoun agreed that the initial philosophical struggle that produced the formation of parties in 1792 still raged: virtue versus corruption; the people versus an elite; liberty versus power. "An issue has been fairly made, as it seems to me," wrote Calhoun to Jackson at this time, "between *power* and *liberty*."[18]

To reconcile past differences among all the Republicans that Van Buren and Calhoun hoped to corral into their reconstituted party, as well as to hold down the number of candidates that might be put forward by individual states, the two men agreed to sponsor a national nominating convention.[19] Van Buren believed that the idea accorded with popular sentiment. The old congressional caucus method of nomination was despised as another instrument by which the powerful few maintained control of the government. The *Albany Argus*, mouthpiece of the Albany Regency, later announced that a convention was under advisement in Washington, but that nothing would be done until the public had a chance to react to the idea. It was generally understood, however, that with or without a convention Jackson and Calhoun would constitute the party's ticket.[20]

Van Buren then began his campaign to unite all those Republicans who abhorred the philosophy and policies of Adams and Clay, arguing that this could be achieved through the election of General Jackson to the presidency in 1828. But there was something, he said, "of still greater importance." Through Jackson's election, he wrote in a letter to Thomas Ritchie, leader of the Richmond Junto, the machine that controlled Virginia politics, we can bring about "the substantial reorganization of the old Republican party." In the past, personal relationships and local factions dominated politics, Van Buren continued, but the 1828 election presented an opportunity to substitute "*party principle* for *personal preference* as one of the leading points in the contest." Party distinctions must be maintained, he added, "& the most natural & beneficial to the country is that between the planters of the South and the plain Republicans of the North. The country once flourished under a party thus constituted & may again."[21]

Obviously, Van Buren's sense of party was different from the view that had typified the Era of Good Feelings. "He hoped for a band of Democrats," one historian, *has* written " . . . loyal to an organization rather than to a leader or an issue. From such a base, he expected the Democracy to become a disciplined majority."[22] In March 1827, Van Buren toured the South, consulting with leaders in Savannah, Charleston, Raleigh, and Richmond and, seeking to revitalize Jefferson's old North-South coalition. He wheedled Crawford of Georgia into accepting the new alliance, and regularly conferred with Congressmen whose philosophy or political objectives coincided with his own.[23] He wrote to other influential Republicans around the country. Together Van Buren's coalition urged the formation of central committees (called Jackson Committees, sometimes Hickory Clubs) to organize local and state campaigns. In a very real sense, Martin Van Buren was the organizational genius behind the ultimate formation of the Democratic party.

## THE LEADERSHIP OF ANDREW JACKSON

---

Perhaps the most important of these committees, as it subsequently developed, was the Nashville Central Committee, important both because of its immediate connection with Jackson and the amount and significance of the political propaganda it generated throughout the campaign. Prominent Nashville politicians established this committee in the spring of 1827 for the stated purpose of detecting and arresting "falsehoods and calumny, by the publication of truth, and by furnishing either to the public or to individuals, whether alone or associated, full and correct information upon any matter or subject within their knowledge or power, properly connected with the fitness or qualification of Andrew Jackson to fill the office of President of the United States."[24]

But General Andrew Jackson provided the real leadership of the Nashville Central Committee, just as he would provide the leadership of the Democratic party until the end of his life. His charisma, popularity, authority and attractiveness to the electorate made him unique among candidates, and made it possible to bring about a restructuring of the existing "Republican" party. Around him, a lasting organization could be fashioned.

Unquestionably, Andrew Jackson and Martin Van Buren created the Democratic party in its modern form. Without Jackson or someone of his commanding personality and appeal, Van Buren could never have achieved his intended goal of resuscitating the "old Democratic" party. The Little Magician needed Old Hickory more than Old Hickory needed the Little Magician. Jackson possessed the essential element required for the process of restructuring the "old Democratic" party: he could win the election. He could always win. And against any opposition. Even after he died, and especially during the crisis of 1860-61, many Americans fervently wished they could restore him to life, to save the nation from secession and impending civil war.

## THE PRESIDENTIAL ELECTION OF 1828

The many political leaders around the country and the numerous committees they formed eventually revitalized the party structure. Some of them continued to call their handiwork the "Republican" party; others the "Republican-Democratic" party; later Jacksonians called themselves members of the Democratic party almost exclusively, although Clay took exception to their use of the term. The Adams-Clay coalition was generally known as the National Republican party, but during Jackson's war against the Second Bank of the United States, it changed its name to the Whig party.

One of the earliest and wisest actions taken by the leadership of the emerging "Democratic" party, to win Jackson's election in 1828, was the establishment of "a chain of newspaper posts, from the New England States to Louisiana, and branching off through Lexington to the Western States."[25] For example, North Carolina started nine new Jackson newspapers and Ohio added 18 to the five that already existed. During a six-month period, three journals were established in Indiana and several were founded in Pennsylvania, Massachusetts, New Jersey, and Illinois.[26] It was reckoned that by 1828 the United States had over 600 newspapers—including 50 dailies, 150 semi-weeklies, and 400 weeklies—an overwhelming number of which took partisan positions in the election.[27]

In no way was this fledgling Democratic party a fully organized operation, such as later developed. Many of the committees sprang up as needed in 1827 and disappeared after the election. No ongoing central committee was established to keep the organization operational in the years between presidential elections. Nevertheless, this loose structure was the essential beginning of the modern Democratic party, and it had purpose, direction, and a commitment to Jeffersonian principles. Most important, it enjoyed the inspired efforts of a large cadre of politicians in every section of the country, dedicated to winning the election for Old Hickory and expelling Adams and Clay from office. "What a pleasure it is," wrote one politician, "to see that party almost unbroken rising in almost every part of the Union to put down the men who would have corrupted and betrayed it."[28]

The manner in which the party went about attracting popular votes for its ticket delighted the masses. Local and state committees planned and conducted street rallies, parades, and barbecues. Men wore hickory leaves in their hats to show their preference for Old Hickory; they carried hickory canes as they marched in parades; and they erected hickory poles in town squares, on steeples and steamboats, and at crossroads. "Many of these poles," wrote one contemporary, "were standing as late as 1845, rotten momentoes [sic] of the delirium of 1828."[29]

"Grand Barbecues" also figured prominently in Democratic campaigning. "Those who fear to grease their fingers with a barbecued pig," announced one Democratic leader, "or twist their mouths away at whisky [sic] grog, or start at the fame of a 'military chieftain' or are deafened by the thunder of the canon [sic] . . . may stay away."[30]

These campaigning tactics were not especially new, but with a popular war hero in the person of Andrew Jackson as their candidate, Democrats demonstrated a level of inventiveness and audacity in their application that lifted electioneering to a height never before achieved. All of which signalled the rejection of the genteel, elitist politics that had characterized the early national period.

Democrats marched voters to the polls on election day behind banners emblazoned with the words "Jackson and Reform." Andrew Jackson, they trumpeted, "is the *candidate of the People*." "If you wish for the restoration of pure, republican principles, support him—if you are a patriot and love your country, support him." In short, declared the Democratic press, "the parties are Jackson and Adams, democracy and aristocracy."[31] Nevertheless, this was not a personal contest between Adams and Jackson, notes one historian, which makes it vastly different from the previous election.[32]

Some 1,155,340 white males voted in the election of 1828 compared to less than 366,000 four years earlier, and Jackson won a tremendous victory. He received 647,276 popular and 178 electoral votes, while Adams won 508,064 popular and 83 electoral votes. In the electoral college, Adams carried all of New England, New Jersey, and Delaware, most of Maryland, and approximately half the New York vote. Jackson garnered all the rest—that is, everything south of the Potomac River and west of New Jersey.[33]

A "great revolution has taken place," sighed one National Republican. The coalition of Adams and Clay, commented Massachusetts preacher and orator Edward Everett, was defeated "by a majority of more than two to one, an event astounding to the friends of the Administration and unexpected by the General himself and his friends. . . . [They] are embarrassed with the vastness of their triumph and the numbers of their party."[34]

## THE JACKSON ADMINISTRATION

At Jackson's inauguration on March 4, 1829, some twenty thousand people poured into Washington to witness the triumph of their hero. "Persons have come five hundred miles to see General Jackson," exclaimed Daniel Webster, *"and they really seem to think that the country is rescued from some dreadful danger!"*[35] At the conclusion of the inauguration ceremonies the crowd followed Jackson to the White House and, in their enthusiasm and exuberance, almost tore the house apart. Men stood with muddy boots on chairs and sofas to get a glimpse of the President. Liquor spilled on the floor and cut glass and china were smashed. Jackson himself was "nearly pressed to death & almost suffocated and torn to pieces by the people in their eagerness to shake hands with Old Hickory." But to the Democratic press, "it was a proud day for the people. General Jackson is *their own* President."[36]

In assuming office, Jackson had a clear sense of what he wanted to accomplish as President and he called it a program of "reform retrenchment and economy." Specifically, he was determined to observe the strictest economy in governmental expenditures, liquidate the national debt, root out corruption in the executive department by opening government employment to all, obtain a "judicious" tariff, and distribute the surplus to the states after the debt was paid, for the construction of public works and the improvement of education within their respective jurisdictions. He would adhere, he said, "to a Just respect for state rights and the maintainance [sic] of state sovereignty as the best check of the tendencies to consolidation."[37]

In his inaugural address, Jackson also wanted to mention his concerns regarding the Second National Bank of the United States. He harbored great suspicions against the Bank and wanted changes in its operation. But his advisers convinced him that any mention of the Bank really belonged in his first message to Congress.[38] Some of them even hoped that he would forget about it altogether.

The new President also advocated the removal of the Indians, which he intended to bring to the attention of Congress at the earliest possible moment, and—since Indian affairs fell under the War Department—he took particular pains to appoint a secretary of war whose opinion on the matter coincided with his own.

This highly conservative set of principles and objectives constituted the basic Democratic creed and agenda for the next several years. Not surprisingly, Jackson achieved most of his objectives, because he presumed to take charge of the government and dictate national policy. He also maintained absolute control of the Democratic party because of the enormous personal support he enjoyed from the American people.

One of his first objectives, as he wrote in an "Outline of principles" on February 23, 1829, was "a strict examination" into the operation of executive departments to find out "what retrenchments can be made without injury to the public service, what offices can be dispensed with, and what improvement made in the economy and dispatch of business." Because of "widespread corruption" in the Adams administration, he said, he wanted those guilty of fraud and incompetence and those "appointed against the manifest will of the people" removed from office. "It is rotation in office that will perpetuate our liberty," he declared.[39]

Jackson's "rotation" policy immediately drew heated criticism from the National Republicans, who dubbed it a "spoils system" in which dedicated and intelligent federal employees were summarily dismissed to make room for political hacks. True, a large number of Democratic journalists found lucrative employment to augment their income, but Jackson contended that rotation was essentially democratic. A popular government had been established through his election, he argued, and any form of elitism in its operation violated the principles upon which this nation was founded. Each one of those ousted from office, he wrote, "believes he has a life estate in it, a vested right, & if it has been held 20 years or upwards, not only a vested right, but that it ought to descend to his children, & if no children then the next of kin. This is not the principle of our government. It is rotation in office that will perpetuate our liberty."[40] And, to a considerable extent, he did dispel the notion that class or any other elitist category determined government employment.

The Bank of the United States was another threat to liberty, according to Jackson. It was a "hydra-headed monster," he scolded, that subverted the electoral process, impaired "the morals of the people," bought up

Congressmen, and sought "to destroy our republican institutions." And it also dared to use its money to influence the outcome of national elections.[41]

When a bill to recharter the Bank passed Congress, a bill initiated and sponsored by Henry Clay and the National Republican party, Jackson vetoed it. And what a thunderclap his veto produced! It was one of the most important and explosive state papers in American history. Not only did Jackson condemn the bill for reasons other than its constitutional flaws—the only justification for vetoing any congressional legislation, according to Clay and Daniel Webster—but he denounced special interest groups who would use the government to satisfy their greed. "It is to be regretted," the message declared, "that the rich and powerful too often bend the acts of government to their selfish purposes." Distinctions will always exist in society, Jackson admitted, "and every man is equally entitled to protection by law; but when the laws undertake to add to these natural and just advantages artificial distinctions, to grant titles, gratuities, and exclusive privileges, to make the rich richer and the potent more powerful, the humble members of society—the farmers, mechanics, and laborers—who have neither the time nor the means of securing like favors to themselves, have a right to complain of the injustice of their Government."[42]

Once again Jackson raised the moral issue: the few were robbing the many. And the government assisted them. The Bank of the United States, which had been granted "exclusive privileges" by federal law, used those privileges to enrich its stockholders.

Jackson's veto was not an attempt to injure or retard the growth of business in this increasingly industrialized society. Rather it was an attempt to halt special interest groups who would manipulate government for their own "selfish purposes." The monied class, according to Jackson, will always be a problem in society. Members of that class have a right to "the fruits of superior industry, economy, and virtue," he acknowledged; but that right does not include making the government their ally to compound their wealth and power. Government, he said, must provide "equal protection" to all, "and, as Heaven does its rains, shower its favors alike on the high and the low, the rich and the poor."[43] Put simply, elitism and privilege must be driven from the political system.

## THE PRESIDENTIAL ELECTION OF 1832

In provoking this Bank War by the introduction of a recharter bill four years before the existing charter expired, Henry Clay believed he had an issue by which he could defeat Jackson for reelection in 1832. For the first time, both parties held national nominating conventions to gear up for the elections.[44] The Democratic convention simply endorsed the many nominations Jackson had already received from different states. Its principal purpose was the nomination of a vice presidential candidate. Jackson chose Martin Van Buren as his running mate, and his wishes were ratified on the first ballot. To show the solidarity of Democratic support for Jackson's choice, the party adopted the two-thirds rule for nomination.[45]

The Bank issue dominated the election, along with Jackson's presidential style. He was accused of behaving like a monarch, and cartoons in the National Republican press depicted him as "King Andrew I." His many vetoes of congressional legislation provided the ammunition for this complaint. Jackson used the veto more times than all his predecessors combined. He even inaugurated the use of the pocket veto, whereby a bill automatically is vetoed if the President fails to sign it during a congressional recess.

But the American people loved and trusted Andrew Jackson and overwhelmingly reelected him to office.[46] They felt that he was "honest and patriotic; that he was the friend of the people, battling for them against corruption and extravagance, and opposed only by dishonest politicians."[47] Although his declared intention of destroying the monster Bank troubled some Democrats, it did not shake their confidence in his leadership.

There were many reasons for that confidence. For one thing, the American people believed Jackson was absolutely committed to democratic rule. His public statements resonated with his devotion to democracy. "The people are sovereign," he wrote, "their will is absolute." "The people are the government, administering it by their agents; they are the Government, the sovereign power." In his first message to Congress he announced his fundamental creed: "*The majority is to govern.*"[48]

For many Americans Jackson symbolized democracy. His popularity no longer rested solely on his past military accomplishments. By 1832, he was seen less as the "Hero of New Orleans" and more as the embodiment of popular rule. "*Democracy and Jackson*," declared one man, are one.[49] In effect, Jackson had loosed the power of the masses, something never done before in American history.

The American people also applauded Jackson's fiscal conservatism. He vetoed many appropriation bills as extravagant. He struck down the Maysville Road and the Washington Turnpike bill and annulled legislation for building lighthouses, beacons, dredging harbors, and other such internal improvements. He also killed a bill to purchase stock in the Louisville and Portland Canal Company. "Now I stand committed before the Country to pay off the National Debt, at the earliest practicable moment," he said, adding, "this pledge I am determined to redeem."

And redeem it he did. By adhering to a policy of strict economy and wielding his veto power every time the Congress attempted a "raid upon the Treasury," he wiped out the national debt. When he took office the debt stood at $60 million; by 1835 it had been completely extinguished. "The National debt is paid!" boomed Senator Thomas Hart Benton at a Democratic celebration to honor the event, "and the apparition, so long unseen on earth, a great nation without a national debt! stands revealed to the astonished vision of a wondering world!"[50]

Still another reason for Jackson's extraordinary relationship with the American people was the fact that the electorate recognized and appreciated his profound love for and devotion to the Union. "There is nothing that I shudder at more than the idea of a seperation [sic] of the Union," he told South Carolina Senator James Hamilton, Jr. "Should such an event ever happen, which I fervently pray god to avert, from that date, I view our liberty gone."[51] When South Carolina nullified the Tariff of 1832 and threatened secession if the government attempted to force compliance Jackson did not hesitate to warn the people of South Carolina that "disunion by armed force is treason." And "nullification . . . means insurrection and war."[52]

Secession and civil war were averted by both the passage of the Compromise Tariff of 1833 and Jackson's firmness and resolve. He was the first person in an official capacity to state publicly that the Union was indivisible and perpetual, that there was no legitimate way to dissolve it. But he foresaw a larger danger. "The tariff was only a pretext," he insisted, "and disunion and a southern confederacy the real object." He predicted what the next excuse would be. "The next pretext," he warned, "will be the negro, or slavery question."[53]

## RACIAL QUESTION AND JACKSONIAN DEMOCRACY

While the Democratic party did not have a corner on racism, its record on the "slavery question," during this period and for many decades to come, was abysmal. So too was its record on the Indians. Jackson personally decreed the removal of the Indians, and the first major piece of legislation enacted under his administration was the Indian Removal Bill. Jackson argued that the southern tribes—the Creeks, Cherokees, Choctaws, Chickasaws, and Seminoles—had to be relocated west of the Mississippi River, for their own survival as well as for national security. Unless they were removed, he contended, they faced eventual annihilation. They will "disappear and be forgotten," he warned.[54] More important, the security of the United States was at stake. He recalled all too vividly the Creek War of 1813 which occurred during the War of 1812. Had the Creeks waited until the British invaded from the Gulf, and synchronized their uprising with the invasion, the War of 1812 might have ended differently—and disastrously. Indeed, the British might have made good their attack on New Orleans.[55] Thus, Jackson meant removal as a means of preserving Native American life and culture in the West while, at the same time, seeking to ensure that Indian uprisings would never again threaten the safety of the United States.[56] Although Jackson personally welcomed the integration of the two races, it was clear that neither Indians nor whites wanted it. And racist disregard for the rights of the Indians only compounded the problem.

Virtually all white Americans in the Jacksonian age were racists. Not that they knew or understood the problem. White Americans only became widely concerned about racism during the civil rights movement of the twentieth century. Yet the virus of racism still rages—even today when Americans supposedly know better.

Blacks in America were especially victimized by racism, and the Democratic party has a reputation in some quarters as having been the party of the slaveowner—the party committed to the perpetuation of slavery in the United States. Some historians even have contended that the Democratic party came into existence in order to protect "the peculiar institution."[57] But this is a distortion. The position of the Democratic party and Jackson on slavery is far more complicated.

Jackson and his party contended that the Constitution expressly recognized slavery and made provisions for representation in the House of Representatives based on its existence. Only with this concession could the Constitution win both the approval of a majority of the delegates who wrote the document and ratification by the several states. Thus, in the minds of the Jacksonians, the Constitution itself settled the slave question once and for all. "There is no debatable ground left upon the subject," declared Jackson's newspaper, the *Washington Globe*. "Has it ever been pretended," the editor asked, "that Congress has any power to subvert . . . the rights guaranteed to individuals by the Constitution?" To Democrats, therefore, the discussion of abolition was akin to discussing the right of the government to confiscate individual property. Like liberty itself, the right to hold slaves was a fundamental right. It was as natural to Jacksonians as capitalism, nationalism, or democracy. It was, as James Oakes has said in his book, *The Ruling Class*, as natural as racism.[58]

Like Thomas Jefferson, whose republican philosophy he professed to follow, Jackson owned slaves much of his life, bought and sold them, believed they were innately inferior, and freed none of them, although he expressed a hope on his death bed that he would meet them all in heaven. He believed that abolitionists, nullifiers, and followers of Adams and Clay (now called Whigs) were troublemakers intent on either disrupting the Union or discrediting democracy. They "propose commotion," the *Globe* asserted. "Out of this they hope they will brew a storm which will unsettle all the Institutions of the country". . . . The "moneyed power" in the country hated the notion of majority rule and sought to crush democracy and restore federalism: "The sole object of the agitators has been to make sectional parties North and South to SEVER the democracy, and defeat that unity of action in support of the popular cause which can alone prevent the triumph of the coalition of federalism working for the cause of corruption—for the moneyed power seeking to command the Chief Magistracy and the Government through the election by States in the House against the will of the majority of the people."[59]

Claiming slavery as a right protected by the Constitution, and claiming that Whigs, abolitionists, and other dissidents raised the issue to foment "revolution" to restore Hamiltonian federalism for their own selfish designs, Democrats sought to muzzle all discussion of the subject in Congress and leave the management of the "peculiar institution" to the "plantation states" where the institution existed. Many Democrats endorsed what Harrison Gray Otis, Mayor of Boston, wrote in a letter on October 17, 1831: "The existence of slavery is a deplorable evil," he said, as had been known at the time of the adoption of the Constitution. Nevertheless, a "compact" was struck and "it is our [northerners'] duty and our interest to adhere to it. . . . I am desirous of leaving the affair of emancipation of your [Southerners'] slaves to yourselves, to time, to the Providence of God."[60] To do otherwise invited bloodshed and the dissolution of the Union.

The moral dimension of the slavery issue never occurred to Jackson or most other Democrats. Nor did they think that the Whigs or the abolitionists really cared about black people or their welfare. All efforts "to cast odium upon the institutions of any state and all measures calculated to disturb the rights of property or the peace of any community," said Jackson in his farewell address as President, "are in direct opposition to the spirit in which the Union was formed, and must endanger its safety." Weak men will persuade themselves, he continued, that their motives are "the cause of humanity and . . . the rights of the human race." Not so. "Everyone, upon sober reflection, will see that nothing but mischief can come from these improper assaults upon the feelings and rights of others."[61]

The accusation by Democrats that Whigs intended to discredit the Democracy over the slavery issue was a real concern. Many Whigs genuinely feared the masses and what they could do. And they already had a terrifying example. The Jackson administration, as far as the Whigs were concerned, was one long disaster for the nation. A "military chieftain," as Clay described Old Hickory, rode into power on the enthusiasms of the masses. His so called "reforms" had produced a "spoils system," a Bank War and the establishment of an executive despotism. "*The Republic*," wailed the *Richmond Whig*, "*has degenerated into a Democracy,*" and democracy had brought only chaos and social unrest.

"Yes," responded Jackson's *Globe*, "Democracy is the cause of all this fury on the part of the aristocratic faction." And all because "it will not suffer a minority to rule. It will maintain the rights of the People. It will not consent that the Government shall succumb to a Bank monopoly. It will not surrender the Constitution to factious incendiaries, and hence it is chargeable with all crimes which those enemies of the country commit."[62]

But the slave question could not be resolved by Democratic insistence that the Constitution had settled the matter or that abolitionism disguised a conspiracy to disrupt the Union and destroy democracy. Nor could it be resolved by ignoring it or muzzling criticism. When petitions from northerners to end slavery were introduced in the House of Representatives, Democrats passed a resolution directing that all petitions, memorials, resolutions, and the like relating in any way to slavery or its abolition "be laid upon the table" without "either being printed or referred . . . and that no further action whatever shall be had thereto." This gag rule, as it was called, attempted to silence mounting demands for abolition, and each year it triggered violent arguments in Congress, with John Quincy Adams, now a Representative from Massachusetts, leading the attack against the rule. The question of abolition had become, in the minds of many Democrats, a vicious scheme "of evil disposed persons to disturb the harmony of our happy Union through its agency." So said Martin Van Buren.[63]

The disturbance to the peace and harmony of the nation continued when Texas won its independence from Mexico and tried to gain admission into the Union. Abolitionists feared the spread of slavery into the Southwest and vigorously opposed annexation. Jackson, who retired from the presidency in 1837 and was succeeded by Martin Van Buren, argued that annexation was not a party or a sectional question, "but a national one." He, like many others, was imbued with the spirit of what John L. O'Sullivan, editor of the *Democratic Review*, called "Manifest Destiny." This concept offered the conceit that American claims to western territories came "by the right of our manifest destiny to overspread and to possess the whole of the continent which Providence has given us for the development of the great experiment of liberty and federative self government entrusted to us. It is a right such as that of the tree to the space of air and earth suitable for the full expansion of its principle and destiny of growth." Once Texas was absorbed into the Union, declared Jackson, and "our laws extended over Orragon [sic]" and California, then "the perpetuation of our glorious Union" will be "as firm as the rocky mountains, and put to rest the vexing question of abolitionism, the dangerous rock to our Union."[64]

The annexation of Texas in 1845 under the nominally Whig President John Tyler, and the acquisition of California and New Mexico as the spoils of a war with Mexico under the Democratic President James Knox Polk, did not "put to rest the vexing question of abolitionism," as Jackson predicted.[65] They only exacerbated it.

The Democratic party during the Jacksonian era can be faulted for failing to recognize slavery as a moral question, for ducking it at every turn. It can be faulted as well, for its neglect or indifference to any opportunity to address the suffering of those held in bondage. Its adherants chose not to notice blacks. Their sole concern was with the rights of the white man. It was a party of and for white men. Blacks, Indians, and women did not enter the political thinking of its members—or the thinking of most white male Americans at the time—when dealing with basic civil rights. If the failure of the party to come to grips seriously with the slavery question teaches anything to succeeding generations, it is that fundamental moral questions cannot be indefinitely postponed or evaded, not without inviting dreadful consequences.

## THE RECORD OF THE DEMOCRATIC PARTY

The record of the Democratic party during the Jacksonian era is far from bleak, however. That record, despite all its inadequacies and failures, had broad appeal to ante-bellum Americans of all classes and sections. And that appeal continues today. Jacksonian Democracy speaks meaningfully and profoundly to both modern liberals and conservatives. Basically, it preaches equality, democracy, and freedom as its principal message; but it balances that creed with a commitment to limited government, laissez-faire economics, fiscal restraint, and support of the states in all their rights and prerogatives.

Conservatives find the doctrines of limited government, fiscal restraint, and support for states' rights very appealing. They are also attracted by the Jeffersonian-Jacksonian reverence for traditional standards of public virtue by all members of society, especially elected officials.

Liberals are attracted to the Jacksonian call for greater democracy, by the belief that the people are sovereign and rule the country through the free exercise of the suffrage. The Jacksonian rhetoric about how the people acting together are somehow wise and good and virtuous and that their will is sovereign still strikes a responsive chord in a wide audience. The Jacksonian Democratic party offered an optimistic view of the people's ability to rule themselves, as well as an optimistic view of the nation's future. On the Friday before he died in 1845, Jackson voiced this optimism. "All is safe," he wrote. "There will be patriots enough in the land . . . to maintain sacredly our just rights and to perpetuate our glorious constitution and liberty, and to preserve our happy Union."[66] Not for a moment did he doubt the ultimate triumph of democracy. He even called for the direct election of the president, senators and judges, along with the right of voters to instruct their representatives.[67]

At various times in the history of this nation Americans have been captivated by Jackson's efforts to curb the greed of the wealthy elite who seek to control the direction of government in pursuit of their financial interests. "The democracy," Jackson wrote at one point, will always give

> evidence of their virtue and patriotism, and that they will never surrender their liberty to the mony [sic] King or *bow the Knee to Ball* [Baal]. It has been a noble stand against the corrupt money power, and let the result be as it may, it affords ample proof that the peoples eyes are opening to the corruption of the times—the danger of their liberties from the mony power, and their determination to resist it. . . . Fear not, the people may be deluded for a moment, but cannot be corrupted.[68]

Many Jacksonians did oppose and fear industrialization; many hated paper money and the credit system and wished to see America remain a nation of farmers and small property owners. But they did not oppose business per se. Rather they feared the ability of corporate interests to control the affairs of the nation. Jacksonians felt it incumbent upon themselves to keep one eye peeled for the threat of corporate power to democracy and the other eye alert for the threat of centralized governmental power to liberty. And the twin dangers will probably never cease. For example, in more recent times the illegal use of corporate funds to finance the Watergate burglary and other "dirty tricks" to assist Richard Nixon in his reelection campaign in 1972 is one of the most notorious instances of this danger. And a recent writer insists that in the 1980s and 1990s Washington became a "Grand Bazaar" where moneyed interest groups regularly bought influence and power from public officials, betraying American democracy in the process.[69]

Jacksonian Democracy has provided an ideology for many reformers of the past 150 years. Populists, Progressives, New Dealers, Fair Dealers, New Frontiersmen, champions of the Great Society, and all those who care about liberty and equality, have found in Jacksonian Democracy an appealing and dynamic source of inspiration. Hopefully, that Democracy, without distinctions or limitations based on race, gender or class, will continue to provide a real and positive difference in the nation's future.

## NOTES

1. *Niles' Weekly Register*, July 5, 1828.

2. Ibid.; and Robert V. Remini, *The Election of Andrew Jackson* (New York: Lippincott, 1965), 28-29.

3. The convention met from December 15, 1814 to January 5, 1815, and issued a report calling for major changes in the Constitution reflecting the New England Federalists' frustration with the war. Because the convention met in secret, and because the war had already come to an end by the time representatives of the convention reached Washington, its opponents charged the gathering with treason and sedition.

4. The best discussion of the changes taking place at this time is George Dangerfield, *The Era of Good Feelings* (New York, Harcourt, Brace & World, 1952).

5. Robert V. Remini, *Henry Clay: Statesman for the Union* (New York: W. W. Norton & Co., 1991), 210-213.

6. However, it should be stated that the Jackson campaign issued a document known as *The Letters of Wyoming* which forcefully reasserted the basic doctrines of republicanism, namely a belief that the struggle between liberty and power continued, and that those committed to the increase of governmental power endangered individual freedom. John Henry Eaton, *The Letters of Wyoming, to the People of the United States, on the Presidential Election, and in Favour of Andrew Jackson* (Philadelphia: Simpson & J. Conrad, 1824), 10-15, 24, 36, 93-94.

7. Jackson had a plurality of 99 votes, principally from the South, the West, New Jersey and Pennsylvania. He also received 152,901 popular votes, the largest number of the four candidates. John Quincy Adams had 84 electoral votes, mostly from New England and New York, and 114,023 popular votes. Crawford was third with 46,979 popular and 41 electoral votes, representing Virginia and Georgia, while Henry Clay came in last with 47,217 popular and 37 electoral votes, representing Kentucky, Ohio, and Missouri. James F. Hopkins, "Election of 1824," *History of American Presidential Elections, 1789-1968*, eds. Arthur M. Schlesinger, Jr. and Fred Israel (New York: Chelsea House Publishers, 1971), 1:409.

8. It will be remembered that Jefferson was Washington's Secretary of State; Madison was Jefferson's Secretary of State; Monroe was Madison's Secretary of State; and Adams was Monroe's Secretary of State.

9. Adams received a majority of 13 votes (New England, Kentucky, Ohio, Missouri, Illinois, Louisiana, Maryland, and New York) while Jackson received seven (Tennessee, South Carolina, New Jersey, Pennsylvania, Indiana, Alabama, and Mississippi) and Crawford four (Delaware, Georgia, Virginia, and North Carolina). *National Intelligencer*, February 10, 1825.

10. Jackson to William B. Lewis, February 14, 1825, *Miscellaneous Jackson Papers*, New York Historical Society. It is unlikely that a "bargain," corrupt or otherwise, transpired. See Remini, *Henry Clay*, 251-272.

11. Jackson to D.G. Goodlett, March 12, 1844, *The Correspondence of Andrew Jackson*, ed. John Spencer Bassett (Washington, D.C.: Carnegie Institute of Washington, 1926-1933), 6:274.

12. Martin Van Buren, *Autobiography*, ed. John C. Fitzpatrick (Washington,

D.C.: Government Printing Office, 1920), 125; Richard Hofstadter, *The Idea of a Party System: The Rise of Legitimate Opposition in the United States, 1780-1840* (Berkeley: University of California Press, 1969); and Robert V. Remini, *Martin Van Buren and the Making of the Democratic Party* (New York: Columbia University Press, 1959), 22. There are two excellent biographies of Van Buren: John Niven, *Martin Van Buren: The Romantic Age of American Politics* (New York: Oxford University Press, 1983); and Donald B. Cole, *Martin Van Buren and the American Political System* (Princeton: Princeton University Press, 1984).

13. Jackson to James K. Polk, December 4, 1826, in Polk Papers, Library of Congress; Jackson to John Sevier, February 27, 1797, Emil Hurja Collection, Tennessee Historical Society, Nashville.

14. Van Buren to James A. Hamilton, February 21, 1829, in James A. Hamilton, *Reminiscences of James A. Hamilton: at Home and Abroad, During Three Quarters of a Century* (New York: Scribner, 1869), 94; Van Buren to Jackson, September 14, 1827, Van Buren Papers, Library of Congress.

15. *A Compilation of the Messages and Papers of the Presidents, 1789-1897*, ed. James D. Richardson (Washington, D. C.: Government Printing Office, 1908), 2:866-868, 872, 879, 882.

16. Quoted in Mary W. M. Hargreaves, *The Presidency of John Quincy Adams* (Lawrence: University Press of Kansas, 1985), 165-166.

17. Thomas Hart Benton, *Thirty Years* (New York: Appleton and Co., 1854-1856), 1:54; and Charles M. Wiltse, *John C. Calhoun, Nationalist, 1782-1828* (Indianapolis: Bobbs-Merrill, 1944), 321.

18. Calhoun to Jackson, June 4, 1826, John C. Calhoun, *The Papers of John C. Calhoun*, Robert B. Meriweather et al., eds. (Columbia: University of South Carolina Press, 1959—), 10:10.

19. A general convention, wrote Van Buren, "would remove the embarrassment of those who have or profess to have scruples as to [a congressional caucus], would be fresher and perhaps more in unison with the spirit of the times. . . . The following may, I think, justly be ranked among its probable advantages. First, it is the best and probably the only practical mode of concentrating the entire vote of the opposition [to Adams]. . . . 2nd its first result cannot be doubtful. Mr. Adams. . . will not submit his pretension to the convention. . . . 3rd the call of such a convention, its exclusive Republican character, and the refusal of Mr. Adams and his friends to become parties to it, would draw anew the old Party lines and the subsequent contest would reestablish them; State nominations alone would fall far short of the object. 4th it would greatly improve the condition of the Republicans of the North and Middle States by substituting *party principle* for *personal preference* as one of the leading points in the contest. Instead of the question being between a northern and southern man, it would be whether or not the ties, which have heretofore bound together a great political party, should be severed." The fifth and sixth reasons cited by Van Buren are the good effect the convention would have in New England and the South. "We must always have party distinctions and the old ones are the best of which the nature of the case admits. Political considerations between the inhabitants of the different states are unavoidable and the most natural and beneficial to the country is that between the planters of the South and the plain Republicans of the North. The country has once

flourished under a party thus constituted and may again." Van Buren to Thomas Ritchie, January 13, 1827, Van Buren Papers, Library of Congress.

20. *Albany Argus*, January 9, 1827. National nominating conventions did not become common practice until the presidential election of 1832.

21. Van Buren to Ritchie, January 13, 1827, Van Buren Papers, Library of Congress.

22. Jean H. Baker, *Affairs of Party: The Political Culture of Northern Democrats in the Mid-Nineteenth Century* (Ithaca and London: Cornell University Press, 1983), 127.

23. Among the Congressmen consulted were Thomas Hart Benton of Missouri, John Henry Eaton of Tennessee, Mahlon Dickerson of New Jersey, Richard Johnson of Kentucky, Louis McLane of Maryland, James Buchanan and Samuel Ingham of Pennsylvania, Thomas Patrick Moore of Kentucky and Sam Houston of Tennessee, among others. Of the eighteen members comprising the Central Committee, the most important included John Overton, Hugh Lawson White, William B. Lewis, John H. Eaton, Felix Grundy, Sam Houston, and George W. Campbell. Robert C. Foster sometimes served as the "chairman pro tem."

24. *United States Telegraph*, April 9, 1827.

25. *National Intelligencer*, March 13, 20, 1827.

26. No doubt the principal sheet of the reorganized party was the *United States Telegraph* begun in Washington under the editorship of Duff Green. Other important journals included the *Albany Argus*, *Richmond Enquirer*, *New York Courier* and *Evening Post*, *Boston Statesman*,*Charleston Mercury*, *Baltimore Republican*, *Philadelphia Palladium*, *Nashville Republican*, and *Frankfort (Kentucky) Argus of Western America*.

27. Washington, *National Journal*, February 27, March 10, 22, 31, July 24, 1827; *National Intelligencer*, March 13, 20, 1827; and Remini, *Election of Jackson*, 76-80.

28. T. Bradley to Gulian C. Verplanck, November 13, 1827, Verplanck Papers, New York Historical Society.

29. James Parton, *Life of Andrew Jackson* (New York: Mason Brothers, 1861), 3:144.

30. Quoted in Remini, *Election of Jackson*, 110.

31. Robert V. Remini, *Andrew Jackson and the Course of American Freedom*, (New York: Harper & Row, 1981), 144-145; Remini, *Election of Jackson*, 102; and *Telegraph*, January 24, 1828.

32. Joel H. Silbey, *The American Political Nation, 1838-1893*, (Stanford: Stanford University Press, 1991), 21.

33. *History of American Presidential Elections: 1789-1968*, eds. Arthur M. Schlesinger, Jr. and Fred L. Israel (New York: Chelsea House Press, 1971), 1:492.

34. Robert Wickliffe to Clay, October 7, 1828, H. Shaw to Clay, January 9, 1829, Clay Papers, Library of Congress; Edward Everett to A. H. Everett, December 2, 1828, Everett Papers, Massachusetts Historical Society.

35. Daniel Webster to Mrs. E. Webster, February 19, 1829, Daniel Webster, *The Private Correspondence of Daniel Webster*, ed. Fletcher Webster (Boston: Little, Brown, 1857), 1:470.

36. *The First Forty Years of Washington Society in the Family Letters of Mar-*

*garet Bayard Smith*, ed. Gaillard Hunt (New York: Scribner, 1906), 295; and *Argus of Western America*, March 18, 1829.

37. "Rough Draft of the First Inaugural Address," Jackson Papers, Library of Congress.

38. See endorsement in James K. Polk's letter to Jackson, December 23, 1833, Polk Papers, Library of Congress.

39. "Outline of principles," February 23, 1829; and Memorandum Book of A. Jackson commencing April 1829, Jackson Papers, Library of Congress.

40. Memorandum Book of A. Jackson commencing April 1829, Jackson Papers, Library of Congress. "In a country where offices are created solely for the benefit of the people," Jackson told Congress, "no one man has any more intrinsic right to official station than another." Richardson, *Papers of the Presidents*, 2:1011-1012.

41. Jackson's criticisms of the Bank can be found in his many letters and official publications. See, for example, Jackson to William B. Lewis, April 29, 1833, Jackson-Lewis Papers, Library of Congress; Richardson, *Papers of the Presidents*, 2:1304, 1224-1238; and Amos Kendall to Jackson, March 20, 1833, Jackson Papers, Library of Congress.

42. Richardson, *Papers of the Presidents*, 2:1153.

43. Ibid.

44. A third party, the Anti-Masonic party—the first third party in American history—held the first national nominating convention on September 26, 1831.

45. Van Buren received 208 votes, Richard M. Johnson of Kentucky, 26, and Philip P. Barbour of Virginia, 49.

46. Jackson received 688,242 popular votes, while Clay won 473,462. Jackson took approximately 55 percent of the popular vote. In the electoral college he obtained 219 votes against 49 for Clay. The Anti-Masonic candidate won 101,051 popular and 7 electoral votes. Sved Petersen, *A Statistical History of the American Presidential Elections* (New York: Ferdinand Unger, 1963), 20-21.

47. Nathan Sargent, *Public Men and Events from the Commencement of Mr. Monroe's Administration in 1817, to the Close of Mr. Fillmore's Administration in 1853* (Philadelphia: Lippincott, 1875), 1:347.

48. Jackson to A.J. Donelson, May 12, 1835, in Donelson Papers, Library of Congress; Richardson, *Papers of the Presidents*, 2:1011. These sentiments are repeated regularly in Jackson's state papers.

49. George Dallas to Edward Livingston, May 30, 1831, quoted in Remini, *Andrew Jackson and the Course of American Freedom*, 386.

50. Martin Van Buren, *Autobiography*, 324; and *Washington Globe*, January 14, 1835.

51. Jackson to Hamilton, June 29, 1828 in Bassett, *Correspondence of Andrew Jackson* (Washington, D.C.: Carnegie Institution of Washington, 1926-33), 3:412.

52. Richardson, *Papers of the Presidents*, 2:1215, 1217-1219.

53. Jackson to Reverend Andrew J. Crawford, May 1, 1833, in, Bassett, *Correspondence of Andrew Jackson*, 5:72.

54. Jackson's address to the Chickasaws, August 23, 1830, Record Group 46, E 326, National Archives.

55. On the Creek War, see Frank L. Owsley, *Struggle for the Gulf Borderlands:*

*The Creek War and the Battle of New Orleans, 1812-1815* (Gainesville: University of Florida Press, 1981).

56. Robert V. Remini, *The Legacy of Andrew Jackson: Essays on Democracy, Indian Removal, and Slavery* (Baton Rouge: Louisiana State University Press, 1988), 81-82.

57. See Richard Brown, "The Missouri Crisis, Slavery, and the Politics of Jacksonianism," *South Atlantic Quarterly* 65 (1966): 55-72. Brown cites Van Buren's letter to Thomas Ritchie of January 13, 1827 in which Van Buren mentioned past party attachment as a "complete antidote" to sectional prejudices. "It was not until that defence had been broken down," wrote Van Buren, "that the clamour agt [sic] Southern Influence and African Slavery could be made effectual in the North." The revival of party attachments, he continued, would still that "clamour." For a denial of the charge that the Democratic party was instituted to protect slavery, see Remini, *The Legacy of Andrew Jackson*, 83-86.

58. James Oakes, *The Ruling Class: A History of American Slaveholders* (New York: Knopf, 1982), 135ff.

59. *Washington Globe*, May 1, 1833; May 28, 1836.

60. Letter reprinted in *Washington Globe*, September 5, 1833.

61. Richardson, *Papers of the Presidents*, 2:1516-1517.

62. *Washington Globe*, August 22, 1835.

63. *Congressional Globe*, 24th Cong., 2d sess., 1581ff; *Washington Globe*, April 26, May 28, June 11, September 2, 1836, January 28, February 4, 1837; Jackson to Blair, July 19, 1838, Jackson Papers, Library of Congress; and Van Buren to Nathaniel Macon, February 13, 1836, Macon Papers, Duke University Library, Durham, N.C.

64. Jackson to Blair, June 7, 25, 1844, Jackson Papers, Library of Congress.

65. Within a month after Van Buren took office as President, the nation suffered a serious economic depression in 1837 and the Whig party won the presidency in 1840 with a ticket consisting of William Henry Harrison and John Tyler, "Tippecanoe and Tyler, Too." Harrison died after a month in office and was succeeded by Tyler. A former Democrat, Tyler had deserted the party in protest over Jackson's policies and presidential style.

66. Parton, *Life of Andrew Jackson*, 3:676.

67. Remini, *Legacy of Andrew Jackson*, 32-36.

68. Jackson to Van Buren, May 1, 1838, Van Buren Papers, Library of Congress.

69. William Greider, *Who Will Tell the People: The Betrayal of American Democracy* (New York: Simon & Schuster, 1992).

## Chapter 3

# The Ambiguous Legacy of Jacksonian Democracy

*Harry L. Watson*

While the roots of today's Democratic party stretch back to the organizing efforts of Thomas Jefferson and James Madison, it was actually a generation later, during the administration of President Andrew Jackson (1829-1837), when the party as we know it found its permanent identity, its first institutional structure, and its renewed ideological vitality. The reestablishment of the Democratic party (or as it was often called, the "Democratic-Republican" or even the "Republican" party) was one of Andrew Jackson's proudest boasts. "I have long believed," he wrote in 1835, "that it was only by preserving the identity of the Republican party as embodied and characterized by the principles introduced by Mr. Jefferson that the original rights of the states and the people could be maintained as contemplated by the Constitution."[1] During Jackson's administration, the president's political rivals organized themselves in a party of opposition, first known as the "National Republicans" and later as the "Whig" party.

The period of rivalry between Jacksonian Democrats and anti-Jacksonian Whigs has become known as the "second American party system," to distinguish it from the earlier rivalry between Thomas Jefferson's Democratic-Republicans and Alexander Hamilton's Federalists.[2] In retrospect, it is clear that the years of the second American party system, from the election of Jackson in 1828 to the election of Abraham Lincoln in 1860, were one of the two long periods in American history in which the Democratic party maintained a prevailing majority in American politics, usually controlling both Congress and the White House. The other, of course, was the period during which Franklin Roosevelt and his successors dominated American politics, from 1932 to 1968. The Jacksonian and Rooseveltian eras were clearly the glory days of the Democratic party, when most of its characteristic themes, slogans, and programs first took shape and its personalities imbedded themselves in the consciousness of the American people.

Once habituated to the experience of stable two-party competition,

American politicians came to develop a pragmatic perspective on political parties, acknowledging that each of two major parties were legitimate contenders for public favor. They came to accept the experience of occasional electoral defeat and often professed to believe that an occasional reversal at the polls could be good for the country and even for their own parties, as trading places with the opposition forced party members to reexamine programs, tighten internal discipline, and renew direct contact with the electorate.[3]

General Andrew Jackson held no such milk-and-water views. For him, the Democratic party was the permanent voice of the many against the few. He despised his rivals in the opposing Whig party and never admitted their legitimacy as a loyal opposition, whose occasional electoral victories might somehow benefit the country. "I have labored to reconstruct this great Party," he insisted, "and to bring the popular power to bear with full influence upon the Government, by securing its permanent ascendancy."[4] Jackson's success in reestablishing his party, if not its permanent ascendancy, has since been commemorated in thousands of Jefferson-Jackson day celebrations by local party activists, and by widespread use of the phrase "Jacksonian Democracy," not only to describe the prevailing political ethos of ante-bellum America, but also to refer more particularly to the Democratic party itself in that period.

Many aspects of Andrew Jackson's view of government continue to speak directly to current American problems and still inspire his party's faithful. An outstanding example is the seventh President's approach to economic and political equality. Andrew Jackson did not propose to level what he regarded as just and necessary social differences, but he was determined that every American citizen should get equal protection from his government. "It is to be regretted," he intoned in his famous veto of the proposed recharter of the Bank of the United States, "that the rich and powerful too often bend the acts of government to their selfish purposes." When the government departs from the ideal of equal protection, "to make the richer and the potent more powerful," as he put it, "the humble members of society—the farmers, mechanics, and laborers—who have neither the time nor the means of securing like favors to themselves, have a right to complain of the injustice of their Government."[5] Outside the federal government, the goal of political equality likewise inspired state-level Jacksonians to attack property requirements for the right to vote and hold office, and to welcome foreign-born Americans to full political participation in American society. Many aspects of Jacksonian equality continue to echo in party rhetoric and policy today, as modern Democrats strive to make their party reflect the diversity of American society and to challenge the persistence of special privileges for the few.

Taken as a whole, however, Jacksonian Democracy has left an ambiguous legacy for the late twentieth century. On the surface, the party's early slogans seem to be at variance with the positions taken by Democrats over much of the twentieth century. As an obvious example, consider what Jacksonian Democrats said about the size and power of government itself. In 1837, John L. O'Sullivan, a sterling Democratic editor, coined the phrase "the best government is that which governs least" as the epitome of Jacksonian Democratic doctrine.[6] Speaking as the party's principal media organ, the *Washington Globe* echoed these sentiments in its motto, "The World Is Governed Too Much." Andrew Jackson's close ally and Democratic successor, Martin Van Buren, faced the task of shaping the national government's response to the disastrous Panic of 1837 and the serious recession which followed it. Did this Democratic president announce a multi-point program of positive government measures to relieve the effect of economic collapse on families and communities around the nation? Far from it. Addressing a special session of Congress, the president warned that "all communities are apt to look to government for too much" and stoutly opposed all current proposals to revive business confidence or stimulate new business activity.[7]

We need only compare the pronouncements of the Democratic president of 1837 with those of the Democrat who held that office in 1937 to see how much the Democratic party changed over the years from the days of its Jacksonian rebirth. "Government has a final responsibility for the well-being of its citizenship," ran a typical pronouncement from Franklin Roosevelt. "If private cooperative endeavor fails to provide work for willing hands and relief for the unfortunate, those suffering hardship from no fault of their own have a right to call upon the Government for aid; and a government worthy of its name must make a fitting response."[8] By comparison, the thrust of Jacksonian rhetoric bears a greater surface resemblance to the sentiments of Herbert Hoover or Ronald Reagan. When Reagan declared in his first inaugural address that "government is not the solution; government is the problem," he plucked a vibrant Jacksonian chord that resonates deeply in the cultural memory of American politics.[9]

Jacksonian stands on racial questions must arouse even deeper discomfort among present-day Democrats who take pride in the party's modern record on civil rights. For long periods of its history, racial positions taken by the Democratic party reflected its origins as an actively proslavery and anti-Indian party which drew its strongest electoral support from the southern and western states. The rival Whig party also left a flawed racial record, but there is little question that the Whigs made more room in their ranks for critics of racial injustice than did the Jacksonian Democrats.

What are modern Democrats to make of the disparities between their party's founding myths and its current positions? For many of us, the now-unsavory aspects of Jacksonian ideology must loom as skeletons in the family closet, which would be better left unmentioned in public discussion. Practical-minded activists may simply dismiss them as irrelevant to present-day concerns and get on with the business of winning votes in a very different electoral arena. Cynics may go further, and remark that political rhetoric has nothing to do with political reality anyway. According to this reasoning, the supposed ideology of Jacksonian Democrats probably had little or nothing to do with Democratic actions even in antebellum days, so it should hardly concern historians, let alone planners and policymakers of the present. Several decades ago, this view was enshrined in the work of Jacksonian historians who shrugged off the party's ideology as "claptrap," and their view still commands a respectable following today.[10]

Properly understood, however, party rhetoric is far from "claptrap." The slogans of Jacksonian Democracy may seem awkward to contemporary Democrats, but they made the party a tower of political strength from the administration of Andrew Jackson to the election of Abraham Lincoln. As the late twentieth century success of Ronald Reagan demonstrated, moreover, the slogans and values of Jacksonian Democracy are deeply inscribed in the culture of American politics comprising a rhetorical legacy too influential to ignore. Instead of shrugging off Jacksonian slogans it would be more useful to ask how the party's opposition to governmental power could have shifted to a willing use of government for certain purposes. We may likewise ask what made it possible for the party to change its stance on race, even while it retained some continuity with its antebellum past. At the very least, we are unlikely to understand how Jacksonian slogans may be transcended or improved upon until we understand what gave them their enormous power and appeal.

Instead of taking the Jacksonian condemnation of state power at face value, let us ask instead what Jacksonians hoped to accomplish with small, weak government? What strategic political purpose lay behind this essentially tactical demand? Were their ultimate goals more like Roosevelt's, or more like Reagan's or Hoover's? Can the answer help to revitalize the role of government, as we struggle to cope with the problems of a century very different from Andrew Jackson's? More troublingly, what exactly did Jacksonians hope to gain with the race card? How was their racism linked to their parallel conviction that they alone spoke for "the great body of the people?"

The place to begin is with "republicanism," the complex of ideas and assumptions which inspired the American Revolution and which Jefferson and Madison evoked when they dubbed their movement to resist Alexander Hamilton the "Republican" or "Democratic-Republican" party. Drawing on sources as near to it in time as eighteenth century political science but also as ancient as classical Greek political philosophy, republicanism taught Americans that free government was the greatest and rarest blessing in human history. Why was freedom rare? The motto of another major Jacksonian newspaper gave the reason: "Power is Always Stealing from the Many to the Few," warned the masthead of Washington's *U.S. Telegraph*, and republicans saw themselves in a never-ending struggle to reverse the nearly inevitable process that had kept most of mankind under one form of despotism or another for most of human existence.[11]

Republicans saw an endless battle between liberty and power. The urge to dominate others was embedded in human nature, they believed, and even the best rulers and the most benign private interests were perpetually drawn towards schemes for extending or perpetuating their influence. More specifically, tyranny resulted from any effort to use government for private advantage, for anyone who learned to use the levers of the state for personal advantage would not stop voluntarily until he had made himself a despot over everyone else. The overweening urge to dominate had thus lain behind Great Britain's drive to tax the colonies, Americans reasoned, and would even corrupt the Founding Fathers if countervailing influences did not restrain them.

Power could be checked by what eighteenth century republicans called "virtue," which republicans defined as a moral willingness to put the public good before private advantages. Repeating the maxims of his youth, Andrew Jackson recalled the concept in his Farewell Address of 1837. "No free government can stand without virtue in the people and a lofty spirit of patriotism," he prophesied. "If the sordid feelings of mere selfishness shall usurp the place which ought to be filled with public spirit, the legislation of Congress will soon be converted into a scramble for personal and sectional advantages."[12]

Though virtue was clearly a moral quality, it was not instilled by moralizing alone. The disposition to put public interests before private vices could only flourish among independent men of middling means. Ideal republican citizens were those too poor to harbor serious ambitions of exploiting others, but too prosperous to be bribed and too numerous to be overpowered. English political theorists had assumed that no one but landed country gentlemen would be sufficiently prosperous and independent to resist the blandishments of a corrupted monarchy, but American thinkers put their faith in a large population of small property-holders, especially in the farmers of small-to-medium holdings who filled the American countryside. In the famous words of the Democrats' founding father and patron saint, Thomas Jefferson, "those who labor in the earth are the chosen people of God, if ever he had a chosen people, whose breasts he has made his peculiar deposit for substantial and genuine virtue."[13]

For Jefferson and the Democratic-Republicans who followed him, liberty and virtue could best be saved by preserving America as a nation of small landowners and staving off the economic forces that would build up great cities, where, he reasoned, a population of propertyless wage-earners would have no choice but to vote according to their employers' dictates, leaving liberty a hostage to the greed of an urban elite. "The mobs of great cities add just so much to the support of pure government," he concluded, "as sores do to the strength of the human body."[14]

Jefferson was not quite the agrarian purist that his words suggested; in an adjoining passage he acknowledged that skilled craftsmen were also necessary to support the labor of farmers in a republican economy. His professed desire to trade American foodstuffs for European manufactures implied that merchants and shipmasters would also be needed to effect the exchange.[15] Even so, the Jeffersonian commitment to a yeoman's republic was so strong that the third president suspended his constitutional scruples to acquire the Louisiana Territory as a landed preserve for future generations of smallholders.

As they passed from the scene after 1815, the Jeffersonian generation left their successors with a strong preference for a "natural" economy dominated by men who depended on their own labor in their own fields, or at the very least, owned their own shops and produced handmade articles with their own skills for consumers who knew them personally. For Americans in the Jeffersonian tradition, this was the only social environment where liberty and virtue could hope to flourish.

Powerful as it was, this vision of the good society was profoundly endangered in the 1820s and 1830s. Successful yeoman farmers were powerfully tempted to turn themselves into even more successful plantation owners and land speculators, while successful shopkeepers and artisans were inspired to turn themselves into wealthy merchant princes and expansive businessmen. As the Industrial Revolution quickened in Britain and New England, the demand for cotton fiber grew and new inventions hastened the flow of worldwide commerce. Canals, steamboats, railroads, and turnpikes proliferated, each one promising a fortune to successful investors and lower costs to producers who purchased their services. The credit economy expanded, as bankers appeared, to finance the increasingly complex transactions of a far-flung market.[16]

Americans of the Jacksonian generation were acutely aware that these new institutions and technologies did not arise spontaneously. Most of the time, they required the strenuous intervention of the government to bring them into existence and to sustain them thereafter. Businessmen of all kinds clamored for special acts of incorporation, to give their enterprises the otherwise unavailable shield of limited liability. Going further, capital-starved railroads and canal companies lobbied frantically and successfully for direct government investments in their stock. Banks did likewise, arguing that the paper banknotes they put into circulation were indispensable to private trade and inestimable as public blessings. Indeed, it is probably safe to say that the typical American corporation of the period before 1840 was not a wholly private enterprise, but a mixed public-private endeavor, with state and local governments joining private shareholders in the ownership and sometimes the management of the firm. Describing themselves as public benefactors, moreover, who provided the poor with jobs and the nation with a secure domestic source of manufactured necessities, factory owners won high tariff protection to shield their infant industries from foreign, usually British, competition. In state after state, for most of the nineteenth century, these efforts were often successful, as America began the long, difficult transition from colonial, agrarian backwater to world industrial giant.[17]

In other words, to an extent almost entirely forgotten today, the economic transformation which eventually made the United States an urban, manufacturing nation did not result from the pioneering independence of a handful of rugged individualists. Instead, what many scholars are now calling the "Market Revolution" came about through the massive intervention of the American state, involving the concerted actions of the federal, state, county, and municipal governments over the course of many decades. Not only did these governments invest millions in the construction and maintenance of turnpikes, canals, railroads, lighthouses, and the like, which they called "internal improvements" and we today call "transportation infrastructure," they also made direct investments in risky new forms of corporate enterprise. In effect, the implementation of a national "industrial policy" is not a recent innovation from Japan, but an old American tradition.[18]

It is also important to remember that the economic changes which probably seem like "progress" to most of us today had not yet won universal acceptance in the 1820s and 1830s. The expansion of banks meant the spread of the privately-printed paper money which all banks of the early nineteenth century issued to their borrowers. Since the federal government issued no paper money itself, these bills were the only paper currency available, but their value fluctuated wildly with the strength of the economy and the fortunes of the bank which issued them. Ordinary farmers and mechanics who were forced to accept such notes might well find that a sudden change in business conditions could turn these notes into "rags" indeed.

By the same token, the expansion of market opportunities through improved transportation technology could increase the pressure on subsistence farmers to reduce their production of food crops and cultivate a market crop instead. The new product might bring a higher cash income, but an unpredictable twist in prices could throw the farmer into bankruptcy, leading to the loss of his farm, his family's livelihood, and his own cherished republican independence. In the rapidly growing cities, moreover, the skills of trained artisans went begging, as merchant capitalists broke complex tasks like shoemaking into numerous component operations and assigned each one to a different unskilled, lowpaid pieceworker. Production rose and prices fell, but the independent artisans of preindustrial society were stripped of their trades, their incomes, their independence, and what they regarded as their rightful place in the social order. If rural folk decided to embrace the new economy, sending their daughters into the new textile mills of New England, or their sons into the urban vortex of a booming city like New York, how could their children's new future as insecure wage-earners ever guarantee the independence and dignity that republican theory demanded for a fully equal member of American society? In retrospect, the early years of the Market Revolution may look progressive to us who see in them the dawning of our own world, but ordinary participants often saw the creation of menacing new forms of social, economic, and political inequality.[19]

For many Jacksonians, the unnatural growth of "monster banks" and "chartered monopolies" threatened to despoil the promises of the Declaration of Independence at the very moment when they were beginning to come true. To make matters worse, the soft-handed men in ruffled shirts who ran these pernicious institutions were demanding government assistance for their underhanded schemes! It was enough to make a freeman's blood boil, and much of the appeal of the Jacksonian Democratic party grew out of a not-unreasonable fear that social and economic change was bringing greater class inequality to American life.

The proponents of America's government-sponsored shift to industrialization had reams of ready arguments with which to defend their departure from Jeffersonian dogmas. The most popular justifications drew directly on the republican tradition itself. If America is a free country, spokesmen reasoned, why shouldn't the power of government be used to promote the welfare of the citizenry? There is no liberty in the poorhouse, they contended; true freedom requires that Americans be prosperous and successful.[20]

The answer Jacksonian Democrats gave to these contentions was complex and variable. In some states, at some junctures, Democrats accepted the reasoning of business interests and distributed state favors with a generous hand. Others, taking their cue from Andrew Jackson himself, were adamantly opposed. When these Jacksonians denounced big government, they were thinking specifically about the use of state power and public funds to subsidize those whom Jackson himself called the "money power," and "the multitude of corporations with exclusive privileges which they have succeeded in obtaining in the different States and which are employed altogether for their benefit."[21] Their reasons for doing so deserve close examination.

Like Jefferson, Jackson believed that republican values could only survive in a society based on independent yeoman producers. He explained why in his Farewell Address:

> The planter, the farmer, the mechanic, and the laborer all know that their success depends upon their own industry and economy, and that they must not expect to become suddenly rich by the fruits of their toil. . . . [T]hese classes of society form the great body of the people of the United States; they are the bone and sinew of the country—men who love liberty and desire nothing but equal rights and equal laws, and who, moreover, hold the great mass of our national wealth, although it is distributed in moderate amounts among the millions of freemen who possess it.[22]

Convinced that the economic changes breaking all around him were undermining such a society, Jackson concluded that government aid to these economic changes would end in the collapse of republican government itself. In his veto of the Maysville Road bill, which had authorized a congressional purchase of stock in a Kentucky turnpike company, Jackson acknowledged that transportation improvements could strengthen the economy, but insisted that "the preservation and encouragement of the republican principle" fulfilled a higher obligation for "the fostering care of the Government."[23] His famous veto of the recharter of the Bank of the United States elaborated on the same idea. A corporate charter, he maintained, was a special legislative privilege available to some citizens but not to all. Such privileges could never be equally distributed; they would always be sought most effectively by the wealthy few and used to exploit the virtuous many.[24]

Legal discrimination in favor of the wealthy was more than just unfair, Jackson argued; it was inimical to republicanism. By making government the locus of conflict between contending private interests, pro-development policies discarded "virtue" (used in the traditional republican sense of a willingness to put public interests ahead of private gain) and made "corruption" (virtue's evil opposite) the mainspring of politics. Once this fatal step was taken, nothing could prevent men from tearing the republic apart in a frenzied scramble for personal advantages. The lessons could already be seen in a recent tumultuous confrontation between supporters and opponents of a high protective tariff. "By attempting to gratify their desires," Jackson pointed out, "we have . . . arrayed section against section, interest against interest, and man against man, in a fearful commotion which threatens to shake the foundations of our Union."[25]

For Andrew Jackson, then, the use of positive law to encourage some economic sectors over others was invariably an act of oppression by the rich against the poor. Even worse, a pattern of such legislation would set off a violent competition between rival interest groups which might tear the country apart, as the recent tariff controversy with South Carolina had almost done.[26] Finally, the use of government power to create an urban, industrial nation would destroy the social bases of republicanism by undermining yeoman communities idealized by Jefferson, for the benefit of urban capitalists. Embedded in Jackson's argument was the clear implication that the use of government power to promote or subsidize the capitalist transformation of American society was directly subversive of popular liberty and the equality of men. When Andrew Jackson attacked big government, in other words, he was not attacking what today's liberals would recognize as social welfare programs, or health and safety regulations, but a systematic policy of favoritism to the business corporations of his day.

Other Democrats made this point more elaborately. One of the most notable was Andrew Jackson's vice president and successor in the White House, Martin Van Buren. After a long life of political activity, Van Buren spent much of the 1850s in composing his memoirs, parts of which were published by his survivors as *Inquiry into the Origin and Course of Political Parties in the United States*. Van Buren wrote candidly as a committed Democratic partisan, and few historians today would endorse the specific details of his analysis of American political development. Precisely because of the ex-President's partisanship, however, his history of party politics is a superb evocation of the Jacksonians' conception of history and their place within it.

Beginning with an account of Democratic party genealogy, Van Buren declared that "the two great parties of this country, with occasional changes in their names only, have, for the principal part of a century, occupied antagonistic positions upon all political questions." The same divisions had existed in the mother country. "Men of similar and substantially unchanged views and principles have, at different periods of English history, been known as Cavaliers or Roundheads, as Jacobites or Puritans and Presbyterians, as Whigs or Tories." In America, according to Van Buren, "with corresponding consistency in principle, the same men have at different periods been known as Federalists, Federal Republicans, and Whigs, or as Anti-Federalists, Republicans, and Democrats."[27]

Van Buren not only identified his opponents as Whigs, Federalists, Tories, Jacobites, and Cavaliers, he associated them with an enduring love of hereditary privilege, centralized government, broad construction of the United States Constitution, favoritism to financial and commercial interests, and support for corrupt, self-interested legislation of all kinds. For Van Buren, like Jackson, the opponents of the Democratic party were ever the power-mad enemies of virtue, waging an endless war of the few against the many by employing the overwhelming power of the state to line their own pockets.

Tracing this struggle through the politics of his own day, Van Buren linked Alexander Hamilton and the founders of the Bank of the United States to the earlier founders of the Bank of England, and went on to include "almost every business class in the community" in the ranks of the so-called "money power." Van Buren took pains to condemn virtually all the major institutions of fledgling industrial capitalism, including

> those who hold the stock of our banks, and control their action. . .[,] our insurance companies which have been invested with special privileges of various grades . . . [, and] our incorporated companies invested with like privileges, and established for the manufacture of articles made of cotton, of wool, of flax, of hemp, or silk, of iron, or steel, of lead, of clay. The same of companies with like privileges for the construction of railroads, of bridges, of canals, where they can be made profitable and other constructions to which the invention and industry of man can be successfully applied.[28]

Fully understanding the power and importance of culture and ideology to the designs of those he regarded as the enemies of popular liberty, Van Buren also swept up intellectuals and the newspapers in his indictment. "The press, men of letters, artists, and professional men of every denomination, and those engaged in subordinated pursuits who live upon the luxurious indulgences of the rich, are all brought within the scope of this influence," he claimed, and used this observation to explain to his readers why most American newspapers had always opposed his party, despite the protection which liberty of the press afforded them.[29]

It is important to emphasize that there was nothing bizarre or irrational about Jackson's and Van Buren's condemnations. These men were both Presidents of the United States, each a sober and mature politician with a firm grip on reality and a sure feel for the public pulse. Given their assumptions about the necessary social basis for a republic, there were indeed grounds for concern about what economic development was doing to America. The economic transformations favored by their Whig opponents were unquestionably creating new forms of domination and social hierarchy, in which hundreds of independent yeomen might be transformed into the wage-earning "hands" of a corporation. The independent farming communities which Jefferson relied on as the social foundations of republicanism were in fact becoming the subjects of distant market forces, symbolized by the mammoth Bank of the United States. An America based on social and political equality, as men like Jefferson, Jackson, and Van Buren understood that term, was indeed impossible in an advanced industrial society, and clear-headed men with views such as theirs had every reason to oppose its development if they could.

They fought the "monster" (as Jackson called the Bank of the United States) with laissez-faire. Supporters and opponents of the new economic order both assumed that the transition could never take place without active and prolonged state intervention. If that was true, Jacksonians reasoned, nothing would be needed to stop the engine of destructive social changes than to yank away the artificial props of government support—the tariffs, the corporate charters, the purchases of stock, the myriad other forms of monopoly privilege which eager promoters had solicited—and the whole movement would collapse. When Jacksonians proclaimed that "the best government is that which governs least," they were hoping to strangle business, not promote it.

In retrospect, it is obvious they failed. Even if their program had been rigorously implemented—and it wasn't—it is highly doubtful that a simple hands-off policy would ever have been sufficient to halt the Market Revolution in its tracks. Jacksonians also were inconsistent. State studies have shown that Democrats in state legislatures were more likely to oppose business subsidies than their Whig counterparts, but the number of exceptions mounted as the depression of the 1840s faded before the prosperity of the 1850s. Party leaders began to tolerate in states what they would not allow to the federal government, reassuring themselves that the hometown bank or railroad could not possibly be so pernicious as a distant monster in Washington or Philadelphia, especially if its board of directors was generously seeded with good, sound Democrats. When Democrats met Whigs on the broad plains of a developmentalist consensus, the collapse of the Jacksonian party system was not far distant.[30] The specific structure of Jacksonian economic policy thus collapsed, but the rhetorical commitment to economic and political equality has endured in party doctrine to the present.

If knowledge of historical context can help us understand the ambiguous legacy of Democratic attitudes towards matters of economic class and public power, what can it tell about the highly charged contemporary issues of race and gender?

In one important sense, the Jacksonian Democratic party made a major and enduring commitment to the principle of openness and inclusiveness in American politics. In keeping with its insistence on the political equality of all white men, the Jacksonian Democratic party made remarkable and largely successful efforts to attract the allegiance and participation of foreign-born white voters. The 1830s and 1840s saw a marked surge of immigration to the United States, particularly from Catholic regions of Ireland and Germany which had furnished few American settlers in earlier periods. Whig patricians were pleased to employ the newcomers in docks, factories, and construction projects, but viewed the prospect of foreign and Catholic political participation with distaste.

Democratic organizers responded quite differently, and welcomed the new Americans enthusiastically. Party organizers insisted that it was devotion to republican principles that defined a good American, not language, religion, or nativity, and stressed to laboring immigrants that Democratic doctrines on economic and political equality were just the answer for the problems of the urban working class. While Whigs insisted on strict naturalization requirements, Democrats in several states offered ballots to all white male "residents" rather than citizens, and opened their tickets and neighborhood party clubs to Irishmen and Germans. The newcomers responded with equal enthusiasm, and the Democratic voting preference of immigrant working class neighborhoods soon became a truism of American politics.[31]

The Jacksonians' approach to nonwhite Americans contrasted sharply with their policy of openness towards white immigrants and also differs from the civil rights record of the modern Democratic party. In 1856, Stephen A. Douglas, Democrat of Illinois, spoke classic Jacksonian doctrine when he declared that "we do not believe in the equality of the negro, socially or politically, with the white man. . . . Our people are a white people; our State is a white state; and we mean to preserve the race pure, without any mixture with the negro."[32] The discrepancy between Jacksonian views of white and black ethnic diversity poses a serious interpretative challenge for historians and party activists alike.

In part, the racial views of Jacksonian Democrats simply reflected the views of white Americans at large. The party emerged in an era when racism was a well-established feature of national policy. African slavery was protected by the federal Constitution and formed the basis of politics and society in almost half the states. Even where slavery itself was banned, equal treatment was rare. Only four New England states in 1840 allowed free black men the right to vote on an equal basis with whites. The Jacksonian era was also a period of rapid westward expansion, and contempt and resentment of the Indian nations that blocked the path of white settlement was widespread among European Americans. In this environment, racial prejudice against blacks and Native Americans was nearly universal among the white population. When the tactic seemed to promise success, white politicians of almost every stripe seemed willing to pander to white prejudice by accusing their opponents of insufficient support for slavery or white supremacy.

Even when we make allowances for widespread popular prejudice, however, the Jacksonians' strong insistence on racial inequality usually distinguished them from their opponents. The core of Jackson's electoral strength lay in southern and western states, where relations with blacks and Indians had paramount public importance. In these regions, voters were well aware that presidential candidate Andrew Jackson was himself a cotton planter who owned nearly 200 slaves, and who had won his early military reputation as a ruthless Indian fighter. Most of these voters were confident that General Jackson would be a reliable defender of African slavery and Indian removal, especially when compared to John Quincy Adams, Jackson's National Republican rival from Massachusetts. Once in office, Jackson and his fellow Democrats did nothing to disappoint this expectation. In the first major policy battle of his administration, Jackson fought successfully for authority to force the Indian tribes still remaining east of the Mississippi to exchange their traditional lands for new territory in what is now Oklahoma. This policy was especially popular in the states of Georgia, Alabama, and Mississippi, where thousands of Cherokees, Creeks, Choctaws, Chickasaws, and Seminoles still controlled much valuable acreage. It was strongly opposed by National Republican leaders, however, who claimed that these Indians were adopting white culture and religion and deserved protection from aspiring cotton planters and gold-seekers. As the campaign mounted to abolish African slavery, moreover, Andrew Jackson defended the "peculiar institution" vigorously. He allowed postmasters to bar abolitionist literature from the U.S. mails and denounced the abolition movement in his Farewell Address. "Nothing but mischief can come from these improper assaults upon the feelings and rights of others," he declared, and his fellow Democrats largely echoed these sentiments.[33]

Even in the North, Democratic leaders supported the proslavery stand of the national party and touted the presidential aspirations of favorite sons like Martin Van Buren, Franklin Pierce, and James Buchanan on the grounds that they were "northern men with southern principles." Within the northern states, Jacksonian Democrats frequently took the lead in attacking local blacks' efforts to gain or preserve the right to vote. This was particularly true in New York and Pennsylvania, the northern states with the largest share of the free states' black population.[34] In the realm of popular culture, historians have documented the close connections between blackface minstrel shows and Democratic politics among the northern working class.[35] When a northern Democrat like David Wilmot of Pennsylvania did break ranks on the subject of slavery's expansion, he did so on the explicit grounds that the power of slaveholding aristocrats was unfair to ordinary white people, not that slavery was unjust for blacks.[36]

The Jacksonians' Whig opponents were as mindful as Democrats of widespread prejudice among the electorate, and their attitude toward non-whites mixed condescension with benevolence. Even before the formal organization of the Whig party, however, Jackson's National Republican rivals fought vigorously against his policy of Indian removal, and the Cherokee Indians relied heavily on Whig lawyers and funding from Whig-dominated benevolent societies in fighting the policy in the United States Supreme Court.[37]

In matters directly concerning African Americans, the Whigs were more closely divided. Southern Whigs were vigorously proslavery and sought political advantages by unfairly accusing Martin Van Buren of abolitionist leanings. In the northern states, however, the Whigs harbored a significant faction that condemned slavery on moral grounds. After he lost the White House to Andrew Jackson, John Quincy Adams made a new career in the House of Representatives, attacking the "gag rule" which forbade the reception of antislavery petitions. Whig leaders such as Horace Greeley and William H. Seward of New York defended equal black suffrage in principle, and deep divisions between antislavery "Conscience" Whigs and proslavery "Cotton" Whigs ultimately contributed to the Whig party's collapse. The various movements for benevolent reform, including temperance, missionary activity, women's rights, and abolitionism, always found a warmer reception among northern Whigs than among Democrats.[38] Recognizing the Whigs' imperfect record on the slavery question, many black abolitionists became disgusted with both major parties, but where they kept the vote, black Americans recognized the Whigs' marginally superior record on racial issues by supporting the party consistently at the polls.[39]

The contrasting positions taken by Whigs and Democrats on matters of race and ethnicity seem to have stemmed from the parties' differing views of equality itself. For Jacksonians, equality was absolute and indivisible. If a man was entitled to some of the privileges of citizenship, he was entitled to all of them, and there could be no intermediate classes of partially enfranchised or semi-equal citizens. As bona fide white men, therefore, Irish and German immigrants were deserving of every political consideration. As long as majority opinion subjected African Americans to slavery in the South and social discrimination in the North, however, there could be no question of political equality for black voters. "If [anti-black] sentiment should alter," declared a Van Burenite delegate to the New York constitutional convention which abolished equal black suffrage in 1821, "if the time should ever arrive when the African shall be raised to the level of the white man—when the distinctions that now prevail shall be done away—when the colours shall intermarry—when negroes shall be invited to your tables—to sit in your pew, or ride in your coach, it may then be proper to institute a new Convention, and remodel the constitution so as to conform to that state of society." Some fifteen years later, a Democratic leader of the Michigan constitutional convention expressed the same sentiment when he opposed black suffrage "until we [can] consent to treat them as equal with us in all respects."[40] Because most of the electorate were not ready to accept blacks so broadly, the Jacksonians were unwilling to accept them at all.

Whig spokesmen were far more willing than Democrats to think in terms of graded hierarchies of citizenship, or indeed, of humanity. Firmly believing in the refined, self-controlled, Protestant urban gentleman as the model citizen, they were prepared to accept others in stages as they approached the status of their civic ideal. The Whig view of equality therefore put great stress on Americans' equal opportunity for self-improvement, implicitly affirming that many Americans needed a great deal of improvement before they could presume to claim equality with such Whig luminaries as Henry Clay or Daniel Webster. "I hold to no aristocracy except the aristocracy of nature," proclaimed a typical Whig spokesman. "To genius, talents, moral worth and public services I render due honor; and I care not whether the claimant to that honor is clad in robes of purple and fine linen, or in the squalid rags of poverty." This orator expressed a Whig version of egalitarianism, but Jacksonians were more likely to assert that all aristocracies were suspect, "natural" or otherwise. Similarly, the *Whig Review* worried about "too strong a tendency to reduce all the elements of society to a common level," and advocated a system where "each takes the place appointed to him by nature." For foreign immigrants who had yet to prove themselves worthy of American republican citizenship, the "place appointed by nature" was a respectful distance from the ballot box. Whig Senator Willie P. Mangum of North Carolina thus deplored the offer of equal treatment to "the bandit of the Appenines, the mercenary Swiss, the hungry loafer of the cities of the Old World, the offal of the disgorged jails, penitentiaries and houses of correction of foreign countries." For native-born American blacks, however, who had proved their worthiness of citizenship by accumulating enough property to testify to their thrift and stability, the right to vote was a fit reward.

By the same token, Protestant Indian farmers deserved at least as much consideration as "wild Irish" immigrants, though Whig leaders were not prepared to admit either group as fully equal to themselves. Even in slaveholding North Carolina, prominent Whig and former Federalist Judge William Gaston urged that free blacks should keep the right to vote if they met a property requirement. "Let them know they are part of the body politic, and they will feel an attachment to the form of Government, and have a fixed interest in the prosperity of the community, and will exercise an important influence over the slaves," he argued.[41] The Judge's position failed narrowly in North Carolina's constitutional convention of 1835, but his tolerance of a gradation of political rights and privileges which did not depend solely on color remained a fixture of Whig thought throughout the antebellum period.

Beyond the conspicuous topics of slavery and race, there is also some evidence of a distinction between the two antebellum parties in the related matter of gender. American women were legally barred from voting in the Jacksonian era, and it was not until 1848 that a handful of female reformers demanded suffrage at the world's first women's rights convention in Seneca Falls, New York. No mainstream politicians defended this demand for many years, yet some historians find subtle differences between Whigs and Democrats on the proper place of women in public life. One study of the 1840 presidential election has called attention to the Whigs' use of "feminine" symbols and Whig efforts to recruit women's aid in persuading their menfolk to vote for William Henry Harrison. "Whig Husbands or None," announced a Tennessee woman's banner, while Democrats protested "this way of making politicians of their women." More recently, it has been argued that the Whig use of women in politics was limited to the passive theatrics of party rallies, and that Democrats were not slow to see the advantage of a corps of handkerchief-waving females at party rallies and parades. When northern middle class women warmed to the reform causes of temperance and abolition, however, supporters of these "women's issues" found a somewhat warmer reception in the northern Whig party.[42]

Jacksonian demands for white male equality, and the Democrats' indifference to the claims of women, blacks, and Indians, evidently stemmed from similar convictions, for the inequality of women and nonwhites served to magnify the egalitarian claims of white men. Rhetorically speaking, a true Jacksonian Democrat was master in his own house, shop, or farm, and would not submit to the feminized status of dependency on another. Nor would he accept the domesticating influence of female moral reformers. The jokes and songs of minstrel shows likewise pounded home the message that blacks were hopelessly lazy, thoughtless, dishonest, drunken, and irresponsible. Whether bond or free, their only conceivable role in American life was to obey the orders of white men. The implied message was equally clear: white men were everything that blacks were not, regardless of where they had come from or how low the vagaries of the market economy had brought them. In a nation where slavery was a daily reality in the southern states, and only recently abolished everywhere else, white racist rhetoric cried out that white men were not and never would be slaves.

This message was especially popular among southern whites, but it was just as eagerly received by northern workers. In rough urban neighborhoods like New York's Bowery, thousands of white men struggled against "wage-slavery," seeking to survive and support their families by competing for daily or weekly earnings and taking orders from other white men—the very things that Jefferson had said would forever disqualify them from true republican equality. Presumptuous elitists—whether banks or bosses or abolitionists or Whig politicians—who wished to dominate white freemen were warned by Democratic racists that white inequality was "un-American" and contrary to the order of nature. During the Civil War, a Democratic party song book made the connection explicit in a protest against Black Republican abolitionism:

> A white American was once
> Thought equal to a King,
> When men the nation founded,
> And law did justice bring;
>
> Now, speak against the nigger
> In Bastilles you'll repent
> For you are not a loyal 'Merican
> Of African descent.[43]

Even at its worst moments, in other words, the Jacksonian Democratic party sought the electorate's approval by defending the liberty and equality of its core constituency.

Familiarity with the Democratic party's Jacksonian roots hardly requires that modern Democrats embrace the identical slogans which aroused their antebellum predecessors. Despite Jacksonian pessimism, we have long since learned that democracy can and must survive the transition to industrial society. The politics of racial and gender inequality have still less place in the modern Democratic agenda. Most of us would like to hope that Democrats have now abandoned these tactics forever, if only to see them adopted by their opponents.

It may be reassuring to realize, however, that the Democratic party has not been as inconsistent and indifferent in its ideology as surface appearances might indicate. In each of its defining generations, the Democratic party sought to protect the eroding position of the electorate's majority class. In Jackson's day, the threat came from a restructuring market economy. In Roosevelt's, a mature industrial economy fell victim to the stranglehold of the Great Depression. Though Andrew Jackson opposed government activism and Franklin Roosevelt supported it, both had similar purposes in mind. For Jackson as for Roosevelt, the most fundamental role for government was to maintain the material social conditions most necessary for the survival of republicanism itself. Jackson hoped to do so by withholding government support from what he regarded as pernicious economic innovations. Roosevelt and his successors would extend government assistance, not for its own sake, but to promote the twentieth century equivalent of the independence and equality among the population that early republicans rightly saw as vital to their experiment.

Those today who cite Jacksonian slogans of rugged individualism to justify unlimited power for the corporate sector are misappropriating the emotional energy of Jacksonian Democracy and turning it to a vastly different purpose than that envisioned first by its creators. Many voters still share a deep need to believe that the world is a boundless frontier. All that stands between us and our dreams, we are told, is to cast off restraints, get the government off our backs, cut out the waste, fraud, and mismanagement, and the path back to the white man's yeoman republic will be clear.

It will do little good for Democrats to protest that this is a distortion of their cultural heritage, and is unfair. They have no copyright on individualist rhetoric and no one will listen to partisan claims of prior ownership. At the same time, Democrats should not walk away from their history, nor abandon efforts to update Jeffersonian or Jacksonian egalitarianism.

Rather, Democrats should keep alive an invigorated consciousness of their own traditions. Without dismissing the contradictions in their own history, Democrats can remember what voters were looking for in the seemingly conflicting rhetoric of the Jacksonians and the New Dealers. Americans in both periods were anxious for a government of liberty and equality for the average household. However unsuccessful in the end, Jacksonian anti-statism was part of an effort to guarantee those qualities. After America had a century of experience with industrialization, the New Dealers would conclude that active government was not inimical to equality, but essential to it. Their turn to "big government" was not an abandonment of the Jacksonian tradition, but a logical fulfillment of it.

In its own twisted fashion, Jacksonian racism supported the claims of the ordinary white person for equality in the public sphere. Today, armed with different assumptions about who deserves to be considered a person, the Democrats' aggressive civil rights record demonstrates that the Jacksonian commitment to an absolute standard of civic equality is still a vital legacy. Following the example of an earlier generation that acted to include the foreign-born in their definition of qualified citizens, modern Democrats have fought to expand the circle of equality, to include minorities and women. As they have done so, their Jacksonian notions of equality have contributed more to the fight against public and private discrimination than older Whig notions of a graduated social hierarchy.

The rhetorical themes of Jacksonian Democracy have left an abiding, though ambiguous, legacy for the Democrats' third century. Torn from the circumstances that inspired them, Jacksonian slogans can be easily misapplied, but they have never been "claptrap." Properly understood, the legacy of the Jacksonian Democrats remains a central aspect of their party's continuing appeal.

# NOTES

1. Andrew Jackson to Joseph Conn Guild, April 24, 1835, in *The Correspondence of Andrew Jackson*, ed. John Spencer Bassett (Washington, D.C.: Carnegie Institute of Washington, 1926-1933).

2. Richard P. McCormick, *The Second American Party System: Party Formation in the Jacksonian Era* (Chapel Hill: University of North Carolina Press, 1966); idem., "Political Development and the Second Party System," in William Nisbet Chambers and Walter Dean Burnham, *The American Party Systems: Stages of Political Development* (New York: Oxford University Press, 1967), 90-116; and William G. Shade, "Political Pluralism and Party Development: The Creation of a Modern Party System: 1815-1852" in *The Evolution of American Political Systems*, Paul Kleppner et al., eds. (Westport, Conn.: Greenwood Press, 1981), 77-112.

3. Richard Hofstadter, *The Idea of a Party System: The Rise of Legitimate Opposition in the United States, 1780-1840* (Berkeley: University of California Press, 1972), 212-271. Hofstadter held up Martin Van Buren as the prototype of the pragmatic party wheelhorse who accepted the legitimacy of the opposition's right to rule. Certainly some antebellum politicians began to feel this way, but I will argue here that Van Buren himself was not one of them.

4. Andrew Jackson to Joseph Conn Guild, April 24, 1835, in Bassett, *The Correspondence of Andrew Jackson*, 5:339.

5. Andrew Jackson, Bank Veto Message, July 10, 1832, in *A compilation of the Messages and Papers of the Presidents*, comp. James D. Richardson, 20 vols. (New York: Bureau of National Literature, n.d.), 3:1153.

6. John L. O'Sullivan, "Introduction," in *The United States Magazine and Democratic Review*, I, 1 (October 1837): 6.

7. Martin Van Buren, "Special Session Message," September 4, 1837, in Richardson, *Papers of the Presidents*, 4:1561.

8. Franklin D. Roosevelt, quoted in *The American Way*, comp. Dagobert D. Runes (New York: Philosophical Library, 1944), 13.

9. Ronald Reagan, quoted in *President Reagan's Quotations*, ed. Clark Cassell (Washington D. C.: Braddock Publications, 1984), 9.

10. For classic examples, see Lee Benson, *The Concept of Jacksonian Democracy: New York as a Test Case* (Princeton: Princeton University Press, 1961), 81; and Bray Hammond, *Banks and Politics from the Revolution to the Civil War* (Princeton: Princeton University Press, 1957).

11. Key works in the history of republican thought include Bernard Bailyn, *The Ideological Origins of the American Revolution* (Cambridge: Harvard University Press, 1967); Gordon S. Wood, *The Creation of the American Republic, 1776-1787* (Chapel Hill: University of North Carolina Press, 1969); and J. G. A. Pocock, *The Machiavellian Moment* (Princeton: Princeton University Press, 1975). For further discussion of how republican principles were applied in the Jacksonian era, see Harry L. Watson, *Liberty and Power: The Politics of Jacksonian America* (New York: Hill & Wang, 1990).

12. Andrew Jackson, "Farewell Address," March 4, 1837, Richardson, *Papers of the Presidents*, 3:1515.

13. Thomas Jefferson, *Notes on the State of Virginia*, ed.William Peden, (Chapel Hill: University of North Carolina Press, 1954), 164-165.

14. Ibid.

15. Drew R. McCoy, *The Elusive Republic: Political Economy in Jeffersonian America* (Chapel Hill: University of North Carolina Press, 1980).

16. For a penetrating recent depiction of the American experience during these years of transition, see Charles Sellers, *The Market Revolution: Jacksonian America, 1815-1846* (New York: Oxford University Press, 1991). For an older, still useful view which stresses commercial and technological change, see George Rogers Taylor, *The Transportation Revolution, 1815-1860* (New York: Holt, Rinehart & Winston, 1951).

17. Richard L. McCormick, "The Party Period and Public Policy: An Exploratory Hypothesis," in idem., *The Party Period and Public Policy: American Politics from the Age of Jackson to the Progressive Era* (New York: Oxford University Press, 1986), 197-227.

18. Watson, *Liberty and Power*, 26-32.

19. Ibid., 30-31; Sellers, *Market Revolution*, 23-27; and Sean Wilentz, *Chants Democratic: New York City and the Rise of the American Working Class* (New York: Oxford University Press, 1980).

20. Alexander Hamilton's report on manufactures (1791) was a classic Federalist foil to the agrarian arguments in Jefferson's *Notes on the State of Virginia*. See also McCoy, *Elusive Republic*.

21. Andrew Jackson, "Farewell Address," March 4, 1837 Richardson, *Papers of the Presidents*, 4:1524-25.

22. Ibid., 4:1524.

23. Andrew Jackson, Veto Message, May 27, 1830, Richardson, *Papers of the Presidents*, 3:1046-1056.

24. Andrew Jackson, Veto Message, July 10, 1832, Richardson, *Papers of the Presidents*, 3:1153.

25. Ibid.

26. Led by Vice President John C. Calhoun, the cotton and rice planters who dominated South Carolina became convinced that the federal tariff was destroying their prosperity and undermining slavery itself. Unable to achieve repeal of the tariff in Congress, in 1832 they called a special convention to declare it null and void, and thus unenforceable, in South Carolina. President Jackson had no great love for protective tariffs, but he would not tolerate the subordination of federal authority to state power, and threatened to invade South Carolina to restore the supremacy of federal laws there. Armed conflict was averted by compromise in 1833. See William W. Freiehling, *Prelude to Civil War* (New York: Harper & Row, 1966).

27. Van Buren was referring to political factions in seventeenth and eighteenth century England. "Cavaliers" and "Jacobites" had supported the arbitrary powers of the Stuart monarchs, while "Roundheads," "Puritans," and "Presbyterians" had opposed the "divine right of kings," in favor of Parliament and the authority of representative institutions. After the Stuarts were permanently expelled, "Whigs" continued to champion the rights of Parliment, while "Tories" supported the prerogative powers of the Crown. Martin Van Buren, *Inquiry into the Origin and*

*Course of Political Parties in the United States* (New York: Hurd & Houghton, 1867), 7-8.

28. Ibid., 222, 224-225.

29. Ibid.

30. Michael F. Holt, *The Political Crisis of the 1850s* (New York: John Wiley and Sons, 1978), 101-138.

31. Robert Kelley, *The Cultural Pattern in American Politics: The First Century* (New York: Knopf, 1979), 170-176.

32. Ibid., 195.

33. Andrew Jackson, "Farewell Address," Richardson, *Papers of the Presidents*, 4:1517.

34. In New York, leading Democratic-Republican (and future president) Martin Van Buren framed constitutional "reforms" in 1821 which gave nearly unlimited suffrage to white men, but imposed a discriminatory property requirement for prospective black voters. In Pennsylvania, Democratic mass meetings in 1837 successfully pressured the state constitutional convention to strip all black inhabitants of the right to vote. Leon F. Litwack, *North of Slavery: The Negro in the Free States, 1790-1860* (Chicago: University of Chicago Press, 1961), 74-93.

35. Jean H. Baker, *Affairs of Party: The Political Culture of Northern Democrats in the Mid-Nineteenth Century* (Ithaca: Cornell University Press, 1983), 212-260; and Alexander Saxton, "Blackface Minstrelsy and Jacksonian Ideology," *American Quarterly* 27 (May 1975): 3-28.

36. Eric Foner, *Free Soil, Free Labor, Free Men: The Ideology of the Republican Party Before the Civil War* (New York: Oxford University Press, 1970), 267; and David Potter, *The Impending Crisis, 1848-1861* (New York: Harper & Row, 1976), 37.

37. Some recent historians have condemned leading Whigs as hypocritical on matters relating to Indians, pointing out that party leaders abandoned their opposition to Indian removal once they replaced the Democrats in office. In the early days of the Jackson administration, however, before the policy of Indian removal had become an accomplished fact, the actions of National Republicans offered clear support to the Indians's own views of their rights. No one saw this more clearly than the Cherokee leaders who worked closely with Whigs Daniel Webster and William Wirt in contesting their removal before the Supreme Court. For a contrasting view, see Robert V. Remini, *The Legacy of Andrew Jackson: Essays on Democracy, Indian Removal and Slavery* (Baton Rouge: Louisiana State University Press, 1961), 179-180, 318-320.

38. Daniel Walker Howe, *The Political Culture of the American Whigs* (Chicago: University of Chicago Press, 1979), 32-42.

39. Litwack, *North of Slavery*, 80-81, 85; Benson, *The Concept of Jacksonian Democracy*, 179-180, 318-320.

40. Litwack, *North of Slavery*, 77-78; and John Ashworth, *'Agrarians' and 'Aristocrats:' Party Political Ideology in the United States, 1837-1846* (London: Royal Historical Society, 1983), 222.

41. *Proceedings and Debates of the Convention of North Carolina Called to Amend the Constitution of the State* (Raleigh: Joseph Gales & Son, 1836), 79.

42. Robert Gray Gunderson, *The Log Cabin Campaign* (Lexington: University of Kentucky Press, 1957), 127, 135-137; and Mary P. Ryan, *Women in Public: Between Banners and Ballots, 1825-1880* (Baltimore: The Johns Hopkins University Press, 1990), 132-141.

43. Baker, *Affairs of Party*, 234.

## PART TWO

# Democrats and the Civil War Legacy

### 1840s–1890s

## Chapter 4

# A Portrait of Democratic America in the Mid-Nineteenth Century

*Robert Kelley*

The Democrats entered the 1850s as the nation's majority party. Their great adversaries, the Whigs, whose home base was in Yankee New England—or wherever Yankees predominated as they migrated westward into upstate New York and the Middle West—could rarely win either the presidency or majorities in Congress. Democrats could be confident in the knowledge that it was their party, first as Jeffersonian Republicans and then as Jacksonian Democrats, that had ruled the country from Washington, D.C. with few intermissions for half a century.

The Democratic rank and file, furthermore, were passionately loyal, commonly speaking of the party as if it were an army fighting a noble cause, even, indeed, as if it were a church and therefore an almost holy vessel. Turn-outs for state, local, and federal elections—which seemed to come along every few months—were massive and highly organized.[1] Since the 1830s, American politics had been the country's folk theater, with a cast involving tens of thousands of ordinary citizens. Within an intricate network of committees and party meetings, with all power lodged in the national conventions, absolute loyalty and obedience to the cause was demanded. The ethic of being a "party man," formerly condemned, had by that time acquired new legitimacy, especially among Democrats, who appeared to display a particular relish for party combat. The Whigs, meanwhile, never comfortable with party discipline, stepped back. The Democrats were supreme party men, endlessly preaching "*everything for CAUSE, nothing for men.*"[2]

In 1852, the belief that the Democracy—as the Democrats were fond of referring to their party—was America's natural governing party appeared once more to be confirmed. The party achieved a smashing national victory, their eleventh in the fourteen presidential ballotings since Jefferson's election in 1800 began their ascendancy. They not only won the presidency for Franklin Pierce, but also gained a huge majority in Congress.[3]

Meanwhile, even the federal judiciary was solidly in the hands of the party of Jefferson and Jackson, since only Democrats, with one exception, had been appointed to the U.S. Supreme Court since Andrew Jackson's administration.[4]

## DEMOCRATIC AMERICA AND WHIG AMERICA: TWO SEPARATE CULTURES

Who were the Democrats, and who were the Whigs? Within the white, male American population in the mid-nineteenth century, these groups formed two large and enduring communities, two great archipelagoes of peoples and ways of life which spread across the entire country, from East to West and North to South.[5] We may think of them as "Whig America" and "Democratic America," and though the two parties could claim roughly equal shares of the electorate, the decisive fact was that their social centers of gravity were quite different from each other.[6]

Democrats and Whigs differed in their religions, ethnicities, living areas, and lifestyles—including even forms of recreation, and tastes in music, foods, and dress—as well as in their political visions, values, and causes. They had conflicting ideas about what America was or could be, and where it should be going; and they differed on what was admirable and honorable in human behavior. Above all, Whigs and Democrats saw themselves as fighting different enemies.

The enemy, of course, is the eternally powerful force that drives people to join ranks behind the banner of a particular political party. Ever on the horizon, the enemy's presence arouses and inspires people to collective thought and action. What and who people are against, what threatens their way of life and their economic interests, on both an individual and a national level, shapes all political languages, and thus the agenda of every ideology and movement. When enemies disappear, even ethnic groups tend to fade in self-consciousness and dissolve, while political parties are reduced to bickering internecine squabbles and confusion, and pass from history.[7]

Who was the enemy, the "negative reference," for Democratic America? Its constituency was held together by a shared dislike, for many even a hatred, of New England Yankees, and by a fear of what, if given power over the nation, the Yankees might do to the ways of life of everyone else. The preeminent historian of ethnocultural politics, Paul Kleppner, writes:

> Few Yankees were loved by others. Their distinctive "nationality" typically was carried by a "blinding prejudice," for the Yankee was not only conscious of "being a New England man," he was

> also convinced that Yankees collectively "brought in themselves the germs of every quality essential to national greatness." And their "blinding prejudice" was fused with a nearly inexhaustible energy for minding the business of others. Yankees helped their neighbors, even when those neighbors resisted that assistance, for their determination to correct wrongs, to extirpate sin, to refashion others in the Yankee [Puritan] image, was fueled by moral imperatives. It was their divinely mandated task "to produce in the nation a more homogeneous character." Yankee behavior in pursuit of that goal, and the reactions to it, created the . . . intersecting fault lines of the [nation's] . . . party system[s].[8]

As a Tennessee editor put it during the crisis of the late 1850s, "The Puritans of today, like the Puritans of 1700, conceive themselves to be better and holier than others, and entitled—by divine right as it were—to govern and control the actions and dictate the opinions" of their fellow men. New England was "always putting itself forward as the accuser & maligner of its brethren, the marplot & busybody of the confederacy, always crying over its grievances & always arraigning the other states for pretended usurpations. . . ." New Englanders had "persuaded themselves that they had a prescriptive right to impose their politics, their habits, manners and dogmas on the sister States and aspired to convert the whole people of the United States to Yankeedom." For them, "nothing exists that may not be improved."[9]

The Democrats, therefore, had their fundamental demographic base (when it came to winning national elections) among those masses of white Southerners who literally for centuries had hated the Puritans. About half of the white Southerners had long before migrated to the American colonies from the southern and western counties of England. These regions, in the seventeenth century, were characterized by an intensely rural, aristocratic, military, and honor-bound way of life. Their society centered on large estates with many tenant farmers—who were an illiterate folk in a region without public schools. In their mansions, meanwhile the elite indulged their tastes for drink, opulent houses and dress, elaborate equipages, and lordly personal styles. This culture, this way of life, was transferred almost en masse, southern drawl and all, across the Atlantic. Settling in around the Chesapeake Bay, it joined with slavery to form the core of the southern colonies and later of the southern states.

While in England, these Southerners had hated the very different English of the eastern shires, the region called East Anglia, who in the 1600s had sent thousands of their own to America to settle New England. East Anglia was the land of the Puritans, of bustling commerce and cities, of a distaste for violence and a preference for disciplined, austere ways, and of a classically Calvinist passion for learning. In the seventeenth century, these two ethnic communities, the Puritans and the southern English, fought each other in a great civil war in which the southern English—the Cavaliers—battled for the king, while the Puritans of the eastern shires—the Roundheads—rallied sternly behind Oliver Cromwell, and beheaded Charles I. The bloody events of that period still resounded in the historical memories of the Southerners and Yankees in the America of the 1850s, and continued clamorously so to do during their next (and last) great battle, the American Civil War.[10]

In the 1700s, a quarter of a million Scotch-Irish—a sternly Presbyterian (i.e., Calvinist) people who had emigrated from Scotland to occupy northern Ireland (Ulster) in the 1600s—migrated, in a number of famine-driven pulses, across the Atlantic to the British colonies. They settled in the lower Hudson Valley in New York, and shared central and western Pennsylvania where they congregated thickly, joined by a multitude of Lutherans and "plain people"—such as the Amish and the River Brethren—coming in from Germany. In a long stream of migrating families, thousands of the Scotch-Irish and Germans then journeyed southwestward from Pennsylvania to occupy the piedmont foothills and long Appalachian valleys in the back-country South, where they inhabited a vast region running hundreds of miles from north to south, clear to South Carolina.[11]

The Germans were a quiet, inward-turning people who avoided politics, but the Scotch-Irish were militant activists in the Revolutionary era. A fighting, almost tribal, folk who had glorified war in their homeland (against the hated Catholic Irish), they had their own bitter and bloody historical reasons for despising the English, who had been their oppressive overlords in Ireland and traditional enemies of Scotland. In America, the caustic Anglophobia of the Scotch-Irish focused on the Yankees of New England who, as a homogeneously English people proudly claimed that identity as uniquely their own. It was no coincidence that America's first "ethnic" president would be the Democrat and Scotch-Irishman Andrew Jackson, who had been born of immigrant Ulster parents and called himself an "Old Irishman," had fought the English in the Revolution and the War of 1812, intensely disliked Yankees (who regarded him with equal distaste) and spoke in a North-of-Ireland burr all his days.[12]

Together, the English and Scotch-Irish formed a great mass of peoples in the vast region of the South. Instinctively anti-Yankee, they were thus instinctively Jeffersonians and Jacksonian Democrats. This is not to say that the South was monolithically anti-Yankee. In the pre-Civil War years, the Whigs had an enormous following there, at least until their catastrophic defeat in 1852. Thousands of white men in the southern states, including the Whigs' towering figure, Henry Clay, and one of its then obscure personages, Abraham Lincoln, admired Yankee ways: their industrious work ethic, their entrepreneurial energy, bustling and productive cities, common schools, and literacy.

New England seemed, by contrast to the South, such a *civilized* society. Whigs like Abraham Lincoln looked about them at the violence and disorder, the hostility toward book learning and schools, and the heavy drinking and carousing that seemed so markedly to characterize Democratic communities in these years and yearned for the spread of Yankee civility.[13] Certainly, it was common within Lincoln's Whig-Republican world to view Democrats as made up largely of the dregs of society. "Republicans," writes Joel Silbey, made it clear that "two out of every three of the more uninformed, the intemperate and vicious portion of most communities" were Democrats. Or, more directly, "the ragged infantines of steeves and brothels, the spawn and shipwreck of taverns and dicing houses" formed the core of the Democratic support aided only by some "weak-minded men of respectability."[14]

## THE CRISIS OF THE 1850s CREATES A NEW PARTY SYSTEM

Despite this admiration for things Yankee among the Whigs south of Pennsylvania and the Ohio River, the politically crucial fact in the pre-war and post-war South was the deep, persisting hatred of Yankees that most Southerners felt. Intensifying that ancient cultural and ethnic antipathy was the powerful reality that the South was a slave society. From a vocal minority among the New Englanders, either in their homeland or out in the Middle West, came torrents of abolitionist rhetoric, both in the open air and in print. It was an outcry filled with loathing for southern ways of life. Southerners, who tended to believe that all Yankees were abolitionists, were alarmed to see the slavery extension issue swelling enormously in national politics, beginning with the Wilmot Proviso measure of 1846—to ban slavery within territory acquired through the Mexican War—and continuing into the 1850s.

In 1853, American public life was shaken by one of the mightiest earthquakes ever: the enactment of the Kansas-Nebraska Act by the Democratic Congress and a Democratic President. This measure opened at least potentially to slavery an enormous part of the national domain that had been closed to that institution, and preserved for free society, since the Missouri Compromise of 1820 (admitting Missouri as a slave state). This territory was the still unorganized portion of the Louisiana Purchase, a vast region running a thousand miles north from Arkansas to the Canadian border. The Kansas-Nebraska Act set off tornadoes of rage in the North. Angry anti-southern rhetoric erupted in state after state, especially from the Whigs, who saw their cherished Yankee civilization—a civilization of free labor, the work ethic, public schools, and sweeping progress toward an industrial, urban future with opportunity for all (whites)—as being in grave danger of being cooped in by a powerful and expansive slavocracy.

A massive rearrangement of voting groups, already underway in the 1850s for other reasons, accelerated. Tens of thousands of white Southerners, former Whigs who were alarmed by the angry anti-southern tone emerging among Whigs—their party nationally—crossed the line and marched into the Democratic party.[15] This sweep toward enfolding essentially all white Southerners into one party, the Democrats, picked up speed in the 1850s when the Whigs in the northern states, unable to contain within themselves the explosive impulses aroused by the Kansas-Nebraska Act, simply broke apart and collapsed. In their place arose a wholly northern party, the Republicans, which was far more intensely Yankee in its makeup and anti-southern in its attitudes than the Whigs had ever been before it.[16]

Thus was the Democratic political base in the South, from which the party traditionally had gone on to win presidential elections, vastly expanded. All the Democrats had needed to add to their southern bloc of votes were enough victories in the Lower North—in Pennsylvania or New York or Indiana and Illinois—to gain electoral college majorities. (Through the Kennedy and Johnson presidencies of the 1960s, this composition would continue to make up the basic sectional architecture of Democratic victories, when they were achieved.)

Democrats were able to win these victories in the Lower North because, in the southern portions of the East-West band of states running from New York and Pennsylvania out to Illinois—especially in the parts of these states below the 41st Parallel—there were strong economic links to the South, as well as thousands of voters who shared the southern Democrats' anti-black racism and their dislike of Yankees. Pennsylvania for one had its tens of thousands of passionately Democratic Scotch-Irish, lined up behind the memory of their beloved Andrew Jackson, as well as a great host of Lutheran (and Reformed) Germans, who voted en bloc for the Democrats. Since the Germans' arrival in the eighteenth century, the ethnically English in the northern states had held them in scorn. Traditionally anti-immigrant, these northerners disliked the Germans' "foreign" language and stolid, "unprogressive" ways.[17]

There were also the Dutch and other non-English minorities of the New York City and the lower Hudson Valley regions, who, repelled by the Yankees, and their dream of a homogeneous America molded in their image, voted Democratic. In the Jacksonian years and in the 1850s, indeed, wherever the Dutch and Germans settled in the midwestern states, there were Democratic votes to be found.[18] Westward from Pennsylvania, too, stood rich harvests of votes to be gathered in that immense region in southern Ohio, Indiana, and Illinois which in the 1820s and 1830s had been settled by Southerners and was forever afterward predominantly southern in culture and loyalties.[19]

From the 1820s onward, Yankee America launched two fervent crusades which would resound through the coming decades: one for alcoholic temperance, and the other for Sabbatarian laws aimed at halting all non-religious activities on Sunday.[20] Both these efforts offended the non-Yankee peoples. Like the Scotch-Irish with their whisky, the Germans also had an ethnic beverage at the core of their culture, beer, and liked to recreate freely, in the Continental fashion, on Sundays. The Germans were not a Puritan people, save for the intensely religious pietistic sects among them—such as the Amish, Mennonites, and River Brethren. The Democrats, in their unending scornful attacks on temperance and sabbatarianism—indeed, on all of the "blue laws" governing dress, sexual relations, and recreation that Yankees pressed on the states where they congregated—regularly proclaimed the message that they were the Jeffersonian party of "personal liberty." On this ground the Germans and Dutch were strongly with them.

In 1848, a wave of failed democratic revolutions in continental Europe sent another stream of Germans to America, in this case a highly voluble, highly visible group of journalists, reformers, political activists, scientists, and professors. They immensely broadened the cultural life of Germans in the United States, inducing a sophistication not formerly present in that community. However, the "Grays"—as the Germans, usually farmers, of traditional and often long-standing American residence were called—drew back from the "Greens," as they termed the liberal reformers. On their part, the Greens referred scornfully to the Grays as provincial, conservative, and politically apathetic.

As the Greens swung enthusiastically behind the anti-slavery, anti-southern reforming Whigs (as learned and professional people, they were naturally Whigs in temperament) and marched en masse into the new Republican party, giving Abraham Lincoln their warm support, they made it appear through their many journals and newspapers that the Germans generally were voting Republican. However, the German voting masses held strongly to their Democratic partisanship in most states. They disliked the Yankees, recoiled from the anti-Catholic and anti-immigrant prejudice that flowed with the Yankees into the new Republican party, loved their beer and Sunday picnics, and cared little for African Americans.[21]

## THE OTHER EARTHQUAKE: THE CATHOLICS ARRIVE

Meanwhile, in the decade from 1845 to 1855, the entire political context in America was being transformed by a great natural catastrophe and human tragedy in Europe. Both Catholic Ireland and southern (predominantly Catholic) Germany were scourged by a terrible potato famine in the 1840s. This crisis sent hundreds of thousands of their peoples fleeing to America in what was "proportionately . . . the heaviest influx of immigrants in American history."[22] During these ten years, three million people, Irish Catholics as well as Catholics and Lutherans from Germany, arrived in eastern port cities—the equivalent of 15 percent of the entire American population in 1845. Before that year—in fact, since the Revolutionary era—there had been relatively few new immigrants living among the American people.[23]

This sudden massive influx of strangers into primarily the northern states, and especially of Catholic strangers arriving in what was to that point an overwhelmingly Protestant country (in fact, territorially the largest Protestant country in the world, a circumstance regularly broadcast from pulpits and taught triumphantly in the public schools) came as a tremendous shock to the native Anglo-American core culture.[24] Americans had always said they believed in religious toleration, but they had thought of this only in terms of toleration among Protestants. Catholics, hated literally for centuries in overwhelmingly Protestant Britain, were outside the pale. As David Potter writes:

> Though it is largely forgotten today . . . it is . . . true that for a considerable part of the nineteenth century the Catholic church was chronically under fire. Its beliefs were denounced; its leaders were assailed; its convents were slandered, and its property was threatened or even attacked. With both the Protestant press and the secular press keeping up a constant barrage of abuse . . . serious riots, with loss of lives, occurred. . . . Convents were attacked . . . while [between 1834 and 1860] probably as many as twenty Catholic churches were burned in cities or towns from Maine to Texas.[25]

The German ethnic community grew with great speed in the 1850s. German immigrants arrived in the United States during that decade in larger volume than even the Irish, who represented some 1,200,000 of the great 1845-1855 influx. There were 600,000 German-born people in the country in 1850; by 1860, there were 1.3 million. Avoiding regions where Yankees predominated, they formed large colonies in New York City, Buffalo, and

Baltimore, and migrated into the huge middle western interior to settle as farmers in the countryside of Ohio, Illinois, Wisconsin, and Missouri. Cincinnati, Milwaukee, and St. Louis became special centers of German culture.

Intensely religious, German Catholics and Lutherans established their own parochial schools to maintain their separateness. This brought them, and the Irish Catholics, into immediate conflict with the Yankees, who insisted that all children attend the public schools, where (under proper English language tutelage, and reading the King James Bible, along with anti-Catholic histories) they would be turned into mainstream Americans. By the mid-century decades, indeed, battles over the parochial school question were beginning to become an explosively partisan issue between Democrats and Whigs in the northern states.[26]

Americans in general paid far more attention to the Irish Catholic influx than to that of the Germans. For one thing, they headed right to such centers of American life as New York City and Philadelphia, where, already made politically adept by their long fight against English domination in the British Isles, they quickly became an actively militant and well-organized group that regularly voted Democratic, making them the center of all eyes.

Also, they settled right among the Yankees of urban New England, who protested loudly. A third of the Boston electorate in 1855 was Irish Catholic, their numbers having tripled since 1850. This was why, said one politician, the Yankees "want a Paddy hunt & on a Paddy hunt they will go." After all, in England itself, the Catholic Irish were commonly regarded as practically a sub-human species, ignorant, violent, drunken, and by virtue of their Catholicism, addicted to ancient medieval idolatries—and this contempt was widely shared among New Englanders. Also, the very nature of the Catholic church, a body under apparently authoritarian rule by a foreign potentate, the pope, seemed at war with the core values of American republicanism. How could the Catholics possibly be loyal Americans? Were they not here to subvert the republic, certainly to destroy its Protestant faith?[27]

Thomas Jefferson, however, who scorned militant Yankee Protestant clerics trying through government to supervise everyone else's moral lives, had specifically welcomed immigrants of all faiths. Indeed, the Democrats from their beginnings had diverged most sharply from the Whigs in opening their ranks to immigrants (though of course, the Whigs were delighted with the newcomers from England who, in the 1840s and 1850s, voted Whig by a three to one margin).[28]

In contrast to Whig and Republican nativism, Democrats celebrated cultural laissez faire. *Equality, equality*: over and over, this was the Democrats' chant—though they frequently would insist that America was a white man's country, and that the inequality of African Americans as human beings was so obvious that the race clearly was not included in the very meaning of Thomas Jefferson's great assertion in the Declaration of Independence that all men were equal. Toward European, non-English immigrants, however, the Democrats opened wide arms of welcome. America as a land enriched and indeed glorified by heterogeneity (among whites)—as opposed to the Yankee passion for homogeneity—was their constant preachment.

As Illinois Senator Stephen A. Douglas, an outspoken racist on black-white issues, said of immigrants in 1852, the Democratic party

> has made this country a home for the exile, an asylum for the oppressed of all the world. We make no distinctions among our fellow citizens. . . . It is this wise, just, and honest policy that has attached the foreign vote to the democratic party. [By contrast, Whigs had waged] a bloody and revengeful war against Irishmen, Germans and Welshmen.[29]

Thus, as Paul Kleppner writes,

> Most post-1790 immigrant groups supported the Democrats. Irish Catholics were the most strongly and consistently Democratic of the newer immigrant groups. And among the German Catholics, French and French Canadian Catholics, the New Dutch, Norwegians, German Lutherans, and German Reformed, the Democracy received strong, though contextually varying support.[30]

Besides, the Jeffersonian and Jacksonian tradition in American politics had always been loudly, persistently anti-English, a quality the Irish particularly relished. It can be easily understood, therefore, why the party of the out-groups, the white minorities, would attract the Irish Catholics—even more, if possible, than it attracted the Germans. While in the 1850s some 80 percent of the latter lined up on the Democratic side, something like 95 percent of the Irish Catholics voted that ticket, and would continue to do so in ensuing generations. Altogether, this tidal wave of immigrants arriving in America during the 1850s brought in more people than voted for the Whig candidate in 1852, and made the Democrats, in the northern states, an increasingly powerful force.[31] Clearly, in the America of the 1850s, what political scientists refer to as the global political universe had been utterly revolutionized.

The Democratic party was becoming what it would remain practically into our own time, the "Catholic" party in national politics. At the same time, the arrival of the Irish and German Catholics immediately produced the brief eruption of an organized nativist, expressly anti-Catholic, and of course militantly anti-Democratic, party. The "American" or "Know-Nothing" party soon achieved startling victories in Congressional elections, drawing off thousands of Whigs as they left their moribund party.[32]

In the northern states, the flood of Catholic Irish pouring into Democratic ranks had the prompt effect of driving the devoutly Presbyterian Scotch-Irish, bloody enemies of the Catholic Irish in Ireland for centuries, out of the Democratic party and over to the other side. (The same decamping to the Whig-Republicans took place among the Baptists and Methodists of New England, formerly Democratic because of their historic oppression by the dominant Congregationalist majority.) Taking New York politics as a case in point, practically all of the non-English Protestants from the British Isles—the Scots, Welsh, and Scotch-Irish—shifted over en masse, to the level of 90 percent, to join their former enemies, the English, amongst the Whig-Republicans. It would appear that they hated Irish Catholics far more than they did their fellow Protestants from England.[33]

This first of the historic crossings-over of major ethnocultural groups from one party to the other signaled the dissolution of the Second Party System of Whigs and Democrats, in place since the late 1820s, and began the transition into the Third Party System of Republicans and Democrats, which would endure for forty years into the mid-1890s.[34] Also, apparent in this crossing-over, was the initiation of the deepest long-term trend in American political culture: the tendency over time of formerly Democratic minority peoples, as they acculturate and win acceptance, to lose the sense of being a minority and fall into the core culture. By so doing, and at the same time joining the Republican party—membership in which has always been a profoundly cutural statement—they in effect joined the "American" club as embodied in the Yankee mainstream.

Thus, the Scotch-Irish were in the process of disappearing. In the South, they would continue until modern times to vote Democratic, but elsewhere, from the mid-1850s onward, this once prominent faction of the Democratic party, these kinspeople of Andrew Jackson himself, lost their self-consciousness as a separate group, joined the Republicans, and faded into the background. The same long-term trend can be seen in the later political history of other former outgroups, such as the Dutch, the Germans, and the Mormons. Only African Americans have gone in the opposite direction, that is, from the Republicans to the Democrats, as they did in the era of Franklin Delano Roosevelt.

## DEMOCRATIC RACISM

Then there was Democratic racism, both North and South, which gave that party in the 1850s a huge and loyal following in the Lower North.

Southern whites, of course, were fundamentalists on the race issue. Among their allies in the northern states, none of the traditional Democratic ethnocultural voting groups shared the readiness of a highly religious vocal minority within the Whigs to argue the cause of African Americans, slave or free, and that of the Indians on the frontier. These groups condemned Jackson endlessly for his warfare against the Native Americans, and his subsequent removal policies. As a general rule, however, Democrats were prejudiced against African Americans, and essentially indifferent to their being slaves.[35] They regularly used a language of contempt, referring to African Americans as "vicious, indolent, and improvident." Seeking to improve black people, they said, would go against the very laws of nature.[36]

In the 1850s, Stephen A. Douglas was the Democrats' great spokesman on race issues, including the spectacularly divisive questions of slavery in the South and in the territories. Douglas, himself a Vermont-born Scot who hated the English and ranted against them year after year on the floor of Congress to Irish Catholic cheers, refused to condemn slavery. Instead, he denounced any hint of racial equality. "We do not believe in the equality of the negro, socially or politically, with the white man [in Illinois]," he said in 1856. "Our people are a white people; our State is a white state; and we mean to preserve the race pure, without any mixture with the negro." As for slavery, he considered it simply a local institution, as he had said as early as in 1848. Slavery's "burdens or advantages," Douglas remarked, "belong to those who chose to retain it, and who alone have the right to determine when they will dispense with it."[37]

Irish Catholics shared Douglas's antipathy toward African Americans. The two groups fought each other regularly in the northern cities, during the 1840s and 1850s, particularly in Philadelphia. Both were poverty stricken folk at the bottom of the employment ladder, and they competed for the same unskilled jobs. The Irish and their Catholic church rejected abolitionism root and branch, the Irish press in America calling its militants lunatics and infidels. The *New-England (Catholic) Reporter* said that the abolitionist William Lloyd Garrison should "be immediately transported to Ethiopia, there to dwell in love and harmony with the wild negroes."[38]

These attitudes were not, of course, confined to Democrats. In the early 1860s, anti-black sentiments pervaded every sphere of life in the northern states, segregation being the norm. Only in New England were African Americans allowed to vote. In the Middle West, "Our people," said a leading congressman, "hate the Negro with a perfect if not a supreme hatred," even though less than one percent of the population in those states was nonwhite.[39]

# DEMOCRATIC POLITICAL ECONOMY: THE PARTY'S VISION FOR AMERICA

During their years as the majority party before the Civil War, what was the Democrats' political economy agenda for the nation? What kind of America did they intend to create?[40] First, following, as always, the principles of Thomas Jefferson, they wanted an America that was highly decentralized, one in which the federal government did little more than conduct the nation's foreign policy.[41] The Whigs, for their part, thought of the community at large as primary and society as "organic" (one of their favorite words). Thus, the Whigs believed, America needed a vigorous central government—and they thought of government as God's magistrate on earth, doing God's business—which confidently intervened in society at the state and national levels to stimulate the development of resources and foster commerce and industry, and, at the local level, to supervise personal morals. They thought the country needed, as Henry Clay sought to provide in his perennial advocacy of an "American System," a centrally developed and implemented economic plan—one that would create a domestic market for manufactured goods, opened up by means of internal improvements (roads, canals, and railroads)—made possible by a national bank that would provide financial supervision, and protected by tariffs from foreign competitors.[42]

Democrats, conversely, thought of their ideal personage—the free, independent, and self-sufficient (white, male) individual—as entirely capable of handling his own affairs. They wanted him free not only to make money as he wished, with government playing favorites for no one, but also to live the moral life he chose, whether this meant drinking or dancing on Sundays or owning slaves. These things, they believed, were what America, by contrast with the old countries in Europe, was all about. Enlightenment rationalism, which came to them through Thomas Jefferson, was intensely secular. It urged a complete separation between church and state, and thus was massively impatient with meddling clerics seeking, by their reading of God's wishes, to supervise the private moral lives of the benighted. Free thinkers, agnostics, and the rare atheist found their political home in Democratic America.

The Democrats, then, wanted a country in which all the governing that was needed—and they thought of it as precious little—would be conducted by small and parsimonious governments, close to the people and under their direct daily supervision: that is, by the states and counties. This was, of course, a self-serving attitude on the part of white Southerners, for it protected slavery, but behind all of this, nonetheless, was a profound Democratic distrust of power, whether lodged in the halls of governments or in those of private corporations. Democrats believed this power to be the unsleeping enemy of liberty, its natural prey. They thought of strong and active government as corrupted by the wealthy elite and their privileged corporations, who would make it their ally in exploiting society at large.[43]

In 1838, a brilliant young Democrat and self-trained economist, Samuel Tilden of New York state—one of Martin Van Buren's closest advisers—rose before a jammed Tammany Hall audience in New York City to warn against the self-seeking power of the brooding colossus of international exploitive capitalism. The wealthy, he said were

> an organized class which acts in phalanx and operates through all the ramifications of society; concentrating property in monopolies and perpetuities, and binding to it political power—it has established an aristocracy more potent, and more oppressive than any other which has ever existed. Such at this moment is practically the ruling power in nearly every civilized nation.[44]

It was on these grounds that Andrew Jackson had electrified and polarized all of American public life by his 1832 veto of the recharter of the Second Bank of the United States.[45] Bankers, Democrats said, were far too powerful and inherently unscrupulous to be given, through a single mighty institution that essentially would be the federal government's banker, supervision over the entire economy through its management of this huge pool of capital and the supply of currency.

For the most part, Democrats won a permanent victory on this point in political economy. Under James K. Polk in the 1840s, the Democrats got lastingly in place the principle that, by means of an Independent Treasury System, there would be an entire separation between the federal government and banking. The Treasury Department, henceforth, cared for its own funds, and hundreds of state-chartered banks issued their own currency. Thus, the United States, alone among Western countries, would from Jackson's veto onward never have one great nationally chartered private bank performing banking services for society at large, but rather many thousands of them, ideally in competition with each other and therefore scattering, not monopolizing, financial power.

## ADAM SMITH: THE DEMOCRATS' TEACHER IN POLITICAL ECONOMY

Among rural Democrats and the world of small farmers, where especially in the widely illiterate South there was little contact with transatlantic economic theorizing, political economy consisted principally of an inchoate distrust of the wealthy, city folk, and bankers, and of economic change. Among the party's national leadership, however, and particularly in its northern urban centers in the Jacksonian years, there was a sophisticated command of, and much talk about, the leading economic theories that had evolved across the Atlantic in Britain, the first industrializing and urbanizing country.

Thomas Jefferson had read closely, and ever afterward proclaimed as his bible in political economy, Adam Smith's famous book *The Wealth of Nations* (1776). Jacksonian Democrats like Samuel Tilden also quoted Smith chapter and verse, as did Democratic political economists right on through the nineteenth century, and up to Woodrow Wilson, another Adam Smith disciple. They did so because Smith was concerned, first, with exploring and explaining the terrible persisting problem of poverty, a grave issue in Britain, and second, with how to create a productive economic system built on social justice.

Freeing up the productive powers of the whole society (not just those of a privileged few, who were given special aids by government) would create, Smith said, a steadily rising standard of living for all, including the poor, *if* the government stood back from the market place and let unfettered competition take charge. That, indeed, was the key: liberating individuals of whatever station or situation to search for profit as their particular wits enabled them to find it, thus mobilizing their talents. This meant a principled clinging to laissez-faire, from which two cardinal results would flow. Since at this stage of economic knowledge it was believed that monopoly was created only by special governmental grants of privilege, laissez-faire, Smith and the Democrats believed, would prevent the rise of what they feared most: monopoly control of markets, with all that this entailed in exploitive power over society.

It was Smith, in fact, who had articulated the need for many small banks, instead of one large one like the Bank of England, in order to protect society from bankers' vast powers. Laissez-faire, he said, would also release powerful entrepreneurial impulses that would ignite a dynamically productive economy. If kept open to all on grounds of equal access the market, as if by an invisible hand, would create widely-shared wealth and shower social justice on all. Even the workers would share in the bounty, if employers could be kept from exploiting them.

The problem, said Smith in a famous utterance, was that businessmen hardly gathered for merriment but they were soon engaged in some conspiracy against the public welfare, whether collusions on raising prices or lowering wages, or schemes looking toward the creation of monopolies.[46] Much cleverer than those who governed the country, they were endlessly imaginative in finding ways to convince lawmakers, perhaps through the judicious distribution of what eighteenth century England called "golden pills," to enact protective tariffs and bounties and monopolistic corporate charters to foster particular enterprises. This diversion of capital away from natural channels and into artificial, government-favored enterprises was said to create a strong economy, and to make Britain more powerful in the world, but all it really aimed at, said Smith, was raising prices and exploiting labor.

The inescapable fact, Smith pointed out, was that no one, certainly not a small group of secretive aristocrats in Parliament or the Cabinet, knew enough to direct the economy in detail so as to make it work better. This was simply beyond the human mind. We may be able roughly to understand what is near to us, Smith said, but things far away are dim, inscrutable, constantly changing, and beyond our daily intellectual command. (A philosopher, Smith had written another book on this score). Such interventions, therefore, interfered irrationally with the economy's natural forces, twisted and warped it into strange, inefficient shapes, and ended up hampering productivity (and, ironically, reducing the nation's power) while enriching a few.[47] The market, the market: this alone, if left wholly free of special privilege, would not only stimulate production, it would by competition discipline prices and aid the always-pressed consumer—and if Whigs were eternally the party of the producer, Democrats were eternally the party of the consumer.[48]

## THE DEMOCRATS ON MONEY AND THE PROTECTIVE TARIFF

To insure justice to the consumer, Democrats since Jackson's time had insisted on a *sound-money* policy; that is, on a currency system backed by gold. Drawing on the towering authority of such leading English economists as David Ricardo and, later, John Stuart Mill, whose ideas were canonical for the Liberal Party in Britain—the party that, led by William Gladstone, called for a political economy on Adam Smith lines—Democrats insisted that a sound money system would produce a stable money supply and therefore stable prices. This would discipline the greedy appetites of bankers, who, hungry for the interest gained from loans, were forever printing off floods of unbacked paper money to hand out to needy debtors, and by this self-seeking process setting off booms and busts—from all of which, being insiders, they could profit.

Democrats insisted that, in crusading for sound money, they were preeminently the party of the worker and the consumer in general, for whom inflation of food prices and the other necessities of life was a nightmare. Forty years after Andrew Jackson left the White House, Samuel Tilden running for the presidency in the election of 1876 was still repeating with obsessive frequency and absolute certainty that in his implacable hostility to an inflated currency—which the Greenbackers called for and the Republicans acquiesced to—he was laboring in the interests of the working person.[49] When his anointed disciple, Grover Cleveland, finally won the White House in the 1880s, he did so on this same sound-money platform, clinging to it on social justice grounds during the great depression of the 1890s. He angrily battled the sound-money cause against William Jennings Bryan, the new free-silverite young Democrat from the High Plains, whom he could not begin to understand.[50]

Democrats joined Adam Smith, as well, in condemning protective tariffs as nothing but handing over to profit-hungry corporations a right, corruptly purchased from Whig-Republican legislators of easy virtue, to build monopolies behind high tariff walls and levy high prices on the consumer. Why should not ordinary Americans be able to buy what they needed in the cheapest market available, whether at home or abroad? Why should there not be a free and unfettered international market for all things?

The Democratic President James K. Polk has become known as the great expansionist who launched the Mexican War, secured the Mexican Cession, and who, joining this accomplishment to his successful diplomacy over the Northwest, gave the United States a 1,500-mile coastline looking out to the Pacific. In this, he followed another Jeffersonian and Jacksonian tradition, that of expansionism, hallowed on the Democratic side and much condemned by Whigs.

Less known is his role in economic policy. With American farmers in mind, it was Polk who put his Secretary of the Treasury, Robert J. Walker, to work in 1846 carrying out, through an extraordinary feat of transatlantic cooperation, a drastic lowering of the American tariff against British goods in implicit return for the famous repeal by Gladstone's Liberals, in 1846, of Britain's Corn Laws, or protective tariffs, against American wheat. For decades thereafter, Whig-Republicans would hold up the Walker Tariff as the highest example of Democratic economic folly, and a historic error that essentially began destroying American industry and laid open the country forever to price-gouging by the English.[51]

By the 1850s, the British Liberals and the Democrats in the United States had the substance of one of their dreams in political economy: an essentially unfettered transatlantic trading community between a Liberal Britain and a Democratic United States—linking American farms with British cities and British factories with American consumers. Sixty years after his death in 1790, Adam Smith finally seemed to have triumphed on both sides of the Atlantic. Mercantilism in its traditional form appeared to have been quashed, as Britain swung to free trade and the United States got very close to it.

Tariffs were now low in order to stimulate trade and subject all producers to competition. Also, a reasonably complete separation between government and business (at least at the federal level in the United States) had been achieved. Meanwhile, "sound-money" principles, embodied in the international gold standard, would keep prices low and thereby damp down the economic oscillations that created so much social misery. Wealth, access to which was equitably shared—so Democrats and Liberals now believed—because it was no longer artificially diverted by governments into the hands of selfish capitalists, would begin to mount, and everyone's standard of living would rise.

This, ironically, in response to discoveries of enormous gold supplies in the American West from 1848 onward, actually did occur. Both the American and the British economies took off, having been freed to do so by the Democrats' and Liberals' recent achievements in removing constricting barriers to free internal and international trade. It was a startling upward surge that would create the economic euphoria of the mid-Victorian years. Not until the grave economic collapse of the mid-1870s would the transatlantic boom subside.

## NOTES

1. For a superb description of the upsurge of the partisan spirit and of a new "political nation" organized around parties from 1838 onward, see Joel H. Silbey, *The American Political Nation 1838-1893* (Stanford: Stanford University Press, 1991), 16-45. On frequency of elections and degree of organization, see "Organize! ORGANIZE! ORGANIZE!", chap. 3, 46-71. On near-religious attitudes toward party, see "The Shrine of Party," chap. 7, 123-40. In "'To the Polls': The Structure of Popular Voting Behavior, 1838-1892," chap. 8, 141-158, he describes and discusses the massive turnouts.

2. Ronald P. Formisano brilliantly evokes the party atmosphere of the time and its cultural origins in, *The Birth of Mass Political Parties: Michigan, 1827-1861* (Princeton: Princeton University Press, 1971), 22, 57-58, 70, 77-78.

3. David M. Potter, *The Impending Crisis 1848-1861* (New York: Harper & Row, 1976), 141-144, 228-238. Pierce's popular majority and electoral college margin was greater than any achieved since the 1820s, in James Monroe's second election. "The six states of the lower South gave [Whig candidate General Winfield] Scott only 35 percent of their vote. The same states had given 49.8 percent to [Whig candidate, Zachary] Taylor in 1848. Any reader . . . will recognize that the southern Whigs had suffered one of the sharpest losses in American history."

4. On Supreme Court partisan membership, see Don E. Fehrenbacher, *Slavery, Law, and Politics: The Dred Scott Case in Historical Perspective* (New York: Oxford University Press, 1981), 115-18.

5. "Southerner," "South," and other such terms all refer, scholars now agree,

to an ethnic community, just as do the words "French," "Irish," or "Yankee," and these terms are capitalized in my chapters.

6. By now, it will be clear that, as a historian of political culture, I will not in this essay be making use of what was for many years the reigning model, class-analysis. Universally relied on for decades in what may be called the Charles Beard era in historiography, it depicted the Democrats—as they did themselves in the nineteenth century—as the party of the workers and farmers. That had always seemed inherently absurd to me, because of course if that were true, the massively outnumbered Whigs would never have won an election anywhere. In the 1950s and 1960s, Richard Hofstadter made us sensitive to cultural milieu when seeking the origins of political behavior. So guided, I found what seemed to me rich support for this approach when researching a comparative work, Robert A. Kelley, *The Transatlantic Persuasion: The Liberal-Democratic Mind in the Age of Gladstone* (New York: Knopf, 1969). Meanwhile, in what was called the "new political history" when it flooded in during the 1970s, inspired by the seminal work of Lee Benson we learned conclusively that the economic class model was fatally inaccurate, *The Concept of Jacksonian Democracy: New York as a Test Case* (Princeton: Princeton University Press, 1961).
To the present time, it is difficult to do more than say that the very wealthy and the very poor tend to lean in different directions politically, which, as an analytical model, hardly takes us very far. As Benson insisted thirty years ago, and as the distinguished historian of nineteenth century American politics, Joel H. Silbey, concludes in a recent summing up of the issue, in the mid-nineteenth century, even workers in the cities, let alone farmers (the overwhelming majority of the people) did not exhibit much class consciousness in their political behavior but rather were far more influenced by their ethnoreligious identity and values. See Silbey, *American Political Nation*, 160-69; Robert Kelley, *The Cultural Pattern in American Politics: The First Century* (New York: Knopf, 1979), 3-38, I have sought to see how different political history looks, when examined from this perspective. In its introduction I have discussed the scholarly origins and evolution of the ethnocultural model, as has Richard L. McCormick in the first chapter of his *The Party Period and Public Policy: American Politics from the Age of Jackson to the Progressive Era* (New York: Oxford University Press, 1986).

7. As happened, for example, to Thomas Jefferson's Republican party after the Federalists died away in the 1820s, and to the Whigs in the 1850s when they lost to new competing parties—the nativist American party and the Republicans—control over defining who was in fact the enemy. As to the power of the enemy in holding together ethnic groups, see John A. Armstrong's magisterial study of ethnicity over thousands of years, *Nations before Nationalism* (Chapel Hill: University of North Carolina Press, 1982).

In the two works above cited Kelley (*The Transatlantic Persuasion*, and Kelley *The Cultural Pattern in American Politics*), I have emphasized the role of the enemy as the shaping influence in public life.

For a valuable overview of the "negative reference group" concept in historical studies of political culture, see McCormick, *The Party Period and Public Policy*, 30, 39-40, 42-43, 54, 61-62.

8. Paul Kleppner, *The Third Electoral System, 1853-1892: Parties, Voters, and Political Cultures* (Chapel Hill, University North Carolina Press, 1979), 48.

9. Quoted in Kelley, *The Cultural Pattern in American Politics*, 222, drawing from a paper read by Joel H. Silbey at that 1976 annual meeting of the American Historical Association.

10. The foregoing, and following, discussion of the English origins of Southerners and New Englanders, their ways of life and feelings toward each other, and the differing proportions of ethnic peoples from the British Isles in the South, draws upon two remarkable recent works, Daniel Hackett Fischer, *Albion's Seed: Four British Folkways in America* (New York: Oxford University Press, 1989); and Grady McWhiney, *Cracker Culture: Celtic Ways in the Old South* (Tuscaloosa: University of Alabama Press, 1988). Essential also is William R. Taylor's classic work, *Cavalier and Yankee: The Old South and American National Character* (Cambridge: Harvard University Press, 1961).

11. See McWhiney, *Cracker Culture*, and James G. Leyburn, *The Scotch-Irish: A Social History* (Chapel Hill: University of North Carolina Press, 1962).

12. Robert V. Remini, *Andrew Jackson and the Course of American Empire, 1767-1821* (New York: Harper & Row, 1977), 2-3; and especially, on Jackson's "North-of-Ireland" qualities, see the still essential biography written by an Englishman living in America in Jackson's time, James Parton, *Life of Andrew Jackson* (New York: Harper & Row, 1967).

13. See Carl N. Degler, *The Other South: Southern Dissenters in the Nineteenth Century* (New York: Harper & Row, 1974); Daniel Walker Howe, *The Political Culture of the American Whigs* (Chicago: University of Chicago Press, 1979); Kelley, *The Cultural Pattern in American Politics*, 214-16. Benson, in *The Concept of Jacksonian Democracy: New York as a Test Case*, has excellent material on the "hell of a fellow" complex among major Democratic voting groups, such as riverboatmen and lumbermen. Of course, the Scotch-Irish and the Irish Catholics, who would begin arriving in America in droves in the 1840s, were heavy users of whisky, their ethnic beverage. The urban saloon became a central institution in Irish Catholic political life.

14. Joel H. Silbey, *A Respectable Minority* (New York: Norton, 1977), 23.

15. For this general period, and its political and political culture dimensions, see Michael F. Holt, *The Political Crisis of the 1850s* (New York: Wiley Press, 1978); Eric Foner, *Free Soil, Free Labor, Free Men: The Ideology of the Republican Party Before the Civil War* (New York: Oxford University Press, 1970); David Brion Davis, *The Slave Power Conspiracy and the Paranoid Style* (Baton Rouge: The Louisiana State University Press, 1969); and William E. Gienapp, *The Origins of the Republican Party* (New York: Oxford University Press, 1987); and Potter, *The Impending Crisis* (New York, Harper & Row, 1976), *1848-1861.*

16. Kelley, *The Cultural Pattern in American Politics*, 197-216.

17. Ibid., 70-80, 101-105, 128-129.

18. Ibid., 192-93.

19. Foner, *Free Soil, Free Labor, Free Men*, 186-216; James A. Rawley, *Race and Politics: Bleeding Kansas and the Coming of the Civil War* (Lincoln: University of Nebraska Press, 1979), 168-72, a book that is essential on the psychology of the 1850s, points to the division along the line of the forty-first parallel.

20. Clifford S. Griffin, *Their Brother's Keepers: Moral Stewardship in the United States, 1800-1865* (New Brunswick: Rutgers University Press, 1960); S. J. Rorabaugh, *The Alcoholic Republic: An American Tradition* (New York: Oxford University Press, 1979); Bertram Wyatt-Brown, "Prelude to Abolitionism: Sabbatarian Politics and the Rise of the Second Party System," *Journal of American History*, 58 (September 1971), 316-341; and Ronald P. Formisano, *The Birth of Mass Political Parties: Michigan, 1827-1861.*

21. James M. Bergquist, "People and Politics in Transition: The Illinois Germans, 1850-60," in *Ethnic Voters and the Election of Lincoln*, ed. Frederick C. Luebke (Lincoln: University of Nebraska Press, 1971), 196-226; Robert Henry Billigmeier, *Americans from Germany: A Study in Cultural Diversity* (Belmont, Calif.: Wadsworth, 1974), 62-81; and George H. Daniels, "The Immigrant Vote in the 1860 Election: The Case of Iowa," *Mid-America* 55 (July 1962):146-62.

22. Potter, *The Impending Crisis*, 241.

23. Ibid., 241-242.

24. Ibid. Also, on the sense in the pre-Civil War years of America being a great Protestant nation, see Martin E. Marty, *Righteous Empire: The Protestant Experience in America* (New York: Dial Press, 1970), and Robert T. Handy, *A Christian America: Protestant Hopes and Historical Realities*, 2d. ed. rev. & enl. (New York: Oxford University Press, 1984), esp. 24-56.

25. Potter, *The Impending Crisis*, 243, citing Ray Allen Billington, *The Protestant Crusade, 1800-1860: A Study of the Origins of American Nativism* (Chicago: Rinehart, 1964).

26. Kelley, *The Cultural Pattern in American Politics*, 189-190; and n. 20 above.

27. The literature on the Irish is voluminous. See Edward M. Levine, *The Irish and Irish Politicians: A Study of Cultural and Social Alienation* (Notre Dame: University of Indiana Press, 1966); William V. Shannon, *The American Irish* (New York: Macmillan, 1963); John B. Duff, *The Irish in the United States* (Belmont, Calif.: Wadsworth Publishing Co., 1971); L. Perry Curtis, *Apes and Angels: The Irishman in Victorian Caricature* (Washington, D.C.: Newton, Abbot, David & Charles, 1971). I have discussed their role extensively in British and American political culture in *The Transatlantic Persuasion*, 22-23, 34-41, r8, 84-86, 193, 267-268, 303-337, 372-373, 406-407.

28. See Benson, *The Concept of Jacksonian Democracy*, 278-287.

29. Quoted in Silbey, *The American Political Nation*, 83.

30. Paul Kleppner, *The Third Electoral System 1853-1892*, 61.

31. Potter, *The Impending Crisis*, 245.

32. See Eric Foner, *Free Soil, Free Labor, Free Men*, 237-260; and Michael F. Holt, *Forging a Majority: The Formation of the Republican Party in Pittsburgh, 1848-1860* (New Haven: Yale University Press), 139-141.

33. Benson, *The Concept of Jacksonian Democracy*, 166-171.

34. The subject of "party systems" has been the subject of a large scholarly literature. For major discussions of it, see Paul Kleppner, et al., *The Evolution of American Electoral Systems* (Westport, Conn.: Greenwood Press, 1981), esp. Kleppner, chap. 1, "Critical Realignments and Electoral Systems," 3-32. See also

chap. 2, "The Realignment Synthesis in American History," in McCormick, *The Party Period and Public Policy*, 65-88.

35. Jean H. Baker has a powerful description of Democratic racism, its origin and nature, in chap. 6, "The Negro Issue: Popular Culture, Racial Attitudes, and Democratic Polity," in her extraordinary work, *Affairs of Party: The Political Culture of Northern Democrats in the Mid-Nineteenth Century* (Ithaca: Cornell University Press, 1983).

36. Silbey, *A Respectable Minority*, 80-83.

37. Robert W. Johannsen, *Stephen A. Douglas* (New York: Oxford University Press, 1973), 162, 233, 340, 501.

38. Joseph M. Hernon, *Celts, Catholics, and Copperheads: Ireland Views the Civil War* (Columbus: Ohio State University Press, 1968), 65-75; and Gilbert Osofsky, "Abolitionists, Irish Immigrants, and the Dilemmas of Romantic Nationalism," *The American Historical Review* 80 (October 1975): 889-912.

39. Leon F. Litwack, *North of Slavery: The Negro in the Free States, 1790-1860* (Chicago: University of Chicago Press, 1961); George M. Fredrickson, *The Black Image in the White Mind: The Debate on Afro-American Character and Destiny, 1817-1914* (New York: Harper & Row, 1971); and V. Jacque Voegeli, *Free but Not Equal: The Midwest and the Negro During the Civil War* (Chicago: University of Chicago Press, 1967), esp. 1-6.

40. For a succinct summation of the mid-nineteenth century Democratic mind, see chap. 4, "The Connecting Tissue: Ideas, Principles, and Policies in American Politics," in Silbey, *The American Political Nation*, 72-89.

41. On the Democrats' obsession with their guiding spirit, Thomas Jefferson, see Merrill D. Peterson, *The Jefferson Image in the American Mind* (New York: Oxford University Press, 1962).

42. For the Whig mentality taken in large and in detail, see Daniel Walker Howe's brilliant *The Political Culture of the American Whigs* (Princeton: Princeton University Press, 1979)

43. For the following on Democratic political economy, including the role of Adam Smith as Democratic party authority on matters economic, see the chapters on Smith, Thomas Jefferson, Samuel Tilden, and Grover Cleveland, in Kelley, *The Transatlantic Persuasion*.

44. Kelley, *The Transatlantic Persuasion*, 256-257.

45. In the voluminous literature on the Bank War, see Peter Temin, *The Jacksonian Economy* (New York: Norton, 1969); and John McFaul, *The Politics of Jacksonian Finance* (Ithaca: Cornell University Press, New York, 1972), as well as the brilliant work which awakened historians to the centrality of the Bank War, Arthur M. Schlesinger, Jr.'s *The Age of Jackson* (Boston: Little, Brown, 1945).

46. Adam Smith, *An Inquiry into the Nature and Causes of the Wealth of Nations* (London, 1776). His statements as to businessmen will be found in the Modern Library edition (New York: Knopf, 1937), 128, 508.

47. In the New York State constitutional convention of 1846, Tilden would take the lead in carrying through a great reform Jacksonian Democrats had been calling for for years: ending the ancient system of granting corporate charters only by special legislation. This process, they said, was eternally open to corrup-

tion. To replace it, and to tap that capital-mobilizing instrument for everyone and stimulate the economy without special privilege or monopoly, Tilden got the convention to establish a General Incorporation law, which would allow any group to receive a corporate charter as a matter of right (rather like getting a driver's license) if they met certain minimum financial and other requirements. See Kelley, *The Transatlantic Persuasion*, 261.

48. See Kelley, chap. 2, "The Inherited World View: Adam Smith and the Dynamic Economy," *The Transatlantic Persuasion*, 55-79.

49. This possibility was scoffed at by generations of historians enamored of the inflationist, free-silver cause of William Jennings Bryan. In our own time the rise and victory among most economists of monetarist theory, which says essentially what Tilden and the Jacksonian Democrats (and British Liberals in the same period) were saying about the relation between inflation and high prices, has placed all of this in an entirely new light.
For the currency question in the 1870s, see two masterful works, Robert Sharkey, *Money, Class, and Party: An Economic Study of Civil War and Reconstruction* (Baltimore: The Johns Hopkins University Press, 1959), and Irwin Unger, *The Greenback Era: A Social and Political History of American Finance, 1865-1879* (Princeton: Princeton University Press, 1964). They make it clear that Republicans, always eager for abundant supplies of capital and comfortable with the fact that inflation acts like a protective tariff, were surprisingly soft on the currency issue, and leaning toward inflationary measures.

50. See Kelley "Grover Cleveland: The Democrat as Social Moralist," chap. 8, *The Transatlantic Persuasion*, 293-350.

51. Kelley, *The Cultural Pattern in American Politics*, 156-58. For a typical Gilded Age version of the Republicans' history of America's economic history, in which the Walker Tariff of 1846 stands forth as a gross historical error, see two Congressional speeches by William McKinley: "The Tariff Commission," April 6, 1882, and "The Morrison Tariff Bill," April 30, 1884, in William McKinley, *Speeches and Addresses: From His Election to Congress to the Present Time* (New York, 1893), 70-105, 146-147.

## Chapter 5

# In Eclipse: Democratic Culture and the Crucible of the Civil War

*Jean Baker*

In the years after Andrew Jackson's presidency ended in 1837, an energetic quickening of purpose and organization occurred within the Democratic party. What had been a loose confederation of local factions now became the most powerful, and eventually the most durable, institution in the United States. By no means the elite expression of a few leaders delivered to the masses, this freshly reminted party was accurately characterized in the descriptive cliche of American politics as a "grass-roots movement." Not only did the mid-century Democratic party organization bridge the divide between the values of citizens and the policies of state and national leaders, but—in a development so foreign to late twentieth century practice as to be nearly incomprehensible—the Democratic party emerged as a beloved affiliation for generations of white men who understood themselves to be Americans because they were Democrats. How was it that this organization became so strong? And, after so many years of an antiparty faith that held partisan affiliations to be dangerously unAmerican, how did the Democrats move into the sunlight of national prominence?

No sooner had the Democrats emerged as a significant force, than they soon faced daunting tests. From the end of the Mexican-American War in 1848 until the "stolen" presidential election of 1876, the party was nearly overwhelmed by national events surrounding the secession of eleven southern states (during 1860-1861), the liberation of nearly four million slaves in the Border States and the South, the Civil War, and the Reconstruction of the Union after 1865. External forces that had once favored the party's rapid advance now undermined it as a long period of eclipse ensued. With other institutions, including churches and the Republic itself, collapsing or dividing along sectional lines, how did the Democrats survive? The answer to this question emerges not so much from an evaluation of leaders and national platforms as from the Democratic party's culture and behavior.

## PARTY CULTURE

Earlier political associations in the United States, including the "Democratic-Republicans" which the Democratic party claimed as its ideological ancestor, had been based on kinship relations, personal followings, and a sense of deference to the great men of a community.[1] But by the middle of the nineteenth century, Democrats accepted a two-party system based, as Joel Silbey has written, "on collective behavior and regularized, impersonal institutions."[2] In the party, as in the nation at large, citizens whose lives had been barely brushed by the hand of the government—save for the postmaster and U.S. land commissioner—were simultaneously becoming members of a more centralized, more formal party organization and a modernizing nation.

In the United States, it was a time for creating the organizations believed by one outsider, the French visitor Alexis de Tocqueville, to be a noteworthy activity of the American people. The results of what de Tocqueville called the Americans' "march across these wilds, draining swamps, turning the course of rivers, peopling solitudes and subduing nature," appeared in thousands of churches, lodges, and associations.[3] The Democratic party was part of that joining together to create a society within the wilderness. But, unlike most prewar voluntary organizations, the Democrats wrapped themselves in the national symbols of the American flag—the eagle, the red, white and blue, and the Declaration of Independence. Through practice and doctrine, they conveyed a sense of nationalism, accomplished in part by means of a racial and gendered exclusiveness based on their members' enjoyment of a sense of fraternity. Such sentiments were balanced by the party's inclusionary pledges to accept the thousands of white immigrants pouring into the United States during this period, most of whom came from Germany and Ireland.

Reflecting the centralizing changes imposed by railroads, roads and new inventions like the telegraph, the Democratic party in 1848 established a National Committee in Washington—with one member allocated to each of the thirty states—to oversee its affairs in between presidential elections. It was also at this time that the party's national conventions began to provide openly stated general principles in a formal platform whose resolutions could be applied to a range of specific local and state concerns. Such a body of doctrine differentiated Democrats from other Americans, binding the party's members together in what Martin Van Buren praised as a "political brotherhood" loyal to the organization.[4] Democrats came to accept the view enunciated in the party's unofficial journal *The*

*United States and Democratic Review* that "parties are schools of political science and no principle can be safely incorporated into the fabric of national law until it has been digested, limited and defined by the earnest discussion of contending parties."[5] In the corollary to this process, Democrats came to view their organization as an essential component of a popular government that, no longer considered a fragile experiment, they now celebrated as the oldest in the world. A new generation of professional politicians promoted, along with the American Revolution and the Constitution, the Democratic party as an engine of self-government. (The metaphor itself reflected the party's sensitivity to the changing technology of the period.) The Democrats' newly developed notion of party was that of a disciplined permanent majority of believers not a transitory coalition, a legislative caucus, or an amorphous fraternity of all Americans.

So important was this new subnational party identification that it came to be taught as a family value. In countless homes throughout the land, young American boys now learned to be Democrats from their fathers. While they received civic instruction in how to be Americans in their district schools, history books and schoolmasters' lessons were by design nonpartisan. On the other hand, partisan habits, consigned to individual practice, were the legacy of family training and observation. In some communities this partisan kinship and sense of being a Democrat was felt so strongly that members buried their dead in Democratic graveyards.[6] Such a process of political socialization was so intense, that in some cases, it transcended even the older institutional force of church affiliation. According to Thomas Marshall of Indiana, "My father and grandfather were notified during the Civil War that their Methodist preacher would have to strike their names off the role if they continued to vote Democratic. My grandfather announced that he was willing to take his chance in Hell but never on the Republicans."[7]

To some extent, other political organizations were a part of this changed culture. Yet, before the formation of the Republican party in the middle of the 1850s, the other major party—the Whigs—continued to fear political parties as potential threats to a young Republic. "The Democrats," complained a Massachusetts Whig, "are always at their posts and [they] always act together." On the other hand the Whigs, who had developed principally in opposition to Andrew Jackson rather than in support of a principle, tried to manage "on their own hook."[8] In time, of course, Whig leaders adopted the Democratic model of a platform, a structure, and an instructed following, but their initial failure to appreciate the benefits of political socialization proved to be one reason for their collapse in the 1850s.

Thus, to be a Democrat in mid-century America was to understand the advantages of a partisan culture in which opponents, however wrong-headed, were nevertheless granted the status of a loyal opposition. Institutionalized antagonisms, the Democrats came to recognize before their opponents, were necessary elements of democratic practice. Unknown at the time, such an understanding would serve as good preparation for their status as a minority party. Members held their appreciation of the virtues of a two-party system to be the legacy of a special insight into the principles of self-government from which they took their name. A competitive two-party system, in their view, limited the possibilities for the corruption of power, and also dampened the potentially disruptive jealousy between regions of a vast nation whose size, in the view of James Madison, made its government by consent perpetually tenuous and vulnerable to demagoguery.

By mid-century, the brief, one-party arrangement of the early Republic— remembered as "The Era of Good Feelings" during James Monroe's administration—was no longer appropriate. Instead, as one faithful Democrat, Congressman Samuel Cox of Ohio, concluded, "In all free countries an opposition is an element of government. It is as indispensable to the safety of the realm as a free press or a free pulpit. To dispense with it is to endanger, if not to dispense with liberty."[9] So believing, the party moved from the informality of amateurs to an organization of professionals, and from an earlier existential defensiveness to an exuberant assertion of principles and behavior.

To be a Democrat at mid-century was to be able to fuse nationalism and localism, while rendering allegiance to a particular place, such as a county or state (and increasingly for those in the South, a section), or to an occupational, religious, or ethnic group. At a time before the emergence of the single-issue lobby, there was no exclusivity in these identifications. Instead, such associations of place and status reinforced each other in what historians have identified as ethnocultural patterns of voting behavior. Accordingly, a Baptist born in the South but "removed" to southern Illinois was almost invariably a Democrat; and a second-generation Irish Catholic residing in an Eastern city was almost surely a Democrat as well.

When one branch of the large Scotch-Irish Presbyterian family of Stevensons ended its migration from North Carolina and Kentucky in central Illinois, its baggage included an unshakable affiliation with the Democratic party. A century later, the family's most famous member, Adlai Stevenson, acknowledged that he had "a bad case of hereditary politics." So too did the Allen family of Ohio, whose inheritance included the story of its original Democrat, William Allen, later a governor of Ohio. As a child, William Allen had met Andrew Jackson who, according to family lore, had inquired "And what is your name, my brave little Democrat?" Henceforth, given the family's Southern Baptist heritage, its affiliation was fixed.[10] In the process of being Democrats particular ethnic and religious alliances were not destroyed, but rather were incorporated into an organization of boastful nationalism.

In some communities like Hunterdon County, New Jersey, residents were influenced by a pervasive Democratic culture and were single-mindedly Democratic.[11] In others, the party was connected through social and geographic networks that served as lines of political communication. A reliable study of midwestern Democrats in 1860 indicates that nine out of ten of the party's voters turned out in subsequent presidential elections, eight out of ten to repeat their Democratic ballots.[12] Groups within the party believed that while their party membership grew out of special characteristics that separated them first from Whigs and later from Republicans, it was the essence of their Americanism. "I cast my ballot for the Democracy," explained one newly naturalized Baltimorean, "and became an American."[13] In striking contrast to today's politics, partisans held "being a Democrat" as a natural and expectable part of their lives. Mid-century Democrats loved politics.

"Show me a man that belongs to no party," said one Democrat, "and I will show you a man without principle. Show me a man who has no party feelings and predilections and I will show you a fool or knave. . . . Party is the salt of the nation. It establishes a wholesome guardianship over the institutions of our country; it checks and restrains the reckless ambition of those in office and never fails to expose the nonfeasance, misfeance, or malfeasance of those in power."[14]

As the earlier fear of parties as subversive special interest groups diminished before such forceful arguments, being a Democrat became synonymous with being a patriot. "The Democracy is national; it is America, it embraces the continent. It is universal and catholic," celebrated the editor of the *Democratic Review.* Party rhetoric connected Democrats from New York to California and from Maine to Mississippi. "Union of Lakes, Union of Lands, Union of Hearts, Union of States"—in the words of a party song.[15] Granted that this was a time in American political history when the lack of a party affiliation was exceptional and considered unworthy of any man (those who didn't vote or who were uninterested in party activities were often likened to women). Still, during the tumult of the Civil War and its aftermath, no other organization could claim the Democrats' universality and ubiquity.[16]

Considering themselves nationalists, Democrats invariably portrayed their opponents as particularists, representing not all American people but some special, usually privileged group of them. Democrats were, in party rhetoric and conviction, the party of "all the people." In contrast, the Federalists and then the Whigs—along with the more ephemeral Liberty, Free Soil, Southern Rights, and Unionist parties of the period—emerged as associations of the rich and powerful, willing to twist the power of the government to their ends. More than a cynical effort to get votes—for there would always be more non-rich than rich—this connection grounded the party's ideology in a fervent objection to government favoritism. Thus Democrats saw banks, tariffs, and internal improvements as hazards to freedom, because federal activism was inevitably based on a form of special treatment.

As Michael Holt has written, "Throughout the country, but especially in northern states, Democratic opposition to active government interference in the society attracted those who resented the aggressive do-goodism of the evangelical Protestants who joined the Whigs to press for prohibition and legislation outlawing activities on Sunday."[17] Meanwhile, opponents objected that the Democrats themselves did not always follow their own pledges, were themselves increasingly the special messengers of southern interests, and were sympathetic to private corporations on the state level.

Yet, in the minds of the faithful, such criticism barely shook the integrity of an organizing principle. As one Democrat explained in 1854, "a monopoly of the old aristocracy promises us roast-beef but feeds us on the shadow of beef-steak."[18] In Alabama, a party newspaper conveyed the sense of class implicit in Democratic rhetoric: "There is an incessant war waging in every commercial country between the moneyed interests and the rights of labor. . . . Separate these town, striped-breeches gentry from the rest and [the Alabama Whigs] will dwindle to a handful."[19]

In the land of centrist politics, however, the often wealthy Democratic leaders rarely rose from the ranks of the poor or even the working class. Lacking polls and survey data, the social and economic backgrounds of mid-century Democrats are difficult to ascertain. In broad terms, it appears that Democrats were less likely than their opponents to draw their support from the urban rich and middle class and more likely to find it in the less developed, less prosperous counties and among the newly naturalized. Overall, however, class-based voting is a modern imposition on mid-nineteenth century politics.[20]

In the 1850s, when the Republicans replaced the defunct Whigs and Know-Nothings as the opposition party, Democrats naturally viewed them as representing not the American people, but only the North. Southern Democrats especially diminished their Republican opposition into a mere arm of the abolitionist movement—again a special interest, according to Democrats, that did not speak for the people. By creating the image of a two-class society, divided between producers and non-producers, the Democratic ideology dampened status differences, with the party positioning itself as the great body of the Americans—a collection of the "industrious, honest, manly, intelligent millions of the people." Only the party's opposition had the defiling characteristics of a class held together by wealth, control of "monied corporations," and single-issue platforms.[21]

Part of the Democratic perception of its nationalistic tendencies rested on an understanding of the necessity of making different appeals to different groups. By no means the ideological trimming of their opponent's scorn (what Samuel Cox once called "saddle-bagging"), localism was perceived by Democrats as the core of their nationalism. It was in their view no connivance to offer a policy of tariffs for revenue in the South, while promoting the principle of "home valuation" of coal and iron imports in some Pennsylvania counties. The latter was a local issue and the Democrats' flexibility demonstrated the importance of protecting individual miners whose jobs were threatened by the unfair advantages of owners whose interests in turn were protected by government.[22]

In the Democratic view, the United States was properly understood as a confederation or a federal union based on a Constitution that institutionalized concentric but overlapping circles of power. The first words of its preamble—"We The People of the United States in order to form a more perfect Union"—spoke to this pluralism and recognized what Democrats had come to celebrate as the amorphous theme of their faith: "Our whole country, the Democracy and the Constitution."[23]

From this conviction Democrats derived a body of faith that detested the centralization of the Whigs and later the Republicans. Fearing power, Democrats would use their local communities as firebreaks and thereby avoid the possibility of the arrogant corruption of authority all Americans believed themselves to have experienced during the colonial regimes of English governors. (It was this sentiment that soon resonated through both the rhetoric and the behavior of southern Democrats who accused the North of violating the property rights of individual slaveholders.) Within a federal system that included what Democrats liked to call "the general government," "the states," and "the home places," party faith channeled parochial allegiances into a larger framework. As described by Morton Grodzins, loyalties to family, religion and, in this case, party were the structural undergirdings of a larger nationalism. "One fights for the joys of his pinochle [or Democratic] club when he is said to fight for his nation."[24]

In the 1850s, because of the Democrats' broad-bore refraction of American antebellum culture, party history became an agonizing preview of national affairs. Split into factions before the Civil War, Democrats battled each other from 1861-1865 in a war carried out through partisan means. During Reconstruction, their efforts to restore the white South to the Union foretold the story of the Confederacy's so-called redemption by southern Bourbons. The resistance of the Democrats to changes in the status of freed African Americans previewed a national acceptance of the doctrine of separate and unequal. Democratic party affairs thus served as precursors to national events, as party, like nation, struggled to survive. And the party's continuity, like the nation's continuity, depended on a combination of remembered traditions, ancient principles, family instruction, inherited behaviors, and community endeavors—the party culture that persisted beneath the external episodes of a troubling time in Democratic history.

In the end, this would not be an era that carried the name of some proud party leader like Jefferson, Jackson, Cleveland, or Franklin Roosevelt. Nor would it be remembered for some public policy or cluster of principles that elevated the nation. Instead, the quarter century from 1848 to 1873 was memorable in party annals for the Democrats' endurance. On the margins of the celebrated episodes of party history, this was a period in which the Democratic future was assured. For by the end of the nineteenth century, the existence of the Democratic party was incontestable, just as in the larger society no more civil wars would threaten the United States. But in mid-century, could it withstand the cataclysm—and by what means?

## PARTY BEHAVIOR

The external story of the Democratic eclipse is easily told, at least from the perspective of presidential elections and national nominating conventions. What is less well understood is the internal means by which the organization that had been the majority party for much of the republic's history was able to sustain itself. Although other American political parties disappeared—from the Whigs and Know-Nothings to the more ephemeral Free Soil, Liberty and, after the war, the Greenback, Greenback-Labor, Anti-Monopoly and Prohibition parties—the Democrats survived to become the oldest political party in the world. The tools they used are worth remembering.

In 1848, the Democratic ticket of Lewis Cass of Michigan and William Butler of Kentucky lost the presidential election to the Whig nominee, Zachary Taylor. Before the election, the party's enduring tenet was offered to the electorate in a popular song: "The NORTH and SOUTH in union joined/The EAST and WEST shall vie/In harmony and peace combined/ 'Neath freedom's watchful eye."[25] In the coming years the party would often reassert this ideal of national harmony out of regionalism—the partisan version of e pluribus unum. Opposing abolitionists and the power of Congress to interfere with "a domestic institution," the Democrats' call for unity came so often that cynics complained that party leaders were displaying not conviction but the Democrats' perpetual fear of schismatic factions.

Democrats held otherwise. With the confidence of a powerful majority party that had elected nine of the thirteen presidents who followed George Washington's two terms and that, since Andrew Jackson's second inauguration, had controlled either the United States House or Senate in five of six sessions, Democratic leaders dismissed their loss of the presidency as a temporary eclipse.

Through the party's national organ, the *Washington Globe*, and the hundreds of county newspapers that carried the Democratic message to its followers, opinion-makers explained that their division over the issue of the extension of slavery had led some to drift off and vote for former Democrat Martin Van Buren's Free Soil party. This was the case especially in New York, which the Whig General Zachary Taylor (nicknamed "General Mum" by scornful Democrats who were proud of their well-advertised ideology), had carried. Such a third-party movement could be expected to fade away. Moreover, Taylor had won only a plurality, not a majority of the popular votes.

In the next presidential election—for this was the key to winning in a period of closely margined electoral outcomes—faithful Democrats would organize more effectively and "do their duty" by getting out the vote. Today's party inconstancy was unknown at a time in which variations in turnout, not commitment, were crucial to election victory. Using the metaphors of war that still survive in today's political idioms of campaigns, electoral casualties, battles, and survivors, Democrats were exhorted "to close ranks and stand firm"; "Falter not before the enemy"; "Use your paper bullets!" "Prepare for conflict at the Ballot Box. We'll welt them with our full divisions and our brave soldiers." The apocalyptic note of such rhetoric, which was similar in tone and purpose to battle-eve oratory, was intended to get every Democratic soldier to the polls. At the same time, such martial appeals conflated party activity with the patriotic behaviors of military service.[26]

Naturally, Democrats depended as well on their traditional appeals to a light and simple government, run frugally. They also displayed, in their party idiom, their suspicion of any extension of the power of the government, especially in the case of Whig efforts to transform American market and class relations through tariffs, national banks, and federally funded internal improvements. Like the Jacksonians of earlier decades, they accepted the complex of ideas dubbed "republicanism" by modern historians, fearing that authority inevitably would steal from the many to the few, through conspiracy or favoritism.

Two years later in 1850, a compromise worked out in Congress, with its supposedly careful balancing of northern and southern interests, seemed to have ended the sectional tensions that Democrats feared—or as least so the optimists in the party hoped. At the state level, traditional and therefore more reassuring controversies over the proper role of government in the lives of Americans continued to divide the Whigs and Democrats. What the astute Illinois Senator, Stephen Douglas, recognized as routine "old issues," might divert attention from the growing divisions within the Democracy over the extension of slavery. If the party could dampen the controversy over the status of slavery in the territory wrested from Mexico after the war that lasted from 1846 to 1848, then its natural majority would assure its future dominance.[27]

In 1852, Democrats turned to the national nominating convention that had become the organizational centerpiece of their party apparatus and its engine of mobilization. In the party's early years, informal caucuses of congressional and state leaders had nominated party leaders and established policy. But by mid-century, Democrats convened everywhere—at the county, district, ward, and state level; at the state senate and congressional level; and at the top of the pyramid, in the national nominating convention.

By 1852, Democrats had held five such national conventions. The structure of these assemblies fulfilled several party ideals—from the egalitarianism manifested by electing delegates locally to the eventual hierarchy created within the convention where state and regional leaders channelled support for their favorites. As a result, as James Chase has written, "a layered pyramid of conventions developed, each level composed of delegates chosen by the one immediately beneath it." In theory, every Democrat was represented. But as the United States grew from a population of four million spread over thirteen states in 1790 to one of twenty-four million dispersed through thirty-one states in 1850, delegates actually represented other Democrats in an indispensable spiralling process.[28]

In the presidential year of 1852 the Democrats looked forward to retaking the White House and controlling the national patronage that, in this period, consisted of numerous post office jobs and the more important cabinet positions and collectorships that bound state leaders to the national party. Though centrally organized after the creation of a National Committee in 1848, the "Democracy," in the affectionate party nickname that linked partisanship to a national ideal, must mobilize all its members. Most remained as faithful to the party as they were to their church. According to one Ohio Democrat, "it has been the pride of my life to rank myself as a Democrat. [I have] a Democratic ancestry where from grandfather to grandson no vote has been cast other than for Democrats from Thomas Jefferson down to Franklin Pierce."[29]

In this era before the emergence of the independent voter who voted for the "best man" rather than the party, and of the no-party Americans who did not vote at all, Democrats rarely "scratched a ticket" to substitute the name of another party's candidate. Voting, controlled by the local party, which paid for the printing of the paper ballots that were handed out on election day, was a private act beyond government sanction or regulation. Even the voting places were private. Taverns, homes, sometimes even the verandahs of hotels were used in a process whose rituals revealed its informality. But at the same time that voting was personal, it was also public. Every neighbor knew who took the Democratic ballots and handed them to the judges. Every neighbor knew who the Democrats were in the party lists kept by local leaders. And, of course, every neighbor knew who subscribed to the local Democratic newspaper. Being a Democrat was an association to be proud of, not one to hide.

With party politics serving as ceremony, habit, and boisterous entertainment, Democrats of the 1850s marched in military-like units in torchlight parades, erected—and then protected from Whig and Republican opponents—huge poles of over a hundred feet that soared into the sky with a Democratic banner on top, and listened avidly to long stump speeches often lost in the wind in this age before microphones. (Among the period's most important qualifications for party leadership, along with a good sturdy horse and a wide front porch, was a durable voice.) Then they cast their Democratic ballots—many decorated with a drawing of their hero Andrew Jackson, an Irish harp, or the rooster that signified their party had much "to crow about." Such ceremonies helped to dampen the class and economic differences between individual Democrats. A rich man like the land speculator Matthew Scott in McLean County, Illinois, paid for the uniforms for the Democratic stalwarts, but decisions over the arrangements for floats and even the timing of parades were collectively reached by local Democrats of every class.[30]

In this era of participatory politics, Democrats enthusiastically went to the polls. Turnouts for presidential elections routinely exceeded seventy percent of the eligible voters, and in 1856 reached over eighty percent. Nor were the roll-offs and turn-downs (that is, off-year voting and voting for lower offices) significant, as the electorate enjoyed politics at every level. In Hunterdon County, New Jersey, a party leader calculated that over ninety percent of the Democrats listed in his registration lists voted in 1852. Limited to white males over 21 (blacks could vote only in five New England states and in New York if they fulfilled certain property requirements), party politics was a distinctively male process that bound white males together in sexual solidarity. In an ancient understanding that gave way only at the end of the nineteenth century, each man acted for his family. In this political culture, women, minors and slaves were "virtually" represented by the white male "head of family."

In 1852 the Democrats met in Baltimore to nominate their presidential ticket and to write a platform. Few of the three hundred delegates, earlier chosen at county and district conventions, were committed to any candidate. In this age before primaries, delegates waited for a state or local leader to tell them whether, as a state under the unit rule, they should vote again for Lewis Cass of Michigan, an acknowledged "Northern man with Southern principles." Of those who did not support Cass, some preferred a younger man, such as Stephen Douglas, the popular five-foot four-inch "Little Giant" from Illinois. Still others hoped that the wealthy bachelor from Pennsylvania's Lancaster County James Buchanan would be chosen. Whatever the outcome, both the membership and the presidential aspirants venerated the convention process, which by that time had been raised "to an American art form."[31] In this decade of the unravelling of parties, Democrats intended their post-Jacksonian structure of the convention to provide unity.

To that end, the pledges enumerated in the party's national platform were actually efforts to diffuse the growing tension over the extension of slavery, as the convention promised "a faithful execution" of all the Compromise of 1850 measures, including the controversial Fugitive Slave law, which made it easier for slaveowners to "repossess" slaves seeking freedom in the North. Praising as always the states' rights principles of the Kentucky and Virginia Resolutions of the 1790s, the Democratic party also proclaimed its desire to end agitation over slavery.[32]

As better-known leaders blocked each other, the convention remained stalemated. Finally, on the forty-ninth ballot, the Democrats nominated the dark-horse Franklin Pierce, a former Senator from New Hampshire whose principal asset was his anonymity. After his nomination, Pierce did not campaign in an era in which Democrats understood that they had conveyed the so-called "gift of the people." Their candidate must not brazenly seek votes but must stay home, limiting his efforts to a few discreet letters. More so than the Whigs and later the Republicans, the Democrats, writes Daniel Howe, "put party first and treated the candidate as the instrument of the party."[33] Accordingly, it was the party, not Pierce or his vice presidential running mate William King, that American men were called on to support. And it was the party organization, led by local and state Democratic leaders and Democratic editors, that took the partisan message to the people affirming that a leave-alone government would prohibit national banks, federal support of commerce, and any interference with "the domestic institutions of the states"—that is, with slavery.

Pierce won easily over the Whig Winfield Scott in the fall elections, carrying all but four states. Some said his victory came because he was a truer friend to compromise than Scott. Others concluded that the Democratic party was the normal choice of the majority, especially since it held as a basic tenet "embracing and upholding the Union as it was, the Union as it is and the Union as it shall be." In any case, the party's vote rose by nearly four hundred thousand votes over that of 1848 as Democrats attracted disproportionate numbers of new voters and mobilized their members. Yet those Democrats who looked beyond this election and the immediate satisfaction of a return to power and control over the national patronage worried about the Republic's future. Not only had their party displayed a dangerous factionalism in a convention that was designed to bring harmony, not dissension, but the Whigs were crumbling and with them the Second American Party System that had been in place since the days of Andrew Jackson.

The bankruptcy of this two-party arrangement and the subsequent realignment of voters' allegiances revealed the influence of society's new political concerns. While the Democratic party survived this sea change and kept its broad-based ideological commitment to localism, Unionism, and small government (while adding racism), by 1856 its strongest component was made up of southern slaveholders. At the same time, in a process of party sectionalization after the passage of the Kansas-Nebraska Act under the leadership of Stephen Douglas installed the principle of local decision on slavery in the territories, some Democrats left the party. Northern Democrats who believed in "free soil" were outraged at a piece of legislation that undid the Missouri Compromise of 1820. "The lion of the Democracy has become the jackal of slavery," lamented one party dissident who, after a struggle with his conscience over the abandonment of the party of his ancestors, joined the Republicans.[34]

Yet, what Senator Douglas intended, among other motivations, was the characteristic Democratic solution of letting the people of each territory decide for themselves about slavery. Popular sovereignty, it was called, and it emerged from his partisan conviction that as communities organized, they should determine for themselves whether or not, and if so when, to have slavery. Many Democrats, especially in the South and Border States, recognized this solution as a cardinal principle of a party faith grounded in localism.

Douglas was also responsible for the party's foreign policy initiatives. Representing a group of Democrats nicknamed "Young America," the Illinois Senator promoted "the mission of progress in the development and advancement of human rights throughout the world." Supporting revolutionary movements in Europe in 1848 with words and money, Douglas, Democratic businessmen, newspaper editors like John O'Sullivan, and especially younger party members were self-conscious nationalists. Again the link between party and country was reaffirmed in beliefs intended to drown sectional interests through expansion. Such a position was placed within a prideful ideology that held America to be the best hope of mankind. While other parties would not argue with such patriotism, these views set Democrats apart from the Republicans and the Whigs, who viewed the enlargement of the United States as a threat to national integrity. By mid-century, the Democratic platforms included aggressive statements on Cuba, an interoceanic canal, Canada, and the hegemony of the United States in the Gulf of Mexico. While such policies attracted southerners who wished to expand their slave empire, nothing seemed to divert attention from the growing controversy over slavery, sectionalism, and immigration that was refashioning the parties.[35]

During this rare occasion of realignment—which occurred only twice more in American history and which in the personalist, nonpartisan politics of the late twentieth century is impossible—some Democrats left the party to join the new nativist organization, the "Know-Nothings." The latter addressed concerns raised by the immigration of the nearly four million Irish and Germans who, between 1846 and 1860, flooded into Eastern cities—and within a short time (sometimes before naturalization, according to Know-Nothings and Republicans) were voting Democratic. The Know-Nothings also attracted former Democrats who feared the intrusion of the Roman Catholic church in local matters such as schools. A third group of former Democrats who were abandoning what had been their "shrine of party" accepted the Temperance party's calls for state legislation to prohibit or at least control the sale of alcohol. Eventually, the Republican party absorbed these defectors into a powerful coalition that ran the federal government until the 1870s.

Meanwhile, southern Whigs were joining the Democrats because that party stood for the strict construction of the Constitution and the localism that the Democrats believed would prevent any interference in the privileged matter of slave property. Southerners were also attracted to the Democrats because that party for twenty years had supported the removal of the sensitive matter of master-slave relations from national politics. For years, Democrats had associated their Whig competitors with interfering abolitionists. Now southern Whigs remembered that connection. As a Maryland slaveholder explained: "I am forced into the Democratic party after twenty years of opposition because I behold in that party the only bulwark of Southern rights and the only political organization capable of stemming the tide of Northern fanaticism and of supporting in their integrity the Constitution and the Union."[36]

Amid these agonizing shifts, in 1856, Democrat James Buchanan won the presidency he had long coveted. Ominously for his party, he had been challenged by candidates representing two new parties—the Republicans and the Know-Nothings—whose total popular vote exceeded his. Moreover, the Democrats carried very few counties north of the forty-first parallel, and the Republicans carried none south of the Mason-Dixon line running through northern Maryland. The Whigs, the Free Soilers, the Free Democrats and even the ephemeral Liberty Party and Southern Unionists had all disappeared. Now the North and South were so polarized that in Washington congressmen and senators who had previously followed the party line on roll calls (much more faithfully than would be the case during the twentieth century) divided as representatives of their section.[37]

Even the election of a speaker of the House became a nearly impossible task, with members not only refusing to vote for the member of the opposite party but also opposing a candidate from another section. For the first and last time in its history, the United States had a multi-party system. Unlike the Whigs and the Know-Nothings, the Democrats survived this realignment. But in the face of growing sectional intransigence, how long could they do so? And how could they maintain a national organization whose strongest faction was threatening to leave the Union?

The partial answers came in the spring of 1860. When the Democratic party met in Charleston, South Carolina, to nominate a presidential ticket and to write a platform, it could do neither. First the platform committee splintered over the South's demand for congressional protection of slavery in the territories, which violated party principles in its assertion of federal authority. In a fateful decision that acknowledged the Democratic commitment to party over candidate, the Douglas supporters agreed to have the platform voted on before any nominations were made. Eventually three platforms on territorial slavery reached the floor. Then, seven southern delegations walked out. Earlier, during the call of Douglas supporters for a roll call, a riot erupted on the floor. Encouraged by the gallery, northern and southern Democratic delegates punched and bit and slapped each other in a less lethal preview of the 1860s.

By November, voters confronted the results of this unusual but not unique party schism in two Democratic presidential tickets, one led by Stephen Douglas of the Democratic National Party and the other by Kentucky's John Breckinridge of the National Democratic Party. Unable to employ the local and individual issues that had earlier cut across sectional lines, these factions nevertheless were united in their labelling of the opposition Republicans as dangerous sectionalists. Nor did they differ in their attitude toward slavery in the South, both holding that slaves were private property under the jurisdiction of the states. Again, it was the future of slavery in the territories that divided the two factions.

Supporters of Douglas and Breckinridge also agreed, in the official beginning of the party's antiblack politics that lasted until after World War II, that their opponents were "Black Republicans"—"nigger-lovers intent on elevating the African race to complete equality." "Elect Lincoln and the Black Republican ticket," argued the Democratic *Indianapolis Daily Sentinel*, "and you will have Negro equality."[38] For mid-century Democrats, who held out the hand of friendship to white male immigrants and incorporated them into the party on the basis that the United States was a haven for the oppressed, blacks were an inferior species, even in their Biblical origins. Shaping an ideological position that denied an analogical viewing of slaves as having the same relation to corrupt southern masters as prerevolutionary colonists did to English kings, Democrats—North and South—included blacks as impossible citizens whose inferiority would corrupt the white man's democracy. As potential pollutants of the Republic, slaves could not be included in the body politic, and the standard "Negro speech" delivered by Democratic leaders from 1850 to 1870 might begin with other issues such as wartime taxes, higher tariffs, and the war. But by the end of this period the African American had emerged as the cause of public disorder and war-driven changes.

Within weeks of Abraham Lincoln's election (the winner of a plurality in a four-party race, this first Republican President had carried only sixteen northern, but heavily populated states with high electoral counts), seven southern states led by Democrats left the Union. Later four more seceded. From the perspective of these soon-to-be Confederates, by opposing such Republican interferences as those in Kansas or in Virginia under John Brown, they were the party's true loyalists. Like Americans on the eve of the Revolution, Democratic secessionists saw themselves as preventing the corruption of power by northern Republicans.

At first, most northern Democrats tried to conciliate and cautioned against coercing the South. "Let them go in peace" was their refrain, for at this point they preferred to appease their "erring sisters." "War," insisted a Democratic Congressman from Ohio, "is no remedy." These particular party appeals that reached out to southerners and to individual Democrats were subsumed in the secession winter of 1860-1861 into a national concern to keep the Union that was entirely congruent with the party's faith.[39]

But when the fighting began in the spring of 1861, thousands of northern Democrats volunteered. Following Stephen Douglas's impassioned plea to be patriots, not traitors, they followed the Union. Fernando Wood, a former New York Mayor notorious for his Southern sympathies, called upon Democrats in his organization "to form a phalanx." By July, his Mozart Hall regiment (a local competitor to the better-known Tammany Hall) was training in Yonkers and soon was fighting with McClellan's forces in Virginia. New Jersey's Third Congressional District, which became one of the Democrats' safe seats during the Civil War, sent hundreds of volunteers, officered by the district's Democratic leaders.

The concept of what Albert Riddle called "sinking the partisan in the patriot" came easily to Democrats who had always understood their political life as an act of service to the Republic.[40] Even those who did not fight remembered Senator Stephen Douglas's symbolic act when he reached out to hold Lincoln's top hat as the new President began his first inaugural address in March of 1861—or so the story went.[41] Such acts of loyalty and fidelity to the Union did not, however, assure the party's survival at a time in which, unlike today, political parties could be transitory institutions that rose, flourished like a spring flower, and by fall's election time had disappeared.

## PARTY CHALLENGES

When the South seceded, the Democrats lost their electoral stronghold and became for many years the minority party. Their eclipse continued into the 1870s during Reconstruction, with their largest constituency either out of the Union or not voting because of local boycotts or disenfranchisement. Meanwhile, in the North after the realignment of the 1850s, the party had been losing its appeal to a new generation of voters and to former stalwarts who drifted off to the Republicans during a time in which the issues of slave extension and southern intransigence were of preeminent concern. In Illinois, for example, the Democrats gave up their normal majority to the Republicans whose candidates during the Civil War routinely won statewide elections, taking over fifty-five percent of the vote. "By 1860," writes Joel Silbey, "the Republicans held fourteen of eighteen governorships in the states north of the Mason-Dixon line, controlled all but three northern legislatures, occupied 102 of 146 seats in the House of Representatives (six others were held by anti-Democratic Unionists) and had won twenty-nine of the thirty-six United States Senate seats in the northern states."[42]

During a war fought under the auspices of the now dominant Republican party, Democrats in the North struggled to maintain their organization, their electorate and their ideals. First they faced the structural challenge of avoiding a bipartisan wartime coalition cleverly proposed by Lincoln as a Unionist movement. Briefly in the fall of 1861, some Democrats did run as Unionists, though they soon resisted what one described as "being swallowed up."[43] Thereafter, the Republicans, wrapping themselves in the flag of wartime patriotism, converted the Democrats into an organization of "Copperheads," traitorous snakes in the grass who had become the party of "Dixie, Davis and the devil."[44] Such overstated party rhetoric had long marked political campaigns, but during a civil war, its vituperativeness became especially threatening for the minority party. Although the war lasted four years, it would be nearly half a century before the Republican "waving of the bloody shirt" of wartime memories disappeared as a popular image in American politics.

Certainly, there were examples of Democratic disloyalty, though never as many as the Republicans created in their effective wartime imagery. Individual Democrats (probably more often than Republicans) did desert from the army, did evade the first draft in American history, did oppose Lincoln's programs—especially the Emancipation Proclamation, and in 1864, did encourage a negotiated peace with the Confederate government rather than its unconditional surrender. As a result, it was easy for Republicans to stamp the mold of traitor on the entire Democracy by using the words and actions of its most vehement prosouthern peace wing. Thus, after Congressman Clement C. Vallandigham of Ohio sprinkled the blood of a Democrat supposedly assassinated by the Republicans over an audience during a speech in which he violated a military order prohibiting declarations of southern sympathy, he was arrested and became a star exhibit in the Republican catalogue of traitors.

To survive such associations, Democrats relied on a number of tactics. First, they came to see themselves as a loyal opposition. As the party of government in the period after Andrew Jackson, they had rarely served in such a capacity. Now, using the ideological construct of their own devising, they legitimized the concept, perceiving themselves as opposing, within acceptable limits of disagreement, the tyrannies of their opponents. As the Republicans made Vallandigham into a representative Democratic traitor, so Democrats reversed the image and made him into a victim of Republican oppression.

Democrats protested the closing of newspapers; they fulminated against the arrests and trials of civilians like Vallandigham in military courts; they called attention to the government's suspension of the ancient protection of habeas corpus, especially in Maryland where a Democrat was arrested—but never tried—for blowing up railroad bridges. Their forty-four Congressmen (of 146) voted as a bloc against the administration's program of high tariffs, a national banking system, the Homestead Act granting 160 acres of land to settlers, and the confiscation of rebel property. Eventually, the Democrats fastened onto the Republicans the enduring label of radicals, while holding themselves to be true to the tradition of states' rights and limited government—undertaken in the name of individual liberty.[45]

For the wartime Democratic party, the most serious transgression of the Republicans was their effort to change the status of African Americans. By 1863, former slaves were not only emancipating themselves through individual acts of liberation and by means of federal policy, but they also were fighting, as Union soldiers, for their freedom against white southerners. When Lincoln announced his preliminary Emancipation Proclamation in the fall of 1862, Democrats universally condemned it as both unconstitutional (on the grounds that the President held no such power) and dangerous (on the grounds that the United States must remain "a white man's country"). For Democrats, the African American now emerged as a symbol of the party's core beliefs of "conservative naturalism."[46]

As the war dragged on, Democrats adopted the slogan "the Constitution as it is, the Union as it was, and the Negroes where they are."[47] Through their party-stipulated image of black immutability, Democrats saw themselves simultaneously as citizens of a unique nation of white men and as members of a particular political faith. In keeping with their party culture, they relegated their "Puritan" Republican opponents to the role of coercionists, intent on usurping local authority, trampling on individual liberties, and bullying private opinion and behavior in order to establish a revolutionary new social system.

Besides these appeals, the Democrats depended on the local nature of American politics. In a testament to the vibrancy of their earlier partisan imperatives, Democrats remained active during the war years. Statewide and national elections were frequently scheduled on different days in the fall, whereas city, town, and district voting took place in the spring. Even in wartime, the political calendar was crowded with rallies, speeches, conventions, and elections. Typical of other states in the frequency and recursiveness of their elections, Marylanders voted for the president of the United States in November of 1860. Then the following June, they elected their congressmen, and in September, they again cast ballots—this time for a new governor. Such frequency of voting sustained the Democrats because there was always some success somewhere to celebrate. War did not wipe away partisanship, and through local victories, Democratic leaders came to understand that a loyal core of party members would never defect.

In 1862, the Democrats celebrated their morale-boosting off-year gain of thirty-five seats in the congressional elections. Even to the drumbeat of Republican charges of disloyalty, the party had been able to sustain itself through successful local appeals to such groups as miners in Pennsylvania's Schuylkill County, Irish Catholics in Baltimore's second district, and small farmers in the rural Illinois county of Metamora. Before the nationalizing of American politics in the twentieth century, local contests made the Democratic party more than the sum of its parts.

Using the code words of racism and localism, the Democrats also elected governors in New Jersey and New York and carried statewide contests in Illinois, Pennsylvania, and Indiana. Though they lacked a powerful national voice after Stephen Douglas died in 1861, the Democrats faced the presidential elections of 1864 with hope, but no obvious candidate. Remembering the gathering tradition of one-term presidencies after Andrew Jackson's two terms, they observed the factionalism within the Republicans. Meanwhile, they hoped to diminish their own divisions over the degree of support they should give to a war effort controlled by their partisan enemies. Not only did Democrats expect their convention in 1864 to serve as a rallying point for their efforts to defeat Lincoln, they also intended to demonstrate that free elections, even during a civil war, must be maintained.

Nominating on the first ballot a popular symbol of their patriotism—General George B. McClellan—delegates at the Democratic National Convention in Chicago in 1864 included a "peace before reunion" pledge in a platform that also condemned the Republicans' "four years of failure to restore the Union by the experiment of war." With the restoration of the Union a centerpiece of their ideals, Democrats pledged an end to the Lincoln government's interference with individual liberties. While McClellan accepted his party's complaints against Republican tyranny, he later explained that he supported the surrender of the Confederacy before negotiations began.

The wartime campaign was short, with the nation's attention riveted on the fall of Atlanta and Sherman's march through Georgia. In the election that followed, although Lincoln was easily elected amid optimistic reports from the front, the tenacious Democrats received forty-four percent of the vote. Closed into their minority status with the South out of the Union, the party remained competitive because its organization was well-developed, its members loyal, and its platforms salient to many Americans. Under the leadership of Samuel F.B. Morse, party notables created a nineteenth century version of Paul Butler's Democratic Advisory Committee of the 1950s in the Society of the Diffusion of Political Knowledge which furnished tracts and pamphlets to voters.[48] In local communities, the party organization depended on their poll books to contact Democrats, and they made special appeals to first-time voters and conservative Republicans weary of war.

When Robert E. Lee surrendered at Appomattox and the war ended in 1865, the Democrats impatiently awaited their return to power after an aggravating period of Republican control. No group celebrated peace more expectantly; no group anticipated a place in the sun more fervently. Tactically, Democrats saw their emergence from a wartime eclipse as dependent on their Southern and Border State coalition and on an end to the divisive issue of slavery that had started the conflict. As Horatio Seymour, New York's war governor predicted,". . . the war issue is dead; the slavery issue is dead and on all living issues the Democratic party are united . . . (and) confident that their policy commands the approval of a large majority of the people."[49] Conscious of their long history, Democrats transformed the Republican party into a heterogeneous war-driven opposition. Like all their previous competitors, it would soon disappear, they believed.

Closing "our lips upon the questions of the past," Democrats now supported the return of the South to white domination, the removal of federal troops, amnesty even for Confederate leaders who had served in the United States government before the war, and no national interference with the local authority of southern communities. Applying this creed to the postwar period, the party continued to hold that the "town must do nothing which the school district could do as well, the state . . . nothing which the county or city could do, and the federal government nothing the states could as completely and safely accomplish."[50] In the twentieth century, this definition of negative liberalism would be reversed as Democrats would seek to employ the government to protect individuals from the ravages of unfettered industrial capitalism and social and economic discrimination. In the mid-nineteenth century, Democrats instead found government the most likely agent of abuse. The consistent thread in both efforts was a reach for freedom.

After Lincoln's assassination, party leaders hoped to ride President Andrew Johnson's coattails to the White House. The President from Tennessee who had received his vice presidency from Lincoln because he was a Democrat, by 1866, had challenged Republican reconstruction policies. Hopeful Democrats interpreted his vetoes of the Freedman's Bureau Act and the Civil Rights Act as a reassertion of his party roots. But Johnson had his own ambitions and tried unsuccessfully to create a new conservative alliance.

In response to Johnson's efforts, Democratic solidarity proved unassailable. As the *Baltimore American* explained in 1866, "the children of a Protestant or Roman Catholic Church usually attach themselves to the church of their parents and think all other denominations [are] on the road to perdition. So it is with the Democrats. They live and die in the faith of their fathers and are not easily drawn to any new organization."[51]

Thus, when the Democratic national nominating convention met in the new Tammany Hall near New York's Union Square on July 4, 1868, according to John Hope Franklin, "the 781 accredited delegates were a remarkable cross-section of the nation's Democracy." They included a new generation of northern leaders—the Wall Street financier and long-term Democratic party chairman August Belmont, "Boss" Tweed, and Samuel Tilden (the latter of the party's swallow-tail faction known for its wealth, elegant dress, and generosity to the party). Also among the delegates were 172 former party activists from the Confederate South including: Zebulon Vance, the Confederate governor of North Carolina; Nathan Forrest, notorious for his role in the massacre of African American troops at Fort Pillow; and Samuel Cox, who had moved to New York when his Ohio district turned implacably Republican.[52]

The platform of the party retooled many familiar principles. Accepting the end of slavery and secession, the Democrats called for the immediate restoration of the Union, the payment of the billion dollar war debt, a tariff for revenue only, equal rights for naturalized citizens, and the control of suffrage by the states. They reserved most of their attention for attacks on the Republicans who, according to traditional party idiom, represented an arrogant corruption of power—a despotic force installed in the South. Just as Democrats before the war had condemned Know-Nothings for their violations of the rights of Catholics and the foreign-born, just as during the war they had attacked Republicans for illegal arrests, so now they accused "the radicals" of violating the rights of southern states and the region's white citizens.

The white South's importance to the Democracy was by no means simply an issue of electoral support, any more than the Republican fostering of black male voting in the South occurred just for partisan advantage. For Democrats, a true peace assumed the return of the region into an harmonious Union. Holding to the idea that southerners resumed their allegiance to the United States immediately—like a lung reinflating—in a process of "restoration" without reconstruction, Democrats referred freedmen's issues to states and local communities. But because they did not control the government, for the next decade the former Confederacy was portrayed in Democratic cartoons and iconography as well as in national and local resolutions as a dignified but tormented goddess of liberty. "The people of the South," complained delegates in Maine, "have been deprived of their full rights."[53]

Out of step with twentieth century civil rights convictions, Democrats opposed the Freedman's Bureau; they resisted the Fourteenth Amendment which gave citizenship rights to black males and the Fifteenth Amendment which established black male voting. Briefly they flirted with the possibility of seeking black votes, especially in the South, moving toward their opponent's position on this major issue in a so-called "New Departure." But as the Democrats of the South competed with the Republicans for the African American vote, "a large segment of its membership was unable to accept it," writes Michael Perman,". . . they were convinced that the party was committing suicide." Again, a strategy which offended the party's understanding of partisan differences was dropped.[54] For how could a true Democrat accede to policies that, no matter what their substantive content, denied his conviction that Republicans were "the other" to his partisan being?

Instead, the image of the African American as a defective candidate for any form of citizenship continued to animate the party. In the North, Democrats overwhelmingly opposed eight state plebiscites on black suffrage. In the process, what might have been an abstract national policy was transformed into an important Democratic local issue throughout the United States.

For several years, exterior events surrounding the end of the war preoccupied Democrats. But by the late 1860s, economic concerns involving the currency, inflation, and low farm prices replaced issues arising from Reconstruction. Now the Democrats created an alternative to the Republican "waving the bloody shirt" in their "showing of an empty purse," drained by Republican fiscal policies.

In the election of 1868, the Democratic ticket of Horatio Seymour and Francis Blair lost to the popular Republican war hero Ulysses Grant, but with an encouraging forty-seven percent of the vote. Neither this defeat, the twenty-two ballots needed to nominate Seymour, nor the continuing tension between its factions discouraged Democrats. Instead, the 1868 nominating convention and election celebrated, according to one loyalist, "our pedigree and ancestry." Announced another, "We are the spontaneous instinct of the average national character always imbued with intense national feeling."[55]

Four years later, the corruption of Grant's administration split the Republicans. Hungry for a national victory after over two decades of eclipse, Democratic party leaders mistakenly accepted the strangest bedmate of their history. They nominated the crusty Liberal Republican editor of the *New York Tribune*, Horace Greeley, wrote a separate platform, and lost the national election to Grant. From this experience, Democrats concluded that fusion was no solution. Better, as a party leader had predicted earlier, to "lose as 'life-long Democrats' . . . than win as a fresh and vigorous party."[56] Not until 1876 were the party's presidential ambitions fulfilled when Samuel Tilden won the popular vote but lost the election through the subterfuge of the Republicans over the electoral count.

Two years earlier, in 1874, aided in the North by urban machines based on local patronage and a populist administration of city affairs, Democrats had begun their return to national power by winning two-thirds of the seats in Congress. Heralded as "the Overturn," the party's success had been accomplished locally—in district races where loyalists could mobilize their followers over community issues. "This election," crowed one Democrat, "is not a victory but a revolution."[57] He exaggerated, for it was another five before the Democrats controlled the Senate and another ten years before Grover Cleveland was elected. Nonetheless, in electoral terms, the elections of the 1880s had become highly competitive.

On the local level, the party's true followers—men who had been raised as Democrats by their families—had persisted. Democrats who had grown up in the 1840s and 1850s retained their partisan heritage based on a party culture grounded on a set of convictions, a loyalty to organization, and a variety of behaviors such as parading, voting, and attending conventions. The long eclipse had ended for a political party that by now had become the oldest in the world.

The Democratic experience during the middle years of the nineteenth century revealed the critical importance of the party's development before the Civil War when attitudes, values, and behaviors had been inculcated among a loyal following. In contrast to the twentieth century, nineteenth century politics was the most compelling secular activity of Americans, although by the end of the century political reformers would try to clean up public life by eroding party authority. Soon, single-issue lobbyist groups, regulatory bodies, and commissions, rather than the Democratic party, would hold immense power over the lives of individual Americans. Even the power of the family to inculcate partisan attitudes would dissipate as state agencies became more influential.

While the external events of slave emancipation, war, and Reconstruction had worked against the Democratic party, a partisan culture that only existed in the nineteenth century had assisted its survival. Above all, the Democrats of mid-century America had been members of an organization that pervaded their lives and offered entertainment, sociability, psychological identification, a belief system, and most notably an understanding that serving party was a form of patriotism. The source of the Democrats' partisan light had been sometimes obscured by the event-filled decade of the 1860s, but by the mid-1870s, the eclipse—not the party—was over. The party of the past had become a party with a future.

## NOTES

1. Ronald Formisano, "Deferential-Participant Politics: The Early Republic's Political Culture, 1789-1840," *American Political Science Review* (June 1974), 473-487.

2. Joel Silbey, *The American Political Nation, 1838-1893* (Stanford: Stanford University Press, 1992), 8.

3. Alexis de Tocqueville, *Democracy in America* (New York: Vintage Books, 1957), 2:78.

4. "The Autobiography of Martin Van Buren," *Report of the American Historical Association* , ed. John Fitzpatrick (1920), 163.

5. *United States and Democratic Review* 9 (October 1841): 345.

6. Jean H. Baker, *Affairs of Party: The Political Culture of Northern Democrats in Mid-Century America* (Ithaca: Cornell University Press, 1983), 132.

7. Thomas R. Marshall, *The Recollections of Thomas R. Marshall* (Indianapolis: Bobbs-Merrill, 1925), 70-71, 189.

8. Silbey, *American Political Nation*, 36.

9. Samuel Cox, *Three Decades of Federal Legislation*, (Providence: J. A. & R. A. Reid, 1885), 28; and Cox, *Eight Years in Congress, 1857-1865, Memoir and Speeches* (New York: D. Appleton, 1865); 5-6, 235. On the theory of a loyal opposition, see George Dennison, "The Idea of a Party System: A Critique," *Rocky Mountain Social Science Journal*, 9 (April 1972): 31-52.

10. John Bartlow Martin, *Adlai Stevenson of Illinois* (New York: Doubleday, 1977), 6; and Baker, *Affairs of Party*, 42.

11. Ibid., 46-52.

12. Ray Miles Shortridge, "Voting Patterns in the American Midwest, 1840-1872" (Ph.D. dissertation, University of Michigan, 1974), 1-94, 116, 157, 200.

13. Thomas Courtenay to Robert Brune, October 15, 1858, Frederick Brune Papers, Maryland Historical Society, Baltimore, Md.

14. Quoted in Silbey, *American Political Nation*, 35.

15. *Democratic Review* 9 (October 1841): 345; and Broadside collection, 1860, Library of Congress

16. *Democratic Review* 5 (October 1855): 345; James Raymond, *Political; or, The Spirit of the Democracy in '56* (Baltimore: John Wood, 1850).

17. Michael Holt, *Political Parties and American Political Development from the Age of Jackson to the Age of Lincoln* (Baton Rouge: Louisiana University Press, 1992), 56.

18. J. Mills Thornton, *Politics and Power in a Slave Society, 1800-1860* (Baton Rouge: Louisiana State University Press, 1978), 42.

19. Ibid., 42-45.

20. Silbey, *American Political Nation*, 164; and Holt, *Political Parties and American Political Development*, 53-54.

21. *New York Evening Post* (April 20, 1844); and *Democratic Review* 1 (October 1837): 2, 7.

22. Roy Franklin Nichols, *The Disruption of American Democracy* (New York: Collier, 1962), 197-198.

23. *United States and Democratic Review* 5 (October 1855): 345; and Raymond, *Spirit of Democracy*, 72.

24. Morton Grodzins, *The Loyal and the Disloyal: Social Boundaries and Treason* (Chicago: University of Chicago Press, 1956), 29.

25. Jean Baker, *The Politics of Continuity: Maryland Political Parties from 1858 to 1870* (Baltimore: The Johns Hopkins University Press, 1972), 41; *Baltimore American*, (July 19, 1860).

26. Baker, *Affairs of Party*, 289.

27. Michael Holt, *The Political Crisis of the 1850's* (New York: John Wiley, 1978), 98-99.

28. James E. Chase, *The Emergence of the Presidential Nominating Convention, 1789-1832* (Urbana: University of Illinois Press, 1973), 3.

29. *The Democratic Party as It was and as It is: Speech of Hon. Timothy Day* (Washington: Buell & Blanchars, 1856).

30. Matthew Scott Notebook, 1855, Scott-Hardin Papers, Cornell University Library; and Michael McGerr, *The Decline of Popular Politics* (New York: Oxford University Press, 1986), 30-33.

31. James McGregor Burns, *The Vineyard of Liberty* (New York: Knopf, 1982), 594.

32. Roy and Jeanette Nichols, "Election of 1852," in Arthur M. Schlesinger, Jr., ed. *History of American Presidential Elections*, 2, 951-952.

33. Daniel Howe, *The Political Culture of the Whigs* (Chicago: University of Chicago Press, 1979), 54.

34. Day, *The Democratic Party*, 3.

35. Robert Johannsen, *Stephen A. Douglas* (New York: Oxford University Press, 1973), 344-346.

36. Baker, *The Politics of Continuity*, 24.

37. Joel Silbey, *Shrine of Party: Congressional Voting Behavior* (Pittsburgh: University of Pittsburgh, 1967), 118.

38. Quoted in Holt, *The Political Crisis*, 187.

39. *Congressional Globe*, 36th Cong., 2d sess., 35; also Stephen Douglas's speech, ibid, 39.

40. Albert Riddle, *Recollections of Wartime*, 164; and William Claflin to Joseph Holt, October 20, 1862, Holt Papers, Library of Congress.

41. Baker, *Affairs of Party*, 330.

42. Joel Silbey, *A Respectable Minority, The Democratic Party in the Civil War Era* (New York: Norton, 1977), 18.

43. Quoted in Silbey, A *Respectable Minority*, 42.

44. Baker, *The Politics of Continuity*, 129.

45. Baker, *Affairs of Party*, 143-176.

46. Ibid., 177-218.

47. Silbey, *A Respectable Minority*, 51.

48. Papers of the Society of the Diffusion of Political Knowledge, microfilm edition, Library of Congress.

49. Chandos Fulton, *The History of the Democratic Party* (New York: 1892), 457.

50. Silbey, A *Respectable Minority*, 177; and *New York World*, March 7, 1865.

51. Quoted in Baker, *The Politics of Continuity*, 157.

52. John Hope Franklin, "Election of 1868," in Schlesinger, *American Presidential Elections*, 1252.

53. *Appleton's Encyclopedia*, 1866, 404, 408, 461; and "Honest Democrats Read This," Broadside Collection, New York Public Library.

54. Michel Perman, *The Road to Redemption: Southern Politics, 1869-1879* (Chapel Hill: University of North Carolina Press, 1984), 58.

55. *New York World*, July 4-10, 1868; and Democratic National Committee, *Official Proceedings of the National Convention*, 12-18.

56. Quoted in Silbey, A *Respectable Minority*, 208.

57. Ibid., 208.

# Chapter 6

# Democrats and Blacks in the Gilded Age

*Lawrence Grossman*

Popular perceptions of the Democratic party's record on the race issue tend to oscillate between two extremes. For those whose familiarity with our politics goes back no further than a generation, the Democratic party is the party of civil rights and racial equality, the political haven for racial minorities, the foe of white supremacists. But for those who know something about American politics in the nineteenth century, the Democratic party is tainted by racism. After all, the rival Republicans freed the slaves, granted blacks civil equality, and gave them the ballot, while Democrats fought these measures and repeatedly sought to stimulate a white backlash against black rights.

Each of these images of the Democratic party is accurate, but incomplete. The bridge between them is the complex and fascinating process through which the nineteenth century racist Democracy evolved into the modern civil rights party. This essay examines the first phase of the metamorphosis, the development of Democratic racial attitudes and the party's changing relationship with black Americans from Reconstruction through the 1890s. What happened in this period set the stage for more dramatic political shifts in the twentieth century.

## THE RACIST DEMOCRACY

By the mid-nineteenth century, the Democratic party was on its way to becoming the political embodiment of white racism in America. One reason was the potent influence of the party's southern wing, whose justification for the maintenance and spread of slavery rested on the doctrine of black inferiority. The disproportionate power of southerners within the national party was ensured by a Democratic rule that party nominations must be approved by two-thirds, not just a majority, of delegates to the national convention. This enabled the southern minority to veto candidates considered insufficiently tolerant of slavery, and thus dictate the national ticket. As the sectional conflict over the spread of slavery intensified, so did southern control over the Democratic party.

But southern clout was not the sole reason why Democrats stood for white supremacy. Since its beginnings in Jackson's day, and even in its prehistory as Jefferson's Republican party, the Democracy had attracted the votes of many immigrants, especially in the big cities, who stood at the bottom of the economic ladder, struggling to obtain and hold on to low-paying, unskilled jobs. This brought them into direct conflict with urban blacks, who were vying for those very same employment opportunities. Thus, racial prejudice, fortified by economic competition, made many of these immigrants eager allies of the white supremacist forces in the Democratic party.

Another factor, not directly related to the race issue but bearing important implications for its political resolution, was the traditional Democratic preference for states' rights and distrust of federal power. In the abstract, the expression of the states' rights doctrine said nothing about a person's racial views; but in the real world of American politics—in the 1860s as in the 1960s—opposition, on constitutional grounds, to federal protection of black rights was often a transparent disguise for white racism. Even in those cases where it was not, belief in a limited central government set constraints on what even fair-minded Americans could do to ensure equal rights.

## LEGACIES OF THE WAR

In 1861, shorn of its southern wing by secession and the Civil War, the Democratic party of the North was itself splintered by these events. Some Democrats—the "Copperheads," as they were called—opposed the war, some backed the Republican administration's efforts to subdue the Confederacy, and others hoped for a reunited Union but objected to President Lincoln's way of achieving it. What all agreed on, though, was that blacks must be kept subordinate; even Democrats who favored the Union cause insisted that this was a "white man's war."

Every step taken during the war to help blacks—from military confiscation of southern slaves to letting blacks fight for the Union to emancipation—elicited complaints from Democrats that the administration favored black equality, a black invasion of the Midwest, and racial amalgamation. Since white supremacist feeling was widespread among Republicans as well, Democratic politicians calculated that racism would gain them votes. They continued this strategy on into Reconstruction, opposing the Fourteenth Amendment, which granted blacks civic equality, and the Reconstruction Act of 1867, which mandated black voting in the

South. There was, then, much truth to the Republican taunt that "the only test of Democratic soundness is hatred of the Negro."[1]

Yet perceptive Democrats recognized that appealing to white racism was a two-edged sword, that also could alienate voters. For one thing, this approach reminded them that the party had recently included, and would once again include, in leadership positions, slaveowners who had made war on the United States. For another, it recalled that the party had exhibited an equivocal attitude, at best, toward the suppression of the rebellion. Furthermore, many northerners who were personally prejudiced toward blacks believed that the nation had a moral obligation to protect the newly freed slaves from mistreatment. These voters could only be repelled by the Democrats' anti-black rhetoric and insistence on white supremacy in the South.

The Democratic party had to resolve an internal struggle between two contradictory forces: the impulse to gain power through stimulating a white racist backlash, and the calculation that long-term success depended on burying the issues that arose out of the sectional conflict and the war—even if that meant partial acquiescence to changes in the racial status quo for which Republicans were responsible.

The first national expression of this Democratic dilemma surfaced in the 1868 presidential election. With blacks now voting for the first time throughout the old Confederacy, should Democrats contend for the White House as the party of white supremacy, arousing the enthusiasm of their rank and file but giving credence to Republican charges that they were seeking to reverse the results of the war? Or should they accommodate themselves to the new reality, reassuring northerners and possibly even competing for the black vote, but dampening the fervor of old-line Democrats?

Those Democrats seeking to distance the party from the political burden of its recent record were fascinated with the idea of nominating Chief Justice Salmon P. Chase for president. Chase had been a major architect of the Republican party and an early advocate of emancipation and black rights. But he had alienated the Republicans and his intense desire to be president left open the possibility that he might be willing to run as a Democrat.

Chase negotiated a platform with the Democrats. At first he insisted that the party accept universal suffrage in return for blanket amnesty for all disfranchised Confederates.[2] Chase argued that such a course would win the South for the Democrats: if Dixie Democrats would but accept and protect black voting, he reasoned, they would be "welcomed back to their old lead with joy and acclamation."[3]

On June 8, the *New York World*, which spoke for moderate eastern Democrats, issued an implicit response. While not quite calling for formal acceptance of black voting, and without mentioning Chase, the paper editorialized that "since we can *do* nothing about negro suffrage, why not practice the dignity of silence and *say* nothing?"[4] An avalanche of Democratic attacks on Chase's position buried the *World*'s strategy. Judging by public reaction to the editorial, Senator James Doolittle of Wisconsin estimated that the nomination of Chase "should lose two Democrats to every Republican gained."[5]

Hungering for the presidency, Chase moved further to accommodate the Democrats. He stated his willingness to settle for Democratic recognition "that universal suffrage is a democratic principle, the application of which is to be left in the States, under the Constitution, to the States themselves. . . ."[6] Yet even this concession to states' rights was not enough for old-line Democrats, who wanted to continue to fight openly for white supremacy. Abandoning that struggle, explained Ohio Senator Allen Thurman, would "take all the fire and zeal out of the people and enable the radicals to obtain a very easy victory."[7]

Chase and his views were virtually ignored at the Democratic National Convention, which resolved in its platform that congressional Reconstruction in the South was "unconstitutional, revolutionary and void." The delegates nominated for vice president Frank Blair of Missouri who stated before his nomination that the next president should order the army to "disperse" the new state governments in the South and "allow the white people to reorganize their governments. . . ."[8] Burdened with this platform and running mate, presidential candidate Horatio Seymour was unable to focus the campaign on economic issues, as he had intended. Republican Ulysses S. Grant was elected President, with 214 electoral votes to Seymour's 80, but the Democrats polled an impressive 47 percent of the popular vote—evidence, to some, that appeals to white supremacist feeling might yet sweep the party to power.

## TOWARD A NEW DEPARTURE

Republican sponsorship of a Fifteenth Amendment in 1869, nationalizing black suffrage and providing it federal protection, aroused solid Democratic opposition, first in Congress, then in the state legislatures. Even if black voting in the former Confederacy could be justified on the ground that those states had lost the right to regulate their suffrage by seceding, the proposed new amendment changed the voting qualifications in northern and Border States that had never been in rebellion against the government. This enabled Democratic critics to combine racist appeals with states' rights arguments. In Indiana, for example, Democrats insisted that a Republican-controlled legislature elected before any mention of a

Fifteenth Amendment had no right ratifying a constitutional change that would affect voting rights in the state. They also declared their belief that "the Government was formed *for* white men, in the *interest* of white men . . . *by* white men."[9]

But the tide was turning in the other direction. Once ratification of the new amendment became a foregone conclusion, pragmatists in the party took the initiative once again. "The nigger question has to be dropped," counseled the *New York World*.[10] The course taken by Samuel S. "Sunset" Cox, a shrewd and articulate New York congressman, demonstrates a Democratic party in transition. On the floor of Congress, Cox sounded the old racist themes as he described southern black legislators as "mulatto barbers and black field hands, who had sharpened their minds on the razor-strap and cudgelled their brains with their ox-goads." Yet several weeks afterward, Cox privately suggested to the editor of the *New York World*:

> What would be the effect of a policy of acceptance of the inevitable Colored Cuss: He is here! in Senate and as a voter, and he will soon be everywhere whether we like it or not—If you would back me up—I would issue a pronunciamento from the Halls! I think it's foolish—we are—not to look into the *Whites* of his eye, '*Squar*! He's an element of the future![11]

Despite apprehensions of Democratic-inspired violence in the North, the spring elections of 1870—the first conducted under the Fifteenth Amendment—went smoothly. "Some of the residents," remarked a leading midwestern Democratic paper, "looked a little hard when the sooty-faced, wooly-headed citizens handed in their ballots, but we are happy to say that no objection was offered."[12] But just as in the twentieth century it took southerner Lyndon Johnson to enact landmark civil rights laws and cold warrior Richard Nixon to recognize Communist China, so too the nineteenth century Democratic party could not officially accept black political rights until challenged to do so by a prominent dyed-in-the-wool Democratic leader with a Copperhead past.

The man was Clement Vallandigham of Ohio, who had attained notoriety among Union supporters and had even been deported from the country for his pro-Confederate activities during the war. Hoping to reestablish his political career in 1871, Vallandigham got the Democrats of Montgomery County (Dayton), and then the statewide Ohio Democratic organization, to adopt a "New Departure" platform recognizing the Thirteenth, Fourteenth, and Fifteenth Amendments as "accomplished facts" that were "no longer political issues before the country."[13] National party chairman August Belmont was overjoyed with this "return of reason and sound common sense. . . . The game of charging us with disloyalty and Copperheadism is played out."[14]

To be sure, neither Vallandigham nor Belmont—nor, indeed, any other New Departure Democrat—was prepared to endorse federal protection for blacks seeking to exercise their rights under the amendments. While ready to take the humiliating step of swallowing the recent changes in the Constitution, they insisted, in Vallandigham's words, that the amendments be interpreted according to "the old doctrines of the fathers of the Republic, of the Whig party, of the Democratic party in former times, the sound doctrine of strict construction."[15]

Thus, formal Democratic acceptance of equal rights for blacks in 1871 could—and, in fact, did—go hand-in-hand with opposition to Republican-sponsored legislation to protect black voting in the South, despite the fact that the Reconstruction amendments contained enforcement provisions. New Departure Democrats also opposed a civil rights proposal by Republican Senator Charles Sumner of Massachusetts barring racial discrimination in public accommodations, places of amusement, schools, cemeteries, and jury selection.

New Departure Democracy was a long-term strategy to regain the trust of northern public opinion and thereby reassert white, Democratic control of the South, and, ultimately, Democratic power in national politics. If the mistrust of northerners could only be dispelled by guaranteeing the legal equality of blacks as enshrined in the Constitution, it was a price worth paying, since such theoretical equality might be ignored and subverted in practice, when and where necessary.

So quickly did the New Departure approach win over influential Democrats that by 1872 it was possible to envision a Democratic coalition with anti-Grant Republicans in the presidential election. Despite the contrast between their original positions on Reconstruction, little separated the two groups now: Democrats accepted the civic equality of blacks that Republicans had espoused, and many anti-administration Republicans—known as Liberals—like the Democrats, wanted an end to federal intervention in southern affairs.

This coalition strategy might have worked if the Liberals, who held their nominating convention first, had not chosen a candidate with a number of glaring weaknesses—not the least of which was his identification in the public mind with the cause of racial equality. The nominee was Horace Greeley, editor of the *New York Tribune*, whose anti-slavery record and recent support for Republican Reconstruction—and even for Sumner's civil rights bill—were too much for old-line Democrats to stomach. U.S. Representative Daniel Voorhees of Indiana explained to his constituents that he and his Democratic congressional colleagues had hoped to use the proposed civil rights bill against the Republicans in the upcoming campaign. But "what harmony will there be," he asked, "between the entire

Democratic side of the House . . . and their candidate . . . on the point of [racial] equality in schools?"[16]

The Democratic party proceeded to endorse Greeley, though without enthusiasm. Asserting that the Greeley Republicans were as responsible as the Grant supporters for Reconstruction, some disgruntled Democrats ran a separate, "straight-out" party ticket in several states. Many more Democrats stayed home on election day, and a good number of Democrats who did vote for Greeley were like the man in southern Illinois who considered it "enough to make the master of ceremonies in the bottomless laugh in his own face to see men who believe in their inmost hearts, in the exclusive rule of *White Men*, voting for the man who had proudly carried Cuffee in his pocket for 30 years."[17] In November, Greeley suffered a humiliating defeat.

## BURYING THE RACE ISSUE

The Democratic coalition with anti-Grant Republicans, so demoralizing in the short run, paid long-term dividends. By agreeing to cooperate with the Democrats, Liberal Republicans—some of whom boasted enviable records in the cause of racial equality—had given legitimacy to the New Departure Democracy. It was, perhaps, worth the cost of losing the election in a landslide to hear Senator Sumner, who hated Grant, proclaim that the Democrats, by accepting the results of the war, had "set their corporate seal to the sacred covenant. They may continue Democrats in name, but they are in reality Republicans."[18] Now, Republicans disgruntled with their party would feel much freer to change their party affiliation without fear that by doing so they might hand the Confederacy a posthumous victory.

This blurring of partisan lines over the question of black rights accelerated after 1872. Northerners grew increasingly reluctant to let federal authorities intervene in southern affairs. The passage of time gradually cooled war-inspired passions, and new issues—an economic depression, government corruption, currency reform, labor-management strife—excited the political energies of the American people. The Republican hold over both the executive and legislative branches of the federal government—and thus their ability to push through Reconstruction legislation—came to an end in 1875 when the Democrats took control of the U.S. House of Representatives, just after the lame-duck session passed a weakened version of Senator Sumner's civil rights bill. Not for another 14 years would the Republican party control both Houses of Congress and the White House simultaneously.

By 1877, all the southern states were in the hands of white Democrats. The party met evidence of anti-black violence in the South with a combination of denials and claims that the region was more peaceful than it had been under Republican rule—even as northern Democrats privately worried that their southern colleagues' behavior was costing them precious votes. The Democrats paid lip service to black rights, but insisted on leaving their enforcement to the individual states. A disgusted Republican senator, George Edmunds of Vermont, aptly characterized the Democratic stand:

> It is all very nice for a few dozen gentlemen on the other side to get up and say that they are in favor of the Constitution of the United States with all its trimmings and refuse to do anything about it . . . when it comes . . . to proposing to do anything about it, then the gentlemen say, Oh no; oh no; it is too late, or it is too early; it is too vague, it is too mysterious, it is too something; never let us do anything about it at all.[19]

Though they were committed to white (Democratic) supremacy, when northern Democrats urged voters to "let the southern people influence and impress the negroes in their own way"[20] they were not necessarily justifying racial violence. The upper-class southern Democrats who "redeemed" their states in the 1870s tended to take a paternalistic, rather than a viciously racist, stance toward blacks. Attracting black support served their own political interests in fending off challenges from lower-class whites, while entailing no commitment whatsoever to racial equality. For a while, however, these southern regimes did hold in check the kind of intimidation and outright physical terror that would spread through the region when the regimes began to falter in the late-1880s, ushering in the age of wholesale black disfranchisement, segregation, and lynchings.

## A NEWER DEPARTURE[21]

The collapse of Reconstruction created new opportunities for northern Democrats to build bridges to black voters. Democrats could ask, and some blacks seriously wonder whether continued near-unanimous black fealty to the Republican party of emancipation and enfranchisement made sense now that the condition of race relations in the South was effectively beyond the reach of federal authority. Did not automatic black Republicanism cause the party to take such support for granted, and remove any incentive for Democrats to ingratiate themselves with the race? Would blacks not gain more by making the two parties bid for black favor, if not in national elections where the fate of the South might be at stake, then at least in state and local contests?

For their part, the northern Democrats proved remarkably willing to compete for the black vote, both with patronage and with favorable state legislation—especially after the U.S. Supreme Court invalidated the federal Civil Rights Act in 1883, forcing blacks to look to northern state governments to protect their rights. The attempt by northern Democratic leaders to win over black voters began in the 1870s, accelerated in the 1880s, and continued on into the 1890s. The motives of these leaders—like those of most politicians most of the time—were mixed. Some, who came from Republican backgrounds, had long been seriously committed to fair treatment for blacks. Others, old-line Democrats, now said that they had been wrong in opposing black rights. All saw the potential benefit that might be derived from black support at a time when the balance of political power in many northern states was extremely close. They also hoped that Democratic liberality toward blacks would win white votes as well, by providing concrete new evidence to wavering Republicans that the Democracy had indeed purged itself of its old negrophobia.

The New York Democratic party dropped appeals to racism as soon as ratification of the Fifteenth Amendment became a foregone conclusion, and the Tammany Hall machine in New York City went after the black vote just as it had pursued the votes of other minorities. By the 1880s, Democratic mayors were appointing blacks to city jobs, and in 1891, Democratic municipal authorities invited the first black juror to serve at the court of general sessions. In neighboring Brooklyn, a Democratic-controlled school board integrated the public schools in 1888, and a Democratic mayor named a black to the school board and appointed the city's first black policeman.

Similar tendencies became evident on the state level after Grover Cleveland was elected governor of New York in 1882 and appointed a black engineer to the state engineer and surveyor's staff—the first time that a black had been given more than a menial position in the New York state government. In 1884, Cleveland had to confront the issue of school integration. Although by state law a black child could attend any public school, there were two "colored schools"—remnants of the past—in New York City. When the municipal board of education sought to shut them down as an economy measure, the principals and teachers objected on the grounds that some black children benefitted from an all-black educational environment, and that the move would bar black teachers from the profession, since they would not be hired by white schools. The governor and the Democratic legislature satisfied the black educators by keeping the two schools open, officially as regular ward schools accessible to both races, but likely to remain predominantly black in fact.

Cleveland's Democratic successor in Albany, David Bennett Hill, also sought black support through the extensive use of patronage. The high point of Democratic outreach to New York blacks occurred when Hill ran for reelection in 1891 against a Republican who had strong ties to insurance interests and, as a legislator, had abstained on a bipartisan bill barring racial discrimination by life insurance companies. The Democratic state platform played the issue for all it was worth, viewing "with gratification the growing friendly feeling toward the Democratic party of our colored fellow citizens in this State, and they are welcomed to our ranks with the assurance that within our party discrimination on account of race is discountenanced."[22] After a sweeping Democratic victory, New York's leading black newspaper blamed Republicans for taking the black vote for granted and treating blacks "as if they were the scum of the earth."[23]

Democratic efforts to attract black support in New Jersey began in earnest when Leon Abbett became governor in 1884. Abbett had entered politics as a race-baiting Copperhead during the Civil War, but now he sang a different tune, distributing patronage to blacks, steering a civil rights bill through the legislature, and—what aroused greater public interest—sponsoring the baptism of the son of the black Newark city messenger.

Abbett, the former racist, did something even more surprising when a mulatto church sexton was denied burial in a Hackensack cemetery. The governor sent a special message to the legislature noting that cemeteries could only deny burial on "reasonable" grounds. Racial prejudice, he went on, was not reasonable, and he demanded remedial legislation. Democrats in the legislature prepared a bill barring such discrimination, and Abbett stood firm against a Republican amendment that would have exempted religious corporations from the scope of the proposal. The Democratic measure became law.

In Pennsylvania, two prominent blacks tried to initiate better relations with the Democrats. In 1874, William Still and Robert Purvis backed an independent candidate for mayor of Philadelphia who was running with Democratic support against the Republican machine nominee. Denounced and even threatened by angry black Republicans, Still responded in a public speech: "I think that colored men who have been so long bound under the yoke, and have been so long compelled to think and act only at the bidding of the dominant race, should be the last people on earth to institute or encourage this kind of political tyranny." Many Democrats, he added, "are no longer in sympathy with pro-slavery doctrines and ideas," and Still recently had been unable to find "in any of the Democratic papers any sneers against the colored man."[24]

While the independent candidate lost that year, the potential value of the black vote was not lost on local Democrats. In 1881, Democrat Samuel King was elected mayor, and proceeded to appoint the first blacks to the city police force. When Republicans recaptured city hall three years later and took steps to remove those policemen, the staunchly Republican

*Harrisburg Journal*, the state's leading black newspaper, stated that King had been "the best mayor in the interest of the colored citizens" in Philadelphia's history, and wondered "whether it would not serve our interests better to pay a little attention" to the Democracy.[25]

Connecticut Democrats made their first bid for the black vote in 1878 by exploiting the state government's refusal to recognize privately organized black militia units as official components of the state national guard. After Republican majorities in the legislature blocked a Democratic bill granting the black militiamen equality with their white counterparts, the minority leader of the Connecticut House of Representatives told a black protest meeting in New Haven: "We tax the colored man . . . make him liable to draft in time of war, but will not permit him to learn military science before war comes." Whether or not they decided to vote Democratic, he announced, blacks "could rely on him."[26] In 1883, newly elected Democratic Governor Thomas Waller called for legislative action on the militia issue, and both houses quickly approved the proposal. The next year, a Democratic legislator introduced a civil rights bill which passed unanimously.

The first Democratic inroads into the Massachusetts black vote were the work of Benjamin F. Butler, who returned to the Democratic party in 1880 after years as a Radical Republican and then a Greenbacker. Two years later he was elected governor, aided by the votes of some blacks who recalled the racial egalitarianism of his Republican years. Butler appointed the first black ever named to a judgeship in the state, and renominated him after a rejection by the Republican-controlled common council. After a second rejection and Butler's own defeat for reelection, the lame-duck governor appointed another black to the bench. This appointment achieved confirmation. In Boston, Democrats put the first black on the police force in 1885, and nominated a black to the state legislature in 1891.

Midwestern Democrats also reached out to blacks. In 1885, Illinois and Indiana enacted civil rights statutes, and six years later Illinois strengthened its law. The Indiana bill was signed by a Democratic governor, and all three of these measures received significant Democratic legislative support, especially from Democrats with relatively large black constituencies. On the local level, Democratic mayors Carter Harrison of Chicago and Thomas Taggart of Indianapolis provided blacks with liberal patronage and made deep inroads into their support.

Of all the northern states, it was in Ohio—where the balance of power between the parties was exceptionally close—that the political independence of blacks and the political flexibility of Democrats were most highly developed. In the mid-1880s, Ohio blacks were able to play the two parties off against each other and gain substantial benefits.

Peter H. Clark, a black schoolteacher in Cincinnati, led the drive for black political independence. After years of complaining that Ohio Republicans took black support for granted, Clark declared himself a Democrat in 1882. The rewards were substantial: Democratic financial support for a new black newspaper edited by Clark, the appointment of his son as a deputy sheriff, and the naming of the first black policeman in Cincinnati history.

Ohio's 1883 gubernatorial election gave Clark the perfect opportunity to proselytize the Democratic faith among fellow blacks: the Democrats nominated George Hoadly, a former Republican abolitionist who still believed in racial equality, while the Republicans put up Joseph B. Foraker a prominent lawyer who, on several occasions, had represented defendants accused of violating the civil rights of blacks. Hoadly won by a razor-thin margin that he attributed to a split in the black vote. The new governor dispensed patronage to blacks, aided the formation of additional black militia units, and named blacks as trustees of two universities and of the state asylum for the blind. More important, Hoadly called on the legislature to enact a civil rights bill, and the two parties vied with each other to demonstrate support for racial equality. Two bills were passed in 1884, the second more stringent than the first. As was the case in other states, Democratic legislators representing large black constituencies, particularly in urban areas, were especially supportive of black rights. "The world moves," noted Ohio's major black newspaper, "and with it even the Bourbon Democratic party."[27] Governor Hoadly sought to enforce the new civil rights laws, on one occasion forcing a segregated skating rink out of business.

With the Ohio black vote now up for grabs, Republicans in the legislature raised the stakes, introducing a bill ending school segregation in the state. The Democratic governor announced his support for the measure, and even criticized black educators who worried that they would lose their jobs if separate black schools disappeared. The desegregation bill passed the Ohio House of Representatives with considerable Democratic support, but narrowly failed in the state Senate.

The 1885 gubernatorial election was a rematch between Hoadly and Foraker, and both sides went all-out for the black vote. After the Republicans won in a landslide, the lame-duck Hoadly once again called for an end to separate black schools. Later, when black legislators submitted a new proposal to abolish all remaining racial distinctions from state law—including not only segregated schools but also the ban on interracial marriages—one of the black members warned his Republican colleagues: "Defeat this bill and the wrath of the colored voters will bury you beneath their ballots."[28] The bill passed in 1887.

Looking back on the three-and-a-half years since George Hoadly's election, Peter Clark claimed that events had proven the value of black political independence. For too long, he wrote, "there was a sort of notion prevalent, that to ask the Republicans of Ohio to do justice to her colored citizens would embarrass the party in its alleged fight against wrongs in the South." But a few thousand "colored 'kickers'" helped elect the Democrat Hoadly, starting a virtual bidding war by both parties for black support. "If you ask the question of any 'kicker,'" he concluded, "'who abolished the Black Laws?' he will slap himself on the breast and say, 'I did it, with my free ballot.'"[29]

## A DEMOCRAT IN THE WHITE HOUSE

When George Hoadly ran for reelection in 1885, the Foraker campaign brought southern Republicans into the state to address black voters. These southerners had a simple, irrefutable message: If Governor Hoadly were to express his racially egalitarian ideas in Mississippi, his fellow Democrats would lynch him.

Did the new Democratic approach to race relations in northern cities and states have any application nationally? The election of Grover Cleveland as President in 1884 marked the first time that Democrats had captured the White House since 1856. However forthcoming the party had proven to be in the North, southern blacks feared that a national Democratic administration might bring further deterioration of their rights. Many blacks in both the North and the South worried that federal patronage would now be for whites only. Here was a clear test of whether the northern Democratic New Departure—of which Grover Cleveland, as Governor of New York, had been a prominent practitioner—could be nationalized.

In a sense, the challenge facing Democrat Cleveland resembled the challenge confronting Republican Ronald Reagan a century later. Both men led political parties distrusted by the great majority of blacks—parties that argued against a strong federal role in the enforcement of racial equality—and both presidents sought to allay black fears of the new administration and build up a cadre of black supporters.

In his inaugural address, Cleveland "pledged to do equal and exact justice to all men" and said that "there should be no pretext for anxiety touching the protection of the freedmen in their rights of their security in the enjoyment of their privileges under the Constitution and its amendments."[30] Cleveland was a firm believer in the New Departure doctrine of allowing southern whites a free hand in running their states, and, during his administration, there were no federal prosecutions for violations of the election laws. In this respect Cleveland hardly differed from his Republican predecessor. After 12 blacks were murdered in a Carrolton, Mississippi, courtroom in 1886 in the most serious racial outbreak of his first term, Cleveland called the incident "a blight to our civilization" and expressed surprise that state authorities were taking no action. Yet he did nothing.[31] On two occasions he did take political action against white southerners who had terrorized black voters: in 1885, when he revoked a commission he had already signed appointing a Mississippi postmaster, after finding out that the man had engaged in intimidation; and in 1888, when he forced a federal district attorney from the same state to resign for trying, in the words of the Attorney General, "to suppress the colored vote . . . and to prevent colored people from running for office by violence and intimidation."[32]

For American blacks, whose status as full-class citizens was only shallowly rooted in the recent Fourteenth and Fifteenth Amendments, federal patronage was a potent symbol of political recognition. Republican administrations had awarded blacks a few visible appointments as well as more numerous subordinate positions in the bureaucracy. President Cleveland came into office pledged to the merit system for officeholders: only incompetents and those who had campaigned for the Republicans while holding office would be fired. He told a black visitor: "Let the same rule apply to white and black alike."[33] Blanche K. Bruce, the black former senator from Mississippi, was removed from his post as register of the treasury because he had worked in the Republican campaign, and was replaced by a white. Yet Frederick Douglass, the most prominent black in the country and an outspoken Republican, retained, for a full year, the office of recorder of deeds in the District of Columbia. Indeed, the Democratic president invited Mr. and Mrs. Douglass to White House receptions—a courtesy that his Republican predecessor Chester A. Arthur had not extended—even though Douglass's new wife was white and southern guests were offended.[34]

President Cleveland recognized blacks in his appointments to the diplomatic corps. He adhered to the tradition, instituted by Republican presidents, of appointing blacks as ministers to the "black" nations of Haiti and Liberia, and named another black as consul in Luanda, Angola. In addition, despite protests from the all-Democratic Louisiana congressional delegation, the Cleveland administration retained in office the incumbent black Louisianan serving as consul in Santo Domingo.[35]

While there is no evidence that blacks were dismissed from jobs in government departments on racial grounds, the thirst of Democrats for office—which frequently overrode Cleveland's commitment to the merit system—undoubtedly had the effect of reducing the number of black employees: Republican job holders, blacks included, were fair game for dismissal, and there were few black Democrats with legitimate claims to the spoils of office to take their places. Partially offsetting the erosion of black representation, however, were the close ties between black Republican politicians and certain southern members of the Democratic administration. The latter, out of a sense of personal obligation and political quid pro quo, intervened to save the jobs of numerous black incumbents. Another factor boosting black presence on the federal payroll was the use, in conformity with the Pendleton Act of 1883, of civil service examinations in hiring for low-level positions. Although whites in many parts of the South found ways to subvert the civil service rules, the examinations were administered in a color-blind manner in the North, and, as a result, many blacks got post office jobs.[36]

The most dramatic black patronage episode of the Cleveland administration began on March 4, 1886, when the President nominated James C. Matthews, a black lawyer from Albany, New York, to replace Frederick Douglass as recorder of deeds in the District of Columbia.[37] At first, the choice of Matthews aroused opposition only from Washington residents and some southern Democrats who, while voicing their disapproval on the grounds of Matthews' non-residency in the District, were clearly motivated by resentment that a white man had not been named. Soon, however, Republicans in the Senate—where the confirmation would be decided—resolved to defeat Matthews. Ostensibly, they too objected to a non-resident in the position. But Senator John J. Ingalls of Kansas frankly explained their real motivation in a private conversation that was later leaked to the press: "it would be bad politics to take a man like Matthews—of his ability and character and standing among his people—and place him in a prominent position" because to do so would contradict the Republican insistence that a black Democrat was a "monstrosity."[38]

The battle lines were drawn. On July 31, a Senate coalition of 29 Republicans and eight southern Democrats defeated the nomination, while 13 Democrats and one maverick Republican supported the President. Cleveland, in defiance of much of the southern wing of his own party, publicly stated that Democratic political recognition of blacks was a matter of principle, and named Matthews to a recess appointment. But in January 1887, when the nomination was resubmitted, the Senate responded with another rejection, with 22 Republicans and nine southern Democrats besting 14 Democrats and three Republicans. Not to be outdone, the stubborn President named James M. Trotter, a Massachusetts black, to the post. This time, the Republican Senate contingent, sensitive to black complaints about the treatment given Matthews, decided to cut its losses: Trotter was confirmed on March 3—though he was no more a D.C. resident than Matthews.

Black public opinion clearly sympathized with President Cleveland, who, throughout the episode, had skillfully positioned himself, in contrast to southern extremists, as a New Departure Democrat eager to recognize blacks, and had made the Republicans appear blindly partisan in their insistence on punishing a black because he had the temerity to support the Democrats. "The most stalwart Republicans of the race," reported a black paper, "men who never had a kind word for the Democracy whenever it did anything that was good, speak in complimentary terms of the President's action all through the Matthews affair down to the nomination of Trotter."[39]

## "THE SOUTHERN TAIL WAGS THE NORTHERN HEAD"

Cleveland's 1888 reelection campaign made a strong appeal for the black vote, even to the point of subsidizing a national convention of black Democrats in Indianapolis in July. But this was to be the high point of black-Democratic relations, for as soon as Republican Benjamin Harrison defeated Cleveland in November, the race issue in the South reemerged, and for most of the black community, far outweighed in importance matters of patronage.

In 1889, facing the prospect, for the first time in 14 years, of a Republican President, Senate, and House of Representatives—which together would have the power to interfere with state control over race relations—southern Democrats reacted angrily and fearfully. A spectacular increase in anti-black violence was the result. Under pressure from political insurgents in their states, several of the formerly benevolent Bourbon leaders called for an end to black voting.

Northern Democrats, still eager to attract the black vote and, with it, respectability in the eyes of those white northerners who still cared about the welfare of blacks, faced a quandary. "The great Democratic party of the wide North and West," advised the racially egalitarian Louisiana writer George W. Cable, should "withdraw its support from the Southern policy now, as it did in 1860."[40] But northern Democrats were too politically dependent on their southern white allies and too tied to the doctrine of states' rights to take effective action. When New York Governor David B. Hill met privately in Atlanta with Democratic leaders and advised them, instead of interfering with the black vote, to emulate northern New Departure Democrats and win black support, he was rebuffed. "The Negro that Governor Hill has seen at the North," editorialized the *New Orleans Times-Democrat*, "is not the Negro that is now being discussed; he is not the Negro that must be known by all who desire to speak intelligently of the race issue."[41] It was clear that despite all that had changed in the northern Democracy, "the Southern tail wags the Northern head of the Democratic party."[42]

When the Republicans sought to protect the black franchise by proposing a bill in Congress that provided for some federal oversight of congressional elections, the Democratic party unanimously condemned it as a "force bill" and denounced any such "interference" in southern affairs. Using opposition to the federal elections bill as one of the most critical campaign issues, the Democrats won control of the House of Representatives in the 1890 elections and skillfully maneuvered to sidetrack consideration of the bill in the lame-duck session of 1891.

Then, in 1892, with former President Cleveland running once again against President Harrison, the Democrats raised the specter of a Republican revival of the federal elections bill. Advised by his campaign manager to exploit the issue, Cleveland recalled "the saturnalia of theft and brutal control which followed another Federal regulation of State suffrage."[43] The solidification of ties between northern and southern Democrats in opposition to federal protection of black voting led some blacks who had previously backed the Democracy to switch sides and support Harrison. But this had no impact on northern Democrats. The *New York Sun* commented, "The possible loss of the votes of the few colored men . . . counts for nothing against the great duty which the Democracy owes to Democratic principles, and to the happiness and fortunes of millions in the South."[44]

Indeed, what is surprising is the large number of blacks who campaigned for the Democrats in 1892 despite the situation in the South. Democrats exploited black grievances over patronage and argued that the Republican high-tariff position hurt blacks by raising prices on goods they had no choice but to buy. A Democratic official in New York, assigned to attract the black vote, bragged: "I have gotten the colored contingent into wonderfully good shape. . . . They have had no recognition from the Republican party, and they are tired of . . .'Hewing wood, and drawing water.'" A black newspaper, the *Detroit Plaindealer*, noted the Democrats' opportunism: "In the South, it is 'no force bill,' while in the North the managers are proud of the increasing intelligence of the Afro-American, if he but votes the ticket."[45]

The Democrats won in a landslide. The new administration repealed the remaining federal election laws; the Republican party, refusing any longer to risk political suicide, gave up all hope of protecting black voting in the South, even when the party regained control of the national government four years later; and southern states were now free, without fear of federal interference, to find ways to disfranchise their black citizens—even while the Fourteenth and Fifteenth Amendments remained in the Constitution. Thus, with the race issue removed from the national agenda and the South solidly Democratic, Democrats could continue to vie with Republicans in the contest for the black vote in the North. It had taken a generation, but the New Departure had finally succeeded.

Democratic racial policy had certainly changed since the early days of Reconstruction. Official opposition to black legal equality was gone, and, in northern politics, Democratic racist appeals had been replaced by an approach that viewed blacks as a possible source of votes—which was more or less the way Republicans now looked at blacks as well.

Yet, in other ways the old Democracy survived. The party's northern wing still took orders from Dixie Democrats when it came to southern race relations, which meant that they were willing partners in the degradation of blacks in the region. And the ancient Democratic preference for states' rights and limited government provided a firm ideological barrier against any federal role in ensuring the civil rights of Americans. The emergence of the Democratic party in the mid-twentieth century as the champion of racial equality could only occur when these two inhibiting factors were overcome.

## NOTES

1. *New York Independent*, March 12, 1868.
2. Salmon P. Chase to Alexander Long, April 19, 1868, Jacob Schuckers to Long, May 9, 1868, Long Papers, Cincinnati Historical Society.
3. Chase to August Belmont, May 30, 1868, Manton Marble Papers, Library of Congress.
4. *New York World*, June 8, 1868.
5. Doolittle to George H. Paul, June 15, 1868, Paul Papers, State Historical Society of Wisconsin.
6. Chase to William Cullen Bryant, June 19, 1868, Bryant-Godwin Papers, New York Public Library; and "Mr. Chase's Views," Jacob Schuckers Papers, Library of Congress. Both are reprinted in Jacob W. Schuckers, *The Life and Public Services of Salmon Portland Chase* (New York: D. Appleton, 1874), 588-89, 567-68.
7. Thurman to William Bigler, June 24, 1868, Bigler Papers, Historical Society of Pennsylvania.
8. *National Party Platforms, 1840-1964*, eds. Kirk H. Porter and Donald B. Johnson (Urbana: University of Illinois Press, 1966), 37-38; and William E. Smith, *The Francis Preston Blair Family in Politics* (New York: Macmillan, 1933), 2:405-407.
9. *Indianapolis Sentinel*, March 5, 1869.
10. *New York World*, June 29, 1869.
11. *Congressional Globe*, 41st Cong., 2 sess., January 4, 1970, 499; and Cox to Manton Marble, February 27, 1870, Marble Papers.
12. *Cincinnati Enquirer*, April 5, 1870.
13. James L. Vallandigham, *A Life of Clement L. Vallandigham* (Baltimore: Turnbull Brothers, 1872), 438-439; and *Dayton Herald*, June 2, 1871.
14. August Belmont to George McCook, June 5, 1871, 28, Marble Papers.
15. *Dayton Herald*, June 7, 1871.
16. *Chicago Tribune*, May 26, 1872. Once nominated, Greeley avoided talking about the civil rights bill.

17. P. R. Sawyer to William Allen, July 27, 1875, William Allen Papers, Library of Congress.

18. Charles Sumner, *The Works of Charles Sumner*, 15 vols. (Boston: Lee & Shepard, 1883), 15:184-85.

19. *Congressional Record*, 45th Cong., 3 sess., February 5, 1879, 1007.

20. *Albany Argus*, March 11, 1879.

21. This section is based on the more extensive treatment of black-northern Democratic relations in Lawrence Grossman, *The Democratic Party and the Negro: Northern and National Politics, 1868-1892* (Urbana: University of Illinois Press, 1976), chap. 3.

22. *New York Times*, September 17, 1891.

23. *New York Age*, December 12, 1891.

24. William Still, *An Address on Voting and Laboring* (Philadelphia: James B. Rodgers, 1874). The Still Papers, part of the Leon Gardiner Collection at the Historical Society of Pennsylvania, contain correspondence from other blacks, most of it critical, about his role in the campaign.

25. *New York Times*, August 29, 1881; and *Harrisburg State Sentinel*, April 12, 1884, May 10, 1884.

26. *New Haven Palladium*, March 20, 1878.

27. *Cleveland Gazette*, February 9, 1884.

28. Benjamin W. Arnett and Jere A. Brown, *The Black Laws* (n.p.: n.d., 1886), 27.

29. *New York Freeman*, March 26, 1887.

30. *A Compilation of the Messages and Papers of the Presidents, 1789-1897*, ed. James D. Richardson (Washington: U.S. Government Printing Office, 1897), 8:302.

31. *New York Tribune*, March 26, 1886.

32. *Nation* 40 (1885):512; and Augustus Garland to J.B. Harris, January 3, 1888, Department of Justice Instruction Book Y, 505-506, National Archives.

33. C. S. Smith to John H. Oberly, March 24, 1885, Grover Cleveland Papers, Library of Congress.

34. Frederick Douglass, *Life and Times of Frederick Douglass* (New York: Pathway Press, 1941), 556-558.

35. Grossman, *The Democratic Party and the Negro*, 122-125.

36. Ibid., 125-128.

37. For a detailed description of this nomination and its repercussions see ibid., 128-141.

38. *New York Times*, June 30, 1886.

39. *New York Freeman*, March 19, 1887.

40. George W. Cable, *The Negro Question: A Selection of Writings on Civil Rights in the South*, ed. Arlin Turner (Garden City: Doubleday, 1958), 270.

41. Quoted in *Detroit Plaindealer*, November 15, 1889.

42. *New York Age*, December 28, 1889.

43. *Official Proceedings of the Democratic National Convention Held in Chicago, Illinois, June 21-23, 1892* (Chicago: Cameron, Amberg, 1892), 224.

44. *New York Sun*, September 29, 1892.

45. A. B. Upshaw to Grover Cleveland, September 27, 1892, Cleveland Papers; and *Detroit Plaindealer*, September 2, 1892.

## Chapter 7

# The Democracy of Tilden and Cleveland

*Robert Kelley*

The Civil War inaugurated a new era in American politics. If from Thomas Jefferson's election in 1800 through James Buchanan's in 1856 the Democracy had won practically all of the presidential elections and dominated the federal government, everything changed when Abraham Lincoln became chief executive in 1860. In the fourteen presidential ballotings that would be held during the half-century from 1860 through 1912, only in 1884 and in 1892 would a Democrat—in both cases the same man, Grover Cleveland—win the White House. Similarly, the 1860s marked the beginning of a long "Republican era" on the Supreme Court. From Lincoln's first appointment of a Supreme Court justice to Franklin Roosevelt's, a span of about three quarters of a century, at no time would there be more than three Democrats sitting on the bench.[1]

## THE REPUBLICAN AGENDA FOR AMERICA

In Congress, when the war began in 1861, the Democracy in the northern states was suddenly bereft of its mighty southern wing, and it subsided into a drastically shrunken and weakened role in that body. Though the Democratic vote in the northern states during the war never dropped below about forty percent, sometimes approaching the fifty percent mark, its national primacy was utterly gone.[2]

With their huge majority in Congress during the wartime years, the Republicans finally had their chance to enact Henry Clay's venerable plan for the country, his "American System," while the Democracy looked on helplessly. Implementing what Leonard Curry has called their blueprint for modernizing America, the Republicans enacted a series of economic measures. To foster industrialization they erected a wall of protective tariffs which in succeeding years would mount higher and higher; to create a unified economy they established a national banking system (if not a national bank) and a single national currency; and to speed transport, they inaugurated a program of pouring out large sums and land grants for internal improvements, as in the building of a transcontinental railroad. At the same time, through the Morrill Act of 1862, they issued large land-grant subsidies to support the building of a nationwide system of state universities to train the skilled middle class needed to direct the new economy.[3] By 1865, the Republican agenda for America was essentially a realized program.

After war's end, a sweeping Republican victory in the congressional election of 1866 gave the party a two-thirds majority in that body. Subsequently, over angry but fruitless Democratic protests and Andrew Johnson's presidential vetoes, what history knows as Radical Reconstruction was put into effect. Its goal: to assure the vote and civil rights to the former slaves in the South. As its keystone, Republicans enacted the Fourteenth Amendment, which gave the federal government immense new national authority to enforce "equal protection of the laws."[4] This extraordinary program of federal assistance for economic development and attempted racial justice in the South set the terms of national political debate in the United States for the next half-century.

## CULTURAL DYNAMICS UNDERPIN DEMOCRATIC RESURGENCE

In the mid-1870s, within a decade of Robert E. Lee's defeat at Appomattox Court House, Democratic America surprised everyone by suddenly rising to fresh national strength. Northern interest in reforming southern race relations was dying, and in 1873, a grave national depression which ran on through the mid-seventies shocked the country. Democrats, capitalizing in part on these discontents, achieved a startling turnaround in the congressional elections of 1874, when, having since 1860 been a weak minority in the House of Representatives, they won an astonishingly strong majority (169 seats to 109 for the Republicans). Subsequently, they were able to battle over the next twenty years on remarkably even terms with the Republicans in congressional elections. From the 1870s to the mid-1890s, the "Gilded Age" of common speech, Republicans won presidential elections only by razor-thin margins or by victories in the electoral college only (in 1876 and 1888), the popular vote majority having gone to the Democrats.

Behind this extraordinarily even balance of power was a national patchwork pattern of party domination. If we were to use an increasingly intense shading to indicate places on the map where Republicans held the majority, we would see two very dark patches covering New England and the Great Plains states (particularly Iowa, Kansas, Nebraska, Minnesota, and the Dakotas). Sketching in cross-hatching for Democrats, we would note that as Reconstruction collapsed a dense mat of such lines took form in the South—especially the "Deep South"—a mat which now reached up to cover the Border States, where before the Civil War the Whigs had held sway. The massively Democratic Solid South had taken form, and for almost a century it would stand as an immovable political monolith in national politics, balanced off against another much less noted phenomenon, the Solid North, in New England and out in the western Midwest.[5]

The surge of the Democrats, not only in the former Confederacy but also in the Border States, was driven, of course, by a simple but powerful cultural reality: "Republican" to most white Southerners was synonymous not only with "black rule" but with "Yankee rule." This meant that most whites in that enormous area recoiled en masse from voting Republican, for so doing would have made them disloyal on two grounds: to the "Lost Cause" of the Confederacy, in those states that had seceded; and to white racial supremacy, both there and in the Border States. Thus, four out of every five whites in this vast continental expanse voted Democratic, decade after decade.[6]

Until well into the 1880s, these were the years when, as Paul H. Buck has written, "there was no peace [between North and South]. . . . In the minds of men [the Civil War] still persisted."[7] Republicans were still deeply angered at the South, and in elections they regularly waved the bloody shirt. Their most spectacular national leader, James G. Blaine of Maine, was especially enraged by the post-Reconstruction crushing of the African Americans' vote in the South by white violence. In caustic, wounding oratory he led the anti-Southern charge year in and year out.

Once more, in this lurid debate, the Democrats were the white South's advocates and apologists for its racism. For years they ostentatiously refused to accept any of the great Reconstruction constitutional amendments as the law of the land. When in 1871 a Congress desperate to put down the massacre of African Americans in the South (and their white Republican friends) enacted the historic Ku Klux Klan Act, giving the federal government for the first time a role in criminal justice, Democrats condemned that law too as a violation of localism and states' rights.[8] Indeed, the virulent racism that disfigured the Democratic party before the Civil War continued, through the Gilded Age, to be much of its stock in trade, though as we observe in Lawrence Grossman's skillful and absorbing essay in this volume on that topic, there are surprising complexities in that record.

The South's fixed loyalty to the Democratic party created what C. Vann Woodward calls that region's "half-century of abasement": the years when a grindingly poor South, utterly shattered by the Civil War, bitterly distrusted, and regarded with distaste for its cruel racial oppressions, was by its determined loyalty to the Democratic party unable to win any role or influence in the executive branch or Congress until Woodrow Wilson's presidency, save in a minor way during Grover Cleveland's two separated terms. "If for fifty years," wrote William Garrott Brown in 1910, "there has been a single great general law or policy initiated by Southerners or by a Southerner, or which goes or should go by any Southerner's name, the fact has escaped me."[9]

In the Gilded Age, Democratic America—the world of the social outgroups (save for African Americans)—also benefitted, as it had in the decades from 1840 to 1860, from a renewed tidal wave of immigration from Ireland and the Continent. It was an immigration which by the 1880s began to include Jews, Italians, Poles, Bohemians, and other ethnic peoples regarded by Republican-voting nativists as truly racially inferior and un-American. It was this multitudinous inpouring of new peoples that gave the Democrats the votes they needed in the northern states to challenge the Republican monolith.[10]

As "Catholic" and "Democrat" became ever more closely intertwined, it was asked yet again, as it had been before the war: how could Catholics—subservient, it was said, to a foreign potentate, the pope in Rome—be loyal to a Protestant America? An autocratically appointed and all-powerful priesthood—which was entirely beyond any control by their congregations, which did not choose the priest who presided over their lives—seemed eloquently and, on its face, entirely at odds with a democratic republic, and un-American.

Coincident with the Catholic influx, there also arrived in the States a renewed inpouring of German Lutherans. Their political behavior would be much more mixed and ambivalent than that of the Catholics, since they shared many traits with the Yankees, especially their work ethic and admiration for education and high culture. They were often substantial farmers who had little liking for the increasingly Democratic inner cities, and as Protestants they were powerfully swayed, too, by their historic antipathy toward Catholics.

In the Gilded Age, however, German Lutherans in the mass continued to vote Democratic, as they had before the Civil War. Why? Because they were a special kind of Protestant people who liked to maintain parochial schools, which Yankees so condemned, so they could keep the German language and German culture alive amongst their children; because they spoke a "foreign" language, and clung to it, bringing upon themselves a Yankee charge of not being Americans; and because they loved their beer, their folk-singing and folk-dancing beer gardens, and their Sunday recreations, all of which Yankee temperance workers and sabbatarian blue-law advocates condemned. The Gilded Age was racked with an almost constant political warfare over the drink trade and Republican-supported crusades for prohibition, and the issue sharply and deeply polarized local politics. The Germans, in sum, well knew that on cultural grounds the Republicans disliked them; and the pluralistic Democrats, with arms open wide for all faiths and ways of life, were therefore their usual political home of choice.[11]

In the eyes of the countryside and the small towns, where Republicans predominated, a repellent phenomenon was growing into a fearsome new power in American public life: large industrial cities. Thousands of Catholic immigrants, too poor (save for many of the Germans) to buy land and farm equipment, congregated there, creating solidly anti-Republican working-class precincts, and made "urban," in the industrializing states of the Northeast and Midwest, increasingly synonymous with "Democratic." In Republican eyes,they had therefore made the cities synonymous with drink and crime, with strange and "un-American" languages and faiths, un-American parochial schools, and ethnic-based political machines, which sold votes to the highest bidder in order to share the loaves and fishes—that is, government jobs—amongst their people.

Thus the cities, to multitudes of Republicans, had become cesspools of crime, vice, and unspeakable dangers to the human soul. In the Midwest, this spectacle created a deep mood of crisis amongst Republicans. As old-stock Americans watched the swelling of these foreign worlds, with their culture of drink, dancing, and theatres and their political corruption, they began to fear that America was politically, economically, and morally doomed.[12] Paul Kleppner, writing of such people, notes Republicans saying at the time that the cities "had become 'a serious menace to our civilization,' because in them were 'focalized' the triune dangers that imperiled it: immigrants, Romanists, and saloons."[13] The fact that, in the early 1880s, Catholics began to be elected to the mayor's seat of such major cities as New York City and Boston seemed "a terrifying portent for the future, for Catholics [it was said] were still servants of the pope and always 'ready to do priestly bidding.'"[14]

Religiosity, indeed, was so intense in Victorian America, as it was across the Atlantic in contemporary British society, that it suffused and gave a special cast to practically every aspect of national life. The enormous evangelical campaigns of the nineteenth century, embodied in the Second Great Awakening of the years from the 1820s to the 1850s, had succeeded in transforming a people formerly largely indifferent to organized Christianity into what was literally the largest stronghold in the world of vital Protestantism. By the 1890s, more than seven out of ten Americans, Richard Jensen writes, were church-going people; five of nine were members of pietist and revivalist congregations; and harsh religious controversies within and about the churches constantly provided headline material for the newspapers.[15]

Americans not only flocked to their churches, they carried on business together with fellow church members, intermarried there, and discussed politics obsessively in that setting. They found their personal identities, in heterogeneous America, as Catholics or Lutherans or Methodists. Consequently, religion invaded politics every day. In his study of American politics in the upper Mississippi Valley during the Gilded Age, Richard Jensen concludes, "Religion was the fundamental source of political conflict in the Midwest." For one thing, it was an established mark of the existing American political culture for the churches to participate actively in local and national politics, taking strong stands on the issues—especially on moral questions—and proclaiming them to their crowded and attentive congregations.[16]

## THE REPUBLICAN CRUSADE FOR CULTURAL PURITY

"The Republican party," writes Paul Kleppner, "was above all else the party of morality. As one of its early preacher supporters had informed his Congregational flock, it was 'the *party* of God, the *party* of Jesus Christ, and [it stood] *against* the party of iniquity [i.e., the Democrats].' To that minister, as to most Yankee pietists, *Republican* came to mean a crusading moral movement through which they would make their society holy. And they never doubted success, for to them the Republican ethos was founded on the fundamental truth that 'righteousness alone can exalt a nation.'"[17]

What Republican clerics and pious parishioners set forth was a reform agenda which, though drawn up principally by puritan Yankee clerics, was warmly supported as well by other Protestant groups of a similarly moralistic cast, groups which, like the Yankees, were given to austere, puritan ways of living, and were deeply distrustful of drink and what they defined as loose morals—as well as, on historic grounds, of Roman Catholics. These included, among others, the Quakers of Pennsylvania and of many locations in the middle and far western states, who on rock-solid pietist grounds—that is, for style-of-life reasons—had been on the Federalist-Whig-Republican side of American politics from the nation's beginnings. So, too, on that side were the equally pietist and self-denying immigrant Swedes and Norwegians of Wisconsin and Minnesota, two Lutheran peoples who had a horror of liquor, that legendary scourge in their homelands.[18]

Therefore, in those wide areas in the North and West, where in the Gilded Age the two parties were fairly evenly balanced, cultural dynamics provided the principal force driving the rise of a reinvigorated Democratic party. Mirroring the black-white hatreds that shaped southern politics, what took place after the war in Yankeeland was a vast refueling and re-energizing of tribal hatreds between Catholic and Protestant, Irish and English, the immigrant and the native-born. These lurid controversies had exploded briefly in the 1850s, only to be damped down by the greater crisis of the Union.

It is well known that the new migration settled thickly in the cities of the northeastern states; what is less understood is that by 1890, six out of every seven people in Milwaukee were either born abroad or had foreign-born parents. Three out of four in Chicago, and in the smaller towns such as La Crosse, Wisconsin, Davenport, Iowa, and Peoria, Illinois were foreigners. In Iowa's Des Moines, an otherwise unusually Yankee town, a third of the people were first or second generation immigrants. "With so many of their residents of recent European background," Ballard C. Campbell, Jr., writes, "the larger cities [in the Midwest] possessed a distinctively foreign quality." And yet many immigrants, especially the Scandinavians and Germans, settled densely in the midwestern countryside too. Overall, in 1890 four of ten of the people living in Iowa, just under half in Illinois, and three-fourths of the residents of Wisconsin were immigrants or children of immigrants.[19]

Among these peoples were floods of Roman Catholics from Ireland, Germany, Italy, and eventually Bohemia and Poland. By 1890, Catholics not only loomed large in such traditional lodging places, for them, as Boston and New York and Philadelphia; they had flocked to the Midwest as well, becoming the largest single voting bloc in both Michigan and Wisconsin.[20] It was an invasion that set off waves of alarm within the most zealous Protestant circles in America—that is, among those peoples who formed the heart of Republican America. For one thing, they knew that Catholics had always swung behind the party of Thomas Jefferson, the party which from America's beginnings had insisted on a rigorous separation of church and state, toleration of all faiths, and absolute laissez faire in all matters cultural.

In sharp contrast, the Federalist-Whig-Republican tradition carried within it what, in American terms, was practically a state-church outlook. That is, as the voice of America's most politically active and aggressive Protestants, Republicans believed that government at all levels must carry out the moral reforms that mainstream Protestantism trumpeted, generation after generation: the end of the saloon and of drinking; of prostitution, Sunday recreations, and risque dress; of "dirty books" and contraceptives; and of stores open on the Sabbath.

Their task, they believed, was to purify America, to cleanse it of its sins. Was not the United States, they would ask, fundamentally a *Christian* (by which they meant a Protestant) country? And was that not its claim for God's special solicitude and protection? With this mentality, the Republican party was no place for the culturally deviant or for any of those outside the mainstream, the core way of life.[21]

The result, in the 1870s and 1880s, was a powerful Republican-inspired and pietist-led crusade, carried on at the local level in state after state, to purify American life of its new contagions. At the national level, as we have long known from John Higham's studies of political nativism, Republicans argued for immigration restrictions—though always excepting British migrants, a Republican voting group.[22] And within the states and local communities, where most of this cannonading went on, pietist Protestants fought relentlessly to reform the life styles of the new Americans by enacting "blue laws" aimed at keeping the Sabbath holy and quiet. In other words, they condemned the Catholics' and Lutherans' Continental-style recreational Sunday, trying to outlaw on that day baseball playing, or excursions on steamboats and railroads, commercial or governmental activities, the buying of groceries, the publishing of newspapers, or the operation of factories and mail trains. Most of all, it meant re-igniting the old prewar crusade against "*The Liquor System*," the "dominating curse of our time. . . ," which set off direct crusades against the Germans' beer gardens and the Irish Catholics' saloons.[23]

## SAMUEL TILDEN: THE DEMOCRATS' LINK TO THE AGE OF JACKSON

Searching for a renewed and revivifying connection to the storied Age of Jackson, when the Democracy had bestridden national politics like a colossus, the Democrats of the Gilded Age finally found it in a brilliant, millionaire recluse, Samuel Tilden. Since Martin Van Buren's time, Tilden had been the northern Democracy's towering intellectual authority in political economy. He had played an important role in New York State's constitutional convention of 1850, installing in classic Adam Smith fashion the principle that incorporations were no longer to be allowed only under special legislative charters—traditional sources of corruption and monopoly—but were to be open to everyone under equal conditions.

Adept in, and fascinated by, the new and rare arts of quantitative analysis, Tilden had gone on to amass a great fortune as one of the first railroad attorneys able to bring some order into the chaos of the early railroad era. A widely heard critic of Republican race policies in the 1860s, Tilden had soared to national prominence in the 1870s as an implacable fighter against political corruption. Given the task of investigating the Tweed Ring in New York City, which siphoned off millions from public works construction projects, he ultimately destroyed Tweed and his bipartisan ring—in the process becoming governor of New York in 1874, and subsequently the scourge of the (Erie) Canal Ring.

Tilden had a theory ready at hand to explain why the country was being so assaulted and nearly overwhelmed in the Gilded Age by corruption at every level of government and in practically every community: it simply flowed, he said, from the cozy relations between Republicans and the business community, and the centralist, big-spending doctrines Republicans preached as they sought to aid businessmen in every possible way. Republicans said they were pouring tax money into public works and granting protective tariffs, land grants, bounties, special charters, and other such aids to the business community simply in order to stimulate the economy and produce prosperity. What actually happened, Tilden said, was a carnival of corruption as people bought these special privileges from compliant legislators and administrators. Speaking of the Tweed Ring, he remarked that "[t]he cancer which reached a head in [New York City] . . . gathered its virus from the corrupted blood which pervades our whole country."[24]

Tilden brought a whole new style to Democratic party tactics. The traditional electioneering strategy was based on mobilizing the voters in an unending public display of torchlight parades, marching brass bands, and uniformed marching societies. After describing an 1876 march in New Haven, Connecticut, by thousands of people who, under the illuminations of gaslights and Chinese lanterns, then listened to hours of oratory, Michael E. McGerr writes:

> As the flag-raising in the sixth ward made clear, elections in the mid-nineteenth century required the visible endorsement of the people. Politics in the American colonies and the early republic mainly took place among elites. To be sure, most of the important political decisions of the nineteenth century occurred in private as well. But much of political life was necessarily acted out in the streets. However undemocratic the results, American politics from roughly the 'thirties to the 'nineties demanded the legitimacy conferred by all classes of people through parades and rallies and huge turnouts.[25]

Tilden, however, was impatient with all of this folkish brouhaha, unassisted as it was by a newer and more precise science of politics. He was himself a numbers-obsessed evangelist for the social sciences now being taught in the new universities. As governor, he was an early speaker before the American Social Science Association, founded in 1865, proclaiming his enthusiastic agreement with their idea that a sufficiently exact knowledge of social affairs, rooted in quantitative studies, could yield a knowledge of the laws governing human society.

Tilden was fascinated, too, not only by statistics, but by the advantages organization and orderly administration could bring to public affairs—a phenomenon he had witnessed abundantly in the railroad world. Much more powerful than torchlight parades, he believed, would be the application of careful, disciplined, analytical methods which, for the first time, would make use of informal pre-election polls of voters to locate those precincts most undecided and responsive to persuasion.

A firm believer in the power of mass adult education methods, in New York elections he hired teams of writers, put them on several floors of a downtown New York City building, and set them to turning out floods of circular letters and pamphlets, all of which would be directed to key electoral districts. "Party workers," writes McGerr, "visited each wavering voter and left behind pamphlets, copies of his speeches, and issues of Democratic newspapers. [To the mystification of traditional politicos,] The technique worked. . . ."[26]

In 1876, the Democrats nominated for the presidency their elder from the Age of Jackson, their sorcerer, Samuel Tilden. In these depression years a whirlwind of economic nostrums to revive the national economy were in the air. Among them, the most spectacular was the crusade of the Greenback party. Looking at the more than $400 million in wartime-issued national greenbacks still at loose in the economy without backing in gold, the Greenbackers insisted, in an argument notable for its sophistication and modern aura, that the greenbacks should not only be retained (thus avoiding a return to the war-suspended gold standard) but increased in volume to restimulate the economy. A permanently inflationist national currency policy, they insisted, would insure a steadily rising level of industrialization by keeping interest rates low and making capital available to entrepreneurs.[27]

Tilden, however, had been, since Jackson's time, a leading American advocate of "sound money" and the international gold standard, a position derived from the work of such British Liberal economists as John Stuart Mill. He believed that only the stable prices of the international gold standard, linked to the British pound with its unchanging gold content, could protect workers and consumers in general from exploitation by inflationist speculators, who through their manipulations of paper currency could profit alike from the booms and busts that struck the poor so cruelly. Only sound money, indeed, could induce a revival, Tilden said, of the confidence within the business community that was necessary to bring about an end to the depression.[28] (In 1879, "specie resumption" put the country back on the gold standard.)

To argue the sound money thesis and flood the country with his anticorruption ideas, at the center of his campaign he placed a "Literary Bureau" in New York City where forty writers, editors, and clerks wrote, printed, and mailed out 27 *million* circular letters, leaflets, pamphlets, and other campaign documents. It was the first national "campaign of education" mounted in American politics which aimed at shaping public opinion directly through the party press.

State organizations struggled to follow the instructions in a *Campaign Textbook* of over 700 pages worked up by Tilden's staff. Many scoffed; torchlight parades still marched through America's streets; but in the presidential election of 1876, Tilden won a popular majority. The famous corrupted electoral college count in the House of Representatives then put Republican Rutherford B. Hayes in the White House. But Tilden was widely admired for having run, nonetheless, "the best race by a Democratic presidential candidate in a generation . . . [creating] an example that party leaders would find increasingly compelling. In later years, Tilden's name and methods seemed to awe . . . politicians." Around his name and tradition gathered a group of leading Democrats who, as they "grew powerful in the 'eighties and early 'nineties . . . would convert the Democratic party to educational politics."[29]

## POLITICAL ECONOMY TAKES CENTER STAGE AGAIN

In the 1880s, North-South oratorical cannonading, feeding on the hatreds fostered by the Civil War, finally subsided into a secondary place at the national level of American politics. "[S]omehow or other," observed a contemporary Democratic academic from Columbia University, Harry Thurston Peck, the issue "had, in sporting parlance, gone stale. The new generation which had grown up since the war cared little for these things, and the older generation had grown weary of them."[30] In its place, the country began taking alarmed notice of the erratic and, for thousands of American workers thrown regularly out of work, dangerous state of its economy. During thirteen of the twenty-seven years from 1873 to 1900, the United States was, in fact, in either a serious recession or a severe depression. Industrial warfare, expressed in thousands of strikes annually, raged and flared across the nation.[31]

The crucial question was: how could the country's economic and therefore social health be restored? The farmers of the Great Plains and the South, who suffered from heavy debts and catastrophically slumping international grain and cotton prices, revived the inflationist appeal of the now-defunct Greenback party. They demanded that the money supply be increased by re-monetizing silver, an inflationist step which they believed would turn commodity prices upward again (by itself, currency inflation does tend to have that effect). Their agitations culminated in the spectacular agrarian tumult of the late 1880s and the Populist crusade for free silver in the early 1890s.[32]

Urban consumers, however, especially immigrant laborers, recoiled from the inflationist message coming in from the farming countryside, for they certainly did not want higher food and fiber prices. And the national Democratic party, strong in the immigrant working-class wards in the northeastern and midwestern cities, continued to cling with absolute conviction to the hallowed belief, received through Tilden in undiluted form from the Age of Jackson, that "sound money" was vitally necessary to protect the consumer from inflation. When inflationist economics finally captured the party, it had to be from an entirely different Democratic world, that of the rural High Plains wheat farmers and the cotton farmers of the South, in an evangel trumpeted from the mid-1890s on by William Jennings Bryan.[33]

## THE GREAT GILDED AGE BATTLE OVER THE PROTECTIVE TARIFF

In the populous midwestern and northeastern states where national electoral victories were won or lost, politicians and voters alike focused in the 1880s not only on the currency question but on that fascinating, almost infinitely complex topic that millions of people believed held, one way or another, the answer to the nation's problems: *tariff* policy. The immediate occasion for the eruption of the tariff debate into high prominence was the election to the presidency, in 1884, of Grover Cleveland, governor of New York state and a Tilden protege. He arrived in the White House primarily as a crusader against political corruption and for sound money, in the Tilden mold. In his two presidencies the civil service idea, which went far to replace the corruption of party patronage, slowly became a reality in the federal government.

Cleveland wanted most of all to cleanse of corruption's influence not simply government, but America's *economic* system. "Selfish" and "sordid" were the key words in his political language, popping up in his speeches, writings, and private correspondence again and again to express his disdain for the unscrupulous wealthy and what they and their corrupt partners, the machine politicians, were in their mutual scheming doing to the nation. Alarmed at the plundering of the West by huge fraudulent land claims made by cattle kings, land syndicates, railroad companies, and lumber barons, Cleveland publicly condemned the "colossal greed" of these Americans and forced them to return more than eighty million acres.[34]

Before long, too, Cleveland was yielding to the urgings of his advisers to turn his presidency four-square toward a frontal attack on the protective tariff, a battle which, in his mind, reenacted the struggle against predatory interests that Andrew Jackson had undertaken in his historic war against the United States Bank half a century before. When Cleveland took up his great cause, the United States was fully launched, finally, on a long and angry national debate over whether its political economy should be nationalist or internationalist in its fundamental nature.[35]

For decades, both Henry Clay, as head of the pre-Civil War Whig party, and Henry C. Carey, chief economic theorist for both the Whigs and their successors the Republicans, had been teaching Whig-Republicans to think in nationalist terms. Protective tariffs, they said, by closing out foreign goods (primarily British), would create industries and jobs, from which all manner of good things would flow: in place of simple agrarianism, a complex, many-faceted, and much stronger economy—which in its growing cities would offer many opportunities for the gifted entrepreneur and jobs for the poor, which finally would solve the problem of poverty, and the class warfare it seemed endlessly to stimulate.[36]

At bottom, Republicans were proud—they would say uniquely patriotic—nationalists, who never tired of hurling the epithet "internationalist" at the low-tariff Democrats. The supreme task of government, they would say, is to look after America's welfare, not that of the world at large. Support for the tariff, they maintained, meant working for national economic independence, for outright self-sufficiency. As an increasingly prominent Ohio Republican, Congressman William McKinley, said, in words taken from two addresses in 1878 and 1885:

> We want to be independent in that broad and comprehensive sense, strong within ourselves, self-supporting and self-sustaining in all things. . . . We ought to take care of our own Nation and her industries first. . . . If I were not a Republican for any other reason . . . I would be [one] . . . because Republican protection believes in America as against the world. (great applause)[37]

Republicans were unrepentant, indeed exultant, disciples of the tariff. As a producer-oriented party, they scorned the cry for lower prices. Cheap prices, Republicans Benjamin Harrison and William McKinley said over and over again in one way or another, inevitably made for a poorer, meaner, cheaper society. They pointed as proof to the degraded lives of the working classes in Europe and Asia, where cheap goods were standard.[38]

## DEMOCRATS AND THE TARIFF

From the late 1860s into the 1880s, a sharply diverging definition of the tariff issue had been coming from one of the era's most popular and widely influential economists, David A. Wells. The growing impact of improved technology in America, Wells said, meant that farmers and industrialists were both producing so much that their output would always be in surplus; that is, more than the American market could absorb. The answer? *Enhanced foreign trade*. That is, rearranging national policies so that they encouraged, rather than hampered, foreign sales of those surplus goods.

This, Wells said, could not happen so long as America had high protective tariffs, for the barrier they provided kept foreigners from earning American dollars by selling in the United States market, and thus prevented them from buying American goods. Reducing the tariff would also reduce the costs United States manufacturers had to bear by allowing the import of *cheap raw materials* (to Wells, an extremely crucial point), which at the time were made costly by tariffs on such commodities as foreign wool and pig iron. This, in turn, would solve the great problem Republicans were saying was insurmountable at that time, and indeed was making it impossible for Americans to win foreign markets: it would allow American producers to lower prices for their goods in world commerce and enable them to compete successfully.

The Democrats quickly adopted Wells as their economist and his ideas as their own. From his post as adviser to Grover Cleveland, his concepts found their way directly into the President's tariff messages. Of course, Democrats had traditionally looked on high tariffs as unfair privilege objectified, since such tariffs allowed the prices of American-made goods to be artificially higher than would otherwise be the case if American products were forced to compete evenly with foreign-made goods. To twist the knife, Democrats charged—with embarrassingly abundant evidence—that the tariffs represented an advantage gained by corrupt buying of legislators' votes.[39]

Another group of advisers to Cleveland was also important in swinging him toward launching what would certainly be a long and bitter struggle over the tariff. They were the "Mugwumps" of political history, an offshoot of the Republican party. A highly visible stratum of Harvard-centered northeastern professionals, academics, attorneys, community leaders, writers, and journalists, the Mugwumps looked for their models in ideas and public style across the Atlantic to William Gladstone and the British Liberals, and to their hallowed triumph in swinging Britain to free trade. Fervent supporters of the British concept of an educated and non-partisan civil service to bring efficiency and purity into government, they labored endlessly in its cause. Mugwumps, too, were wary of the established, mainstream Republican party, for to them it was too intimately interwoven with the corrupt business classes. Holding off from it, they had been calling themselves "Independent Republicans" since the 1870s.[40]

In 1884, when the Republicans had nominated James G. Blaine to oppose Cleveland, the Mugwumps, in a spectacular and publicly announced demarche, had recoiled in distaste and headed across the line to become enthusiastic Cleveland supporters. Mugwumps had long distrusted the incontestably brilliant Blaine for his close friendships with the wealthy, his mysterious sources of money, his scoffing at the "corruption" cry and opposition to civil service, and his passionate advocacy of the protective tariff. To the Mugwumps, Blaine had become, indeed, the national symbol of Republican party sycophancy to the business community. In the early years of Cleveland's first presidency, the Mugwumps urged him by every possible means to think of the protective tariff as the nation's transcendent issue.[41]

Since the nation's beginnings, the Democrats and their predecessors, the Jeffersonian Republicans, had insisted that the very concept of an active government intervening in the economy—by means of government aids to business enterprise in many forms—was the source, the ever-flowing bedrock fountain, of all political corruption in American life. It was the precise means, they said, by which the wealthy victimized society: buying favors from the government, and making a mockery of democracy by putting its institutions in their pocket.

The reality of the tariff as a daily fact in American public life, indeed, was that, year in and year out, it produced a kind of policy chaos in Washington, together with ripe, rampant corruption. Congressmen had a continuous field day, adding more and more taxes on foreign goods as manufacturers in their districts persuaded them to do, by means both honest and dishonest. The "tariff schedule" became longer and longer and more complicated, confused, and illogical. It had utterly no relation to the daily flow of commerce, the rise and fall of prices internationally, or the constantly shifting level of costs. Any notion that in some sensible, justifiable way it equalized costs of production in the United States and abroad, as Republicans said it did, was an absurdity. Furthermore, it was ratcheted higher and higher, and with each ratcheting upward, it stayed there, never to come down.

## CLEVELAND'S CRUSADE FOR ECONOMIC JUSTICE

Ever more frequently, the country heard Cleveland saying that the ultimate answer to America's unhappy economics and violent social conflict lay in drastically lowering the protective tariff. It simply created, he said, monopoly, high prices for consumers, and social exploitation by the wealthy. Taxes on imports "increase without corresponding benefit to the people at large the vast accumulations [of wealth] of a few among our citizens, whose fortunes . . . are not the natural growth of a steady, plain, and industrious republic." Through 1886, Cleveland fought hard, in vain, to get a tariff reform bill through Congress.

For his pains, he succeeded principally in setting off a national hysteria of Anglophobia, with the Republicans continually accusing him and the Democracy of being British agents aiming to crush American industry, of selling out to British gold, of being essentially traitors to America.[42] In fact, as Republican America had launched its massive Gilded Age drive toward industrialization, the country's most committed and dangerous enemy in its eyes lay in Great Britain. For the greatest barrier to be surmounted, they said, lay in the ruinous competition that Britain's far more mature factories, and its cheaper labor costs, could mount.

There were complicated ironies here. The heartland of Republican America lay in New England, among the Yankees, who for ethnic reasons traditionally had looked eastward across the Atlantic in great admiration of the English. And yet New England was the heartland, too, of American industrialism. Therefore, jealousy and admiration, frustration and emulation, resentment and cultural Anglophilia all merged together for Republican America, as it looked at Britain, in a curiously ambivalent and contradictory amalgam.

Yet the enmity was firm and implacable. People like Henry Carey and his disciples had been saying for many years that, whatever the means, the British were still using Americans as colonials, as they were currently using the people of India and Ireland. The English idea of world free trade—that is, no one having tariffs—simply aimed at flooding everyone else's domestic markets with English goods, Careyites said, and preventing the rise of domestic industries in America. England, in short, as James G. Blaine put it, wanted to keep everyone else down. As Secretary of State, he would directly defy British commercial supremacy. The British, he believed, "thwarted and limited American aspirations for prestige at every turn; and, even more important, blocked the expansion of America's economic and political power."[43]

Anyone who called for lower American tariffs was condemned as loyal to Great Britain, not the United States of America. William D. "Pig-Iron" Kelley, a staunch campaigner for tariff protection of Pennsylvania's steel mills, set the pattern as early as 1868 by arguing that David Wells's low-tariff principles were in the interest of the British, and therefore treasonous. Thereafter, it was a common reflex for Republican orators to label anti-tariff Democrats as bribed agents of the British. The country was flooded with anti-British protectionist pamphlets in every election campaign.[44]

William McKinley was quite open in his accusations: "There is a lobby here from the other side," he said during a House debate on the tariff in 1883, "wanting to get legislation from the Democratic side of this House to enhance English manufacturing, enrich the coffers of English lords, destroy American industries, and degrade American labor." The Democratic party, he said in the same venue a year later, "stands for a doctrine which will . . . open up the market of this great Nation to the products of English skills, English labor, and English capital."[45] It is in alliance, he alleged, with the manufacturers and the traders of England, who want the American market.

> It is the pro-British party. . . . Do you know of any reason in the world why Americans should not make everything that Americans need? [Then] every man would . . . be employed . . . and employed at a profitable remuneration. Why, everybody is benefitted by protection [he went on], even the people who do not believe in it. . . .[46]

Cleveland was peculiarly vulnerable to the charge of pro-British disloyalty. He and his Secretary of State, the elegant and cosmopolitan Southerner, Thomas Bayard, were unusually notable for their convinced internationalism in America's foreign policy, which they pursued in the style of William Gladstone's British Liberals. Cleveland and Bayard consciously avoided, Edward Crapol writes, any display of anti-British bombast or jingoism.

> Both men were . . . prone to [stress a common] . . . Anglo-Saxon destiny . . . as a joint venture to be realized with the aid and cooperation, if not the lead, of Great Britain. This was especially true of Bayard, an unabashed Anglophile. . . . Try as they [might] . . . Bayard and Cleveland could not simply cut off Anglophobia, and it continued to haunt them throughout the administration.[46]

Campaign posters in the 1888 campaign regularly depicted Cleveland under the British flag, with the American flag flying over Harrison. "Republican campaign slogans," Crapol notes, "included 'Cleveland runs well in England,' and the ever-popular 'America for Americans—No Free Trade.'"[47] With Republican presidential candidate Benjamin Harrison and his mentor James G. Blaine leading the way on thc campaign trail in 1888, the Republicans unmercifully and enthusiastically twisted the lion's tail.

As Cleveland ruminated his failure to get the tariff lowered in the 1886 Congress, he settled on a bold step to make the tariff the *single* focus of national attention, and of his presidency: in an unprecedented step which caused a sensation, he devoted his entire annual address to Congress in 1887 to a dramatic cannonade against the protective tariff. In a typical gesture, the Wisconsin Democrats, delighted with their champion's words, distributed 85,000 copies of Cleveland's tariff message in English, German, Polish, Czech, Norwegian, and Swedish throughout that state during the presidential election campaign of 1888 (in addition, in this Tildenite "campaign of education," to a million other documents).[48] Cleveland went on to win a popular majority, though he lost the election to Benjamin Harrison by being counted out in the electoral college.

Grover Cleveland's extraordinary Fourth Annual Message, issued in late 1888 as he was winding up his first term as president and reflecting on his continued failure on the tariff, was as heated a blast against greedy corporate interests as Americans had ever, or would ever, hear from any of their presidents. In the America of the 1880s, he said, classes were rapidly forming, "one comprising the very rich and powerful while in another are found the toiling poor." Trusts, combinations, and monopolies ruled the land, while the citizen, Cleveland said in what became a deathless passage, "is struggling far in the rear or is trampled to death beneath an iron heel."[49]

In 1890, the Republicans in Congress jacked the protective tariff even higher in the McKinley Tariff of that year, which excluded almost entirely from the American market whole categories of British-made goods. Then at the state level, where as we have seen, cultural warfare rocketed along year after year in the Gilded Age, Republicans succeeded in 1890 in infuriating the Germans of the Midwest, whom they had been trying to win over, with some success, by playing on their anti-Catholicism. Giving in to their passion to expunge "foreign" languages and make everyone speak English, Republicans in the state of Wisconsin enacted the Bennett Law, which decreed that to meet a new legal requirement of school attendance, children would have to go to an institution where English was the language of instruction.

> Never in its history did the GOP labor under such burdens as the 1890 campaign imposed. In nearly every northern state the Germans and Irish looked upon the Republicans as the sponsors of prohibition. In Wisconsin and Illinois, especially, the compulsory education issue [i.e., the Bennett Law] incited the immigrant groups. Every consumer lamented the higher prices sparked by the McKinley Tariff. . . . The economic resented the billion-dollar spending extravaganza [in support of Civil War pensions and public works] the GOP had conducted in Congress—and everywhere men looked in vain for the industrial utopia Harrison had promised them from his front porch.[50]

Cleveland ran a third time for the presidency in 1892, and with his campaign thus powerfully fueled by both cultural and economic forces, he was able to return to the White House in an astonishing national victory which, for the first time since the 1850s, gave the Democrats control of both houses of Congress as well as the executive branch. (Thus, he became the only president save Franklin Roosevelt to win three consecutive popular vote majorities in a presidential election.)

In the fashion of so many other presidents, however, Cleveland was destined to have a deeply frustrating second term. Soon after his administration began, a stunning economic earthquake, the depression of 1893, struck the country with a force never seen before. With his Presbyterian's commitment to "hallowed truths" and "principles," Cleveland held firm, as a depression president, to his inherited Jeffersonian belief in laissez faire and sound money. Thus, he was able to do nothing effective about the economy, and his party turned angrily against him, hiving off in 1896 to swarm behind William Jennings Bryan and free silver.

## THE FOURTH PARTY SYSTEM INAUGURATED

The Republicans had always preached active government intervention in the economy, by means of aids to business enterprise, and the financing of public works. Thus, as William McKinley said over and over again in his presidential campaign in 1896, they were the party of jobs (though of course he had nothing like a New Deal in mind). In the second great crossing-over in American political history, in the congressional election of 1894 and later in the presidential balloting in 1896, urban ethnic groups long in Democratic ranks, such as the Germans and the Italians, switched to the Republican side—save for the Irish Catholics, whose anti-Republican feelings were in their bones. Essentially, Democratic America shrank drastically in the northeastern states; for many years, its political base would be almost entirely in the South.

During the next forty years of the Fourth Party System (1894-1932), Washington and most of the states would be under overwhelmingly Republican control, save for the eight years of the Wilson presidency. Everywhere outside of the South Democratic America slid into what seemed to be a permanent minority status. And as it turned out, the Republicans would win a complete victory on the tariff issue. During his second term, Cleveland's struggles to lower the tariff had been almost entirely in vain. Not only did Congress, in the succeeding administration of President McKinley eliminate such modifications as Cleveland finally got in place, at enormous political cost. They raised, in the Dingley Tariff of 1897, the protective barrier to its highest levels: to an average of 52 percent. The Republicans were finally America's majority party, and economic nationalism was completely triumphant.

## NOTES

1. See Appendix, Table 1, "Information on the Members of the Supreme Court," in Albert P. Blaustein and Roy M. Mersky, *The First One Hundred Justices: Statistical Studies on the Supreme Court of the United States* (Hamden, Conn.: Ardon Books, 1978), 104-109.

2. For the Democratic voting proportion, see Joel A. Silbey, *A Respectable Minority: The Democratic Party in the Civil War Era, 1860-1868* (New York: Norton, 1977), 156-59, 219, 226. For the period on into the 1890s, during which voting loyalties were extraordinarily high, see Joel A. Silbey, *The American Political Nation 1838-1893* (Stanford: Stanford University Press, 1991), 153, citing studies by Paul Kleppner.

3. Leonard P. Curry, *Blueprint for Modern America; Non-Military Legislation of the First Civil War Congress* (Lexington: University of Kentucky Press, 1969), 244-249.

4. On Reconstruction, an immense subject which has created a similarly outsize historical literature, Eric Foner's recent prize-winning study is now the best source. Eric Foner, *Reconstruction: America's Unfinished Revolution 1863-1877* (New York: Harper & Row, 1988).

5. Paul Kleppner, *The Third Electoral System, 1853-1892: Parties, Voters, and Political Cultures* (Chapel Hill: University of North Carolina Press, 1979), 22-23, 29, 37. Other sources, such as Carl N. Degler, *The Other South: Southern Dissenters in the Nineteenth Century* (New York: Harper & Row, 1974), and J. Morgan Kousser, *The Shaping of Southern Politics : Suffrage Restriction and the Establishment of the One-Party South, 1880-1910* (New Haven: Yale University Press, 1974), tell us that the Republicans, though a minority in the South after Reconstruction ended, continued to attract hundreds of thousands of votes until well into the twentieth century; that the "Solid South" was not monolithic, though its role in Washington had that quality. The reader may wish to refer to the 1892 map in the Appendix.

6. Paul Kleppner, *The Evolution of American Electoral Systems* (Westport, Conn.: Greenwood Press, 1981), 131-132. For the mood of the Lost Cause, which suffused the Southern mind for half a century after the Civil War, see Thomas L. Connelly and Barbara L. Bellows, *God and General Longstreet: The Lost Cause and the Southern Mind* (Baton Rouge: Louisiana State University Press, 1982).

7. Paul H. Buck, *The Road to Reunion 1865-1900* (Boston: Little, Brown, 1937).

8. See Foner, *Reconstruction*, 425-44, on passage of the Ku Klux Klan Act. For a Republican reply to Democratic criticism, see Blaine's speech, "The Democratic Party and the Constitutional Amendments," in James G. Blaine, *Political Discussions: Legislative, Diplomatic, and Popular* (Norwich, Conn.: The Henry Bill Publishing Company, 1887), 138-149.

9. C. Vann Woodward, *Origins of the New South 1877-1913* (Baton Rouge: Louisiana State University Press, 1951), 456.

10. Kleppner, *The Third Electoral System*, 22-58, 150.

11. Robert Henry Billigmeier, *Americans from Germany: A Study in Cultural Diversity* (Belmont, Calif.: Wadsworth, 1974), 95-104, and passim; *Ethnic Voters*

*and the Election of Lincoln,* ed. Frederick C. Luebke (Lincoln: University of Nebraska Press, 1971); Kleppner, *The Third Electoral System*, 153-58, and *Kleppner, The Cross of Culture: A Social Analysis of Midwestern Politics 1850-1900*, (New York: Free Press, 1970) 49-50, 82, 95-100, 109-111; and Richard Jensen, *The Winning of the Midwest: Social and Political Conflict, 1888-1896* (Chicago & London: University of Chicago Press, 1971), 67, 82-84, 165, 192-194, 195-199.

12. "The emotional dimension of urbanism," writes Richard Jensen, "was metrophobia, the rural and small town fear of the great metropolis." Jensen *The Winning of the Midwest*, 179. In chap. 7, he discusses Republican fear and hatred of cities at length.

13. Ibid., 206.

14. Ibid., 219.

15. Jensen, *The Winning of the Midwest*, 62-63, 65-67. I have discussed at length the religiosity of American and British life and political culture in the nineteenth century in Robert Kelley, *The Transatlantic Persuasion: The Liberal-Democratic Mind in the Age of Gladstone* (New York: Knopf, 1969), 33, 48-53, 139, 255, 267-268, 307-317, 404-405; and throughout in, Robert Kelley, *The Cultural Pattern in American Politics: The First Century* (New York: Knopf, 1979).

16. Jensen, *Winning of the Midwest*, 58-59.

17. Kleppner, *The Third Electoral System*, 328. Kleppner observes in the associated footnote (54) to this passage: "Throughout the nineteenth century Republican spokesmen frequently made such claims, and the Democrats just as frequently ridiculed them for doing so."

18. On the Quakers, see Kleppner, *The Cross of Culture,* 61-66; on Scandinavians, see ibid., 51-3, and Kleppner, *The Third Electoral System*, 158-163, as well as Jensen, *The Winning of the Midwest*, 80-81.

19. *Representative Democracy: Public Policy and Midwestern Legislatures in the Late Nineteenth Century* (Cambridge: Harvard University Press, 1980), 6.

20. Kleppner, *The Cross of Culture*, 95-111.

21. For the foregoing, see Martin E. Marty, *A Righteous Empire: The Protestant Experience in America* (Chicago: University of Chicago Press, 1970), and Robert T. Handy, *A Christian America: Protestant Hopes and Historical Realities* (New York: Oxford University Press, 1971). On the belief that the United States was legally and constitutionally a Christian country, which meant excluding Jews from the franchise and office-holding, see the long history of this effort (successful for lengthy periods) in Morton Borden, *Jews, Turks, & Infidels* (Chapel Hill: University of North Carolina Press, 1984).

22. John Higham, *Strangers in the Land: Patterns of American Nativism 1860-1925* (Westport Conn.: Greenwood Press, 1981). British immigrants shared the Republicans' distaste for the Irish Catholics. On their voting Whig-Republican since the Age of Jackson, see Lee Benson, *The Concept of Jacksonian Democracy: New York as a Test Case* (Princeton: Princeton University Press, 1961), 324ff; Kleppner, *The Cross of Culture*, 53-54, and ibid., *The Third Electoral System*, 163-166; and Rowland Tappan Berthoff, *British Immigrants in Industrial America 1790-1950* (Cambridge: Harvard University Press, 1953), 186-196, 202-207.

23. Discussed extensively through Jensen, *The Winning of the Midwest.*

24. Chap. 7, in Kelley, *The Transatlantic Persuasion*, "Samuel Tilden: The

Democrat as Social Scientist," explores his life, mind, and career. The quotation is from p. 279. See also Alexander B. Callow, Jr., *The Tweed Ring* (New York: Oxford University Press, 1966).

25. Michael E. McGerr, *The Decline of Popular Politics: The American North, 1865-1928* (New York & Oxford: Oxford University Press, 1986), 5.

26. Ibid., 71.

27. Irwin Unger, *The Greenback Era: A Social and Political History of American Finance, 1865-1879* (Princeton: Princeton University Press, 1964).

28. See chap. 7, "Samuel Tilden: The Democrat as Social Scientist," passim, in Kelley, *The Transatlantic Persuasion.*

29. Ibid., 71-75.

30. Harry Thurston Peck, *Twenty Years of the Republic 1885-1905* (New York: Dodd, Mead, 1913), 33, his tart, brilliant classic.

31. W. Elliot Brownlee, *Dynamics of Ascent: A History of the American Economy* 2d ed. (New York: Knopf, 1979), 267-362.

32. Lawrence Goodwyn, *Democratic Promise: The Populist Movement in America* (New York: Oxford University Press, 1976).

33. The currency question in the Gilded Age, which ultimately became so powerfully intrusive, has been discussed in a large historical literature. In addition to the work of Irwin Unger, *The Greenback Era*, and my own chapters on Samuel Tilden and Grover Cleveland in *The Transatlantic Persuasion*, consult Walter Nugent, *Money and American Society, 1867-1880* (New York: Free Press, 1968).

34. On Cleveland in general, consult, Richard E. Welch, Jr., *The Presidencies of Grover Cleveland* (Lawrence: University Press of Kansas, 1988); and chap. 8, "Grover Cleveland: The Democrat as Social Moralist," in Kelley, *The Transatlantic Persuasion*, 293-350.

35. For general discussions of the Gilded Age tariff debate, see Edward P. Crapol, *America for Americans: Economic Nationalism and Anglophobia in the Late Nineteenth Century* (Westport, Conn., and London: Greenwood Press, 1973); Tom E. Terrill, *The Tariff, Politics, and American Foreign Policy 1874-1901* (Westport, Conn.: Greenwood Press, 1973); W. Walter Poulshock, *The Two Parties and the Tariff in the 1880s* (Syracuse, N.Y., 1965); and Jensen, *The Winning of the Midwest*, 18-20.

36. Irwin Unger, in his *The Greenback Era*, discusses Carey and his ideas extensively. See also Arnold W. Green, *Henry Charles Carey, Nineteenth Century Sociologist* (Philadelphia: University of Pennsylvania Press, 1951), and George Winston Smith, *Henry C. Carey and American Sectional Conflict* (Albuquerque: University of New Mexico Press, 1951).

37. See speeches on, "Wool Tariff Bill," April 15, 1878, House of Representatives, and "What Protection Means to Virginia," Petersburg, Virginia, October 29, 1885, in William McKinley, *Speeches and Addresses: From His Election to Congress to the Present Time* (New York, 1893), 19, 189-190.

38. Jensen, *The Winning of the Midwest*, 19. "Things, however, are sometimes the dearest, when nominally they are the cheapest," McKinley said in 1888 in a typical utterance. "The selling price of an article is not the only measure; the ability to buy, the coin with which to purchase, is an important and essential

element." See speech on "Free Raw Materials," Home Market Club, Boston, Mass., Feb. 9, 1888, McKinley, *Speeches and Addresses*, 254.

39. Crapol, *America for Americans*, 24-33.

40. Gerald W. McFarland, *Mugwumps, Morals and Politics, 1884-1920* (Amherst: University of Massachusetts, 1975).

41. David S. Muzzey, *James G. Blaine* (New York: Dodd, Mead, 1943), passim.

42. Crapol, *America for Americans*, esp. 20-21.

43. Ibid., 21-22, 67-70.

44. Ibid., 24-30.

45. See speech on "The Tariff of 1883," House of Representatives, January 27, 1882, and speech on, "The Morrison Tariff Bill," House of Representatives, April 30, 1884, in McKinly, *Speeches and Addresses*, 111-112, 149.

46. Ibid., 61-63; William McKinley, "The Wood Tariff Bill," House of Representatives, April 15, 1878, in William McKinley, *Speeches and Addresses*, 2-19; ibid., and "What Protection Means to Virginia," campaign speech, Petersburg, Virginia, October 29, 1885, 182-195.

47. Crapol, *America for Americans*, 144-147.

48. Ibid., 171.

49. Jensen, *The Winning of the Midwest*, 4. For the "educational" campaigns in these years, see chap. 3, "Partisanship Redefined" and chap. 4, "Educational Politics," in McGerr, *The Decline of Popular Politics*, 42-106.

50. Fourth Annual Message, Dec. 3, 1888, Richardson *Papers of the Presidents*, 7:5358-5385. In the House McKinley said in 1882: "Much idle talk is indulged in about manufacturing monopolies in the United States, and everything is called a monopoly that prospers; everybody who gets ahead in the world is, in the minds of some people, a monopolist. We have few, if any, manufacturing monopolies in the United States to-day. They can not long exist with an unrestricted home competition such as we have." See speech on, "The Tariff Commission," House of Representatives, April 6, 1882, in McKinley, *Speeches & Addresses*, 96-97.

51. Jensen, *The Winning of the Midwest*, 141. He provides detailed discussion of the Bennett Law controversy.

PART THREE

# Democrats in a Republican Age

## 1890s–1930s

Chapter 8

# The Democratic Party in the Era of William Jennings Bryan

*Robert W. Cherny*

When Woodrow Wilson spoke to the opening session of the 63rd Congress in 1913, it marked the first time since 1895 that Democrats had held both the presidency and majorities in both houses of Congress. They lost four consecutive presidential elections beginning in 1896, and faced Republican majorities in the Senate from 1895 until 1913 and in the House from 1895 until 1911. From 1896 to 1912, as Democrats wandered through the political wilderness, they looked consistently for leadership to William Jennings Bryan, who came to hold the dubious distinction of being the only Democratic presidential nominee to lose three times. Though Bryan failed to win the presidency, the period of his Democratic party leadership witnessed one of the most significant transformations in the party's history. During those years, Democrats abandoned their longstanding commitment to laissez faire and minimal government and endorsed instead a positive role for government in the economy in the form of regulation, protective legislation, and a progressive tax structure. An understanding of Bryan, the Democratic party he led, and its transformation under his leadership must look first at the important political changes in the 1890s and then at Bryan's unique role as party leader.

## THE POLITICAL REALIGNMENT OF THE 1890s

Political scientists and historians describe the years from 1890 to 1896 as a period of critical realignment, comparable to those of 1828-1836, 1854-1860, and 1930-1934.[1] The 1890s saw not only important changes in party loyalties among voters, but also the beginning of a far-reaching transformation of the nature of parties and politics. The realignment involved five historical occurrences. First, during 1890 to 1892, despite a strong record of accomplishment in the 51st Congress, voters rejected the Republicans. Second and simultaneously, a new party emerged—the Populist party—which established a regional political base by challenging important elements in the political agendas of both major parties. Third, the elections of 1892 gave Grover Cleveland the presidency and produced Democratic majorities in both houses of Congress, but Cleveland and the party botched their opportunity to cement voter loyalties. Instead, the Democrats splintered, and party leadership passed to William Jennings Bryan. Fourth, the presidential election of 1896 marked the establishment of a national Republican majority that was to dominate politics for a generation. Finally, throughout the 1890s and into the early twentieth century, Democrats faced fundamental changes in the very nature of political parties, campaigns, and politics.

**The 51st Congress.** With Benjamin Harrison in the White House and Republican majorities in both houses of Congress, the 51st Congress (1889 to 1891) gave Republicans their first real opportunity to make policy since the Grant administration fifteen years earlier.[2] The House took the lead on tariff revision and reduction of the surplus, both issues pushed to the fore of politics by Grover Cleveland in 1887 and 1888.[3] Led by William McKinley, the House Ways and Means Committee tried to cut tariff income (and reduce the federal surplus) without removing protection from American manufacturing, partly by raising rates on some items to prohibitive levels.[4] At the same time, Republicans sought to reduce the federal surplus through increased spending, including large appropriations for a modern navy and expanded pension eligibility for Union veterans. The House also approved a federal elections bill, sponsored by Representative Henry Cabot Lodge of Massachusetts, and labeled the "Force Bill" by Democrats. The bill authorized federal supervision over congressional elections to prevent fraud, violence, or disfranchisement. All understood that southern Democrats formed its chief target.

The Senate, meanwhile, approved two measures named for Republican Senator John Sherman of Ohio: the Sherman Antitrust Act and the Sherman Silver Purchase Act. Passed with broad bipartisan support, the Antitrust Act was a response to widespread concern about the "trusts" and "monopolies" that had emerged during the 1880s. Republicans passed the Sherman Silver Purchase Act to assuage the concerns of western farmers over falling farm prices. The Senate then turned its attention to the House-passed legislation on tariffs and elections. Concluding that a Democratic filibuster against the Lodge bill was likely to prevent passage of the McKinley Tariff, Senate Republicans delayed the elections bill until a later session so that Democrats would not block the tariff. The elections bill, however, was never revived.[5]

In 303 days, Congress approved a record number of new laws, enacting nearly the entire Republican platform from 1888. Although addressing a wide range of issues, the new legislation failed to resolve them and, instead, supplied fuel for the fires of political realignment that burned through much of the 1890s.

**The Populist Party.** While the 51st Congress held forth in Washington through the hot summer of 1890, arguing over silver, the tariff, antitrust legislation, and the Lodge bill, a different political drama unfolded in the nation's heartland. Hard pressed by debt and plagued by low prices for their crops, members of the Farmers' Alliance in Kansas, Nebraska, the Dakotas, Minnesota, and surrounding states proclaimed a new party and nominated their own candidates for office. They soon took the name People's party, or Populists.

The new Populist party emphasized three elements in their platforms, speeches, and other campaign materials: antimonopolism, government action on behalf of farmers and workers, and increased popular control of government.[6] Their antimonopolism came in part from their own experiences with railroads, grain buyers, and the companies that manufactured farm equipment and supplies; it derived as well from a long American tradition of opposition to concentrated economic power, a tradition that included Thomas Jefferson and Andrew Jackson. "From the same prolific womb of governmental injustice," proclaimed the 1892 Populist platform, "we breed the two great classes—tramps and millionaires."

Where the Jacksonian solution to the threat of monopoly was to limit government on the assumption that monopoly derived from governmental favoritism, the Populists called for government action to restrain monopoly on behalf of farmers and workers, including federal ownership of the means of transportation and communication. "The time has come," they proclaimed, "when the railroad companies will either own the people or the people must own the railroads." They also demanded an end to deflation (through the issuing of either paper or silver money, or both, just so there was more of it), the eight-hour day for workers, prohibition of private armies of armed guards for use against strikers, and a graduated income tax to replace the tariff.

Finally, Populists advocated changes to make government more responsive to the people, including expansion of the merit system for appointing government employees, direct election of United States senators, a one-term limit for the president, the secret ballot, and the initiative and referendum.[7] Many also favored female suffrage.

The Populists thus drew upon two major strains in American political thinking. One was a distrust of private monopoly that had provoked Andrew Jackson's attack on the Bank of the United States and that continued to fuel the Democrats' opposition to the tariff and to subsidies. The other was a Republican (indeed, Hamiltonian) willingness to use the powers of government to accomplish economic objectives. But where the Republicans had used the powers of government largely to stimulate economic growth, the Populists wanted to use government to control, even to own, the corporate behemoths that had evolved in their lifetimes. They added to this a commitment to increasing the direct role of the voter in political decision-making, an anti-party attitude derived in major part from distrust of the old political organizations.

The Populists also broke with previous political patterns in presenting themselves as the political spokesmen (and spokeswomen, since women were more active in the new party than they had been in either of the old parties) for an economic class. Their political rhetoric bristled with references to the "producing class": those who, by their labor, were deemed to produce value. "Wealth belongs to him who creates it," proclaimed their 1892 national platform. Where the older parties fed on regional loyalties generated by the Civil War, the Populists declared "the civil war is over" and "every passion and resentment which grew out of it must die with it." Where the Democrats flatly rejected prohibition and focused campaigns against it in some states, and the Republicans cautiously tiptoed around the issue, hoping not to offend prohibitionists, the Populists simply declared such questions "secondary to the great issues now pressing for solution." On the eastern rim of the Great Plains, where Methodist farmers were strongly Republican and Irish Catholic farmers overwhelmingly Democratic, both came together in support of the new party. In the South, where race defined partisan loyalties for a generation, southern Populists called for a biracial coalition of farmers and laborers.[8]

**Deflation and Silver.** The Populists' demands for free silver and the Republicans' passage of the Sherman Silver Purchase Act both reflected aspects of the silver issue, which had to do specifically with the legal status of the silver dollar and more generally and more importantly with the relation between the currency supply and price levels. The post-Civil War era saw a general deflation caused by a variety of factors, including increased productivity and federal policies. This especially affected debtors, and the post-Civil War expansion of agriculture had been accomplished largely on borrowed money. From 1865 onward, falling produce prices meant that farmers had to sell more and more each year just to make the same mortgage payments and buy necessities. Given the relation between supply and demand, the more they raised, the lower prices fell. One historian compared their plight to that of Alice in Wonderland: they had to run faster and faster just to stay in the same place.[9] Beginning in the 1870s, such farmers looked to an increase in the money supply—i.e., inflation—to counteract falling prices.

Some inflationists (the "Greenbackers") favored paper money, but others focused on silver as a less controversial solution. Before 1873, Congress had required the federal Mint to accept both gold and silver bullion in unlimited quantities and to make it into coins without charge; in other words, to provide free and unlimited coinage of gold and silver. Congress specified the weight of silver in a silver dollar and the weight of gold in a gold dollar; in the early nineteenth century, the congressionally established ratio of silver to gold ranged around 15 or 16 to one, silver to gold. The market for silver made it more profitable for owners of silver bullion to sell commercially, so the Mint coined no silver dollars after the early nineteenth century and none had circulated as currency since before the Civil War. In 1873, Congress deleted the silver dollar from the list of authorized coins—an action that reflected not just the reality, but also the policy priorities of some federal officials who wanted the United States on the gold standard, both in emulation of leading European nations and because they were convinced that only the gold standard would permit Americans to compete effectively in international markets.[10]

When the commercial price of silver fell in the mid-1870s, inflationists and silver-mining interests made common cause to remonetize silver. In 1878, Congress passed the Bland-Allison Act, a compromise that authorized limited coinage of silver dollars but satisfied neither inflationists nor proponents of the gold standard. Support for "free silver" (meaning the free and unlimited coinage of gold and silver) grew not just among farmers who wanted inflation but also among representatives—mostly Republicans—of western silver-mining states. The Sherman Silver Purchase Act of 1890, a Republican attempt at compromise, promised more silver dollars but still in limited quantities. Like the Bland-Allison Act, it satisfied neither side.[11]

**Republican Waterloo.** Issues in the elections of 1890 varied from region to region. In the western Midwest, the Populists stood at the center of the campaign, lambasting both the Republican and Democratic parties for ignoring the needs of the people. Until 1890, the Republicans had won most elections there; now western Democrats sometimes retired to the sidelines to watch the Populists and Republicans battle with each other. In the South, Democrats trained their efforts against the Lodge "force bill" as a threat to white supremacy, while members of the Farmers' Alliance tried to work within the Democratic party to secure candidates committed to the farmers' cause. In the Northeast, the campaign turned largely on the tariff, with Democrats pointing to price increases as evidence that the tariff really taxed consumers. In some parts of the region, Democrats even paid door-to-door peddlers (a typical source for household goods) to inflate tinware prices to absurd levels and blame the McKinley Tariff.[12] In the Rocky Mountain West, silver was the issue. In parts of the Midwest, Democrats scourged Republicans for their support of prohibition or their efforts to change laws governing local schools. In German-speaking areas in Wisconsin, Republicans proved vulnerable for passing state laws requiring school classes to be taught in English. A leading Iowa Republican had claimed in the early 1880s that "Iowa will go Democratic when hell goes Methodist," but, pushed by Republican moral reformers, Iowa Germans and Czechs helped elect a Democratic governor.

Republicans found themselves on the defensive everywhere, and they suffered defeat everywhere. The House of Representatives elected in 1888 included 166 Republicans and 159 Democrats; the House elected in 1890 had 88 Republicans, 235 Democrats, and nine Populists. The Democrats counted the largest majority in nearly 60 years. William McKinley himself went down in defeat. What happened to the Republican congressional candidates affected Republican candidates for state and local offices, especially in the Midwest in 1889.[13]

The Populists established themselves as the most successful new party since the Republicans themselves appeared in the 1850s. Kansas Republican Senator John J. Ingalls had earlier dismissed them as "a sort of turnip crusade," but in 1891, a Populist took Ingalls's seat in the Senate. The Populists took control of the Nebraska legislature too, and nearly won the governorship. In several states, they held the balance of power between the two old parties. All across the South, the Farmers' Alliance claimed they had been crucial to Democratic success and looked to the Democrats to redeem promises of assistance to farmers.[14]

In 1892, with little enthusiasm, the Republicans renominated Harrison. Forgiving his defeat in 1888, Democrats made Grover Cleveland their candidate again. The Populists, in their first national convention, gave their presidential nomination to James Weaver, a Union general during the Civil War, and they named a Confederate veteran as their vice presidential nominee. In most western states the Democrats had shrunk to a tiny third party, and they gave open or covert support to the Populists in order to deny victory to the Republicans. In the South, however, Democrats viciously attacked the Populists as a threat to white supremacy, while Republicans sometimes leaned to the Populists as the best means of defeating the Democrats.

Democrats and Populists claimed impressive victories in the 1892 elections. Cleveland won with 46.1 percent of the popular vote to Harrison's 43.0 percent and Weaver's 8.5 percent. The Democrats kept control of the House and, for the first time in twelve years, also won the Senate. Populist gains came largely in the Great Plains, the Mountain West, and the South. Weaver carried five states and placed second in nine more; Populists elected three governors, eight or ten congressmen, some 50 other state officers, and 1,500 local officials and state legislators.[15] In Washington, the Democrats now found themselves in control of both the presidency and Congress and fully able to translate their promises into law.

**Divided Democracy.** By a coincidence unfortunate for the Democrats, the nation entered a severe economic depression at the same time Grover Cleveland moved back into the White House. Some 15,000 businesses failed in 1893, more than ever before in a single year, and more, proportionately, than any year since the depression of 1875-1878. Unemployment estimates for some cities ranged as high as a quarter or even a third of the work force.[16] Cleveland and his party thus confronted not only the silver and tariff issues, but also depression, unemployment, labor unrest, and the challenge of the Populists. In 1887-1888, Cleveland had pointed his party toward tariff revision but had failed to lead, and he and his party went down to defeat in 1888. Given a second chance, he failed on a more spectacular scale.

When Congress met in 1893, Democrats, in addition to the depression, immediately faced decisions on silver and the tariff. Cleveland took action first on silver, calling Congress into emergency session and asking them to repeal the Sherman Silver Purchase Act, which some financial leaders blamed for causing the depression but which many western and southern Democrats defended as better than no silver coinage at all. Given the economic realities of 1893, repeal may have been necessary to prevent further economic disaster for the banking system, but it came at a significant cost: Cleveland divided his party almost down the middle, pitting the Northeast against the West and much of the South.[17] The tariff bill that came out of the House Ways and Means Committee late that year reduced duties, tried to balance sectional interests, and created an income tax as a means of recovering lost federal revenue. The Senate, however, produced so many amendments and compromises that Cleveland characterized the result as "party dishonor."[18]

Rather than seeking to restore party unity, Cleveland typically took positions which conservatives applauded as "principled" and "courageous" but which failed to bring together the increasingly divided Democrats. In mid-summer 1894, for example, Cleveland ignored the objections of the Democratic governor of Illinois, John Peter Altgeld, and sent federal troops into that state, ostensibly to protect the U.S. mail, but actually to break a nationwide railway strike centered in Chicago. Cleveland's Attorney General, Richard Olney, prosecuted the strike leaders, especially the union president, Eugene V. Debs, a Democrat who had campaigned extensively for Cleveland among union members in both 1888 and 1892.[19]

In the midterm elections of 1894, Democrats fared poorly everywhere except in the deep South. They lost not just in New England and the Midwest, in many cases reversing recent gains, but also in the Border States and in some of the former Confederate states. Republicans scored their biggest gain in Congress ever, adding 117 seats while the Democrats lost 113.

In surveying the devastated Democratic landscape of 1894, one exception stood out. In Nebraska, William Jennings Bryan, a young, two-term Democratic Congressman, forged a winning political coalition. First elected to the House in 1890 and narrowly reelected in 1892, Bryan benefitted both times from backing by Populists attracted by his support for silver, the income tax, and direct election of U.S. senators. In 1892, he joined other prominent Nebraska Democrats to urge that Democratic voters support Weaver for president. Then in 1893, when the legislature deadlocked over selection of a senator, Bryan took the lead in convincing the few Democratic legislators to support a Populist. Later that year, Bryan's eloquent defense of silver during debate over repeal of the Sherman Silver Purchase Act moved him into the front ranks of Democratic silverites.

In 1894, Nebraska Republicans nominated for governor a candidate closely associated with the American Protective Association (APA), a virulently anti-Catholic group; the Populists named Silas Holcomb, a respected former Democrat. Bryan formed the Nebraska Democratic Free Coinage League and used it to win control of the state Democratic party, attracting conservative (and Catholic) Democrats with calls to defeat the APA. In the state Democratic convention, Bryan himself nominated Holcomb for governor. Although the coalition amounted to little more than the Bryan Democrats accepting the Populists' candidates for office, a straight Democratic ticket put up by Cleveland's patronage appointees drew only a few voters away from Holcomb. Holcomb's success in Nebraska, and similar Populist-Democratic cooperation elsewhere, seemed to present a clear alternative to the conservatism of Cleveland.[20]

**Bryan vs. McKinley**. In 1896, when Republicans met in St. Louis to chose their presidential candidate, William McKinley already had a commanding lead and won on the first ballot by a three to one margin over four rivals. He hoped to focus his campaign on the tariff, but the convention adopted a platform plank in favor of the gold standard and against silver. When the delegates adopted the gold plank, a small number of western, silverite Republicans, led by Senator Henry Teller of Colorado, walked out of the convention and out of the party.[21]

When the Democrats convened in Chicago, silverites outnumbered defenders of Cleveland but agreed on no single candidate. The platform committee divided on the money issue, presenting the convention with a majority report endorsing silver and a minority report supporting Cleveland's policies. Members of the committee debated the two versions before the convention. For the conventions's closing speaker, the committee chose Bryan, who had spent much of the previous 18 months championing silver throughout the country. Bryan provided a masterful speech. Defining the issue as "the producing masses" against "the idle holders of idle capital," he presented "two ideas of government":

> There are those who believe that, if you will only legislate to make the well-to-do prosperous, their prosperity will leak through on those below. The Democratic idea, however, has been that if you legislate to make the masses prosperous, their prosperity will find its way up through every class which rests upon them.

He closed on a note at once defiant and Biblical:

> Having behind us the producing masses of this nation and the world, supported by the commercial interest, the laboring interests, and the toilers everywhere, we will answer their demand for a gold standard by saying to them: You shall not press down upon the brow of labor this crown of thorns. You shall not crucify mankind upon a cross of gold.[22]

His speech stunned the convention and provoked a half-hour demonstration. Not a declared candidate for the nomination before his speech, Bryan nonetheless won it on the fifth ballot.

The Populists and the Silver Republicans (who had formed themselves into a party) held their conventions next. Given Bryan's commitment to silver, the income tax, and other reforms, and given the close working relationship he had developed with Populists in Nebraska, the Populists felt compelled to give him their nomination, but tried to maintain their independence by naming a Populist for vice president. The Silver Republicans nominated Bryan too. Bryan thus entered the campaign with three parties' nominations and two running mates.

The campaign was closely fought. Bryan broke with precedent to take his case directly to the voters, traveling 18,000 miles by train, visiting 26 states and more than 250 cities, and speaking to as many as five million people. Everywhere, he delivered his central message: the most important issue was silver, and once the silver issue was properly settled other reforms would follow. McKinley stayed at home in Canton, Ohio, and campaigned from his front porch while the Republican party carried the campaign to the voters. His chief campaign organizer, Marcus Hanna, a retired Ohio industrialist, played on business leaders' fear of Bryan to secure a campaign fund of $10-16 million—far more than had ever been raised before, and twenty or forty times as much as the Democrats were able to accumulate.

Bryan hoped his economic message would bring him strong support from farmers—especially those who had voted for the Populists—and workers. Despite some grumbling among southern Populists, the Populist party generally put on the Bryan harness and toiled for his cause

Bryan especially targeted organized labor with a major speech in Chicago on Labor Day.[23] Most labor leaders responded to his candidacy with enthusiasm. Eugene Debs, head of the American Railway Union, had been a leading candidate for the Populist presidential nomination before he withdrew in favor of Bryan; he spoke extensively on Bryan's behalf in October and argued that "the triumph of Mr. Bryan and free silver would blunt the fangs of the money power."[24] Most unionists apparently shared such views, for unions, central bodies, and individual organizers reported virtual unanimity for Bryan among their numbers.[25] Among the labor leaders themselves, only Samuel Gompers, president of the American Federation of Labor (AFL), failed to endorse Bryan—even after Bryan promised to name him to the cabinet—because of an AFL rule against affiliation with a political party.[26]

In addition to his appeals to farmers and workers, Bryan could cite a strong and impressive record of opposition to the anti-Catholic APA. Although personally a teetotaler, his record against prohibition should have lost him no support among those who liked their beer. *If* southern Democrats and Populists could set aside local differences during the campaign, *if* he could attract economically distressed farmers and workers, *if* he could hold the ethnic core of the Midwestern Democratic party, *if* western mining states would deliver votes as anticipated, then he would win.

As it turned out, Bryan was not able to hold the ethnic core of his party in the Midwest. In 1894, the Nebraska fusion campaign had been blessed with a rabidly anti-Catholic Republican opponent. By contrast, the APA had marked McKinley before the Republican convention as the most unacceptable Republican seeking the nomination, and McKinley had condemned the secret order. By election day, however, McKinley benefitted both from some support among Catholics (attracted either by his economic platform or by his condemnation of the APA) and from the resigned APA attitude that the Republican ticket was preferable to the Democratic ticket. McKinley also could point to support from a few labor leaders.[27] The 1888 Republican convention had given an ambiguous endorsement to the temperance movement, but McKinley distanced himself from the cold-water crusade.[28] This and the gold standard helped McKinley's cause among German voters.

Election day saw four of every five eligible voters troop to the polls, a level of participation never since matched. Bryan received 6.5 million votes, more than any previous presidential candidate, but McKinley got even more, 7.1 million. In both the popular vote and the electoral vote,

McKinley scored the largest margin of victory since 1872. Bryan took the South and nearly all the West, but McKinley's victory came in the nation's Manufacturing Belt, the northeastern quarter of the country that included most of the urban population and most of the heavy industry. Of the twenty largest cities, Bryan won a majority only in New Orleans.

The campaign of 1896 had focused centrally on economic matters, and the depression had sharpened the significance of these issues for many voters. Bryan's silver crusade appealed most strongly to debt-ridden farmers and western miners. Although unions endorsed the view that increasing the volume of money would revive business and restore prosperity,[29] many urban residents—workers and the middle class alike—saw in free silver only the threat of higher prices. McKinley forged a more broadly based economic appeal than Bryan by emphasizing both the importance of the gold standard in protecting the value of the dollar against inflation and the benefits of the protective tariff for business and workers alike. Because McKinley put a damper on moral reforms such as prohibition and condemned the APA, he could gain support among Catholics and immigrants—especially Germans—who liked his stand on the gold standard or the tariff; German voters proved important to his success across the Midwest and in some eastern cities.[30] Some companies blatantly pressured their employees and their suppliers, and some loan companies may have pushed their debtors to vote for McKinley, but such direct coercion seems not to have determined the results.[31]

Bryan's defeat spelled the end of the Populist party as a significant political organization. It lingered on in a few places, but split into two factions in 1900, one endorsing Bryan again and the other running a separate candidate, who did poorly. Some Populists moved to the Democratic party, and some to the Republicans. A few joined the Socialist party, and some simply withdrew from politics. A quarter-century later, in 1919, Vachel Lindsay set down his memories of the 1896 campaign:

> In a coat like a deacon, in a black Stetson hat
> He scourged the elephant plutocrats
> with barbed wire from the Platte.
> • • • • • • • • • • • • • • •
> Prairie avenger, mountain lion,
> Bryan, Bryan, Bryan, Bryan,
> Gigantic Troubadour, speaking like a siege gun,
> Smashing Plymouth Rock with his boulders from the West.
> • • • • • • • • • • • • • • • • • • • • • • • • • • • •
> Election night at midnight;
> Boy Bryan's defeat.
> Defeat of western silver.
> Defeat of the wheat.

> Victory of letterfiles
> and plutocrats in miles
> With dollar signs on their coats,
> Diamond watchchains on their vests
> and spats on their feet.
> Victory of custodians,
> Plymouth Rock,
> And all that inbred landlord stock.
> Victory of the neat.
> • • • • • • • •
> Defeat of alfalfa and the Mariposa lily.
> Defeat of the Pacific and the long Mississippi.
> Defeat of the young by the old and silly.
> Defeat of tornadoes by the poison vats supreme.
> Defeat of my boyhood, defeat of my dream.[32]

**The New Face of Politics.** The 1896 election proved one of the most important in American history. Bryan's defeat marked the beginning of a generation for whom the Democrats were a national minority. From the mid-1870s to the mid-1890s, neither of the major parties held a clear majority. After 1896, the Democrats lost six of the next eight presidential elections, and held majorities in both houses of Congress for only six of the 36 years after 1894. Similar patterns of Republican dominance appeared in state and local government, especially in the Manufacturing Belt. Only the Deep South and a few Northern cities remained reliable Democratic strongholds.

Some voters changed parties. In a few western states, enough Populists and Silver Republicans became Bryan Democrats to make those states more closely competitive. In the Northeast and much of the Midwest, enough Democrats became Republicans to make those regions solidly Republican for a generation. However, the realignment of the 1890s did not produce changes in voter loyalties comparable to those of the 1850s (which produced a new political party) or the realignment of the 1930s (which saw both a shift in majority status and the rise to political prominence of organized labor).[33] Most northern Democrats continued to oppose nativism and moral reform, and southern Democrats, during the late 1890s and early twentieth century, solidified their white supremacist regimes by disfranchising and segregating African Americans.

In one way, however, the realignment of the 1890s produced one of the most important changes in the long history of the Democratic party. After 1896, Bryan was the nation's most prominent Democrat. He faced few serious challenges for party leadership from 1896 until 1912 and the nomination of Woodrow Wilson—16 years—and he continued to exert great influence until his death in 1925. Under Bryan's leadership, the party emerged from the 1890s with significantly different policy commitments on economic issues, as Bryan pushed the party away from its commitment to minimal government and laissez faire. Retaining a Jacksonian distrust of monopoly and opposition to governmental favoritism toward business, Bryan and other new leaders of the Democratic party concluded that the solution to the problems of economic concentration lay not in laissez faire but in using government to limit corporate power, especially monopoly power. "A private monopoly," Bryan never tired of repeating, "is indefensible and intolerable." In foreign affairs, too, the years of Bryan's leadership marked a new era in American foreign relations, in which the nation took a much more active role in world affairs. McKinley led the nation to acquire an insular empire consisting of Hawaii, the Philippines, Puerto Rico, Guam, and part of Samoa.[34] Bryan, like Cleveland earlier, rejected imperialism, however, and persistently demanded independence for the Philippines.

**Decline of Parties.** Bryan's tenure as party leader came at a time of far-reaching change in the very nature of American politics. In many ways, the political landscape in 1888 looked much like it had in 1876 or even in 1844. But American politics after 1890 changed in important ways, in terms of structure and issues. After the 1890s, an increasing number of voters came to hold their party commitments less intensely than before. Until then, party loyalty had been, for many, part of a party culture, often linked to ethnicity, described by Jean Baker and others.[35] After the 1890s, outside the South, increasing numbers of voters felt pulled toward one party by their economic situation and toward the other by their ethnicity. These voters became increasingly likely to vote a "split ticket," supporting Republicans for some offices and Democrats for others, a practice made much easier because of widespread acceptance of the Australian ballot after 1890. The decline in party loyalties was both reflected in and accelerated by changes in state election laws that made some offices officially nonpartisan.[36]

The same period saw the emergence of strong, nationally organized groups committed to a single issue or interest—for example, the Anti-Saloon League (formed in 1895), the National Association of Manufacturers (1895), the National German-American Alliance (1901), or the National Child Labor Committee (1904). Such groups sought to cut across party loyalties to focus on a single issue. "The explosion of scores of aggressive, politically active pressure groups into the space left by the recession of traditional political loyalties," Daniel Rodgers has written, produced a "fragmented, fluid, and issue-focused" politics that represented "a major, lasting shift in the rules of the political game."[37]

This erosion of party loyalties and increased emphasis on particular issues coincided with reduced voter turnout. Voter participation fell from 79 percent in 1896 to 65 percent in 1908 to 49 percent in 1920. Part of this decline may have come as some voters resolved conflicting pressures by not voting. More important was the debilitating impact on highly structured party organizations of reduced party loyalties, changes in ballot laws, and civil service reform, which hampered the ability of machines to mobilize the party faithful during campaigns and, especially, on election day.

As a result, campaigns turned increasingly to advertising the virtues of individual candidates, shifting the focus away from party loyalties and toward candidates' personalities, and thereby further contributing to ticket splitting. The Republican campaign in 1896 marked the ascendancy of this new approach, leading Theodore Roosevelt to snort derisively that his party had "advertised McKinley as if he were a patent medicine." Symbolic of this shift was the appearance for the first time in, 1896, of the ubiquitous pinback campaign button.[38]

Voter participation rates also changed, due in part to the most widespread changes in suffrage laws since the expansion of the Jacksonian era and Reconstruction. In some states, changes in registration laws (usually opposed by northern Democrats) reduced eligibility for transient workers and immigrants.[39] Throughout the South, new laws (written by Democrats) greatly reduced eligibility for African Americans and sometimes affected poor whites as well; the virtual disappearance of the Republican party in the region meant that there was little reason to vote once the Democratic party had chosen its nominees.

Although, in the early twentieth century, some states disfranchised African Americans, transient workers, and some immigrants, a number of states expanded the suffrage by removing gender-based barriers to voting. Given the close connection drawn in the nineteenth century between party loyalty and manhood, Paula Baker has suggested that it was no coincidence that female suffrage succeeded only after the decline of intense political partisanship. By 1919, when Congress voted to submit the suffrage amendment for ratification, fifteen states had already adopted full female suffrage, thirteen of them in the West where political parties had been weak before the 1890s and became further weakened afterward.[40]

Thus, within a quarter-century after 1890, many of the characteristics of political campaigning had changed significantly. Voters reassessed the depth of their party loyalty and began to split their tickets. Party organizations lost much of their previous vitality along with some of their previous functions. Voter turn-out plummeted. Personalities, issues, and—with them—advertising played ever larger roles in electoral campaigns. Organized interest groups emerged as significant political actors.

## WILLIAM JENNINGS BRYAN AND THE DEMOCRATIC PARTY

As the party's presidential candidate, Bryan became the titular leader of the party.[41] Labeling Bryan a "titular leader with tenure," Ralph Goldman has pointed out that Bryan filled this "phantom office" more actively and over a longer time than any other defeated candidate has ever done. Bryan received an unintended assist from several who might have challenged his right to speak for the party: Cleveland retired to Princeton and largely withdrew from party struggles; Altgeld lost his bid for reelection in 1896 and was ineligible for the presidency because of his foreign birth; others either left office or tended to the needs of their immediate constituencies.[42] In contrast, immediately after his defeat in 1896, Bryan published his account of the campaign, *The First Battle*. Its message was clear: the campaign was to continue.

Throughout the last thirty years of his life, Bryan made his living from public speaking, writing books, and publishing *The Commoner*, a weekly newspaper launched late in 1900. During the nineteenth century, the central role of speechmaking in politics and religion produced great orators. Few in his day matched the drawing power of his name or the carrying power of his voice. He could speak to thirty thousand people in the open air, without amplification, and those on the fringes of the crowd could understand every word. He took to the lecture circuit every year, and often more than once; nearly every summer he spent three months traveling the Chautauqua circuit, delivering 200-300 speeches in nearly that many towns. He usually spoke twice a day on social, religious, educational, and political questions. Mary Bryan, his wife and political alter ego, confirmed that his tours involved not just speaking: "When he returned from his tours he had not only spoken to, but had listened to, the mind of America. He had had an opportunity to know what America was thinking and he had helped America to make up her mind."

Among those he met during his constant travels across the length and breadth of the nation were local leaders of the Democratic party. William Gibbs McAdoo, with whom Bryan served in Woodrow Wilson's cabinet, concluded that Bryan's travels had given him "a personal acquaintance with more people . . . than any other man in the United States."[43] This sizable personal network, when combined with the subscription list for the *Commoner* and Bryan's own considerable skills in working party conventions, gave him an almost unmeasurable advantage over anyone who might challenge him for party leadership.[44] Yet, while Bryan's travels kept him in touch with a large and politically potent collection of Democrats, this group was largely informal and entirely personal in nature, virtually unrelated to the formal structure of party committees.[45]

**Bryan's Democracy, 1897-1912.** War with Spain in 1898 presented new political issues. The governor of Nebraska appointed Bryan as colonel of the Third Nebraska Volunteer Regiment, but the regiment spent the war in Florida, devastated by typhoid and other illness. During the conflict, the Republican-dominated Congress annexed Hawaii by resolution. Long before the end of the war, most leading silverites had come to share the views of Richard Pettigrew, the Silver Republican Senator from South Dakota, who condemned it as "not a patriotic war" but "a war of plundering and spoils." The treaty with Spain provided for the United States to acquire an insular empire consisting of Puerto Rico, the Philippines, and Guam.[46] Bryan resigned his commission as soon as the peace treaty was signed, proclaimed his opposition to imperialism, but nonetheless urged the Senate to ratify the treaty promptly so that the United States alone could determine the future of the Philippine Islands.

Despite his disagreement with Cleveland's domestic policies, Bryan's anti-imperialism echoed Cleveland's response to events in Samoa and Hawaii. Throughout his first term, Cleveland protested German manipulation of Samoan politics with the object that "no change of native rule shall extinguish the independence of the islands." In 1893, shortly before Cleveland began his second term, members of the white business community in Hawaii, with support from American marines, overthrew Queen Liliuokalani. Although the marines acted without authorization from Washington, the Harrison administration, then in its closing days, quickly concluded a treaty of annexation with the new Hawaiian government. When Cleveland took office, he discovered that the revolution could not have succeeded without the marines' involvement, and he asked the new government to restore the queen. They refused, and Cleveland withdrew the treaty of annexation.[47]

In 1900, Bryan hoped to attract prominent anti-imperialists and to bring back the Cleveland wing of the party, many of whom had taken prominent roles in anti-imperialist organizations. Bryan wrote most of the Democratic platform; it condemned imperialism and militarism, promised independence to the Philippines, attacked monopoly, supported the cause of organized labor, called for direct election of U.S. senators, and reaffirmed support for silver.[48] Most conservative anti-imperialists, however, had a greater distaste for Bryan's economic proposals than for McKinley's imperial adventures. Republicans repeated arguments from 1896 that the election of Bryan would endanger prosperity. Their vice presidential candidate, Theodore Roosevelt, wearing his cavalry hat, carried the brunt of the GOP campaign, including a flag-waving defense of territorial acquisition. McKinley won by a larger margin in 1900 than in 1896.

In 1904, Theodore Roosevelt held sway in the White House, riding the crest of a wave of popularity that derived in major part from his willingness to challenge big business. Bryan evinced no interest in running a third time and made little serious effort to influence the choice of a candidate or the selection of delegates. The Democratic convention opened with a majority firmly committed to "the reorganizers," who hoped to return the party to the conservatism of Cleveland. One of these defined their first task as "to kill Bryanism, root and branch." Even so, Bryan, as a delegate, dictated much of the platform. The conservative majority named Alton B. Parker, a New York judge, as their presidential candidate. Roosevelt won 56.4 percent of the vote to Parker's 37.6 percent, demonstrating that Democratic victory did not lie in running to the right of the Republicans. Bryan began immediately to plan for 1908.

Bryan's drive for a third nomination was unstoppable. By February 1908, his brother Charles had written to more than 120,000 Bryan supporters with directions to organize in every neighborhood so that the platform and candidate would represent "the will of the rank and file of the party." When the Democratic convention opened in Denver, Bryan held the two-thirds majority necessary for nomination. In the platform, he proclaimed the need "to free the Government from the grip of those who have made it a business asset of the favor-seeking corporations," and declared "the overshadowing issue" to be: "Shall the people rule?" The platform called for a long list of reforms, including tariff revision, a requirement that corporations be licensed, a prohibition against any corporation holding more than a fifty percent share of its market, a national insurance fund to protect bank depositors, an income tax, direct election of senators, and independence for the Philippines.[49]

By 1908, primarily in response to an anti-union political initiative from the National Association of Manufacturers, the American Federation of Labor (AFL) had become more involved in politics and presented both parties with a set of proposals for labor legislation. Ignored by the Republicans, the AFL found Bryan and the Democrats highly receptive to their suggestions; the platform promised the AFL everything it asked—an eight hour day for government workers, a cabinet-level Department of Labor, recognition of the right of workers to organize, changes in the laws relating to injunctions, and more. Even so, in keeping with its commitment to nonpartisanship, the AFL did not make a formal endorsement.[50]

In 1896, Bryan had seemed a voice in the wilderness when he spoke against the power of corporations; by 1908, he was one of a multitude. Not only Bryan and his supporters, but many different groups and individuals had come to advocate a variety of proposals for change, a phenomenon that historians treat under the rubric of Progressivism.[51] One major area of concern for Progressives was corporate influence in government. Journalistic exposés—called muckraking—had prompted many states to approve laws limiting the power of corporations in politics, regulating railroads, and establishing the direct primary. As Richard McCormick has pointed out, for the moment, at least, the tenets of antimonopolism had moved from groups on the fringes of political activity—such as the Populists—to those in the political center.[52]

Bryan's calls for the limitation of corporate power found many echoes now; so did his insistence that people had obligations to those less fortunate. His public lectures often emphasized the ideal of service to others, something Bryan considered "applied Christianity." After 1900, his speeches and writings often addressed themes from Protestant Christianity and, in 1903, he suggested that Christ's injunction to "love thy neighbor as thyself" held the potential to "solve every problem economic, social, political, and religious." Such views put Bryan close to the proponents of the "Social Gospel," whose religious outlook led them to advocate social reforms.[53]

In both his antimonopolism and his commitment to a social gospel, Bryan spoke the language of progressivism. Taft and Roosevelt shared some of the phrases of progressivism with Bryan, especially opposition to corporate influences in government. Roosevelt also shared Bryan's views on the need to license corporations, once observing that "about half of Bryan's views are right."[54] Roosevelt, however, picked Taft as his successor and believed that widespread support for his administration's policies meant that Taft would be elected; he proved an accurate prophet.

Prominent African Americans had long been critical of the Republicans for their failure to provide anything more than lip service to black rights in the South, and many became alienated from Roosevelt as a result of a decision in 1906 to punish three all-black companies of soldiers when an Army investigation failed to identify the few culprits in a shooting incident in Brownsville, Texas. Bryan gained support from a number of prominent African Americans, including W.E.B. Du Bois. However, Du Bois, and perhaps others among Bryan's endorsers, saw their support for Bryan as a response to behavior by the Republicans and held no illusions that he might override the racial views of the southern wing of his party. Even so, widespread circulation of a prominent black newspaper that endorsed Bryan brought a sharp protest from southern Democrats.[55]

Bryan mounted his usual strenuous campaign, concentrating on the Midwest and New York, just as he had done in 1896 and 1900. Bryan also won support from the nation's largest German-language newspaper. The AFL mounted the most vigorous campaign it had ever undertaken for a presidential candidate. When the votes were counted, however, Bryan lost for the third time. His 43.1 percent of the popular vote marked a drop of a few points below his previous share; Taft drew 51.6 percent, almost exactly the same as McKinley in 1900. When Bryan accused Taft of being a front for Roosevelt, he only said what most voters believed. Most saw the election as a referendum on the previous seven years of Theodore Roosevelt, and the outcome suggested that a majority not only approved of Roosevelt's strenuous Progressivism but wanted more of the same.

Some of Bryan's respondents attributed his defeat to support for Taft by the liquor trade, apparently out of a distrust of Bryan's well-known personal temperance. From the time he entered politics in the 1880s, Bryan had respected the "personal liberty" tenets of his party and had never spoken in favor of prohibition; within 18 months, however, he announced support for political action against liquor.[56] A year after the 1908 election, Bryan announced his decision never to seek a presidential nomination, but he kept the door open for a draft that never came.

**Democratic Progressivism, 1912-1925.** Bryan's long tenure as titular head of the party ended when the Democrats nominated Woodrow Wilson in 1912. Before the convention, Bryan stayed neutral between the Progressives seeking the nomination, but he dramatically endorsed Wilson in the midst of the convention balloting.[57] In a three-way election, Wilson won with 41.9 percent, a smaller percentage—and fewer popular votes—than Bryan received in any of his campaigns.[58] Wilson offered Bryan the most prestigious cabinet position, Secretary of State, and Bryan accepted.

With a Democrat in the White House and Democratic majorities in both houses of Congress, Bryan took great interest in reform legislation that he considered fulfilled his platform promises: tariff revision, the income tax, a strong role for the federal government in the new Federal Reserve System, a cabinet-level Department of Labor, and the Clayton Antitrust Act. As Secretary of State, he hoped to implement platform promises regarding anti-imperialism and international peace. He was pleased when Congress passed a bill that vaguely promised independence to the Philippines, but he by-passed his anti-imperialist principles when he endorsed the Bryan-Chamorro Treaty with Nicaragua and the Navy's occupation of Vera Cruz. In pursuit of peace, Bryan negotiated treaties with 30 nations that specified a "cooling off" period for disputes, during which the parties were to seek outside fact-finding rather than go to war. He resigned from the State Department when he concluded that Wilson's response to the sinking of the *Lusitania* might drag the nation into war.

Bryan resumed his role as a leading Democrat, Chautauqua lecturer, and reformer. He spoke widely, especially in the West, for Wilson's re-election in 1916, and saw the region provide Wilson with the margin crucial to his narrow victory. After 1915, Bryan focused on social issues, notably female suffrage and prohibition; opponents and supporters of prohibition agreed that Bryan did more than anyone else to ensure the Eighteenth Amendment (prohibition). Democrats remained profoundly divided over prohibition, however, reflecting deeper party cleavages over ethno-cultural issues. In 1924 when the Ku Klux Klan was at its peak strength, Bryan addressed his last Democratic convention to state his opposition to a proposal to condemn the Klan by name; he argued that party unity for economic reform should take precedence over ethno-cultural divisions. During his final years, Bryan focused especially on evolution, which he considered a major social threat for undermining religious faith. Shortly before his death, that cause took him to Tennessee for the trial of John Scopes.

**The Democrats Transformed.** From 1890 on, Bryan filled the role of party leader, first in Nebraska and then on a national level. From the mid-1890s to the mid-1920s, only Grover Cleveland and Woodrow Wilson matched his preeminence. Of the two, Cleveland epitomized the commitment of the Gilded Age Democracy to minimal government and economic conservatism. Wilson shared views close to those of Cleveland until late in his political evolution. When Wilson finally emerged as a Progressive, the Democratic party had already undergone a transformation from a party hostile to the exercise of government to a party committed to use government "to make the masses prosperous," as Bryan put it. Bryan played a key role in that transformation, which revived the antimonopolism of Jackson but interred his belief in minimal government.

Bryan led the party during that transition, his role primarily that of popularizer rather than creator of a new definition of the role of government. The Jacksonian Democrats, and their Gilded Age descendants, had opposed an active role for government in the economy, arguing that any governmental action gave some individual or group an unfair advantage and thus encouraged monopoly. The prospect of securing governmental favoritism, they argued, also encouraged corruption, as greedy men sought to secure privileges by bribing elected officials. The Republicans, from 1861 onward, had used government to stimulate economic development through the protective tariff and subsidies in the form of land grants; except for a few early-twentieth-century Progressives, however, most Republicans opposed using government to regulate, restrict, or even tax economic enterprise. The Populists endorsed Jacksonian notions regarding the dangers of monopoly to both individual opportunity and a republican form of government, but also reasoned that, with giant corporations already in existence, only government could control these great concentrations of economic power. Bryan did not create the idea of using government to control these forces, but he saw the Populists as allies, endorsed some of their ideas, and thrust them to the forefront of political debate by his oratorical prowess. One leading Populist claimed that "we put him to school and he wound up stealing the schoolbooks." Louis Koenig, a political scientist, has agreed that "it was the Populist rather than the Democratic party that provided Bryan with the main planks of his campaign."[60] However, it was the Bryan Democrats who developed those ideas and kept them in the political mainstream.

Bryan was not alone in his efforts to move the Democratic party away from the conservatism of Cleveland. After 1896, he and others worked to maintain the party's new-found commitment to a positive concept of government, to restraining great concentrations of economic power, and to increasing the role of the citizen in the political process. Bryan's compelling voice and engaging smile won him a wide personal following which he could always call upon in support of his principles. He carved out a unique role in American politics by spending three decades traveling about the nation, speaking to grassroots leaders of his party, lecturing to throngs of citizens, sending out his views through *The Commoner*, and battling in convention after convention, whether or not he was a candidate, to write his views into the Democratic platform. He spent little time in public office—four years in the House of Representatives and twenty-seven months as Secretary of State—but made a greater impression on the Democratic party than any other single person between the mid-1890s and the mid-1910s.[61]

For Bryan, every policy proposal had to be tested in the crucible of principle and only those that passed the test earned his support. Once he committed himself, he not only popularized the proposal through his speeches and writings, but typically sought to insert it into the Democratic platform as well. Bryan's political principles emerged especially from his reading of Thomas Jefferson, the founder of his party. Jefferson had written that all men were created equal; Bryan concluded that all voters were, or should be, as nearly equal as possible in fact. (He knew, of course, that voters were as unequal in political influence as in intelligence, virtue, or merit.) The principle of equality had both political and economic corollaries for him.[62]

Like most Democrats from at least the time of Jackson onward, Bryan embraced the notion that, in politics, equality meant that all white males—he eventually added women—stood equally qualified to vote and hold office. Thus, in the 1890s, he opposed the efforts of the APA to exclude Catholics from office, and, in 1924, he opposed the efforts of Al Smith supporters to exclude Klansmen from the Democratic party. Equality for Bryan also meant that personalities carried far less importance than issues and principles. Most Democrats probably would have agreed with Bryan that specialized expertise counted for less than a good heart, a principled outlook, and party loyalty. Bryan quoted Jefferson with approval: "the principles of right and wrong are so easily understood as to require not the aid of many counselors."[63]

Like most Democrats of his day, Bryan saw political equality as only for whites. In one oft-repeated address he speciously argued that where "two groups of people are thrown together and must of necessity live under the same government, the question is not whether the members of each group are capable of self- government, but which group should control the government under which both shall live?" Giving no indication that he ever considered the possibility that different groups might *share* control of government, he concluded that "those who represent the superior civilization always have and always will exercise a dominating influence... the less advanced are themselves better off under laws made by the more advanced, for they have the advantage of living under laws which the more advanced make for themselves."[64] "White supremacy," he once claimed, "promotes the highest welfare of both races."[65]

Beginning with the Jacksonian belief that all white citizens were political equals, Bryan concluded that they should share as equally as possible in the process of governing themselves; he applied that principle to a host of proposals for changes in the structure of political decision making. During the progressive era, a variety of reforms promised the extension of popular participation in government, including the direct primary, the direct election of United States senators, the initiative and referendum, and female suffrage. Bryan thought that all these reforms provided a greater role in government for ordinary citizens, and he gave them his full support, unlike many leading Democrats who viewed both the initiative and female suffrage as opening wedges for prohibition.

Political equality, for Bryan, produced a belief in the unassailable right of the majority to govern. Quoting Jefferson, he proclaimed "absolute acquiescence in the decision of the majority" to be "the vital principle of republics." He did not claim that the majority could do no wrong, only that "the people have a right to make their own mistakes."[66] He criticized violations of majority rule and, throughout his long career, vigorously defended the right of the majority to make any decisions it wished—decisions limiting the property rights of a privileged few, prohibiting the sale of alcohol, and dictating how teachers should present high school biology.

Although Bryan eventually embraced prohibition, he seems never to have seen in that action a contradiction of his party's traditional commitment to personal liberty. He argued that "the chief duty of governments, in so far as they are coercive, is to restrain those who would interfere with the inalienable rights of the individual, among which are the right to life, the right to liberty, the right to the pursuit of happiness, and the right to worship God according to the dictates of one's conscience."[67] He seems never to have considered the possibility that a democratic government itself, operating under majority rule, might threaten the personal liberties of a minority. For Bryan, the major threats to life, liberty, and the pursuit of happiness came not from government, but from "the law-created person, the corporation,"[68] which corrupted both individuals and the political process. In the 1890s, his attention focused on railroads and bankers; by the 1910s, he considered the liquor industry to pose a similar threat to both the individual and the polity.

The economic corollary of equality was that all people deserved an equal chance at success. "Equal rights to all and special privileges to none," Bryan often proclaimed, was the only appropriate rule for "all departments of government."[69] The years after the Civil War witnessed the emergence of huge companies, especially in transportation and manufacturing, many of them monopolistic or oligopolistic. As a good Jacksonian, Bryan traced the origins of these economic concentrations to governmental favoritism. But Jacksonian solutions of minimal government were no longer relevant once the monopolies existed; minimal government, in fact, only gave the monopolies free rein. Like the Populists, Bryan embraced the use of government to remove barriers to individual achievement, especially those posed by the concentration of economic power in private hands. Again and again, he repeated, "A private monopoly is indefensible and intolerable," and he wrote the phrase into five Democratic platforms, those of 1900, 1904, 1908, 1912, and 1924.[70] In the case of the railroads, he concluded that public ownership was the only alternative to private monopoly, but he did not push his party to take that position until after World War I.

Bryan also publicized and popularized proposals for specific changes in economic policy, and often wrote those proposals into Democratic platforms. From his earliest involvement in policy-making in the early 1890s, he focused on tariff reform, following the lead of Grover Cleveland and other party leaders back to Jefferson himself. In his speeches, Bryan categorized the tariff as the leading example of an "indirect tax." Such measures, he maintained, represented efforts to conceal taxes from the taxpayer; Bryan argued that, instead, taxes should be direct and "easily scrutinized." He argued, as well, that the taxpayer should "contribute to the support of his government in proportion to the benefits which he enjoys through the protection of his government," and advocated the graduated income tax as the best means to accomplish that objective. As a congressman, he gained national attention with his defense of an income tax in 1893 (a flat tax rate, but, he thought, better than no income tax at all); he wrote a demand for a graduated income tax into Democratic platforms in 1908 and 1912. Such a tax, Bryan argued, distributed "the burdens of government" according to "the ability to contribute," compensated for the injustice of regressive taxes on consumption, and discouraged large incomes.[71]

Bryan considered taxation one of the "most far-reaching subjects" government faced, and he put monetary and banking policies into the same category. He saw banking policy as closely related to monetary policy, and tirelessly worked for its reform. In the Democratic platforms of 1900 and 1908,[72] and in his speeches and writings, he asserted that the issuance of money was properly a function of government, not of banks, and he insisted on such a provision in the Federal Reserve Act. In 1908, he made a major campaign issue of his proposal for an insurance fund for bank deposits, to be created by taxing banks. His supporters failed to write such a deposit insurance plan into the Federal Reserve Act in 1913, but a few veterans of the 1908 campaign participated, in 1933, when Congress created the Federal Deposit Insurance Corporation. Some of the changes in the Federal Reserve Act made by the Banking Act of 1935 followed pathways Bryan marked when he insisted that the Federal Reserve Board be controlled by representatives of the public, appointed by the president, not by bankers.

Bryan also pushed the Democrats to control large companies through regulation. During the early twentieth century, the federal government came increasingly to regulate economic activities, first during Theodore Roosevelt's administration, and more extensively under Woodrow Wilson. Bryan's campaign and his platform of 1900 had anticipated some of the measures Roosevelt later promoted, and his 1908 platform forecast some features of the Federal Trade Commission Act and the Clayton Antitrust Act, both approved by Wilson, but no regulation ever met Bryan's demand that a company be prohibited from controlling more than 50 percent of its market, or incorporated his concept that "public ownership is imperative wherever competition is impossible."[73] By opposing monopoly, proposing limits on market shares, and advocating government ownership, Bryan—if nothing else—legitimized more moderate reformers such as Roosevelt and Wilson. In the "Cross of Gold" speech and in its innumerable repetitions, he dramatically contrasted economic policies based on creating prosperity from the top down (the "trickle down" approach) with policies oriented toward creating a stable economic base, a theme that Democrats were to employ throughout the twentieth century.

With regard to foreign policy, Bryan failed to make the 1900 election a referendum on imperialism, but his arguments played some role in solidifying public opinion against further acquisition of colonies. He persisted in demanding independence for the Philippines, and wrote that commitment into Democratic platforms in 1900, 1904, 1908, 1912, and 1924.[74] Such persistence finally helped to produce the Jones Act of 1916 with its vague commitment to independence, although fulfillment of this promise came only with further legislation in the 1930s. Like Wilson, Bryan's contributions to foreign policy revealed a strong missionary impulse.[75]

Bryan took a more tolerant position on religious matters than did many Americans of his day, and he vigorously promoted religious toleration within the Democratic party. He worked closely with Catholics from his earliest days in Nebraska politics. When he issued lists of potential presidential candidates in 1912, 1920, and 1924, he pointedly included both Catholics and Jews at a time when most political figures automatically excluded members of both groups from serious consideration. For Bryan, one's religion was always less politically relevant than policy commitments; he preferred a dry, progressive Catholic to a wet, conservative Baptist. Yet he believed it was important that one have a religion and he condemned atheism as a threat to morality.

On race, Bryan's views largely reflected those of his party, but he pushed beyond them when he addressed the issue of colonialism. He argued strongly that people of color were fully capable of self-government, but only where they made up the vast majority of the population. This allowed him to distinguish between the Philippines, Japan, Mexico, or India, on the one hand, and the American South on the other. He did nothing to oppose the segregation of the federal civil service during the Wilson administration; he not only acquiesced in the disfranchisement of African Americans in the South but even defended it as in the interests of both races. Bryan's attitude toward African Americans differed little from those of most Democrats of his day, but he voiced less bias toward African Americans than the majority of southern Democrats. And he stood in advance of most political figures of his day in his advocacy of self-government for the Philippines and India.[76]

The role Bryan defined for himself was that of a crusader, a fighter moved by zealous and principled commitment to a cause. He made the metaphor explicit in his famous speech before the Chicago convention in 1896, likening the commitment of the Silver Democrats to "the zeal which inspired the crusaders who followed Peter the Hermit." "Clad in the armor of a righteous cause" (another metaphor from the same speech), Bryan fought tirelessly throughout his career for one issue after another. In the process, he brought a transformation of the Democratic party.

## NOTES

1. Perhaps the most important statement of the significance of the realignment of the 1890s is Walter Dean Burnham, *Critical Elections and the Mainsprings of American Politics* (Norton, 1970). Other important studies include Jerome M. Clubb, William H. Flanigan, and Nancy H. Zingale, *Partisan Realignment: Voters, Parties, and Government in American History* (Beverly Hills: Sage Publications, 1980); Richard Jensen, *Grass Roots Politics: Parties, Issues, and Voters, 1854-1983* (Westport, Conn.: Greenwood Press, 1983), which downplays the significance of voter shifts except among Germans; and Richard L. McCormick, *The Party Period and Public Policy: American Politics from the Age of Jackson to the Progressive Era* (New York: Oxford University Press, 1986). This section draws upon these sources and upon my own previous work.

2. Homer E. Socolofsky and Allan B. Spetter, in their recent history of the Harrison administration, describe the 51st Congress, 1st session, as setting "a

record for constructive legislation that was not equaled for many years". See *The Presidency of Benjamin Harrison* (Lawrence: University Press of Kansas, 1987), 47. The summary that follows is based largely on the treatment in Socolofsky and Spetter, chap. 4, and in R. Hal Williams, *Years of Decision: American Politics in the 1890s* (New York: John Wiley & Sons, 1978), chap. 2.

3. The federal government took in more money than it spent every year from 1866 through 1893. Throughout the 1880s, when the surplus was largest, it usually ranged above $100 million per year; in 1882, 36 percent of federal receipts went unspent. In addition to the tariff, the other major source of federal revenue was alcohol and tobacco taxes, which carried policy objectives in addition to raising revenue; taxing them increased their cost and thereby put some limits on their consumption. Reducing either of these taxes, especially the one on liquor, was politically risky. See John A. Garraty, *The New Commonwealth, 1877-1890* (New York: Harper & Row, 1968), 246-247.

4. Edward Stanwood, *American Tariff Controversies in the Nineteenth Century*, 2 vols. (1903: New York: Russell & Russell, 1967), 2: 243-295.

5. The Lodge bill never had another chance for passage, due in part to opposition from western Republicans seeking an alliance with southern Democrats on the issue of silver. Not until 1965 did Congress finally act to protect black voting rights, approving a law not greatly different from that Lodge bill—but with the major difference that it was put through by Democrats over the protests of many Republicans and some southern Democrats.

6. This analysis of Populist political discourse derives from my own reading in a wide range of materials; for important treatments of Populism, see John D. Hicks, *The Populist Revolt: A History of the Farmers' Alliance and the People's Party* (1931; reprint, Lincoln: University of Nebraska Press, 1961); Chester McArthur Destler, "Western Radicalism: Concepts and Origins," *Mississippi Valley Historical Review* 31 (1944): 335-68; Norman Pollack, *The Populist Mind* (Indianapolis: Bobbs-Merrill, 1967); Lawrence Goodwyn, *Democratic Promise: The Populist Moment in America* (New York: Oxford University Press, 1976); and Gene Clanton, *Populism: The Humane Preference in America, 1890-1900* (Boston: Twayne Publishers, 1991). For an overview of the historiography, see Martin Ridge, "Populism Redux: John D. Hicks and "The Populist Revolt," *Reviews in American History* 13 (1985): 143-54.

7. Populist policy proposals may be traced through the series of Farmers' Alliance and Populist party platforms in the appendix to Hicks, *Populist Revolt*; all quotations in the previous paragraphs are from the 1892 national platform, which may also be found in *National Party Platforms: 1840-1972*, 5th ed., comp. Donald Bruce Johnson and Kirk H. Porter (Urbana and Chicago: University of Illinois Press, 1975), 89-91.

8. Quotations are from the 1892 Populist national platform, in Johnson and Porter, *National Party Platforms*, 89-91. For Populist appeals that crossed ethnoreligious boundaries on the Great Plains, see Walter T. K. Nugent, *The Tolerant Populists: Kansas Populism and Nativism* (Chicago: University of Chicago Press, 1963); and Robert W. Cherny, *Populism, Progressivism, and the Transformation of Nebraska Politics, 1885-1915* (Lincoln: University of Nebraska Press, 1981), esp. chap. 3, 4; for the South, see Pollack, *Populist Mind*, part 4, or C. Vann

Woodward, *Origins of the New South, 1877-1913* (Baton Rouge: Louisiana State University Press, 1951), chap. 9.

9. Carl N. Deglar, *The Age of the Economic Revolution, 1876-1900*, 2d ed. (Glenview, Ill.: Scott, Foresman, 1977), 69; for treatments of monetary policy, see Milton Friedman and Anna Jacobson Schwartz, *A Monetary History of the United States, 1867-1960* (Princeton: Princeton University Press, 1963), chaps. 2, 3; Walter T. K. Nugent, *Money and American Society, 1865-1880* (New York: Free Press, 1968); Irwin Unger, *The Greenback Era: A Social and Political History of American Finance, 1865-1879* (Princeton: Princeton University Press, 1964); and Allen Weinstein, *Prelude to Populism: Origins of the Silver Issue, 1867-1878* (New Haven: Yale University Press, 1970).

10. Paolo E. Coletta, "Greenbackers, Goldbugs, and Silverites: Currency Reform and Policy, 1860-1877," *The Gilded Age: A Reappraisal*, ed. H. Wayne Morgan, 1st ed. (Syracuse: Syracuse University Press, 1963), 111-40, esp. 119-21; Nugent, *Money and American Society*, chaps. 8-13; Unger, *Greenback Era*; and Weinstein, *Prelude to Populism*, chap. 1.

11. Friedman and Schwartz, *Monetary History of the United States*, chap. 3, esp. 113-119; Nugent, *Money and American Society*, chaps. 14-21; and Weinstein, *Prelude to Populism*. For the platforms, see Johnson and Porter, *National Party Platforms*, 88, 90-91.

12. Stanwood, *American Tariff Controversies*, 2:292; in fact, given the overall impact of the tariff, the cost of living should have been affected very little, or perhaps even reduced slightly.

13. For the elections of 1890 and 1892, see Williams, *Years of Decision*, chap. 3; Paul Kleppner, *The Third Electoral System, 1853-1892: Parties, Voters, and Political Cultures* (Chapel Hill: University of North Carolina Press, 1979), chap. 8; and Richard Jensen, *The Winning of the Midwest: Social and Political Conflict, 1888-1896* (Chicago: University of Chicago Press, 1971), chaps. 4, 5.

14. The most thorough and reliable account of the emergence of the Populist party in 1890 remains Hicks, *The Populist Revolt*, chap. 6; less detailed but no less reliable is Clanton, *Populism*, chap. 2.

15. George Harmon Knoles, *The Presidential Campaign and Election of 1892* (Stanford: Stanford University Press, 1942); Kleppner, *Third Electoral System*, chap. 8; Williams, *Years of Decision*, chap. 3; Hicks, *Populist Revolt*, chaps. 8, 9; and Clanton, *Populism*, chaps. 3, 4.

16. For the depression, see Charles Hoffman, *The Depression of the Nineties: An Economic History* (Westport, Conn.: Greenwood Press, 1970). For unemployment estimates, see Nell Irvin Painter, *Standing at Armageddon: The United States, 1877-1919* (New York: Norton, 1987), 116; and Carlos A. Schwantes, *Coxey's Army: An American Odyssey* (Lincoln: University of Nebraska Press, 1985), 13. National estimates suggest unemployment of 17-20 percent of the nonagricultural work force.

17. Richard E. Welch, Jr., *The Presidencies of Grover Cleveland* (Lawrence: University Press of Kansas, 1988), 117-119, 122-125.

18. Williams, *Years of Decisions*, 90-93; Welch, *Presidencies of Grover Cleveland*, chap. 8; and Stanwood, *American Tariff Controversies*, vol. 2, chap. 18.

19. Williams, *Years of Decision*, 86-90; Welch, *Presidencies of Grover Cleve-*

*land*, chap. 9; and Nick Salvatore, *Eugene V. Debs: Citizen and Socialist* (Urbana and Chicago: University of Illinois Press, 1982), 42, 72-73, 107. For another instance where the Cleveland administration followed an unnecessarily authoritarian reaction and gained criticism for their actions, see Schwantes, *Coxey's Army*.

20. For more information, see Cherny, *Populism, Progressivism, and the Transformation of Nebraska Politics*, 41-47, 62-67.

21. This account of the election of 1896 is taken largely from Robert W. Cherny, *A Righteous Cause: The Life of William Jennings Bryan* (Boston: Little, Brown, 1985; New York: Harper Collins, 1990). Important treatments of the election and its results include Stanley L. Jones, *The Presidential Election of 1896* (Madison: University of Wisconsin Press, 1964); Paul W. Glad, *McKinley, Bryan, and the People* (Philadelphia: Lippincott, 1964); Williams, *Years of Decision*, chap. 5; Jensen, *Winning of the Midwest*, chap. 10; J. Rogers Hollingsworth, *The Whirligig of Politics: The Democracy of Cleveland and Bryan* (Chicago: University of Chicago Press, 1963), chap. 5; Clanton, *Populism*, chap. 6; and Hicks, *The Populist Revolt*, chap. 13. The major full-length biographies of Bryan include Paolo E. Coletta, *William Jennings Bryan*, 3 vols. (Lincoln: University of Nebraska Press, 1964-1969); Louis W. Koenig, *Bryan: A Political Biography* (New York: Putnam's, 1971); and LeRoy Ashby, *William Jennings Bryan: Champion of Democracy* (Boston: Twayne Publishers, 1987). For McKinley, see H. Wayne Morgan, *William McKinley and His America* (Syracuse: Syracuse University Press, 1963); and Lewis L. Gould, *The Presidency of William McKinley* (Lawrence: University Press of Kansas, 1980).

22. Bryan's own account is in *The First Battle: A Story of the Campaign of 1896* (Chicago: W. B. Conkey Company, 1896), chap. 10, esp. 199-206.

23. The speech is given in full in *The First Battle*, 375-383; in it, Bryan professed to speak as a nonpartisan.

24. Salvatore, *Eugene V. Debs*, 156-161; and Philip S. Foner, *History of the Labor Movement in the United States*, 6 vols., 2d ed. (New York: International Publishers, 1975), 2: 336. See also Debs to Bryan, July 27, 1896, in *Letters of Eugene V. Debs*, ed. J. Robert Constantine, 3 vols. (Urbana and Chicago: University of Illinois Press, 1990), 1:120.

25. Foner, *Labor Movement*, 2:336-337; and Coletta, *Bryan*, 1:169.

26. Foner, *Labor Movement*, 2:337-339. Despite holding back from an endorsement, Gompers found himself charged before the 1896 AFL convention with having violated AFL rules by supporting the Democrats; see Philip Taft, *The A.F. of L. in the Time of Gompers* (New York: Harper & Brothers, 1957), 130-131. Bryan's labor support, however, came at a time when organized labor was at a nadir: the Knights of Labor had long passed their prime; Debs's American Railway Union lost most of its members after the disastrous Pullman Strike in 1894; AFL affiliates lost many members during the depression. In the mid-1890s, all union members together made up less than three percent of the total nonagricultural work force.

27. The AFL convention in 1896 refused to seat one such McKinley supporter; see Taft, *A.F. of L. in the Time of Gompers*, 130.

28. A convention resolution in 1888 endorsed "all wise and well-directed efforts for the promotion of temperance and morality," but stopped short of an outright

endorsement of prohibition; see Johnson and Porter, *National Party Platforms*, 82-83.

29. Foner, *Labor Movement*, 2:335.

30. Richard Jensen, *Grass Roots Politics: Parties, Issues, and Voters, 1854-1983* (Westport, Conn.: Greenwood Press, 1983), 9, argues that this was the most significant voter shift in 1896.

31. The evidence is summarized and cited in Coletta, *Bryan*, 1:201-03; Jensen, *Winning of the MidWest*, 48-57, discounts the significance of such efforts in affecting the outcome of the election.

32. Vachel Lindsay, "Bryan, Bryan, Bryan, Bryan," 1919.

33. Coefficients of correlation for the Democrat vote for president, using states as the unit of analysis, suggest that the Democratic presidential vote in 1900, 1904, and 1908 was more closely related to the Democratic presidential vote in 1888 than to the Democratic presidential vote for 1896, and similar patterns are true for the Republican presidential vote of 1892; see Tables 2.2a and 2.2b, Clubb et al., *Partisan Realignment*, 62-65.

34. Lewis L. Gould, *Presidency of William McKinley* (Lawrence: Regents Press of Kansas, 1980); for the foreign policy changes and a good survey of the major works on them, see Robert Beisner, *From the Old Diplomacy to the New, 1865-1900*, 2d ed. (Arlington Heights, Ill.: Harlan Davidson, 1986).

35. In addition to her contribution to this anthology, see Jean H. Baker, *Affairs of Party: The Political Culture of Northern Democrats in the Mid-Nineteenth Century* (Ithaca: Cornell University Press, 1983).

36. Nonpartisan offices typically included judges, school board members and school superintendents, and offices below the county level. California went further in this direction than other states by including all county offices.

37. Daniel T. Rodgers, "In Search of Progressivism," *Reviews in American History* 10 (December 1982): 114.

38. Keith Melder, *Hail to the Candidate: Presidential Campaigns from Banners to Broadcasts* (Washington: Smithsonian Institution Press, 1992), 121.

39. Some states had permitted voting by immigrants who had filed their declaration of intent but had not yet received their final citizenship papers; during the early twentieth century, most states specified final papers, thus disfranchising immigrants for a period of five years.

40. Paul Kleppner, "Politics Without Parties: The Western States, 1900-1984," in Gerald D. Nash and Richard W. Etulain, eds., *The Twentieth-Century West: Historical Interpretations* (Albuquerque: University of New Mexico Press, 1989), 317- 321; and Paula Baker, "The Domestication of Politics: Women and American Political Society, 1780-1920," *American Historical Review* 89 (June 1984): 620-647.

41. Unless specifically noted otherwise, this section is drawn from Cherny, *A Righteous Cause.*

42. Ralph Goldman, *Search for Consensus: The Story of the Democratic Party* (Philadelphia: Temple University Press, 1979), 115-117; and Goldman "Bryan: Titular Leader with Tenure," in *The National Party Chairmen and Committees: Factionalism at the Top* (Armonk, N.Y.: M.E. Sharpe, 1990), 139-157, esp. 139.

43. McAdoo, as quoted in Paolo E. Coletta, "Secretary of State William Jennings Bryan and 'Deserving Democrats'," *Mid-America* 48 (1966): 95.

44. This section, like the previous one, is drawn primarily from Cherny, *A Righteous Cause*, chaps. 4-6. For other treatments of Bryan during this period, see the works cited in note 21.

45. Goldman, *National Party Committeemen and Committees*, chap. 10, 213-231.

46. A treaty with Britain and Germany, late in 1899, gave the United States half of Samoa.

47. Detailed accounts of Cleveland's actions vis-a-vis Samoa and Hawaii may be found in Robert McElroy, *Grover Cleveland: The Man and the Statesman*, 2 vols. (New York: Harper and Brothers, 1923), 1:240-263; 2:45-73.

48. Johnson and Porter, *National Party Platforms*, 112-16.

49. Johnson and Porter, *National Party Platforms*, 144-151.

50. Selig Perlman and Philip Taft, *History of Labor in the United States, 1896-1932*, vol. 4 of John R. Commons et al., *History of Labor in the United States* (New York: The Macmillan Company, 1935), 152-158.

51. Influential recent works have looked at Progressivism in terms of "clusters of ideas" or "social languages," in the terminology of Daniel Rodgers; see Rodgers, "In Search of Progressivism." For a similar analysis, see Arthur S. Link and Richard L. McCormick, *Progressivism* (Arlington Heights, Ill.: Harlan Davidson, Inc., 1983). A different, but not incompatible, approach to defining progressivism may be found in John Whiteclay Chambers II, *The Tyranny of Change: America in the Progressive Era, 1890-1920*, 2d ed. (New York: St. Martin's Press, 1992), esp. chap. 5.

52. Richard L. McCormick, "The Discovery that 'Business Corrupts Politics': A Reappraisal of the Origins of Progressivism," *American Historical Review* 86 (1981): 247-274.

53. Willard H. Smith, "William Jennings Bryan and the Social Gospel," *Journal of American History* 53 (June 1966): 41- 60, esp. 51.

54. Roosevelt, quoted in Paul W. Glad, *The Trumpet Soundeth: William Jennings Bryan and His Democracy, 1896-1912* (Lincoln: University of Nebraska Press, 1960), 90.

55. Koenig, *Bryan*, 449-450. Du Bois, at least, had no illusions, claiming that "An avowed enemy" was "better" than a "false friend"; quoted in Manning Marable, *W. E. B. Du Bois: Black Radical Democrat* (Boston: Twayne Publishers, 1986), 69.

56. In 1910, Bryan tried to convince the Democratic party of Nebraska to endorse county option, a proposal permitting the voters of each county to determine whether liquor would be sold within the county; he failed.

57. William Jennings Bryan to Charles Bryan, no date, William Jennings Bryan Manuscript Collection, Occidental College.

58. This section also draws primarily from Cherny, *A Righteous Cause*; for the 1912 election, see also Bryan's *A Tale of Two Conventions* (New York: Funk and Wagnalls Co., 1912); Coletta, *Bryan*, vol. 2, chaps. 2-3; Koenig, *Bryan*, chap. 24; and Arthur S. Link, *Wilson*, 5 vols.,(Princeton, N.J.: Princeton University Press, 1947-1965), vol. 1, chaps. 10-13.

59. "The Forces that Make for Peace," World Peace Foundation Pamphlet Series, No. 7, Part 2 (Boston: World Peace Foundation, 1912).

60. Koenig, *Bryan*, 245.

61. It may also be argued that Bryan had a greater impact on public policy than most of the fifteen presidents during his lifetime—Buchanan, Johnson, Hayes, Garfield, Arthur, Taft, Harding, and Coolidge; those whose impact was unquestionably greater are Lincoln, McKinley, Theodore Roosevelt, and Wilson. The others are Grant, Harrison, and Cleveland.

62. The remainder of this section is adapted from Cherny, *A Righteous Cause*, 185-204.

63. Bryan, *The Royal Art* (New York: Fleming H. Revell, 1914), 42.

64.Ibid., 19-20. In his assumption that whites represented a "superior civilization," he was reflecting broadly held attitudes.

65. "White Supremacy," manuscript dated March 7, 1923, Bryan Manuscript Collection, Occidental College; Willard H. Smith, "William Jennings Bryan and Negro-White Relations," *Indiana Academy of the Social Sciences Proceedings*, 1967, 3d series, 2:99-111.

66. Bryan, *The Royal Art*, 44, 14.

67. Ibid., 43-44.

68. Ibid., 7.

69. Ibid., 45.

70. Johnson and Porter, *Party Platforms*, 114, 132, 146, 169, 251. He was not a delegate in 1916 and was unable to influence the platform in 1920. In addition, Bryan worked the phrase into many of his speeches.

71. Bryan, *The Royal Art*, 34-36.

72. Johnson and Porter, *Party Platforms*, 114-115, 147.

73. Bryan, *The Royal Art*, 44.

74. Johnson and Porter, *Party Platforms*, 113, 131, 150, 174, 249.

75. Robert F. Crunden described both Bryan and Wilson as responsible for "a Presbyterian foreign policy"; see *Ministers of Reform: The Progressives' Achievement in American Civilization, 1889-1920* (New York: Basic Books, 1982), esp. 226.

76. Bryan's views on the Philippines or India contrast sharply with those expressed by Theodore Roosevelt in, e.g., "Expansion and Peace," *Independent* 51 (1899): 3401-05.

## Chapter 9

# WILSONIAN DEMOCRACY

*John Milton Cooper, Jr.*

At first glance, it might seem tempting to consign the Democrats of the Wilson era to the historical dustbin. But on closer examination it becomes clear that under Woodrow Wilson's leadership, the party began a major metamorphosis. The changes that were to make Democrats less sectional and more strongly reform-minded and progressive at home, and distinctively internationalist abroad, were all set in motion during Wilson's presidency. The foundation for much of this change had been laid earlier during the period of William Jennings Bryan's leadership. Many aspects of the party's ultimate reformation appeared only tentatively during Wilson's time and would not fully capture the hearts and minds of party stalwarts—much less the country as a whole—until decades later. But Wilson's presidency saw the forging of the critical links between the party's complex past and its nascent future. Although Wilson was born in Virginia and raised in Georgia and South Carolina, he was nominated and elected to the presidency as a governor of a northern State, New Jersey, and as a graduate and former president of one of the country's oldest and most socially prestigious universities, Princeton. His background thus made him a symbol of transition, from what had defined Democrats prior to his term to what would define them for the rest of the century.

## SKELETONS IN THE PARTY CLOSET

Many Democrats of three-quarters of a century ago held views, especially on such subjects as racial and gender equality, that inspire nothing but horror almost anywhere on today's legitimate American political spectrum. The Democratic party has changed greatly since that era, both in its major positions on social issues and in its main bases of support. Many of the major concerns of Americans at the end of the twentieth century have little in common with the dominant themes of any of the leading political groups of the Wilson era, neither Democrats, Republicans, nor the various insurgent and third party folk who called themselves "Progressives."

At any time between 1910 and 1920, hundreds of thousands of Democrats would have enthusiastically affirmed the declaration that theirs was a "white man's party." All the elements of institutionalized racism—legalized disfranchisement and segregation of African Americans and open political appeals to prejudice—lay at the heart of the Democratic party's hegemony in all of the former Confederate states, undergirded its strength in Border States, and elicited next to no concern, much less challenge, in the North and West. Sexism, in the form of opposition to female suffrage, held sway among the great majority of southern Democrats and among somewhat smaller majorities of northeastern Democrats. Only western and, to a lesser extent, midwestern Democrats strongly backed female suffrage. In 1919, the Nineteenth Amendment to the Constitution gained final adoption in Congress with more Republican than Democratic votes. Large numbers of Democrats throughout the country also favored discriminatory restriction of immigration before and after World War I, although not with the same breadth of support given by Republicans.

So many Democrats subscribed to such views in those days in part because the party drew much of its following from a far different electoral base than it does today. For over a century, from the 1850s to the 1960s, the white voters of the South formed the party's strongest and most dependable following. Not until the party realignments of the 1920s and 1930s brought Democrats truly substantial northeastern and midwestern strength did the South encounter any real competition for Democratic primacy. During the Wilson era, only the sparsely populated far West offered much leavening of this dominance by Dixie.

The Democratic sweep in 1912 that put Wilson in the White House and gave the Democratic majorities in both houses of Congress also gave the Senate a majority leader from Virginia, and virtually all committee chairmen were southerners. In the House the majority leader was Oscar W. Underwood of Alabama, and 15 out of 17 committee chairmen represented southern states. The executive branch was comparably Dixified, since half the cabinet shared the president's southern birth an upbringing. When one journalist noted that, at the outset of the Wilson administration in 1913, "the flavor and color of things in Washington are all southern," he made a unintentionally cruel pun.

Such sectional dominance underscored the Democrats' greatest political weakness before the 1930s. In a sense, their party had never recovered from being on the losing side in the Civil War. Political upheavals in the 1890s had simultaneously solidified Democratic rule in the South, based upon white supremacy, and cemented an alliance with the West, based upon the two sections' common economic backwardness and poverty.[1] The result was to push the party squarely into minority status, as the Republicans solidified their hold on the more developed, wealthier, and more populous states of the Northeast and Midwest. The political realignment of the 1890s produced a sweeping sectional trade-off, with the Democrats getting the short end of the stick. Their 1912 victory had not altered that fundamental political reality. Wilson's election and the large congressional majorities accompanying it were due to the Republicans having split and Theodore Roosevelt having run as the third-party, Progressive, candidate. 1912 witnessed almost no noteworthy electoral shifts. Roosevelt and President William Howard Taft divided the normal Republican showing, while Wilson held the normal Democratic minority vote (about 43 percent). The only state outside the South to give Democrats a popular majority in 1912 was Arizona, with three electoral votes.

Inordinate white southern influence did not account for everything that most of today's Democrats would find repugnant in their predecessors of the early twentieth century. The party which nominated Wilson as its standard-bearer had two other distinct wings. One was a collection of city machines in the Northeast and Midwest, with their ethnically mixed, though all-white followings and their increasingly Irish-American leadership. In recent years, these organizations have come in for a bit of nostalgic adulation. This newfound appreciation has recast the old-time bosses and their henchmen to make them look like disciplined political warriors on behalf of the poor and warmhearted pluralists who welcomed and aided newly arrived immigrants—in other words, perhaps seamy but nonetheless sincere operators of social welfare agencies. Some retrospective praise may be warranted, but the fact remains that the city machines usually wallowed in corruption and often disintegrated into squabbling, ineffectual factions. They had no ideology and little social vision. Far from being roughhewn early welfare statists, the machine men dispensed paltry favors to the poor and regularly sold them out for their own political and economic profit. They primarily practiced politics for its own sake, clinging to local power and making deals with entrenched interests without benefit of positive programmatic interest.[2]

The other non-southern wing of the party in this era was western, representing the Great Plains and the Rockies. This was by far its most "progressive" segment, favoring not only female suffrage but also such modern advanced political measures as the initiative, referendum, and recall. The western Democrats had their less attractive side, too, however. Merely mentioning the name of their leader, William Jennings Bryan, conjures up their mixed legacy. They favored immigration restrictions, for example, and their strongest social issue, except for female suffrage, was prohibition. From this distant perspective, it is nearly impossible to recapture the benevolent, humanitarian attitudes that partly inspired prohibition.

It raised the first major substance abuse issue in American politics, and it anticipated most of the arguments that have arisen about drugs in the last quarter century. But prohibition also appealed and was responding to repressive, anti-urban, anti-immigrant attitudes. Its main lines of support and opposition were sectional and ethnic. Whereas female suffrage tended to divide southern from western Democrats, prohibition united most of them. Already in 1912, protracted ballots and heated arguments at the Democratic convention foreshadowed the split that was to pit rural, Protestant southerners and westerners against urban, Catholic northeasterners and midwesterners and cripple the party in the 1920s.[3]

All of these elements add up to an unappetizing picture that could reasonably lead someone to forget or reject these Democrats of the 1910s. But to cast aside the memory of the Democrats of the Wilson era would be a mistake for two major reasons. First, this picture of the party's orientation on social issues does not tell the full story of where those Democrats stood and where they were headed even on these matters. Second, the attitudes of the party's adherents in this era existed within a larger context, one which must be considered carefully by their successors in judging their attractiveness and relevance. In particular, the ideological constructions, economic concerns and ideas, and foreign policies of the Wilsonian Democrats require careful attention.

## PROVIDING A CONTEXT

The foregoing, mainly negative picture of Wilson era Democrats needs to be lightened and mitigated in most of its particulars. In particular, while the primacy of the white South and its racial attitudes cannot be denied, the meaning and consequences of that primacy should not be exaggerated. Southern Democrats in the 1910s did not constitute a monolithic bloc, even on white supremacy. Three major factions vied for power within these one-party states—Bourbons, progressives, and agrarian radicals. The Bourbons got their name less from their drinking habits than from their alleged resemblance to the French kings who "learned nothing and forgot nothing." They closely resembled the northern urban bosses, in that they cared most about maintaining their own local power and had few firm convictions on issues, beyond defending white supremacy and reflexively suspecting new ideas. The progressives tended to be well-educated, often business-oriented younger leaders who wanted to bring the South back into the national mainstream, especially economically. Many of these progressives sought to dampen appeals to white racism, and some of them believed that benign neglect might soften and begin to erode the caste system. The agrarian radicals were champions of the region's poor white farmers, although many were themselves members of the substantial planter class. They railed against economic exploitation by outside interests and undemocratic local rule by corrupt machines. Many of these radicals indulged in virulent racist demagoguery, partly out of genuine prejudice and partly as a sure-fire appeal to their lily-white electorate.[4]

This three-way division among southern Democrats produced complicated political developments. As a southern-born national level progressive, Woodrow Wilson drew early and strong support from progressives in the South, but he also aroused opposition from both Bourbons and agrarian radicals. Although some of the Bourbons distrusted Wilson's reformist ideas, they and the radicals objected primarily to his long residence in the north. Ironically, these elements combined to support Representative Underwood as a contender against Wilson for the nomination. He was a Border State native and a progressive, but he had remained a resident in the region and, hence, was presumably a "real" southerner, rather than a yankeefied expatriate. The Wilson-Underwood division in 1912 constituted a fault line between reconstructed and unreconstructed southerners.

After Wilson took office, he drew support from all three factions, although his southern support varied with the issues and the context. The Bourbons proved surprisingly cooperative, thanks mainly to their deep-seated party loyalty and appetite for federal patronage, but they often deserted the administration on more advanced reform measures, particularly female suffrage and abolition of child labor. The progressives predictably formed a bedrock of administration backing. The agrarian radicals likewise supported most of the administration's domestic program, but the chemistry between them and the president was not good. They later provided some of the strongest intra-party opposition to his foreign policy, and they were never satisfied with his stands on racial matters.

Those racist radicals' dissatisfaction did not mean that Wilson was elected as a closet civil rights advocate. One major consequence of the overweening white southern influence in Wilson's administration was an effort by some of his cabinet to segregate the workplace in their departments. That effort collapsed in the face of protests organized by the newly founded National Association for the Advancement of Colored People, but the share of federal jobs that went to African Americans declined precipitously.[5] The president himself did not enjoy good relations with blacks, either. A group of prominent African Americans, led by W. E. B. DuBois, backed Wilson in 1912 because they were sick of the Republicans taking them for granted. But the Democratic nominee gave them no encouragement and never mentioned the subject of race in the campaign. Later, after the reduction in black appointments and the attempt to segregate federal departments, a delegation met with the president, and William Monroe

Trotter threw Wilson's own slogan in his face when he asked, "Have you a 'new freedom' for white Americans and a new slavery for 'your Afro-American fellow citizens?'" An infuriated Wilson shot back, "You have spoiled the whole cause for which you came," and told them to leave. There was a bit more to the incident and Wilson's racial attitudes. He soon regretted that "I was damn fool enough to lose my temper and to point to the door." He also had already stopped the segregation effort.[6]

Wilson actually held fairly typical southern progressive racial views. His public and private statements indicate that he did not believe that blacks were inherently inferior to whites, but rather that slavery and segregation had retarded their progress. With quiet, patient amelioration, he believed, blacks might achieve political and educational equality with whites, though probably not much social mingling—perhaps in a century or so. Such attitudes reeked of paternalism and indifference, but they were a far cry from the truly vicious notions broadcast by such southern radicals as James K. Vardaman of Mississippi and Tom Watson of Georgia. In fact, Wilson's views probably resembled those of a majority of northern whites, Democrats and Republicans alike. Sadly but revealingly, the reduction in federal employment that blacks suffered under Wilson and the Democrats found no redress when the Republicans regained power in the 1920s. Not until the 1940s would African Americans' share of federal jobs regain pre-1913 levels. Overall, this period marked an extension of what the historian Rayford W. Logan has called the "nadir" in post-Civil War race relations. That was true because of both the despicable words and deeds of southern whites and the unconcern of northern whites, and these were not solely Democratic failures.[7]

The best that can be said for the situation was that the seeds of change had already begun to be planted. The NAACP successfully organized the protests that led Wilson to rescind the federal segregation policy, and by that point it also had started to mount its ultimately successful constitutional challenge to disfranchisement and segregation. In 1915, in a rare move against southern political practices, the Wilson administration challenged Oklahoma's "grandfather clause"—the loophole that allowed whites to avoid literacy tests if their grandfathers had voted before 1867 (when no blacks could have voted)—as a blatant violation of the Fifteenth Amendment's bar against racial tests in voting. The NAACP filed an amicus curiae brief, which took the broader ground that this law, among others, violated the "equal protection" clause of the Fourteenth Amendment. The Supreme Court unanimously struck down the Oklahoma statute in *Guinn v. the United States*, but only on the narrower ground advanced by the administration. It was not until the 1930s that the Court would begin to take the broader ground that southern discriminatory practices violated the Fourteenth Amendment. What Richard Kluger has called "simple justice" would be a long time coming.[8]

In fairness to the Democrats of the 1910s, it must be pointed out that their racial attitudes showed most of them at their rock bottom worst. On questions of gender, many gave a considerably better account of themselves, especially as the decade wore on. President Wilson provided the most shining example of improvement. In 1912, he ducked the suffrage issue altogether, neither opposing nor supporting female suffrage and repeating the Democratic platform's dodge that each state must decide suffrage questions for itself. During his first term, however, Wilson underwent total conversion. First, he publicly endorsed and voted for female suffrage in a New Jersey referendum; then he secured a plank favoring a constitutional amendment in the party's 1916 platform; and, finally, he made the amendment an issue in his re-election campaign. During his second term, he supported the amendment eloquently and assiduously. In a speech to the Senate in September 1918, Wilson declared, "We have made women partners in the war; shall we admit them only to a partnership of suffering and sacrifice and toil and not to a partnership of privilege and right?"[9]

Presidential lobbying in 1918 helped secure House passage and brought the amendment within two votes of the necessary two-thirds in the Senate. In the 1918 elections, suffrage organizations targeted four Senators (two from each party) for defeat; three of them lost. Both parties in Congress got the message, and the amendment was passed in May and June 1919. Support and opposition were almost equally bi-partisan. Republican Senators and Representatives favored the amendment by a larger margin than their Democratic colleagues—but only slightly. Western Democrats had long followed the lead of Bryan, who had been the first major male political figure to come out for female suffrage. Majorities of northeastern and midwestern Democrats had swung around, too, and had already helped to secure suffrage in several of their states in advance of congressional action in 1919 and ratification of the Nineteenth Amendment in 1920. Even the South did not stand united against suffrage, as progressives and some agrarian radicals came out in support of the amendment.

## FORCES FOR CHANGE

Several factors underlay changing Democratic attitudes on gender and other social issues. In the South, Wilson's influence unquestionably strengthened the progressives. Indeed, the congruence of feeling and belief that existed between the president and his supporters below the Potomac in this period brought the white South into the greatest harmony it has experienced with the national Democratic party at any time since the Civil War, with the possible exception of the early New Deal. The affinity between Wilson and his native region was so strong that in 1918 he brought off a party purge there, mainly against agrarian radicals on foreign policy issues. No other president of either party has matched that feat in the twentieth century, and several have failed at it, most notably Franklin Roosevelt in 1938, when he attempted to purge conservatives from the party.

In the Northeast and Midwest, two other major influences were at work to alter Democrats' attitudes and expand their constituencies. One influence was external, the other internal. The external influence came from organized labor. Ever since Bryan's rise to national party leadership in 1896, the Democrats had presented a friendly face toward unions, but their pro-labor gestures initially achieved little. Because the Democrats were out of power until 1913, they could not deliver on any promises. The stubbornly non-partisan stance of Samuel Gompers, the head of the American Federation of Labor, prevented much direct union response to Democratic overtures until 1908, when the AFL board overruled him and endorsed Bryan's candidacy. In 1912, however, the competing bid for labor support by Roosevelt's Progressives forestalled any national endorsements. Also, before 1910, the Republicans' protectionist tariff and anti-inflationary currency policies appealed to workers' desires to save jobs and maintain wages against cheap foreign competition.

Multiple influences converged after 1910 to bring labor and the Democrats together. Despite Gompers' discouragement from the top, state and local union leaders readily allied with Democratic politicians, in the Northeast, Midwest, and West. Republican favoritism toward business and comparative coolness toward unions combined with rising inflation to diminish appeals to industrial workers based on high tariffs and a strong dollar. Most important, after 1913 the Democrats were able to come through for labor. The Clayton Anti-Trust Act of 1914 partially fulfilled the AFL's highest legislative priority by granting unions some relief from the anti-trust laws, which had previously been used to hobble their activities. Gompers called the Clayton Act "labor's Magna Carta," and he treasured Wilson's gift of the pen with which the president signed the act into law. Two years later, the Adamson Act met another of labor's most cherished goals by instituting the eight-hour day for interstate railroad workers. During World War I, the Wilson administration gave unions a green light to organize in defense-related industries in return for a no-strike pledge and moderation of wage demands. The acts that Congress and the Wilson administration delivered after 1913 elicited gratitude and enthusiasm from unions. In 1916, AFL affiliates and even more radical labor organizations ardently supported Wilson for re-election and helped supply margins of victory in the critical states of Ohio and California. This labor support carried a price, since in 1916 and again in 1918 Republicans made the Democrats' pro-labor and progressive tax policies major issues. The Adamson Act and war-time aid to unions got tagged as "special interest" measures; graduated corporate, income, and inheritance taxes acquired a sectional twist, as Republicans denounced these levies as southern and western assaults on the well-deserved wealth of the Northeast and Midwest. It is hard to tell how much ice those Republican charges cut with the voters, but they did underline the continuing sharp differentiation between the two parties on economic issues. The strength and warmth of the mutual attraction between the Democrats and labor should at this time not be exaggerated, either. The effective marriage between the party and the unions still lay twenty years ahead; this relationship in the 1910s was, rather, their openly announced engagement.

The second influence that was changing northeastern and midwestern Democrats came from within. The urban machines were spawning a new generation of more sophisticated, more attractive, and much less parochial leaders. The first three Irish-Americans to achieve a measure of national prominence rose through the Democratic ranks in the 1910s. Curiously, the first of them came from the West, when Montana elected Thomas J. Walsh to the Senate in 1912. Two years later, Massachusetts elected David I. Walsh governor. Both Walshes' owed their elevation to some extent to the Republican-Progressive split. Soon, however, all doubt was removed about the strength and appeal of this new breed of ethnic Democrats. In 1918, despite nationwide losses that cost the party control of both houses of Congress, Tom Walsh won re-election to his Senate seat, and David Walsh defeated an incumbent Republican to become Massachusetts' first Irish-American and first popularly-elected Democratic senator. Also in 1918, Alfred E. Smith beat an incumbent Republican to win the governorship of New York.

The victories in Massachusetts and New York were especially significant for two reasons. One was that they marked the first times that Democrats had prevailed in the Northeast against undivided Republican organizations since the 1890s. The other was that they confirmed the statewide electability of urban, ethnic candidates. Thanks to the "battle of the birth rates," and the flood of immigration before 1914, there were now greater numbers of urban-based ethnic voters. But numbers alone did not automatically translate into statewide strength in this region. Tensions and rivalries among ethnic groups continued to plague efforts to build them into disciplined coalitions. Likewise, issues such as prohibition and immigration restriction polarized the electorate, usually to the Republicans' benefit, by strengthening the latter's hold on rural and small town Protestant "natives." Adding to simple numerical strength was the emerging attention of ethnic Democrats to broader concerns. Al Smith and David Walsh epitomized a growing group of ethnic Democratic political leaders, who were transcending the ghettoized outlook of the machines to establish their credibility on state and national issues.

Al Smith's emergence as governor of New York automatically made him a national figure. The 1912 Progressive candidacy of Theodore Roosevelt and the 1916 Republican candidacy of Charles Evans Hughes offered contemporary evidence of how that particular governor's chair furnished the strongest single springboard to a presidential nomination. In the twelve presidential elections during the first half of the twentieth century, only four would not feature a current or former governor of New York as at least one of the candidates. Fittingly, Smith became a contender for the Democratic nomination in 1920, thereby helping to inaugurate a decade of cultural division. The new strength of ethnic Democrats in the Northeast pushed the conflict over such social issues as prohibition and immigration restriction into the center of intraparty politics. Reeling as they did in the 1920s from that internecine strife, Democrats of the period understandably failed to recognize that much of their trouble stemmed from a fresh source of party strength.

In sum, as the 1920s approached, these changes had the potential for making the Democrats a much different party than they had been at the beginning of the decade. They were building a majority coalition based upon relatively disadvantaged groups and sections. Three of the five elements that would give them their electoral edge during the middle years of the twentieth century were either in place or in the process of emerging. First, the western cohort of Bryanites combined farmers with business people and workers who depended upon the region's agricultural and resource-extractive economy. Second, southern progressives brought sophistication and respectability, together with faint hints of racial moderation, to a hitherto recalcitrant white constituency. Third, new ethnic leaders and followers, together with organized labor, energized potent segments of the electorate in the Northeast and Midwest. Only the conversion of African Americans and the attraction of broader middle class elements remained to be accomplished in order to forge the mighty coalition that would give the Democrats majority party standing from the 1930s to the 1970s.

## BECOMING A PARTY OF REFORM, PROGRESS, AND PROSPERITY

The motive forces behind these changes sprang from many sources, and credit for hopeful developments belonged to many hands. Ordinary folk—party workers, reform group activists, comparatively enlightened southern whites, better assimilated ethnics, savvier labor organizers—put in years of patient, often unnoticed effort to help produce these transformations. If any common thread bound these people together, it was an optimistic belief that progress and prosperity in this new industrial era should be open to everybody, regardless of section, ethnicity, gender, or perhaps even race. Such convictions were not confined to Democrats then or later. During the preceding generation, the national Republican party under William McKinley had staked a seemingly preemptive claim to prosperity through its identification with business, especially big business. At the same time, such movements as those headed by Robert La Follette in Wisconsin, Albert Cummins in Iowa, and Hiram Johnson in California had staked a strong Republican claim to "progressive" reform.

But the Democrats enjoyed two advantages in this situation. One was their party's traditional pluralism, at least among whites, which had always given them an edge with northern urban ethnics. Unlike the Republicans, they did not tend to shun the immigrant-based lower classes in cities. Their upcoming intraparty warfare over social issues would be basically a sectional, rather than a class conflict, because it would pit party members from different parts of the country against each other. Although the Democrats would suffer nationally in the 1920s from these conflicts, the Republicans would suffer more from them at the state and local levels in the Northeast and Midwest. The Republicans never had much chance to appeal to the rising ethnic constituencies of northern cities.

The second advantage that the Democrats enjoyed in striving to become what David Sarasohn has called "the party of reform" was the transformation that they had undergone in 1896. The victory of the forces behind William Jennings Bryan had given the party a revolutionary attitude toward the role of government and an unmistakable orientation toward the main economic issues that had arisen out of the industrial revolution. In sum, the Democrats now showed an unprecedented willingness to use existing powers or to create new powers for the federal government, in order to redress perceived inequities and to assist disadvantaged sections and groups. This new stance preserved nineteenth century Democrats' partiality toward underdogs (as long as they were white) but it overturned the earlier insistence on states' rights and limited government. As with prohibition, Bryan's historical reputation would fall victim to the slings and arrows of critics during the cultural conflict of the 1920s. Some of his devaluation would be deserved, since those cultural conflicts might not have grown so nasty or divisive without him. But, on balance, Bryan's memory deserves to be honored by Democrats. Not only did he become one of the handful of truly great non-presidential political leaders in American history, but he also was one of the country's three most significant leaders during the first third of the twentieth century, ranking with Theodore Roosevelt and Wilson. Most important for Democrats, in important respects he was the one who made their party what it remains to this day.[10]

For the Democrats of the turn of the century, Bryan played the part of Moses. He was the prophet who led them through the wilderness, who kept them together, who laid down the basic commandments, and who finally was barred from entering the promised land. Without a leader such as Bryan to keep the party committed to the basic thrust of its 1896 stance and to spearhead the sectional alliance between southern and western agrarian radicals, the Democrats might have divided the way the Republicans did in the 1900s and 1910s, into a pro-business conservative majority and an alienated reformist minority. More likely still, the Democrats might have bumbled along as a loose confederation of parochial machines, made up of southern Bourbons and northern urban ethnics, with no clear ability to formulate a response to overriding national economic issues. To extend the biblical analogy, Wilson was the Democrats' Joshua, who went on to conquer. But, like Joshua, Wilson owed much to his predecessor for having held the band together and kept them committed and zealous in the true faith.

Wilson possessed many qualities that Bryan lacked. Not the least of these was luck. Unlike Bryan, who had run and lost three times, he was a fresh face in 1912, when the Democrats' presidential prospects at last were awarded an electoral opening. Wilson brought to the Democrats an unusual element of electability. His credentials as a graduate, professor, and president of one of the most distinguished northern universities offset the Republicans' usual advantage in social and intellectual prestige, and this proved especially useful in 1912. Since Roosevelt had seized control of the Republican reform forces and bolted to form the Progressive party, national economic issues and questions about governmental responses to those issues became the main focus of the campaign. Moreover, with his "New Nationalism," Roosevelt gave those matters a philosophical grounding that, under other conditions, might have redirected American conservatism toward something like pre-Thatcherite British Toryism.

Wilson was able to meet this challenge by giving the Democrats their own philosophical grounding in his New Freedom. His position emerged as an answer to Roosevelt's immediate charges as well as to longer-running Republican dismissals of Bryanite Democracy. Refuting allegations that Democrats were still wedded to their erstwhile states' rights, limited government approach, Wilson gladly embraced big government. Rejecting his adversaries' devotion to big business as the goose that laid the golden egg of industrial prosperity, Wilson adopted the insights of his newly acquired mentor, Louis Brandeis. He argued that the "trusts" sapped economic efficiency and that government must intervene to foster competition. In opposition to Roosevelt's embryonic vision of a protective welfare state, Wilson painted a countervision of a state that promoted social and economic mobility. Above all, against Roosevelt's classically conservative proposition that a good society depended upon transcendence of individual and group self-interest, Wilson upheld the classically liberal proposition that the only way to maintain a just, healthy society was through the moral, regulated pursuit of individual interests. For all its shortcomings as a philosophical encounter, this dialogue of 1912 was in some respects the finest political debate ever witnessed in an American presidential campaign. For the Democrats, Wilson had duplicated Thomas Jefferson's feat of a century before; building upon Bryan's work in setting the party's main direction in domestic affairs, Wilson gave that direction a philosophical definition that Democrats can still ponder for inspiration and guidance.[11]

Wilson also resembled Jefferson in translating his philosophy into action. His feats of legislative leadership between 1913 and 1916 rivaled those of Franklin Roosevelt in the 1930s and Lyndon Johnson in the 1960s. It can be argued that Wilson's achievements even surpassed Roosevelt's and Johnson's. Unlike Roosevelt, Wilson had no help from a national emergency, and unlike Johnson, he could not draw upon long years of congressional experience and leadership. Wilson did not deserve all the credit for this great legislation, any more than his successors did for theirs. During Wilson's first two years in office, the Democrats enjoyed large congressional majorities, and just about every element in the party was eager to cooperate in making the most of their long-delayed turn at bat. The president also got loyal assistance from Bryan, whom he appointed secretary of state, especially in lobbying. Finally, the first three big segments of the Wilson administration's program—tariff revision accompanied by an income tax (the Underwood-Simmons tariff and revenue act), banking reform (the Federal Reserve Act), and stronger anti-trust laws (the Clayton Act and creation of the Federal Trade Commission)—all embodied ideas whose time had come. The president's chief contribution lay in the patience and diligence with which he got congressional Democrats to stick to their tasks and helped them, with assistance from Brandeis, to thread their way through legal and technical complexities.

Wilson really won his spurs as a legislative leader in 1916. By then, a host of difficulties had beset him. The off-year elections in 1914 had witnessed a Republican resurgence that trimmed the Democratic majority in the House. Foreign affairs had roiled the political waters by spawning conflicts over American responses to the Mexican revolution and World War I. Differences over the war in Europe had impelled Bryan to resign from the cabinet and to oppose Wilson's defense and foreign policies. In spite of those difficulties, Wilson pursued a fresh and more controversial legislative program, which included child labor reform, the eight-hour law for railroad workers, federal aid to agriculture, more sharply graduated federal taxes, and Brandeis's nomination to the Supreme Court. At the same time, the president came out for female suffrage. The impetus for some of these departures was primarily grounded in the Congress, particularly the new taxes, but the strongest force behind most of them came in the White House.

Taken as a whole, Wilson's legislative program from 1913 to 1916 contained either early incarnations or embryonic intimations of most of the major domestic policies of the twentieth century Democratic party. Freer trade would remain a major objective at least through the 1960s, while progressive taxation, or "fairness," remains a hallmark of party policy. Financial reform and public accountability for the performance of the economy persist as leading concerns, as do anti-trust policies and fair trade standards. Protection of children similarly endures as a main theme for the party, and so does aid to labor and agriculture, despite periodic complaints about pandering to "special interests." In sum, there was much in the New Freedom in which New Dealers a generation later could see themselves foreshadowed, and so could devotees of the New Frontier and the Great Society, despite the passage of half a century. Even today, Democrats can still see themselves unmistakably prefigured in their domestic policies and philosophy.

There were no secrets to Woodrow Wilson's legislative success. In addition to patience and persistence, he practiced boldness and partisanship. Some of the 1916 legislative measures such as the child-labor and railroad labor acts, as well as the Brandeis nomination and female suffrage, he pushed despite advice to act differently or go slower. Behind his tactics lay a carefully conceived partisan strategy. In his previous career as an academic political scientist, Wilson had studied and advocated party responsibility as an essential feature of democratic government. Now, as president, he put his ideas into practice. Although he drew some Republican congressional support, he worked almost exclusively through his own party, and he readily claimed partisan credit for legislative accomplishments. At bottom, as a legislative leader Wilson showed how far clear vision of goals, well-set priorities, and reliance upon a disciplined party could take a president.[12]

For their achievements, Wilson and his party earned the most immediate and gratifying reward. They won re-election in 1916. They wrought a political near-miracle that has seldom earned the admiration that it deserves. It was true that Wilson remained a minority president, gaining slightly less than 50 per cent of the popular vote. He also won a narrow victory in the electoral college, where the majority would have tilted the other way if he had not squeaked by to gain California's 13 electoral votes. Congressional Democrats suffered erosion in their strength, and they had to recruit the votes of splinter-party Representatives to organize the House. But more than narrowness clouded this victory. A sense also persisted that the Republicans could and should have won, if only their nominee, Hughes, had run a better campaign and if they had not still suffered from the after-effects of their 1912 split. An air of illegitimacy also lingered in some minds because the Democrats apparently relied on the peace issue—one of their slogans was "He Kept Us out of War"—and then plunged the country into World War I just five months after the election.

Those notions badly misinterpreted the meaning of the 1916 contest. In winning in 1916, the Democratic ticket attracted nearly three million more votes than it had received in 1912. Wilson's popular vote exceeded Hughes's by 600,000 votes, in contrast to his having lagged over a million votes behind his opponents' combined total four years earlier. The Democrats' congressional losses were predictable, inasmuch as they were facing an undivided Republican opposition for the first time in six years. Hughes actually ran a good race during the later phase of the campaign, when he hammered at the eight-hour railroad law as "special interest" legislation and found an excellent manager in Will Hays. The peace issue played a much smaller and murkier part in the election than is usually thought. Wilson's temporary success in the spring of 1916 in getting the Germans to moderate their submarine attacks had removed the immediate threat of war. The Democrats balanced their peace theme with denunciations of "disloyalty" by certain German-American groups, whose support Hughes accepted, even as he also welcomed Roosevelt's vociferously hawkish backing. Many voters felt understandably confused about how to read differences between the candidates and the parties on foreign policy, and in the returns, it is difficult to measure any impact of those issues on identifiable voting blocs. By contrast, domestic issues had an unmistakable impact.

Another reason why the Democrats' feat in 1916 went unsung was that they apparently failed to break the sectional alignment of the preceding twenty years. At the state level, the outcome in 1916 seemed to confirm the pattern set in 1896. Wilson held and somewhat strengthened the Democratic coalition of the South and West, while Hughes retained almost all of the Republicans' strength in the Northeast and Midwest. The crucial difference came in Ohio. That was the only large electoral state that Wilson won; without Ohio, he also would have lost in the electoral college. This pattern of state-level voting, together with the Republicans' resurgence in the 1920s, later led analysts to dismiss the 1916 result as a fluke, mainly a personal victory of Wilson's dependent upon peculiar circumstances. That view is wrong. It overlooks the dramatic improvement that Wilson and most Democratic tickets registered throughout the Northeast and Midwest, and it ignores the major part played by organized labor in making those showings, especially in winning Ohio and California.[13]

The 1916 results conveyed two strong messages. First, the Democrats had become much more competitive with the Republicans nationally. Second, they were building the coalition that would eventually make them the majority party. Several factors would intercede to postpone the Democrats' leasehold on that political promised land. Some of the delay would stem from their intramural conflicts in the next decade. Even more stemmed from the Republicans' skill at putting their old wine of pro-business conservatism into the new bottle of "normalcy" and technology-driven prosperity. Both of those factors got much of their chance to operate through the influence of another element in the political equation—foreign policy. It is interesting to speculate about what domestic policies might have emerged after the Democrats' 1916 victory and what the political consequences might have been if America had stayed at peace. That was not to be. The United States entered World War I in April 1917, and foreign policy issues had already begun to reshape domestic politics.

## ON THE PATH TO INTERNATIONALISM

The debate over imperialism at the opening of the century had left its residue, inclining to polarize the two parties for and against foreign intervention. Roosevelt's record in office and Bryan's criticisms of that record had established them as national figures with clear and opposing reputations in foreign affairs. For the most part, however, inattentiveness had characterized the politics of foreign policy since 1900. At the outset of the Wilson administration, Latin American affairs and the Mexican revolution seemed to bode a revival of earlier conflicts between "big stick" Republicans and peace-inclined Democrats. But those appearances were deceptive. Wilson's lack of reputation in foreign affairs betokened neither lack of interest nor absence of attitude. Years earlier, he had admired Republican imperialism, and in the White House he initially showed a hankering to wield his own "big stick," until experiences in Mexico dampened this enthusiasm.

World War I confronted Wilson and the Democrats, like most of their adversaries, with the need to formulate a clear-cut foreign policy. Actually, the war's outbreak in 1914 tended to confirm established popular attitudes about remoteness from the power politics of the Old World. It took the submarine crisis with Germany in 1915, particularly the sinking of the *Lusitania*, to transform popular and political attitudes by raising the danger of American involvement in the war. At first, responses to this new situation seemed to run in well-worn grooves. Roosevelt began to pursue reunion with his old party under a hawkish banner. He and like-minded Republicans openly embraced bigger defense spending and a hard line against Germany, while they covertly yearned to intervene in the war. Conversely, Bryan resisted any moves that might carry a risk of belligerency, and he resigned as secretary of state in protest against what he regarded as Wilson's harsh diplomatic response to the *Lusitania* incident. Bryan did not stand alone. Democratic congressional leaders warned privately that they would not support war, and many of them publicly sided with the ex-secretary against increased defense spending.

Early on, the foreign policy debate also acquired a broader, more theoretical dimension. Soon after the outbreak of World War I, first Roosevelt and then the other Republican ex-president, William Howard Taft, called for creation of a league of nations to maintain peace among nations. Other Republicans, most notably Senator Henry Cabot Lodge of Massachusetts, endorsed similar ideas for a new method of conducting international relations. Those endorsements marked the political birth of twentieth century American internationalism. The birth of isolationism swiftly followed. No sooner had Taft formed an organization to promote the internationalist cause than Bryan denounced its program as a breeder of war and embroilment in European power politics. Bryan was the first major figure to invoke Washington's Farewell Address and Jefferson's proscription on "entangling alliances" as infallible guides for twentieth century American foreign policy. In the heat of the immediate political conflict over diplomatic and military issues, Roosevelt cooled to the league idea, and few other politicians rushed to embrace or reject it. Nevertheless, the stage seemed set for this larger debate, and the tendencies of the two parties seemed both manifest and familiar.[13]

But the main course of foreign policy debate and political alignment took a different direction, thanks mainly to Wilson. As Bryan's resignation showed, the president did not share his party's knee jerk reaction in favor of peace at almost any price. Wilson did not embrace interventionism either, but he did want a tougher response to Germany. He also came out for greater defense measures, although not to the levels that Roosevelt and some Republicans were demanding. "I wish with all my heart I saw a way to carry out the double wish of our people," he privately told Bryan, "to maintain a firm front in respect of what we demand of Germany and yet do nothing that might by any possibility involve us in the war." Wilson's search for a middle way drew fire from both sides, as Roosevelt denounced him as a coward and Bryan castigated him as a warmonger.

Politically, these issues came to a head early in 1916, at the same time that Wilson started pushing his second domestic program in Congress. On submarine policy, he demanded repudiation of diplomatic moves that Bryan and his congressional followers favored, and he won showdown votes in the House and Senate. Those votes revealed divisions not only among Democrats but also among Republicans, many of whom eschewed the hawkish line favored by Roosevelt and like-minded northeasterners. On defense policy, Wilson made a campaign-style speaking tour early in 1916 to promote his program of moderate increases by putting public pressure on Congress. At the same time, he compromised on a key provision with certain Democratic leaders on Capitol Hill and won nearly all of his program over Bryanite opposition. These moves confirmed the president's leadership of his party and secured his diplomatic freedom of maneuver.

Wilson did not stop there. Ever since the outbreak of the world war, he had privately favored a league of nations. In May 1916, over the objection of some of his advisors and on the eve of the Democratic convention, he went public with his espousal of this new direction for American foreign policy. In a speech before Taft's organization, Wilson endorsed its program in principle and pledged to secure post-war participation in an international organization empowered to enforce peace. When the party convention met, the delegates approved a platform written by the president that explicitly endorsed the league idea and his pledge to make the United States a charter member of a future league. These moves at the middle of 1916 did more than establish Wilson's ascendancy over the Democrats in foreign policy. They gave the party an internationalist direction that it almost certainly would not have had without his leadership.[14]

From 1916 onward, boldness and partisanship also shaped Wilson's foreign policy. The boldness emerged as soon as the president's re-election was assured. During the next two months, he mounted a peace offensive, as he sought to mediate the world war, renewed his pledge to take America into a post-war league of nations, and sketched out his vision of a new world order based upon that league and a "peace without victory." The partisanship emerged at the same time. Roosevelt and Senator Lodge attacked not only the mediation effort and proposal for a compromise peace but also, in switches from their previous stands, the league idea and any diplomatic commitment to it. Likewise, several Republican Senators, most notably William E. Borah of Idaho, took up the cudgels of isolationism from Bryan and denounced all notions of departure from traditional avoidance of international power politics. These developments at the end of 1916 and beginning of 1917 virtually guaranteed that the effort to chart an internationalist course in foreign policy would become a party issue. That is exactly what would happen after World War I. These events provided a dress rehearsal for the post-war conflict over American membership in the League of Nations.

Between the rehearsal and the conflict fell the war. After German renewal and expansion of submarine warfare forced a reluctant Wilson to intervene in April 1917, his administration provided an unprecedented example of efficiency and absence of corruption in managing a war effort. Within less than two years, the president and his advisors, particularly Secretary of War Newton D. Baker, oversaw the raising of an armed force of more than five million men and women, the implementation of the country's first effective draft, and the dispatch of over two million troops and vast quantities of weapons to the fighting front in France. At home the economy was made subject to unprecedented planning and government control, managed by such presidential appointees as Bernard Baruch and Herbert Hoover. Perhaps the highest tribute to the administration's achievement was the inability of bitterly hostile Republican congressional critics such as Lodge to uncover scandals or serious shortcomings, despite their furious digging for dirt.

"Politics is adjourned," Wilson announced in 1918, and he departed from previous administrations' practices of seeking partisan advantage in the prosecution of wars. Major civilian appointments went to such nonpartisan figures as Baruch and Hoover, while the military command of the American Expeditionary Force went to General John J. Pershing, whose deceased first wife was the daughter of a Republican senator. Wilson also made a few stabs at bipartisanship, such as appointing ex-President Taft to the War Labor Board and sending former Secretary of State Elihu Root on a diplomatic mission to Russia. But he drew the line at allowing Roosevelt to raise a division to fight in France, a step the professional military staff also opposed, and he made no systematic attempt to draw the Republican party into partnership in the conduct of foreign and military policy. Wilson's two worst failures of bipartisanship occurred at the end of 1918. First, in October, he asked voters to demonstrate confidence in his leadership by electing Democratic majorities in Congress. Republicans promptly made his appeal a campaign issue, and when they won both houses by narrow margins, they claimed that the country had repudiated Wilson. The second failure came in November, when the president appointed only one Republican, who was not a leading party figure, to the delegation to the peace conference in Paris, which Wilson himself headed. Both his presence and the absence of prominent Republicans lengthened the odds against anything but partisan strife over the peace terms, particularly the League of Nations.[15]

Other aspects of Wilson's war-time leadership also inadvertently contributed to the likelihood of post-war political difficulties. The administration's encouragement of unions fed both labor militancy and employer resistance, with the result that waves of strikes rocked major industries and other sectors of the economy in 1919. The most frightening of those strikes were the radical-led Seattle general strike and the Boston police strike, both of which had to be broken by troops and were denounced by conservatives as harbingers of revolution. Domestic propaganda, governmental and private, fanned a mood of popular hysteria and intolerance. German-Americans, radicals, and pacifists fell victim to official repression, as federal, state, and local authorities took actions such as censoring and suppressing publications, imprisoning citizens, deporting aliens, and banning the teaching of the German language and the playing of music by Bach and Beethoven. Private vigilantism took sometimes vicious, sometimes silly turns. Mobs intimidated citizens and destroyed property; people lost jobs, and some were lynched; dachshunds were stoned in streets; and sauerkraut was temporarily renamed "liberty cabbage," while frankfurters and hamburgers acquired more forgettable but equally short-lived monikers. Some people wondered then and later whether a domestic casualty of World War I may not have been the American people's sense of humor as well as their civil liberties.

The Wilson administration stood uncomfortably in the middle of these actions. Its most controversial deeds—creation of a domestic propaganda agency and passage of war-time sedition and anti-espionage laws—emerged from attempts to moderate more damaging policies demanded by Republicans and some Democrats. The most famous act of official repression—the trial, conviction, and imprisonment of the former socialist presidential candidate Eugene Debs—occurred only after prolonged private negotiations, involving the president himself, in search of a legal arrangement that would allow him to criticize the war. Debs rejected those overtures because of his stated intention to martyr himself to the cause of free speech and opposition to the war. The attempts at moderation met with scorn from conservatives and radicals alike, who found them paltry and feeble for opposite reasons. The worst political damage to Wilson and his party lay in alienating segments of their natural constituency among liberal and labor groups.

## DISINTEGRATION

The chickens of conflict over the war and foreign policy came home to roost all at once for the Democrats during 1919 and 1920. Domestically, the nation was in a mess. The dismantling of war-time rationing and price controls ignited inflation, while the strikes further exacerbated shortages. Rapid demobilization of the armed forces boosted unemployment. Racial tensions exploded in a summer of riots in northern cities, incited by whites who resented the recent migration of African Americans. In the South, a wave of lynchings rose up, often aimed at returning black servicemen. Several cities and states mounted anti-radical crusades, and at the end of

1919 Attorney General A. Mitchell Palmer mounted a massive series of raids against leftist organizations. These actions fed the infamous "Red Scare" of 1919-1920. Politically, the sorriest aspect of the situation lay with Wilson, first in his absorption in foreign policy to the exclusion of nearly everything else and, later, in his physical incapacity. For changing reasons, a dangerous vacuum of leadership existed at the top during most of these two years.

During the first half of 1919, the president was in Paris negotiating the peace settlement and establishment of the League of Nations. Entreaties to attend to domestic problems elicited little response even after he returned home in July. Instead, both Wilson and the Republicans, particularly Lodge, who was now the Senate majority leader and chairman of the foreign relations committee, engaged in an increasingly acrimonious conflict over the treaty and American membership in the League. By September, when his belated efforts failed to win over Republican senators, Wilson hit the campaign trail, as he had done three years earlier for his defense program, in an attempt to sell his foreign policy to the public and put pressure on the Senate. For three weeks, he mounted the most strenuous speaking tour of his career, but his failing health aborted the trip. An ailing president was rushed back to the White House, where on October 2, 1919, he suffered the massive stroke that almost killed him. Partially paralyzed and emotionally impaired, Wilson never again fully functioned as president, although he retained the strength of will to block all efforts at possible accommodation with Lodge and the Republican senators. In November 1919 and again in March 1920, the peace treaty failed to gain the Senate's consent, and the United States never did join the League of Nations.

Three points are most worth making about this familiar, tragic story. First, the final defeat of Wilson's program did not stem from a failure of bipartisanship. Party conflict over the League had been unavoidable in view of the stands taken two years before by Roosevelt, Lodge, and Borah. Wilson deserved blame for not taking a Republican of the stature of Taft or Root with him to Paris, but it is doubtful that even their participation could have won over enough of their party brethren. An internationalist foreign policy was too new to American politics to be amenable to a sincere willingness to submerge differences. It would take another quarter century, a painful flirtation with isolationism, and another world war before an effective internationally minded foreign policy consensus could emerge. Even then, the so-called bipartisan foreign policy of the 1940s would really amount to Republican capitulation, rather than cooperation on equal terms.

The second point about the failure of the politics of foreign policy in 1919 and 1920 is that Democrats were as blameworthy as Republicans.

Until near the end of the debates, Democratic senators played a secondary, curiously passive, rarely constructive role. Republican critics and opponents of the League consistently outgunned them in both oratory and parliamentary maneuver. Although some Democratic senators privately bridled at Wilson's conduct, only a handful of them joined with Lodge in fashioning his alternative program for limited American participation in the League. In November 1919, nearly all the Democrats voted as obdurately against Lodge's alternative as the Republicans voted against Wilson's insistence upon unlimited participation. Only in the second round of voting, in March 1920, did a significant number of Senate Democrats cross over, but not enough of them switched to secure the two-thirds needed for consent. Furthermore, Wilson promised to refuse to ratify the treaty if the Republican alternative did secure the necessary margin.

The final, corollary point about this Democratic failure is that not only Democratic senators but the party as a whole had grown far too dependent on top-down leadership in foreign policy. Such deference to the president would have been unhealthy, even if the story had somehow had a happier ending. Much of the fault lay with Wilson. He practiced patient, collegial leadership in domestic affairs, and he cheerfully delegated authority in both civilian and military aspects of war management. But in foreign affairs, especially regarding war aims and the peace settlement, he played a lone game. Bryan's successor, Secretary of State Robert Lansing, never enjoyed the president's full confidence and rarely got to offer serious advice. Even Wilson's main confidant and war-time diplomatic negotiator, Colonel Edward M. House, seldom contributed to formulating policy. This solitariness was the defect of one of Wilson's greatest political strengths—his boldness. Contrary to the assertions of many critics, no evidence suggests that he harbored a messiah complex; but, he did suffer from tendencies to move fast and take big risks for the highest stakes.

It would be wrong, however, to pin all the blame on Wilson's character. The followers were as much at fault as the leader in the Democrats' excessive willingness to tag along in foreign policy. In this sphere, Wilson himself was playing the part of Moses as Bryan had done earlier. Wilson could not be the conquering Joshua because no one had gone before him to prepare the way for his internationalist program. Not enough groundwork had been laid through debate and reflection. The parallel with Bryan's domestic role is not perfect, because much of Wilson's influence on Democratic foreign policy would be posthumous. Moreover, though, his legacy would undergo eclipse and repudiation during the isolationist heyday of the 1930s, Wilsonian internationalism would endure to become enshrined during the 1940s as the major thrust in foreign policy of the Democratic party. Collective security—in the various forms of the United Nations, the

Marshall Plan, NATO, and intervention in Korea—bore the stamp of the Wilsonian legacy. Although Democratic presidents from Roosevelt to Johnson would indulge in forms of power politics that many latter-day Wilsonians found repugnant, the overarching vision has remained the party's lodestar in international affairs.[16]

## FAILURE TO CONSOLIDATE

Consequences of the political disintegration that occurred during 1919 followed swiftly for Wilson and his party. The result was unmitigated disaster. Forebodings of trouble had dogged the Democrats since early 1919, and by the time of the party convention in June 1920 ill omens were unmistakable. The president's closest friends had to move quietly to quash his delusive quest for a third term in a "great and solemn referendum" on the League issue. Crippled and out of touch with political reality though he was, Wilson retained a fervent following. The biggest demonstrations at the convention were on his behalf, and 38-year-old Franklin Roosevelt helped gain the vice presidential nomination by his conspicuous part in those demonstrations. Domestic issues supplied much more conflict. The delegates fought over prohibition and immigration restriction, and they deadlocked for 44 ballots between the urban, ethnic forces supporting Governor Smith of New York for the presidential nomination, and opposing southern and western elements once more championed by Bryan. It was a foretaste of even worse conflict to come four years hence. In the end, the convention settled on Governor James M. Cox of Ohio as a compromise candidate, mainly because he was a "wet" on prohibition but, unlike Smith, a Protestant, and because he was not associated with the Wilson administration. Franklin Roosevelt got the vice-presidential nomination as a gesture toward Wilsonian loyalists and in fanciful hopes that his famous surname might draw Republican votes.

Cox and Roosevelt mounted a vigorous, exciting campaign that was doomed from the start. Not only were they massively outspent and masterfully outadvertised by the Republicans, but they also failed to strike sparks with their appeals to liberal and progressive economic views. Against his own inclinations, Cox began to emphasize the League issue, partly as a rallying point for his party and partly because it seemed the one issue on which the Republicans might prove vulnerable. Even there, however, through adroit obfuscation and inflamed party sentiment, Republicans sloughed off the challenge.

Nothing availed the Democrats in 1920, as they suffered their worst defeat ever in a presidential election. "It wasn't a landslide," quipped one party leader. "It was an earthquake." The Republicans swept almost everything outside the "Solid South," which they cracked to carry Tennessee. In New York, they defeated Smith for re-election as governor and carried New York City for the first time since the Civil War, a feat they matched in other big cities. In Congress, Democrats lost some of their safest House seats and failed to win a single race for the Senate outside the South. The total result, which gave the Republicans over 60 percent of the popular vote, was at once more and less than the sum of its parts. The Republicans read their triumph as a mandate to pursue "normalcy" at home by reasserting their pro-business conservatism and abroad by pursuing not exactly isolationism but a form of non-internationalism. But much of their swollen margin rested upon temporary disaffections in the electorate. Although the Republicans would also win the next two presidential elections easily, they never again approached this 1920 margin, even though they would face a more deeply divided opposition in 1924 and have a far more attractive candidate of their own in 1928. Congressionally, the Democrats would bounce back in 1922 and again in 1926, and in the congresses chosen in the off-year elections of the next decade effective control would belong to a coalition of Democrats and Republican insurgents.[17]

The 1910s had given the Democrats a roller coaster ride. Early on, they had zoomed to the heights of power and accomplishment. At the middle of the decade, they had taken a dip, but then had enjoyed another exciting rise to even greater heights. Finally, they had plunged to the depths. They had also begun to suffer from the internal conflicts that exposed some of their worst weaknesses and would undermine their strength in the next decade. Yet, on balance and in the longer run, the party had clearly and unquestionably moved in positive, enlightened, hopeful directions. In both domestic and foreign policy, this decade had witnessed the firm establishment of the twentieth century Democratic party. The seeds had been sown, and the first fruits had blossomed. Even the setbacks of the 1920s would not long delay still greater flowerings.

## NOTES

1. For a discussion of this period see Robert W. Cherney, "The Democratic Party in the Era of William Jennings Bryan," chap. 8 in this volume.

2. For sophisticated, well documented presentations of the machines filling social service functions, see Ira Katznelson, *City Trenches: Urban Politics and the Patterning of Class in the United States* (New York: Pantheon, 1981); and Amy Bridges, *A City in a Republic: Antebellum New York and the Origins of Machine Politics* (New York: Cambridge University Press, 1984).

3. The best treatment of Bryan in this period is Lawrence W. Levine, *Defender of the Faith: William Jennings Bryan, the Last Decade, 1915-1925* (New York: Oxford University Press, 1965).

4. On the southern progressives, see C. Vann Woodward, *Origins of the New*

*South, 1877-1913* (Baton Rouge: Louisiana State University Press, 1951); and George B. Tindall, *The Emergence of the New South, 1913-1945* (Baton Rouge: Louisiana State University Press, 1967).

5. Judson C. Welliver, "The Triumph of the South," *Munsey's Magazine* (1913), quoted in Woodward, *Origins of the New South,* 480. On southern domination of the party, see ibid., 456-481; Morton Sosna, "The South in the Saddle: Racial Politics during the Wilson Years," *Wisconsin Magazine of History,* 54 (August 1970): 30-49; and Kathleen Long Wohlgemuth, "Woodrow Wilson's Appointments Policy and the Negro," *Journal of Southern History* 24 (November 1958): 457-471.

6. William Monroe Trotter's address to the President, November 12, 1914, in *The Papers of Woodrow Wilson*, ed. Arthur S. Link, 31 (Princeton: Princeton University Press, 1979): 300; Wilson quoted in Josephus Daniels to Franklin D. Roosevelt, June 10, 1933, ibid., 309, n. 2; see also Stephen R. Fox, *The Guardian of Boston: William Monroe Trotter* (New York: Atheneum, 1971).

7. Rayford W. Logan, *The Negro in American Life: The Nadir, 1877-1901* (New York: Dial Press, 1954).

8. Richard Kluger, *Simple Justice: The History of Brown v. Board of Education and Black America's Struggle for Equality* (New York: Knopf, 1975). On the *Guinn* case, see ibid., 102-104. Ironically, the solicitor general who argued the *Guinn* case was John W. Davis, who would be the Democratic presidential nominee in 1924; 30 years after that Davis would be the main counsel opposing the NAACP and defending school segregation in the *Brown* case.

10. Wilson speech to Senate, September 30, 1918, in Link, *Papers of Wilson*, 51: 159. On Wilson's attitudes and role in the suffrage struggle, see Christine A. Lunardini and Thomas J. Knock, "Woodrow Wilson and Woman Suffrage: A New Look," *Political Science Quarterly* 95 (Winter 1980-81): 655-671.

11. See David Sarasohn, *The Party of Reform: Democrats in the Progressive Era* (Oxford: University of Mississippi Press, 1989).

12. See John Milton Cooper, Jr., *The Warrior and the Priest: Woodrow Wilson and Theodore Roosevelt* (Cambridge: Harvard University Press, 1983), 206-221.

13. See ibid., 229-265.

14. For a fine analysis of one aspect of the election see David Sarasohn, "The Election of 1916: Realigning the Rockies," *Western Historical Quarterly* 11 (July 1980): 285-305. For an example of a mistaken sectional view of the result, see Cooper, *Warrior and Priest*, 255-256.

15. See John Milton Cooper, Jr., *The Vanity of Power: American Isolationism and the First World War, 1914-1917* (Westport, Conn.: Greenwood Press, 1969).

16. See Cooper, *Warrior and Priest*, 266-287.

17. Wilson's speech to Congress, May 27, 1918, in Link, *Papers of Wilson*, 48:164; see also Seward W. Livermore, *Politics Is Adjourned: Woodrow Wilson and the War Congress, 1916-1918* (Middletown, Conn.: Wesleyan University Press, 1966).

18. See, for example, Daniel Patrick Moynihan, *On the Law of Nations* (Cambridge: Harvard University Press, 1990), esp. 25-54.

19. On this election, see Wesley M. Bagby, *The Road to Normalcy: The Campaign and Election of 1920* (Baltimore: The Johns Hopkins University Press, 1962).

Chapter 10

# They Endured: Democrats Between World War I and the Depression

*Allan J. Lichtman*

"They endured," William Faulkner's summary of the black experience in the South, describes the Democratic party in the 1920s. In 1912, after 16 years of exile, Woodrow Wilson led the party to the presidency and control of Congress. But Democratic dominance was short-lived. After losing Congress in 1918, the party would not again hold the presidency, the Senate, the House, or a majority of governorships or state legislatures until the 1930s. In three successive presidential elections of the 1920s, Democratic candidates would gain an average of just 35 percent of the popular vote.

Democratic woes during the decade went beyond the red ink of election returns. The party was strapped for funds and its national organization barely stayed alive between presidential campaigns. Republican views dominated the press, and Republicans won most of the votes cast by the millions of women who had become newly enfranchised in 1920. Programmatically, the Democrats of the 1920s were drawing down the intellectual capital of Thomas Jefferson and Woodrow Wilson; not until the New Deal era would the party replenish its stock of ideas.

Still, Democrats survived the 1920s as a viable opposition, able to regain power and redirect national policy after the Great Crash of 1929. The election of 1920 passed control of government to a staunchly conservative GOP. Republican policies worked well during the prosperity of the 1920s, but were unequal to the challenge of economic distress. Among Democrats, insurgency waned and Jeffersonian principles of localism and limited government made a comeback after 1920. Still, Democrats in Congress and state governments salvaged elements of the progressive agenda: free trade, tax reform, efficiency in government, and investment in public services. The Democratic party remained the only alternative to status-quo politics after a Progressive party movement collapsed in 1924.

Politically, the Democratic party survived the 1920s by melding diverse voter blocs from outside the core of America's economic elite: whites in the South; working-class Catholics and new immigrants in northern cities with Democratic machines (e.g., New York and Chicago); and reformers in the Mountain States, the last bastion of the agrarian insurgency within the Democratic party.

Throughout its history, Democratic pluralism has helped the party to weather periods of adversity, to evolve with changing circumstances, and to succeed in locally based contests for congressional and state offices.[1] To the dismay of critics, however, this same pluralism has made it difficult for the party to rally behind a program for the nation. Democrats have unified only sporadically; for example, in the 1910s, the 1930s, and the 1960s.

Historians of the 1920s have misread Democratic strength in diversity as a source of internal strife and weakness. A "politics of provincialism," in the words of historian David Burner, paralyzed a Democratic party that was split between the insular, rural, native-stock South and West and the cosmopolitan, polyglot cities of the North. "Had the city and country been able to cooperate by naming candidates acceptable to the whole party, the Democrats could have provided the Republicans with a more formidable opposition during the twenties," Burner wrote.[2] In this view, while urban and rural America fought to a standstill during the 1920s, the future of the party belonged to the forward-looking cities. The countryside was fighting a rearguard action for white supremacy, protestant culture, states' rights, and limited government.

The prevailing view of Jazz Age Democrats is triply in error. First, it fails to recognize that Democratic diversity, despite the squabbling it produced, made possible the party's survival in Congress and state governments during the 1920s. Second, it exaggerates urban/rural conflict, ignoring the often shared values of city and country Democrats. Third, it misses the point that challenging parties can rarely influence the outcome of presidential elections. There was no philosophers' stone for Democratic presidential success in the 1920s. The performance of the party in power decides presidential elections, not the strategies devised by parties and candidates.[3] From 1920 to 1928, the record of presidential administrations heavily favored the GOP. Only the Great Depression and President Hoover's failed response opened the White House gates to the Democrats.

The regional and local distribution of the Democratic vote following 1928 is striking. Of 18 Democratic governors, 16 came from the southern, Border, and Mountain States, and one from New York State. Of 40 Democratic senators, 25 came from the southern, Border, and Mountain States, and two from New York State. Of 167 Democratic congressmen, 120 came from the southern, Border, and Mountain States, and 25 from New York City or Chicago.

Although voters surged nationwide to the Democratic party during the 1930s, its base remained the South and the northern cities. By deferring to local Jim Crow traditions, ceding legislative power to southern committee chairmen in Congress and redistributing resources to poorer states, New Deal Democrats tightened their hold on the South. Simultaneously, the Democrats greatly broadened their urban base by toppling Republican machines in cities like Philadelphia, Detroit, and Buffalo; by detaching black voters from the party of Lincoln; and by cementing their alliance with organized labor. After the last election of the Roosevelt/Truman era in 1948, some three-quarters of the Democrats in the House of Representatives came from southern and Border States, and from northern cities of 500,000 or more.

## THE ELECTIONS OF 1920

The midterm elections of 1918 presaged the Democratic party's defeat in 1920 and the demise of the Wilson era. In 1918, the Democrats lost their majorities in both houses of Congress, dropping 26 seats in the House and 11 in the Senate. No incumbent presidential party to date had relinquished control of both chambers in mid-term elections and retained the White House in the next campaign. By 1920, foreign-policy failure, social unrest, economic distress, an exiting president, a nomination struggle, and the lack of an alluring candidate burdened the Democrats. The seven to one odds on the Republicans, offered by Wall Street betters during the fall campaign, made the Democrats of 1920 the greatest presidential underdogs since legal wagering had begun in 1876.[4]

Although President Woodrow Wilson had campaigned in 1916 as the man "who kept us out of war," the tasks of waging war and making peace would dominate his second term. The defeat of the Axis powers in 1919 brought Wilson only a passing triumph. Unable to impose his idealism on the Paris Peace Conference, President Wilson bent his views to the realpolitik of European leaders. He hoped that a League of Nations would compensate for flaws in the peace settlements. But the Senate would not accept the League without substantial revisions, which Wilson rejected. Wilson's failed postwar diplomacy was a wound that wouldn't heal during the election, especially among German-American voters.

Victory in battle also failed to abate the social stress of war. Conflicts arising from black migration to northern cities led to race riots in 25 cities in 1919. A record four million workers walked off the job in that year, including the Boston police. Attorney General A. Mitchell Palmer, a presidential aspirant, exploited fears of foreign radicals to raid the headquarters of left-wing organizations, deport aliens, and arrest thousands of suspected subversives. Economically, the wartime boom was deflating by 1919; a year later, the economy had collapsed into a recession that would not lift until 1922.[5]

The Democratic platform endorsed the League of Nations and pledged to continue Woodrow Wilson's brand of domestic reform. In response to the enfranchisement of women in 1920, the platform advocated federal laws against child labor, federal aid for infancy and maternal care, increased vocational assistance for women, and independent citizenship for married women. The Democrats also formally integrated their leadership structure by requiring that the party's national committee consist of one committeeman and one committeewoman chosen from each state. It would be several decades, however, before these committeewomen gained real clout within the party.

With Wilson incapacitated by a stroke and William Jennings Bryan in decline, the Democrats lacked leadership in 1920. Attorney General Palmer had failed to parlay his "Red Scare" into consensus support, leaving former Treasury Secretary William Gibbs McAdoo, Wilson's son-in-law, as the leading candidate for the presidential nomination. After failing to win Wilson's endorsement, however, McAdoo chose to retreat until 1924. On the 44th ballot, Democrats nominated the little-known but mildly progressive governor of Ohio, James M. Cox. For vice president they turned to the 38-year-old Franklin D. Roosevelt of New York, a lowly assistant Secretary of the Navy. The Democrats hoped that Roosevelt's youthful vigor and magic name might brighten their dark prospects.

The Republicans predictably embraced a solidly conservative platform and presidential ticket. The party of Theodore Roosevelt was visible only among proposals devised for the woman voter. The GOP advocated federal prohibition of child labor, equal pay for equal work in federal employment, and regulation of the hours of working women.

Cox and Roosevelt campaigned vigorously in 1920, but their efforts suffered from a lack of funds and the post-war malaise. After matching Republican spending in 1916, the Democrats fell behind by three to one in 1920.[6] The Republican presidential nominee, Senator Warren Harding of Ohio, called for a return to "normalcy" from the safety of his front porch in Marion, Ohio. Drawing a total of only 34 percent of the popular vote and 20 percent of the electoral college vote, the Democrats of 1920 suffered the worst beating of any incumbent party, before or since. They barely held on in Congress, retaining little more than their base in the southern and Border States. Republicans would control 70 percent of the House and 61 percent of the Senate.

Democratic candidates also lost the contest for women's votes, as women supported Harding in greater proportion than their male counterparts. Throughout the 1920s, women voters would consistently prefer conservative candidates over those who promised change. This endorsement of status-quo politics by women voters dashed feminist hopes that suffrage would revive the impetus for social reform.

The only bright spot for Democrats in 1920 was that enthusiasm had flagged for both parties. Harding's 60 percent of the popular vote translated into less than 30 percent of the voting-age population, as turnout plunged a record 13 percentage points, from 62 percent in 1916 to 49 percent in 1920. A majority of the electorate was politically inactive in 1920, apparently open to recruitment by either party or even an insurgent movement.

## THE ELECTIONS OF 1924

Under Presidents Harding and Coolidge, the Republicans redeemed most of their campaign promises, including opposition to the League of Nations and World Court, tariff protection for business, and immigration restriction. Rather than dismantling the regulatory structures erected by Roosevelt and Wilson, Republican presidents packed federal agencies with pro-business appointees. Under the prod of Treasury Secretary Andrew Mellon, a multi-millionaire banker, Congress restricted the growth of government and its capacity to redistribute income by cutting taxes adopted during the war.

Progressivism was ailing, but not yet dead in the early 1920s. In foreign affairs, the Harding administration was not fully isolationist. It promoted private loans and investments abroad, pushed disarmament pacts, and negotiated agreements to help Germany pay the its postwar reparations. In domestic policy, a "farm bloc" of southern, midwestern, and western legislators sponsored expanded farm loan programs, exemptions from antitrust laws for farmer cooperatives, and regulation of grain markets. The leadership of the farm bloc was heavily Republican, but included southern Democrats such as Senator Claude A. Swanson of Virginia and Representative George Huddleston of Alabama. Farm relief legislation generally received bipartisan support, with voting divided more along sectional than party lines. A Congress and administration still uncertain about the new woman voter reluctantly adopted legislation proposed by women lobbyists: the Sheppard-Towner Act for the health care of mothers and infants (1921), the Cable Act granting independent citizenship for married women (1922), and a Child Labor Amendment to the Constitution (1924).

The scope and duration of reform, however, was limited during the Harding/Coolidge years. The farm bloc failed to gain its top priority of federal intervention to support commodity prices, and after 1922, initiatives for women were confined to the Child Labor Amendment, which fell short of ratification in the states.

By 1922, a Democratic revival appeared to be in progress. A Republican party suffering from weak presidential and congressional leadership could not sustain congressional majorities inflated by the landslide of 1920. In the most successful mid-term elections in party history, the Democrats gained 74 House and six Senate seats. The Democrats controlled 48 percent of the House and 45 percent of the Senate, coming within striking distance of recapturing both chambers.

The following year, the "Teapot Dome" scandals exposed high officials in the Harding administration profiting from the illegal sale or lease of government property, including oil reserves at Elk Hills, California, and Teapot Dome, Wyoming. Insiders speculated that Teapot Dome would disqualify Harding for renomination, opening the GOP to a bloody succession fight and perhaps terminating the new Republican era after a single presidential term. The death of President Harding in August 1923 scrambled the odds once again, however. Vice President Coolidge was untainted by scandal and proved to be a surprisingly popular President, with an appealing anti-hero image. The GOP would unite behind President Coolidge and a stand-pat platform in 1924.

The incumbent Republicans benefitted from an economic boom as business recovered in 1922-23 from the postwar recession. A brief contraction would begin in late 1923 and extend into the beginning of 1924. The economy would start growing again, however, by the summer of the election year.

Democrats provided sporadic opposition to economic policies of the GOP, but failed to develop an agenda of their own. Democrats in Congress joined with progressive Republicans to moderate Secretary Mellon's tax breaks for the wealthy. A handful of western Democrats, representing the legacy of agrarian insurgency within the party, often voted with Republican progressives on tax policy, agricultural price supports, bonuses for veterans, and labor reform.[7] But the Democratic party had no program of its own for easing income inequality, limiting corporate power, or relieving the economic hardship of an estimated 40 percent of Americans who subsisted on poverty-level incomes.[8] Nor did they have any prescriptions for the business cycle or sick industries like agriculture, shipping, mining, and textiles. They only paid lip service to the demands of labor for collective bargaining rights and liberation from anti-strike injunctions. The Democrats of the 1920s had a more limited vision of positive government than the party of Woodrow Wilson a decade before. In 1924 they agreed on assailing Republican corruption, favoritism for the rich, and protective tariffs: a reversion to party platforms of the 1880s.

A more coherently progressive Democratic party would not have toppled the Coolidge administration in 1924. Conditions were too favorable for the party in power. Even many Americans at the edge of subsistence believed that prosperity was within their reach. Poor and working-class Americans would figure more prominently in shrunken Democratic coalitions of the 1920s than their more affluent counterparts. There would be no mass mobilization of the disadvantaged by the Democratic party, however, until the 1930s.

The Democrats scarcely debated economic policy at their 1924 convention in New York City. The hot issues that summer were the League of Nations, prohibition, and the Ku Klux Klan. Newton D. Baker, Woodrow Wilson's Secretary of War, led a one-man crusade for endorsement of Wilson's dream of American entry in the League of Nations. But delegates were unwilling to refight the foreign policy battles of 1920. By a wide margin, the convention ducked a debate on internationalism, advocating a national referendum on American participation in the League. Prohibition divided a party that included ardent Protestant drys in the South and Catholic, Jewish, and German wets in the North. The Democrats' assuaged both camps with a minimalist plank that pledged only "to respect and enforce the constitution and all laws."[9]

Party professionals failed to forge such a consensus on the Klan. America's "second" Klan, founded in 1915, was at the zenith of its power in 1924, with at least three million and perhaps six million members, distributed throughout the United States, in both city and country. The Klan assailed Negroes, foreigners, Catholics, and Jews. It also upheld traditional moral values, cohesive communities, and strict enforcement of the prohibition laws. The Klan's message resonated with America's white Protestants, who largely supported immigration restriction, isolationism, segregation, and Prohibition. In many communities, the Klan was a grassroots movement that challenged local elites for control of government. The profile of Klansmen in the 1920s closely mirrored a cross section of white, Protestant America.[10]

Ironically, the Klan chose the more ethnically homogeneous Republican party as the primary vehicle for its political aspirations in the 1920s. Klan-backed candidates in 1924 competed mostly in Republican primaries and usually ran under the Republican banner in the general elections. But the Democratic party entrapped itself in a sectional debate over denouncing the Ku Klux Klan by name in its 1924 platform. The Klan became the symbolic issue separating the two leading candidates for the Democratic nomination: William Gibbs McAdoo and Alfred E. Smith.

McAdoo believed that his time had come in 1924. But for the Teapot Dome scandal, he probably would have been right. The revelation that McAdoo had been on the payroll of oilman Edward Doheny, one of the principals in the scandal, doomed his quest to become a consensus candidate in 1924. Despite dominating the primaries, McAdoo failed to crush the candidacy of Governor Alfred E. Smith of New York. Smith, the first Catholic to contend seriously for a major party nomination, was the most successful Democratic vote-getter of the era, winning the gubernatorial elections in New York four times. Smith rallied the party's northern delegations, splitting the convention along sectional lines.

By a single vote, delegates defeated a platform plank condemning the Klan. The delegates would have adopted the plank, but for the "unit rule" that empowered state conventions to instruct delegations to cast all votes by majority rule, "regardless of the preferences of the minority." The unit rule applied to all states, except the few selecting delegates in primary elections.[11] Under the unit rule, seven states cast unanimous votes against the anti-Klan plank. Only the state of Alabama—lead by former House Speaker and anti-Klan leader Oscar W. Underwood—cast a unit rule vote for the plank.

Although the unit rule saved McAdoo's position on the Klan, another nineteenth-century throwback probably cost him the nomination. Until 1936, the Democratic party required nomination by two-thirds of the delegate votes cast. Several times, McAdoo edged close to the convention's 550 delegate majority (he peaked with 530 votes on the 69th ballot), but he never approached the 732 votes needed for nomination.

The embarrassing convention sweltered on for more than two weeks and a record 103 ballots before compromising on John W. Davis—a charming, but lackluster moderate—who had consistently finished third in the voting behind McAdoo and Smith. Davis was the nation's leading constitutional lawyer. He had previously served as congressman, solicitor general, and ambassador to Great Britain. The highlight of the convention—the first ever broadcast to a nationwide radio audience—was Franklin Roosevelt's "Happy Warrior" nominating speech for Smith, which marked FDR's recovery from polio.

Davis would not be the only alternative to Coolidge in 1924. Republican Senator Robert M. LaFollette of Wisconsin became the candidate of an improvised Progressive party that sought to win over voters still devoted to opposition to monopoly, restrictions on judicial power, public control of finance and natural resources, progressive income taxes, collective bargaining rights for labor, and price supports for farmers. The neo-progressives of 1924 included the railroad brotherhoods, the American Federation of Labor, remnants of the Socialist party, and progressive farmer groups. La Follette's running mate was progressive Democratic Senator Burton K. Wheeler of Montana. La Follette hoped to run well enough to stalemate the electoral college and precipitate a realignment of the parties. By making opposition to monopoly the centerpiece of a desultory campaign, however, the 69-year-old La Follette was looking backward to the Populist and Progressive eras rather than forward to the liberalism of the next decade. Much of La Follette's support also came not from his economic program, but from his resolute opposition to the war, the Red Scare, and the postwar treaties. Foreign-stock voters, especially German-Americans, were a strong component of the LaFollette vote in 1924.

As in 1920, Republicans outspent the Democrats by more than three to one in 1924, and Wall Street betting odds reached eleven to one for Coolidge, shattering the record seven to one odds on Harding.[12] Neither Davis nor LaFollete gave Coolidge much competition. The Democratic share of the popular vote sank to an all-time low of 29 percent, with 17 percent going to LaFollette. Coolidge easily outpolled both competitors combined, with 54 percent of the vote. The GOP expanded its House majority by 22 seats and its Senate majority by five seats, gaining the cushion needed to withstand the usual reaction against the party in power during midterm elections. Even with a third-party in the field, the presidential race failed to renew interest in politics. Turnout again remained below 50 percent.

The Progressive movement did not survive LaFollette's disappointing showing in 1924. The party had failed to make inroads in Congress or state offices. Its most important sponsor, the American Federation of Labor, would support the Democrats in 1928 and subsequent campaigns. The LaFollette campaign appealed both to Republican and Democratic progressives, but drew most heavily from Democrats who believed that their party had abandoned the policies of the Wilson years. A majority of LaFollette voters, still active in later years, would support Democratic candidates. Taken together, the LaFollette and Davis vote in 1924 foreshadowed elements of the new Democratic coalition of the 1930s.

## THE ELECTIONS OF 1928

The elections held in 1928 marked the end of the Republican era that had begun with the fall of the Democratic Congress in 1918. Hoover's near landslide victory would open the door for Franklin D. Roosevelt's triumph in 1932, as the Great Engineer failed to meet the challenge of economic crisis. Roosevelt would first become a presidential prospect in 1928, with an narrow, upset victory in the New York State gubernatorial campaign.

Although the Democrats nominated Al Smith, the party's strongest personality, in 1928, a generally prosperous economy, a united incumbent party, and tranquility at home and abroad ensured a Republican victory. President Coolidge would continue his conservative policies, with generally feeble opposition from Democrats and Republican progressives. The farm bloc would finally push a form of federal price supports through Congress, but it fell to Coolidge's veto.

The economic boom that had begun in 1924 continued for another two years. The economy would slow to a crawl during the second half of Coolidge's term. Lagging consumer demand stalled an economy where wealth was heavily concentrated at the top and several key industries remained depressed. Overall, growth during the Coolidge years was sufficient to blunt Al Smith's argument that Democrats would be more reliable custodians of prosperity than the GOP.

"Keeping cool with Coolidge," meant more than enjoying prosperity. Labor strife ebbed in mid-decade along with union militancy and membership. The Ku Klux Klan faded rapidly after 1924, as legislation restricting immigration robbed it of a major issue, scandal discredited key leaders, and Klan office-holders proved ineffective. Internationally, the administration scored a public relations coup by negotiating the Pact of Paris that renounced war as "an instrument of national policy." In retrospect, a paper agreement to outlaw war appears naive, but the treaty was a popular success that symbolized harmony among nations in the 1920s. Both major party platforms in 1928 endorsed the outlawry of war.

In 1928, Republican leadership passed smoothly from Calvin Coolidge to Herbert Hoover, who had gained renown for directing American food aid to post-World War I Europe. Hoover was no less impressive as Secretary of Commerce under Presidents Harding and Coolidge. He turned this usually obscure position into a command post of domestic and foreign economic policy. Unlike either Harding or Coolidge, Hoover was a progressive who emphasized efficiency and expertise in government. As Commerce Secretary, Hoover promoted a form of voluntary corporatism in which government would facilitate cooperation among labor, farmer, and business interests.

The Democratic convention met just after the Republican's adjourned. This time there would be no deadlock. On the first ballot, the delegates nominated Al Smith, then serving an extraordinary fourth term as Governor of New York. To placate the South, Smith balanced his ticket with Arkansas Senator Joseph T. Robinson.

As the first Catholic to head a major-party ticket, Al Smith personified Democratic pluralism of the 1920s. Smith was a colorful, blunt-spoken pol from New York City's Lower East Side. He spoke the people's language, punctured stuffed-shirts, and cut through the baloney of politics. In him, many ordinary Americans could see the incarnation of their own hopes and dreams. Al Smith opposed prohibition, but otherwise was a strong defender of traditional moral values.

As Governor of New York, Al Smith was the most prominent among those Democratic state leaders who sustained a semblance of progressive reform through the 1920s. During four administrations, Smith struggled to improve the efficiency of government and expand investments in education and infrastructure. To a lesser extent, he sponsored social welfare programs, especially for women and children. Smith reorganized the agencies of government, overhauled the state's tax structure, and won adoption of an executive budget. He pioneered state bond financing of education and transportation. Smith tired and failed to gain a state housing bank and public power legislation, but managed to win expanded workmen's compensation laws, mothers' pensions, and laws regulating work by women and children.

Democratic reformers in other states shared Smith's commitment to improving the efficiency of government and its delivery of public services. Democratic governors such as Albert Ritchie in Maryland, Harry F. Byrd in Virginia, John M. Parker in Louisiana, Bibb Graves in Alabama, George Hunt in Arizona, Austin Peay in Tennessee, and Dan Moody in Texas all sought to reorganize state government, modernize tax systems, and hike spending on schools and roads, and public health facilities. Democratic governors included both progressives and conservatives, however, and the reformers often found themselves battling old guard members of their own party in state legislatures. The reformers were generally pro-business and won the support of Chambers of Commerce and other trade associations. They favored low taxes and economy in government and either opposed regulation of enterprise or supported curbing only egregious abuses such as the exploitation of child labor. In the one-party South, the reform impulse also took the form of social control, including prohibition, anti-vice, and anti-evolution laws.

Historians have highlighted differences between Hoover and Smith as symbolic of the social tensions that divided Americans in the 1920s. Hoover was Protestant, of rural origin, dry, and associated with the native-stock American and the business elite. Smith was Catholic, urban, wet, and associated with the foreign-stock American and the city machine. It was as though the strife that had racked the Democratic party in 1924 was being replayed in the general election four years later.

In fact, there were broad areas of agreement between the candidates. Despite differences in how they sought public acclaim, they each evoked traditions broadly shared by Americans in the 1920s. Both men represented and defended the American dream of opportunity and mobility for individuals. Both candidates agreed on the values of hard work, traditional morality, limited government, fiscal restraint, and largely unfettered business enterprise. Both were committed to a scientifically designed, professionally staffed government. Both supported a non-interventionist foreign policy and continued disarmament efforts. It is not surprising that

Hoover and Smith, as well as John W. Davis, the Democrat's 1924 nominee, would later denounce the New Deal for excessive taxes, spending, bureaucracy, and regulation.

Like Davis in 1924, Smith ran a cautious campaign that failed to draw a sharp contrast with policies of the GOP. He relied on his personal political skills and sought to dampen fears that he contemplated radical changes in the status quo. Only Smith's position on public control of water power resources and his ill-defined plan for farm relief appeared to offer real alternatives to Hoover's economic program. Even the Democrats' longstanding advocacy of tariff reduction was muted in the 1928 platform. In July 1928, General Motors executive John J. Raskob, Smith's choice to head the Democratic National Committee, wrote to Irenee Du Pont that "Governor Smith's ideas of protecting big business are quite in accord with yours and mine. . . . The Governor believes that there is too much interference of the Government in business. . . . Personally I can really see no big difference between the two parties except the wet and dry question, and, of course, some people say the religious question, which I think both of us agree should form no part of politics."[13]

It was Al Smith's Catholicism that sparked far more interest in 1928 than either the accomplishments or the policies of the two candidates. Responses to Smith's religion preoccupied the party leaders and sharply skewed voter responses to the candidates. A sectarian campaign against Smith ranged from fulminations against "Rum and Romanism" to thoughtful ruminations on the relationship between church and state in Catholic theology.

Religious divisions in 1928 were not a proxy for a supposedly broader conflict between America's rural and urban traditions. The wide gulf between Catholic and Protestant voters that opened in 1928 was independent of voters' place of residence, their economic position, their stand on Prohibition, or their ethnic heritage. Both Protestants and Catholics responded to religious tensions as members of these groups split more decisively in 1928 than in previous or subsequent presidential elections. Hoover benefitted from an anti-Catholic and Smith from a pro-Catholic vote. Although the mathematics favored Hoover, the religious issue accounted for only a small part of his huge lead over Smith.[14]

Other issues divided voters in 1928. As the first presidential candidate to challenge Prohibition, Smith garnered relatively more support from wets than drys. Far more than previous Democratic candidates of the 1920s, Smith also garnered the votes of immigrants and first generation Americans. Foreign-stock voters, however, did not form a relatively larger percentage of his vote than of the vote for Progressive party candidate LaFollette in 1924 or of the vote for Roosevelt in 1932. Yet the composition of foreign-stock support for the Democrats shifted from 1928 to 1932, as predominantly Protestant groups figured much more prominently in the vote for FDR than in the tally for Smith. These findings suggest that the Smith candidacy was not crucial to winning the loyalty of immigrant groups during the New Deal era.

Also contrary to the conventional wisdom was the lack of a significant urban/rural cleavage in the 1928 vote. Independent of religion, ethnic heritage, and Prohibition, the cleft between city and country did not influence the choice between Hoover and Smith. Smith, in fact, carried only five of the nation's 15 largest cities; Roosevelt carried all 15 in 1932 and 1936. The explanation for the heavily urban character of the New Deal vote must be found in the policies and politics of the 1930s rather than in any urban-rural split that predates the Great Crash of 1929.

The politics of race figured prominently in 1928, both in the South and the North. The Hoover campaign sought to crack the solidly Democratic South by exploiting opposition to Smith's religion, his opposition to Prohibition, and his alleged sympathy for racial equality. The Democratic campaign responded by invoking the party's history of racial exclusion. Only by voting for Smith, southern Democrats claimed, could white supremacy be preserved in the South. Although Hoover managed to cut deeply into the usually Democratic South and Border States, the Great Depression postponed the dream of establishing a competitive white-oriented Republican party in the South.

If Smith's candidacy jeopardized white Democratic votes in the South, it also presented an opportunity to garner black votes in the north. Northern black voters could empathize with Smith as a fellow victim of white Protestant bigotry and admire his opposition to the Klan. They could even entertain the hope that his election would advance toleration in American life. Black loyalties to the Republican party were also loosening; not for many years had the party of Lincoln promoted the interests of black Americans. For the first time in history, the black press was more favorable to the Democratic than to the Republican nominee for president. Virtually none of the major black papers supported Hoover; a majority supported Smith or remained neutral. Although a majority of rank and file blacks still supported Hoover, Smith garnered a much greater share of black votes than any previous Democratic candidate. He even gained a greater share of the black vote than Roosevelt in 1932; not until 1934-36 would blacks finally become part of the Democratic coalition.

The turn of black voters and elites to Smith in 1928 did not represent a bright hope that the Democratic party would champion the cause of black people. No black delegates had attended the Democratic nominating convention in Houston, and black visitors to Convention Hall were segregated behind a barrier of chicken wire. Neither the Democratic platform nor the speeches of the candidate appealed to the interests of northern blacks. In their quest for equal rights in the 1920s, black people were confronted on the one hand by a Republican party whose commitment to their people was a tarnished memory and, on the other hand, by a Democratic party still wedded to southern racism. After 1928, the Democrats did nothing to extend their gains among northern blacks. The black vote was actually more Republican in 1932 than it had been in 1928. Not until the New Deal period of 1934-36 did a majority of blacks become reliable Democratic voters.

Although Smith's situation was not as hopeless as that of Cox in 1924 or Davis in 1928, the Wall Street betting odds of 4 to 1 against him showed how confidently the conventional wisdom expected his defeat.[15] Republican betters would not be disappointed on election day as Hoover nearly matched Harding's margin of victory in 1928. Hoover won 58 percent of the popular vote to Smith's 41 percent and 444 electoral votes to 87 for Smith. With victories in both Houses of Congress, the Republicans would control the national government for a third consecutive term.

Contrary to most accounts of 1928, it was not a "realigning election" that moved millions of urban, ethnic voters into the Democratic fold, foreshadowing the New Deal coalition.[16] The election of 1928, as Chart 1 shows, had virtually no effect on Democratic party affiliation among five fairly representative states that reported party registration data. The Smith-Hoover confrontation left the Democrats still clinging to just under one-third of

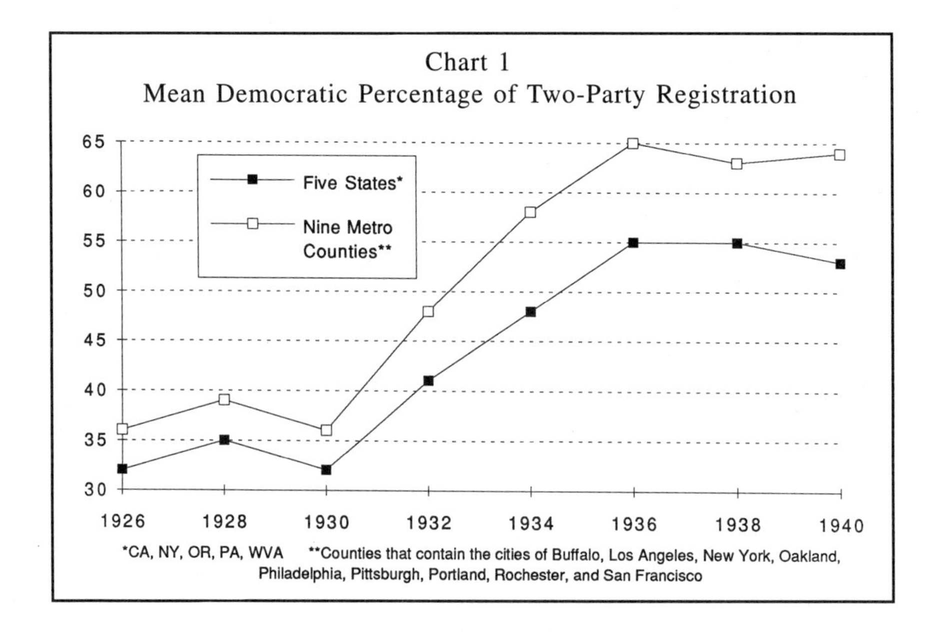

the two-party registration in these states. Not until 1936 did the Democrats become the majority party. Neither did the so-called "Revolution of 1928" affect Democratic party strength in metropolitan areas. As Chart 1 also shows, the Democratic percentage of the two-party registration in nine metropolitan counties from the same five states was slightly more than one-third both before and after 1928. The cities were about two years ahead of countryside in turning to the Democrats. By 1934, the balance of party power had shifted decisively to the Democrats in the metropolitan areas. Analysis of the composition of voter coalitions, moreover, shows that the alignments forged in 1928 did not closely resemble the alignments of the New Deal years. The election of 1928 was notable primarily for sparking a religious division of the electorate that did not contribute significantly to the New Deal coalition.

Neither did the election of 1928 give rise to a new reform tradition within the Democratic party. The old politics still guided the thinking of Democrats. Rather than transforming the structure of their party or devising new issues and strategies, Democratic leaders sought to preserve their own bastions of power and smother potentially divisive issues. For many Democrats, the presidential election of 1928 was a holding action and the nomination of Al Smith a means of appeasing his ardent supporters and keeping the party together until circumstances should turn against the GOP. Smith cooperated by ducking policy issues and relying instead on his personal appeal to voters. The campaign disappointed the party's most prescient leader, Franklin Roosevelt, who lamented the failure to launch "a progressive attack against the Coolidge-Hoover economic program."[17] For years later Roosevelt and would seize the opportunity to both revive and extend his party's progressive traditions.

If the 1928 contest did not durably realign voter commitments, it did awaken the sleeping voters of the 1920s. But the activation of the electorate did not yield the anticipated benefits to the minority party. Historians have stressed Al Smith's recruitment of Catholic and new immigrants, but have slighted the boom in Republican votes that also occurred in 1928. The Republicans gained 5.67 million votes over 1924, compared to a gain of 6.63 million for Democrats, despite the GOP's enormous lead in 1924 and the greater number of votes that would be lost through normal attrition. Moreover, much of the increase in Democratic votes came from 1924 LaFollette voters: about 56 percent opted for Smith; 31 percent voted for Hoover; and 13 percent did not vote. Among previous non-voters who participated in 1928, 58 percent voted for Hoover. The election also produced an especially large upsurge in women voters, the bulk of whom voted for Hoover. For the first time since suffrage, women's turnout closely approximated that of men.[18]

One positive result of the 1928 elections for Democrats was a strengthened party organization. In response to a post-election initiative by Governor-elect Franklin Roosevelt, the Democratic party broke precedent and kept the National Committee functioning between elections. The committee would be an important source of anti-Hoover propaganda during the 1930s.

## CONCLUSIONS

From the perspective of 1928, Republican control of government seemed secure. The GOP had crushed the Democrats in three consecutive contests for the White House, and maintained a decade of control over Congress and a majority of state governments. As one of Franklin Roosevelt's correspondents warned, a Democratic resurgence would require reeducating the public. "I am thoroughly convinced that no candidate can be sold to the public outside of his immediate locality, without a campaign of education. . . . Since the days of the 'Full Dinner Pail,' . . . the Republican party has been constantly hammering into the minds of the voters . . . these slogans, backed up with constant reference in the press to 'good times' until many, many people really believe they are living in an age of prosperity exceeding all expectations."[19] Beginning in 1929, the Great Depression reeducated the public—and the Democratic party—far more quickly than anyone would have dreamed possible in 1928.

A two-tiered realignment of the American party system took place after 1929. First, between 1930 and 1932 the Democrats benefitted from a "depression effect" that swelled the ranks of Democratic voters throughout the United States, but neither yet restored the Democrats to majority status nor reshuffled the composition of voter groupings. Second, between 1932 and 1936 Roosevelt's policies and leadership created a positive incentive for fealty to the Democratic party, especially among city dwellers, blacks, young voters, and persons benefitting most from his economic programs. This "Roosevelt effect" established the party's national dominance, revised the party's ideology, and shaped the economic and social composition of the New Deal coalition.

The Great Depression was thus a necessary, if not a sufficient, condition for the Democratic breakthrough of the 1930s. A generation of historians have been misguided in their criticism of the Democratic party of the 1920s. It was not internal divisions that barred Democrats from the White House, but circumstances beyond party control. No matter how much of a love fest could have been arranged between Albany, New York and

Albany, Georgia, control of the presidency or Congress was unattainable for Democrats prior to the Great Depression.

## NOTES

1. From 1856 to 1992, Democrats controlled the House of Representatives in 38 of the 84 years in which Republicans held the presidency. In contrast, Republicans controlled the House in only eight of the 52 years in which Democrats held the presidency.

2. David Burner, *The Politics of Provincialism: The Democratic Party in Transition, 1918-1932* (New York: Knopf, 1968), 12.

3. For an extended development of this view, see Allan J. Lichtman and Ken DeCell, *The Thirteen Keys to the Presidency: Prediction Without Polls* (Lanham, Md.: Madison Books, 1990).

4. *New York Times*, October 30, 1920, 1.

5. For the best account of demobilization, see generally, Burl Noggle, *Into the Twenties: The United States From Armistice to Normalcy* (Urbana: University of Illinois Press, 1974).

6. United States Department of Commerce, *Historical Statistics of the United States* (Washington, D.C.: Government Printing Office, 1975), 1081.

7. Erik Olssen, "The Progressive Group in Congress, 1922-1929," *The Historian* 42 (1980): 245-263, found that, among Democrats, Senators Burton K. Wheeler and Thomas Walsh of Montana, Clarence Dill of Washington, Henry Ashurst of Arizona, and Max Sheppard of Texas most consistently voted with the progressive bloc.

8. Selma F. Goldsmith, "The Relation of Census Income Distribution Statistics to Other Income Data," in *Income and Wealth*, Conference on Research in Income and Wealth, National Bureau of Economic Research, 23 (Princeton: Princeton University Press, 1958).

9. Robert K. Murray, *The 103rd Ballot: Democrats and the Disaster in Madison Square Garden* (New York: Harper & Row, 1976), 144-145.

10. For recent scholarship on the Klan, see Leonard J. Moore, *Citizen Klansmen: The Ku Klux Klan in Indiana, 1921-1928* (Chapel Hill: University of North Carolina Press, 1991); David H. Bennett, *The Party of Fear: From Nativist Movements to the New Right in American History* (Chapel Hill: University of North Carolina Press, 1988); and Shawn Lay, *The Invincible Empire in the West* (Urbana: University of Illinois Press, 1992).

11. "Convention Manual Compiled by Clarence Cannon for the Democratic National Committee," Washington, D.C., (January 1928), 23.

12. *New York Times*, November 3, 1924, 2.

13. Alan J. Lichtman, *Prejudice and the Old Politics: The Presidential Election of 1928* (Chapel Hill: University of North Carolina Press, 1979), 181.

14. Subsequent analyses of the composition of the 1982 vote are taken from Lichtman, *Prejudice and the Old Politics*, 40-230.

15. *New York Times*, November 2, 1928, 3.

16. For examples of this viewpoint see: Samuel Lubell, *The Future of Amer-*

*ican Politics* (New York: Harper & Row, 1952); V. O. Key, Jr. "A Theory of Critical Elections," *Journal of Politics* 21 (1959): 198-210; Kristi Andersen, *The Creation of a Democratic Majority* (Chicago: University of Chicago Press, 1979).

17. Frank Freidel, *Franklin D. Roosevelt*, 2 (Boston: Little, Brown, 1952): 246.

18. Lichtman, *Prejudice and the Old Politics*, 161, 213.

19. Lichtman, *Prejudice and the Old Politics*, 187.

PART FOUR

# The Rise and Decline of the New Deal Majority

## 1930s–1990s

Chapter 11

# The Democratic Moment: FDR to LBJ

*Alonzo L. Hamby*

The story of the modern Democratic party dates from Franklin Roosevelt's landslide victory over Herbert Hoover in 1932. Before one examines a portion of the landscape on the near side of that watershed, however, it is useful to survey the vista back in the distance for a sense of just how great was the divide of the thirties. Roosevelt was the first Democratic candidate for president since Franklin Pierce (in 1852) to win more than 50 percent of the total popular vote. FDR would do it four times. Only two Democrats have managed it since—Lyndon Johnson in 1964 by an enormous margin and Jimmy Carter in 1976 by a scant one-half of one percent.

Since its establishment in the 1790s as an alliance between liberal southern agrarians and northern city politicians, the Democratic party's strong point has been a diversity of adherents. This truly national base has made it usually a force to be reckoned with in Congress but has also caused it to seem frequently polyglot and formless in presidential elections. Diversity also has contributed to a disjunction between Democratic presidential and congressional parties far more pronounced than among the more homogeneous Republicans.

Although in theory and aspiration the party of the majority—most often defined as the "common people"—the Democrats historically have had difficulty mobilizing that majority in presidential contests. Yet without control of the presidency—in the hands of a charismatic leader with a strong sense of direction—the party has frequently seemed to be less than the sum of its parts, lacking in ideological (or policy) coherence and more devoted to forming firing squads in a circle than to attacking the presumed common enemy. Will Rogers, of course, immortalized the pitfalls of diversity with his famous remark: "I don't belong to any organized political party. I am a Democrat."

The Democratic party of 1932 was obviously considerably different from the one that elected Jefferson and Jackson or the one that put Pierce into the White House. Franklin Roosevelt and the movements to which he attached himself would initiate a second moment of Democratic ascendancy in American politics, lasting until the generational change and new social-cultural values of the 1960s reshuffled American politics. The building of a new majority from diverse elements was briefly characterized by a group of unprecedented public policy innovations that we call the "New Deal" (a label that gives a misleading impression of unified coherence), a "transforming" or "realigning" election in 1936 that seemed to recenter the party around an unbeatable coalition, and then a reaction in which the disunifying tendencies of Democratic diversity reasserted themselves. After Roosevelt, the Democrats would continue as the majority party in American politics, but more in congressional than presidential elections and at the cost of an internal gridlock that contained elements of self-destruction far more potent than most observers realized at the beginning of the 1960s.

## THE DEMOCRATIC SPLIT PERSONALITY

In some respects, the Democratic party of 1932 reflected the split personality that had resulted from the alliance between Jefferson and Burr 140 years earlier. Its most visible segment consisted of the predominantly rural-small town, white, Anglo-Saxon, Protestant South and West; it was here that first, William Jennings Bryan and then, Woodrow Wilson had drawn the bulk of their electoral votes in their runs for the presidency. The party's most dynamic and fastest-growing segment, however, was among the ethno-religious, working-class minorities of the northeastern quadrant of the country. Until that time, this group had delivered few electoral votes to Democratic presidential candidates; but Wilson's paper-thin 1916 success in Ohio and Al Smith's 1928 victories in Massachusetts and Rhode Island were harbingers of the future.

The prevailing outlook of the South-West wing was "Jeffersonian," a term of almost infinite malleability in the 1930s that might be interpreted in one or more of the following senses: (1) small, frugal government; (2) an agrarian fundamentalism that stressed the importance of the small family farmer as an anchor of social stability; (3) a more broadly-based faith in the small enterpriser as the linchpin of society; (4) an often bitter hostility toward the large corporations and enormous financial power centered in the Northeast; (5) a related belief in free trade and resentment of the protective tariff as special interest legislation; (6) a generalized devotion to democracy and the essential virtue of "the common people."[1]

In this multiplicity of meanings, one could find a rationale for a conservatism that stood for as few public services as possible and rejected any interference in such quaint local customs as lynching or child labor. One just as easily could find a basis for certain types of government activism (especially antitrustism), the regulation of big business and finance, or help for the farmer. There was one common denominator: in general, the Jeffersonians looked backward, hoping to recreate a fondly remembered, mythic past in which America was less urbanized, less spoiled, less complicated, and less centralized.

Many of these South-West Jeffersonians envisioned that world as characterized by a high degree of ethnic and cultural homogeneity in which their own norms were dominant. They were willing to resort to such instruments of social control as prohibition and immigration restriction to achieve that objective. Ironically, however, with cultural issues at the forefront of American politics in the twenties, they found themselves less in conflict with the Republicans than with the other large wing of their own party.

The outlook of the northeastern urban Democrats was far less well defined but clearly different in style and content. Based primarily upon the experience of belonging to an urban-industrial working class that was economically and culturally marginalized, with a day-to-day existence frequently at or near the bottom rung in hierarchical systems of industrial authority, this outlook was characterized by a quasi-Marxian (not Communist, not even Socialist) sense of the distribution of power and privilege in American society.

Motivated by feelings of class differences far more intense than those ordinarily found among the South-West Jeffersonians, the northeastern Democrats tended vaguely toward social democracy, or, as some have called it, "bread and butter liberalism." They had far fewer qualms than many of the Jeffersonians about an activist state. Their politics was less about opportunity and support for the small enterpriser than about regulation of working conditions, wages, and hours; social welfare; and encouragement of labor unionism. If the Jeffersonians, in one fashion or another, put the free individual at the center of their philosophy, the northeasterners thought more in terms of the collective.

The policy conceptualizers among them might have had at least a foot in various ideological camps just to the left of the party structure, primarily in the democratic socialism of Socialist party leader Norman Thomas, and labor leaders David Dubinsky, and Sidney Hillman. Stopping short of nationalization of industry, they tended to favor extensive government regulation and economic planning.

The northeastern Democrats also were deeply affected by cultural politics throughout the 1920s. Where the South-West Democrats saw themselves as attempting to protect a traditional America against an alien attack, the northeastern Democrats perceived themselves as under assault from a bigoted majority, intent on forcing its ways upon people who wanted the freedom to continue their cultural traditions (whether these involved the consumption of alcoholic beverages or the education of one's child in a parochial school) and the right to get a job without discrimination. The offensive of traditional America drove together various ethnic groups that under less threatening circumstances would have had little use for each other.

In truth, both sides during the twenties practiced what David Burner has called a "politics of provincialism," their conflicting cultures reflecting the near-even demographic balance between city and country that characterized the period.[2] This situation illustrated a general tendency in the history of American politics: during times of prosperity, ethno-cultural and "social" issues loom large in the political dialogue; during periods of economic distress, they tend to be displaced by distributive questions. Thus it took the Great Depression to refocus the Democratic party and bring a considerable semblance of unity to it.

## THE GREAT DEPRESSION AND THE NEW DEAL

It is all but impossible for the contemporary generation to grasp the seriousness of the economic trauma the Depression inflicted on the country and the world. Beginning as a relatively moderate recession after the stock market crash of 1929, the business cycle accelerated downward after mid-1930, partly as a result of the Hawley-Smoot tariff (the most protectionist U.S. trade legislation of the twentieth century) and egregiously mistimed credit tightening by the Federal Reserve, partly as a result of numerous errors and catastrophes in other countries.[3]

By 1932, the Gross National Product and per capita personal income had fallen to approximately 56 percent of the 1929 total. Unemployment, which averaged an estimated 3.2 percent in 1929, was at 23.6 percent. Farm income was approximately one-third the 1929 level. In the three years from 1930-32, some 5,000 banks failed, with estimated losses to depositors of about $800 million dollars (around $8 billion in today's terms and a far greater percentage of savings than would be the case in today's more affluent society).[4] During the winter of 1932-33, thanks to the strong downward momentum already established and to the uncertainty attendant upon a new administration in Washington, things actually got worse. It would take volumes to describe the suffering summarized by such statistics.

However one wishes to apportion the blame, it is clear that the dominant Republicans, from President Herbert Hoover down, dealt with the economic crisis in a way that neither arrested its precipitous slide nor raised public morale. In 1932, the electorate swept Franklin D. Roosevelt and the Democrats into office in a landslide that was primarily a negative vote against Hoover and his party. FDR in fact had put forth no clear, coherent program during the campaign. In part conscious strategy, this policy fuzziness also reflected the unprecedented character of the emergency and the divided mind of the Democratic party. What was clear was the new President's commitment to policies of relief, recovery, and reform.

The last item in this trinity was in fact a Democratic tradition by 1932. Whether from a Jeffersonian or a northeastern urban perspective, the Democrats had been, on the whole, a party of reform in American life since Bryan, and *the* party of reform since Theodore Roosevelt's failed Bull Moose campaign. Precisely what kind of reform, however, remained a question. For Bryan, and then for Wilson, it had meant, in the beginning, government aid to farmers and small enterprisers, low tariffs, regulation of big business, some social legislation, and tentative ties to organized labor. Still, no observer in 1932 would have identified the party unequivocally with northeastern, working-class social democracy.[5]

Roosevelt had never been firmly aligned with the northeastern wing of the party. He had many personal and emotional ties to the Wilson administration, however, which had been heavily South-West in tone while reaching out to the northeastern Democrats. Throughout the 1920s, he had kept a foot in both camps, a process facilitated by the way in which his struggle with polio had allowed him to remain aloof from day-to-day political combat until he had emerged from his prolonged convalescence to be elected Governor of New York in 1928.

As it developed, Roosevelt owed his nomination largely to the southern and western Jeffersonians, as represented by Wilson's son-in-law and the former Treasury Secretary, William Gibbs McAdoo of California, and the new Vice President, John Nance Garner of Texas. (The northeasterners had predominantly supported Al Smith, the former Governor of New York and Democratic presidential nominee in 1928.) His advisers on relief, labor and industrial policies were northeastern social welfarists (Harry Hopkins, Frances Perkins) and economic planners (Raymond Moley, Hugh Johnson). On agriculture, they included an Ivy League economist (Rexford Tugwell), a former farm machinery manufacturer (George Peek), a western academician (M. L. Wilson), and a former Republican agricultural advocate (Henry A. Wallace). Roosevelt's congressional leadership was primarily from the South and West. His policies over the next six years reflected that diversity.[6]

The New Deal began as a relatively coherent economic recovery program based on "corporatist" planning. Its American antecedents lay in the New Nationalism of Herbert Croly and Theodore Roosevelt and in the institutional economics of FDR's Brains Trusters Rexford Tugwell, Adolf A. Berle, Jr., and Raymond Moley. Its closest working model was the political economy of Italy. Needless to say, Roosevelt did not envision establishing himself as a Mussolini-style dictator. He and his advisors did hope that business, labor, and agriculture, coordinated by the guiding hand of government, could develop a managed economy that would deliver benefits to all concerned and bring the nation out of the Depression.

On paper, the blueprint seemed promising. A National Recovery Administration (NRA) would provide a mechanism by which industry could stabilize prices and production while labor received fair wages, hours, and working conditions. A separate Agricultural Adjustment Administration (AAA) would curtail the surplus of farm commodities and thereby put upward pressure on prices. In the meantime, limited relief payments and public works expenditures would combine with a large increase in the money supply to jump start the economy.[7]

Alas, the history of the 1930s would demonstrate that a managed economy functioned much better under a totalitarian regime—whether Fascist, Nazi, or Communist—than under a democratic one. It was to the credit of the New Deal that compliance to NRA codes by businesses was voluntary (although subject to the pressure of public opinion), and that labor unions retained the right to strike. These democratic safeguards, however, made implementation a slow and uncertain affair; the Ford Motor Company, for example, never signed on. The NRA soon made itself an unhappy example of imperial overstretch by trying to regulate everything from mom-and-pop grocery stores to the New York "burlesque industry," and the cumbersome bureaucratic character of most NRA codes made them widely disliked among businessmen who tried to observe them.[8]

Public works spending, moreover, got underway far too haltingly because of caution on the part of Secretary of the Interior Harold Ickes, and because most states lacked the matching funds they were required to contribute. Only farmers, who clutched at the AAA like drowning men to a life preserver, experienced a significant measure of recovery. (Ruled unconstitutional in January 1936, the AAA was quickly resurrected in the guise of a soil conservation program; in 1938, after the Supreme Court had been tamed, it was reinstated openly.)

When the Supreme Court declared the NRA unconstitutional on May 27, 1935, the agency had become unpopular and was generally judged a failure. Special ad hoc legislation continued corporatist-style planning in a few industries, most notably coal, at the behest of both labor and management. Several enactments, moreover, brought comprehensive federal regulation to trucking, the airlines, and inland waterways in much the same fashion that already applied to railroads, thereby establishing a de facto corporate state for transportation.

In general, however, after the demise of the NRA, the New Deal possessed no consciously administered recovery plan worthy of the name.

Instead, driven by political opportunism, intellectual exhaustion, and sheer frustration, its economic policies featured big business bashing, attacks on the rich, and an intermittent, inconsequential antitrustism. Nonetheless, in 1936, prosperity seemed to be roaring back; industrial production moved up sharply, and unemployment threatened to fall into single digits.

In retrospect, this apparently strong recovery seems to have been in large measure the result of two developments: a greatly expanded relief program centered around the new Works Progress Administration (WPA), and congressional passage, over FDR's veto, of legislation providing immediate payment of the World I veterans' bonus. Together, these measures injected an enormous stimulus into the economy. By the end of 1937, however, the one-time-only shot of the bonus payment had spent its impact, and the administration, worried about the budget deficit, had made draconian cuts in the WPA.

As was the case throughout the thirties, Federal Reserve policy did a lot of inadvertent damage; fearing inflation, although unemployment was still at double-digit rates, the Fed pushed up interest rates. (Roosevelt's Federal Reserve Chairman, Marriner Eccles, is usually remembered as a strong advocate of deficit spending; he was also a sound Mormon banker who spent much of his career fixated on the adverse consequences of loose monetary policies.)

The result was a recession that might fairly be styled a mini-depression. In a matter of months, unemployment rocketed toward 20 percent; as late as 1939, it averaged 17 percent.[9] Looking back, it appears that the Roosevelt administration almost inadvertently had set a recovery process in motion with no real plan for managing it. What could have been the crowning success of the New Deal became instead its most conspicuous failure.

## THE NEW DEAL AND THE PROBLEM OF ECONOMIC RECOVERY

For a generation, the most common perception was that Roosevelt failed to understand the emerging Keynesian formula for restoring prosperity. Intimidated by Republican criticism of his "enormous" deficits, he failed to inject enough fiscal stimulus into the economy to bring it back. The argument is attractive when one considers that the economy waxed and waned during the 1930s in relatively direct proportion to the amount of federal spending. It is probable that the largely unconscious Keynesian policies of 1935-36 amounted to the right path.

If WPA spending had tapered off more slowly over a period of a few years, the country might have turned the corner to prosperity without incurring any serious long-term liability. As it was, the descent back into depression in 1937 created a much deeper pit to climb out of. In the spring of 1938, Roosevelt reversed course and initiated a period of higher relief expenditures which halted the downward spiral. But the renewed spending was too little too late to bring the country back to where it had been in 1936, much less to full recovery; and neither the administration nor Congress was prepared to go much farther. It would take the unrestrained spending of World War II to bring an end to unemployment and lay the basis for postwar prosperity.

The fact of the war suggests to a hindsight-wise second-guesser that Roosevelt would have done well to have piled a hefty military preparedness budget on top of his domestic spending, much as did Hitler in Germany. The military hardware would be desperately needed a few years down the road. Germany, moreover, was the first major power to come out of the Depression, having largely solved the unemployment crisis by 1936.[10]

Yet massive spending on this scale, whether for dams and regional development authorities, aircraft carriers and battleships, or (as Keynes himself suggested to Roosevelt in a moment of frustrated sarcasm and half-jest) pyramids, was never a live option.[11] As an absolute dictator, Hitler could act without regard to the diversity of attitudes and inhibiting diffusion of power that characterize liberal democratic systems. Thus, authoritarian regimes often achieve short-term advantages.

As it was, Roosevelt ran enormous deficits when measured against any previous standard. In the first fiscal year of the New Deal (as well as the last two of the Hoover administration), the budget deficit exceeded 50 percent of expenditures. Until fiscal year 1938, when Roosevelt plunged the nation into recession with his attempt to balance the budget, deficits remained extraordinarily high, running from 33 to 46 percent of total outlays.[12]

It is true that throughout the 1930s, federal spending as a portion of the Gross National Product was small by today's standards. In the climate of the Depression decade, however, it seemed awesome. Policy intellectuals had not yet achieved the widespread understanding of Keynesian economics that would have allowed them to make a coherent case for greater spending. It is not likely that the political system would have accommodated even greater "excess," especially after the Republicans made a strong comeback in the 1938 elections; and even if hyper-deficits had been possible, it is far from clear that they would have had the same effect in peacetime as they did when incurred under the necessity of war.

New Deal planners and Keynesians alike assumed realistically that in the autarkic 1930s a recovery had to be driven by internal consumption rather than by expanded foreign trade. Thus, Roosevelt abandoned a traditional Democratic doctrine. The Hawley-Smoot tariff stayed on the books, altered a bit by numerous bilateral trading deals negotiated under the reciprocal trade program. In truth, however, reciprocal trade was more a smoke screen to conceal the basic pattern of protectionism that persisted through the 1930s than an effort to return piecemeal to the openness of Woodrow Wilson's non-protectionist Underwood Tariff.

The best that could be said in defense of such a policy was that Hawley-Smoot had let the genie out of the bottle, and that it was too late to reverse the trend of protectionism that gripped every major economic power. Postwar Democrats, believing they had learned from the past, would envision interwar protectionism as a leading cause of World War II and would move toward a comprehensive reshaping of the international political economy.

Scholars of both the left and the right agree that New Deal taxation policy did nothing to promote recovery.[13] The most popular target is the Social Security payroll tax. It may, as Roosevelt contended, have been an absolutely necessary method of institutionalizing the program. From the beginning it also served the peripheral function of providing a lot of forced savings to fund the public debt, and thus it sucked money out of the private economy and discouraged a consumption-driven recovery. The processing tax that funded the original agricultural program effectively raised the prices of many ordinary consumer products and was likewise regressive.

The Wealth Tax Act of 1935 became emblematic of a New Deal commitment to income redistribution and "class warfare." It raised marginal tax brackets on incomes of more than $100,000 and increased taxes on gifts, inheritances, and the like—but in truth it was more symbol than substance. Proposed primarily to counter the "share the wealth" appeal of Louisiana Senator Huey Long, it was more a political ploy than a component of an economic recovery program. The act occasioned vituperative rhetoric on both sides of the issue, but in practice did little to extract higher tax payments from the wealthy. It does seem fair to observe that the atmosphere of class conflict that swirled around it could only have decreased the confidence of the investing classes and thereby provided some degree of drag on economic growth.

Perhaps the most ill-considered of all the New Deal taxes, however, was the Undistributed Profits Tax of 1936, a 7 to 27 percent surtax on retained corporate profits, apparently passed in the belief that business was stashing hordes of cash under mattresses and thereby retarding recovery. An extraordinarily effective way of discouraging capital formation, it elicited intense, and mostly justifiable, protests from business. It was repealed in 1938 with Roosevelt's grudging acquiescence.

The primary motive behind New Deal tax policy was an increasingly perceived (and rather conservative) need for revenues to fund new relief and social welfare programs. Here the policy ran up against the problem that all modern welfare states face: how much can be extracted from the haves in order to assist the have-nots, and by what methods, without damaging the engines of productivity that ultimately sustain any safety-net system? Phrased thus, the issue is one of pragmatic judgment rather than fundamental morality, of finding ways to define and balance social responsibility with economic reality.

There was a strong secondary impulse, however, which stemmed partly from cold political calculation but at least equally from visceral emotion. It consisted of a desire to punish the rich and the business classes—and why not? "Business" (a term generally used to denote the large corporate interests and, by extension, the wealthy) had claimed credit for the prosperity of the 1920s, had been unable to cope with the Depression, and now bitterly criticized the New Deal as an assault on the American Way of Life. "Business," by the mid-1930s, had become America's favorite scapegoat, whether in Hollywood films or in Washington.

By then, corporate leaders who could not bear to hear Roosevelt's name called him "That Man," accused him of communistic tendencies, and semi-privately relished rumors that he was a syphilitic. In the campaign of 1936, Roosevelt responded by attacking "economic royalists," "the forces of organized selfishness and of lust for power," and advocates of "a new industrial dictatorship."[14] From the standpoint of political tactics, such rhetoric made a lot of sense. Roosevelt and his core constituencies, moreover, found it emotionally satisfying.

Nonetheless, attacks on business did little to get the economy moving. Just as Roosevelt never understood Keynesian economics, neither did he follow another bit of advice he received from Keynes—to cultivate business leaders, treat their crankiness as that of household animals who had been badly trained, respond to it with kind words, ask for their advice, elicit their support.[15] It was wise counsel, but by the time Roosevelt received it in early 1938, too many bridges had been burned.

Roosevelt and many of the New Deal policymakers had feelings about commerce that ranged from simple disinterest to positive revulsion. The President himself, the product of an "Old Money" family, derived his income from inherited wealth, and had been brought up in the tradition of a socially responsible gentry. The New Deal Brains Trusters and administrators were heavily drawn from an emerging policy intelligentsia of academics and social activists who, to one degree or another, had consciously rejected business as a livelihood.

Many of the southern and western "Jeffersonians" in the Democratic party were neopopulists who thrived on the traditional Jeffersonian-Jacksonian hostility toward big finance. The rapidly growing forces of organized labor were led in some places at the local level by Communists and were almost universally prone to a Marxian-style militance and sense of class conflict that appeared as natural in the hard times of Depression America as it does alien to a more prosperous society.

Neither Roosevelt, nor those around him, nor the Jeffersonians, nor many of the labor leaders wanted to do away with capitalism; rather they talked about humanizing it and finding a "Middle Way." Still, one is forced to conclude, they did not understand how capitalism worked, and they were alienated enough from it that they never found much common ground with "the capitalists," the leaders of American business. They often proclaimed their sympathy for small business, on the other hand, seeing it as a constructive force that they could champion. Few among them, however, understood that small businessmen, as a group, shared the worldview of big business leaders. Indeed small businessman clung to it more tenaciously because they were usually entrepreneurs who had an investment of personal ego in their operations exceeding that of most corporate managers.

Small enterprisers undoubtedly found the burdens of government regulation and the need to negotiate with labor unions harder to deal with than did large corporations. Nor did New Deal tax policy give them any relief. The Wealth Tax Act of 1935, according to William E. Leuchtenburg, "destroyed most of the Brandeisian distinction between big and small business," whatever the intentions of the administration. The Social Security payroll tax provided a new federal requirement at a time when federal taxes were not generally withheld from paychecks.[16]

In the tumultuous thirties, some degree of hostility and misunderstanding between the Roosevelt administration and the business community was probably inevitable. The outlook of both sides was characterized by prejudices and blind spots that made it practically impossible to find common ground. Still, one may wish the effort had been made—and must observe that it was during World War II, with considerable benefit to the nation and to all the concerned social groups. As it was, in the absence of an obvious formula for restoring prosperity and promoting economic growth, class conflict and redistributionism became the natural formula for maintaining and consolidating political power. Never productive as an economic program, no longer a sure-fire political strategy, that formula nonetheless remains an important part of the Democratic worldview.

## BUILDING A DEMOCRATIC MAJORITY: THE ROOSEVELT COALITION

If, then, the Democrats failed to solve the economic crisis they had been elected to meet, how did they emerge from the 1930s as a majority party?

A small part of the answer is that they were lucky in their opposition. The Republicans, shell-shocked by the Depression, produced no ideas, no vision, and no leadership. The emergence of Robert A. Taft as "Mr. Republican" and Thomas E. Dewey as "Most Electable Candidate" by the 1940s suggests not only a party in bankruptcy but one in a desperate search for a suitable receiver.

The parties of the left (Wisconsin Progressives, Minnesota Farmer-Laborites, La Guardia Fusionists, and Socialists) never became a unified force. They failed to develop a domestic program with mainstream appeal, remained hopelessly split on foreign policy, and eventually were unable to resist the overwhelming gravitational pull of the Democrats.

Still, the weakness of the opposition is only the beginning of an explanation. Politicians and parties become winners not just because they have some good breaks but because they know how to take advantage of them. Roosevelt and the Democrats did so superbly.

Roosevelt himself was the party's greatest asset. Political scientists may quibble about whether he was the founder of "the modern presidency," but he surely unlocked its potential. Above all, he demonstrated that a party of diversity requires strong, charismatic leadership to rise above its natural tendency to engage in interest group squabbling. Evoking first the fight against the Depression, then the struggle against fascism, he gave the Democratic party and New Deal liberalism a vision of a national interest that legitimized it for a generation.

Influenced by the examples of his cousin Theodore and his old chief, Woodrow Wilson, FDR was a consummate master of the news media. He opened up the White House press conference, playing it like a virtuoso to get his message across while maintaining a rapport with most of the journalists who covered him regularly. He appeared in newsreels radiating confidence and fortitude. Above all, he emerged as a technical master of the newest and most direct medium of communication—radio.

Possessing an authoritative, Harvard-accented voice that appealed to the sensibility of the age, gifted with a remarkable talent for rhetorical pacing, able to project a sense of empathy with the ordinary people out beyond the microphone, he was the first great communicator of the electronic media age. Words, Roosevelt understood, were no substitute for policy, but they could serve as a powerful adjunct to it, drawing the political support of people who reacted to a leader's vision and who, above all, were convinced that he cared about them in a direct, personal way. Accepting the Democratic nomination in 1936, he declared: "This generation of Americans has a rendezvous with destiny." Spoken by FDR, the sentence was more than a nice rhetorical flourish. It was a declaration of national mission that made a lasting impact on millions of people.

Roosevelt's style and talent facilitated the policies that recreated the

Democratic party as a majority coalition. If ultimately he and the Democrats would fail at achieving economic recovery, they would appear throughout his first term to be marching rapidly toward that goal, with double-digit gains in GNP and a fairly steady reduction in the unemployment rate. Voters, however, responded less to economic statistics than to the immediate assistance they received.

The New Deal programs aimed at helping individuals in distress were so numerous as to defy a complete listing—home and farm mortgage refinancing, work relief, direct relief (also known as "the dole" and constituting a far greater proportion of the total relief effort than is usually recognized), regional development, rural resettlement, farm price supports, wage and hour legislation, and the Social Security system. At one level, as many Republicans charged, this amounted to buying votes by playing Santa Claus. At another, however, it represented an effort by an activist government to meet genuine human needs. Not surprisingly, it was easy for the political and the humanitarian motives to get mixed up with each other.

For example, the most far-reaching of the work programs, the WPA, provided hundreds of thousands of jobs for desperate people and left behind tens of thousands of little monuments in the form of useful public works in almost every county in the United States. WPA was also, pure and simple, a source of patronage for many state and local political bosses; and, in the manner of today's welfare programs, it fostered a sense of dependency among its long-term clients, especially those who lived in low-wage rural areas with little manufacturing or construction.[17]

While Republican criticism resonated with what was left of the comfortable middle class, it was less than devastating because the purposes of New Deal benefits were fundamentally conservative—to preserve a class of farm and home owners, to provide work for those who needed it, and to give handouts only to unemployables. In addition, those who received benefits from the New Deal were generally intensely grateful for them, frequently reacting almost as if the assistance was a personal gift from FDR himself. It was out of such experiences that the New Deal became something more than a failed economic recovery program and a moderately interesting, if altogether incoherent, reform effort. The election of 1936 would mark the last great party realignment in American history and the creation of a Roosevelt coalition that still shows signs of life a half-century later.

The landslide victory of 1936 was a transforming event in American history, but a somewhat deceptive one. What we might call the "core Roosevelt coalition" lay within the 60 percent of the vote that Roosevelt polled. While the coalition was a dominant force in Democratic presidential politics, it was no more than a powerful minority in the larger electoral panorama.

In taking 46 of 48 states, Roosevelt carried virtually every significant group in America other than (for lack of a better term) "the business classes." He also carried in on his coattails the largest Democratic delegations ever in the House of Representatives (331) and the Senate (76).

But much of this majority was produced by a surging economy and a weak, uninspiring Republican opponent. Like Ronald Reagan a half-century later, the President could ask people if they were better off than four years earlier and get a happy response. The longer term question, as the economy fell into recession, was just who would stay with him. A rough sorting-out of several overlapping categories follows:

**Old-stock white, Anglo-Saxon Protestants.** Roosevelt carried only a bare majority of this predominantly middle-class, traditionally Republican group. In the future it would go against him and other Democratic candidates.

**Urban ethno-religious minorities.** Roosevelt won the normally Democratic Catholic and Jewish votes by large majorities. He had actively sought both. Catholics, personified by Democratic National Chairman Jim Farley, Securities Exchange Commission Chairman Joe Kennedy, or young White House aide Tommy Corcoran, were a highly visible part of his administration. Catholic constituencies at the local level included many nationalities—Italian, Polish, German, Portuguese, numerous Eastern European ethnics, French-Canadians. These groups might have little use for each other in the cauldrons of melting-pot politics, but they all loved Roosevelt.

Jews who looked for representation in Washington would find, among others, Secretary of the Treasury Henry Morgenthau and Corcoran's good friend and White House colleague, Benjamin V. Cohen. On the whole, Jews were more likely than Catholics to be drawn to FDR by a liberal ideology.

In the future, both groups would remain important parts of the coalition. Catholic representation, however, would be eroded by upward economic mobility and by concerns that the party was too soft on Communism. Jewish representation would be increased by World War II and by Harry Truman's postwar policies on immigration and Palestine.

**African-Americans.** In a remarkable turnaround, blacks, strongly Republican since Reconstruction, voted three to one for Roosevelt. No demographic group had benefitted so greatly from New Deal programs. When African-American publisher Robert Vann told his readers that the time had come to turn Lincoln's picture to the wall, he was speaking to a population that cared much more about the food Roosevelt had put on the table than about the President's lack of interest in civil rights legislation. The time for the latter would come after World War II.

**Labor.** Organized labor, made a permanent part of the American political economy by the Wagner Act of 1935, emerged as a potent campaign force, a big contributor of money to the Democrats as well as a major source of organization and manpower. Its role would loom larger and larger as traditional urban machines decayed in one city after another over the next couple of decades. From 1948 through 1968, Democratic presidential campaigns would start with the nominee speaking to large union rallies on Labor Day in Detroit's Cadillac Square. For a time, it appeared that the Democrats were well along the path to becoming a de facto counterpart of the British Labor party, a prospect welcomed not simply by the unions but also by an increasingly influential liberal policy intelligentsia.

**The Cities.** Ethno-religious minorities, working classes, and organized labor were of course all centered in the cities, which supported Roosevelt overwhelmingly. "Labor" included heavy representations of the white minority groups listed above, but old-stock working-class Americans voted heavily for FDR also. Roosevelt carried not only ethnic centers like Lowell, Massassachusetts, and Flint, Michigan, but also Tulsa and Oklahoma City; not just Cleveland and Chicago but also Kansas City and Los Angeles. Of the 106 cities in the country with a population over 100,000, Roosevelt carried 104.

**The "Liberal Intellectuals."** From the beginning of his presidency, Roosevelt had enjoyed the support of an emergent group of policy oriented intellectuals who had rejected the conservative, business oriented Republican dominance of the 1920s, but who, unlike those on the independent left, wanted to work within the Democratic party. Some were political journalists, some were lawyers, some were social workers, many were academic social scientists. "Intellectuals" by virtue of education, they were on the whole unconcerned with abstract ideas and dedicated to the use of intelligence to solve practical problems.

Most wanted a society characterized by the social democratic ideal of a more equitable distribution of wealth. Many saw strong government management of the economy as a means of both achieving that goal and smoothing out the business cycle. Increasingly, these intellectuals identified themselves with the causes of (racial) civil rights and expanded civil liberties.

Inside the New Deal, they provided much of the management and policy conceptualization. Outside the administration, they might be writers for such left-liberal magazines as the *New Republic*, the *Nation*, or *Common Sense*; a few might be found on Capitol Hill working for liberal Democratic legislators.

Like all participants in the political process, this group doubtless found the idea of power for themselves and their "class" attractive; all the same, they were less self-interested in the conventional sense than about any of the groups attracted to the New Deal. Most of them deplored Roosevelt's compromises and saw the New Deal as only a very partial realization of their blueprints for a perfect society. At bottom, however, most loved him as they would no other politician. Numerically insignificant, they were important as idea people, publicists, and organizers. They would support FDR to the end, feel just mild about Harry Truman, find a close approximation of their ideal in Adlai Stevenson, be wary of John Kennedy, and reject Lyndon Johnson.

**Farmers.** Perhaps the most volatile segment of the electorate, farmers constituted about 25 percent of the population in the 1930s, and thus were an imposing voting bloc. (By 1960, they would be down to less than nine percent.)[18] Roosevelt carried farm areas easily in a vote that reflected widespread gratitude for the way in which the New Deal had saved rural America from liquidation. After that, however, the relationship would cool quickly. Farm prices fell in the late 1930s, thanks to the recession of 1937-38 and to surpluses that outpaced the government's ability to curtail them. Moreover, the administration's increasing identification with labor and the urban minorities made it less attractive to what was, after all, a culturally traditional segment of the population.

**The South.** Still homogenous, overwhelmingly old-stock WASP, aggressively white supremacist, mainly rural and small-town, distrustful of labor unions and outsiders, the South (i.e., the states of the Confederacy) had been reliably Democratic since Reconstruction, with the one exception of the Smith-Hoover campaign of 1928. The most impoverished region of the country, it had received a disproportionate amount of assistance from the New Deal. In 1936 and subsequent years, it would be solid for Roosevelt, but its ideological and cultural divergences from the overall trajectory of the party raised serious doubts about the future.

Stripped to its enduring essentials, in fact, the Roosevelt coalition looked a lot like the bargain that Jefferson and Madison had made with Aaron Burr in the 1790s, but now the order of power and influence was reversed. The center of gravity (intellectually as well as numerically) in the Democratic party lay not in the agrarian South but in the bustling cities of the industrial North. Roosevelt could not have been reelected in 1940 and 1944 without his overwhelming urban majorities; in both cases, he would have won without a single electoral vote from the South.

## PRESIDENTIAL PARTY V. CONGRESSIONAL PARTY

Yet what Roosevelt had created was a presidential electoral coalition that bore only a tenuous relationship to the realities of power in Congress. In the American constitutional system, presidential and congressional electoral systems are not designed to be in sync, but from the late 1930s into the 1960s, the divergence would become especially pronounced among Democrats, sharply divided between presidential and congressional parties.

The different balance of power in Congress was partly attributable to the under-representation of urban America still common in the state legislatures that redrew congressional districts every decade. It also stemmed, however, from the undeniable fact that minorities (whether ethnic, religious, or racial) were still minorities and were less able to leverage their voting power in 531 House and Senate races than in a national presidential election. The labor and social-democratic characteristics of the worldview that had attached itself to the political emergence of urban dissent was even more an ideological minority.

Roosevelt, who probably was being pushed by events more than purposefully leading them himself, thus had created a coalition that made the Democrats a majority party without ending the divisions among its factions. Within a year of his astounding victory in 1936, his power was waning, and American politics was headed toward a deadlock of democracy.

The immediate precipitants were:

**The Court-Packing Plan.** By common consent, this was the lethal charge that set off the sharp slide in FDR's authority. He had neither made the Supreme Court an issue in the 1936 campaign nor discussed legislation with his leaders in Congress. He much too slickly presented the court reform bill as a method of dealing with tired blood on the Court rather than of getting his way in a dispute with it. The public and many congressmen perceived an attempt to subvert the Constitution. The President had only himself to blame for the disaster that followed, and by the time it was over, he had shown that he could be successfully opposed on an important issue.

**The Recession of 1937-38.** Here, Capitol Hill had to share the blame with the White House. Many safely reelected moderate to conservative Democratic legislators saw no more need for the WPA and allied programs. New Deal tax policy and the generally poisonous relations with the business community surely contributed to the economic debacle.

**The Upsurge of Labor Militance.** Strongly identified with the unions, Roosevelt could not escape a widespread reaction against the tough, angry, class-conflict oriented organizing campaigns that began shortly after his reelection. The sit-down strikes, which captured the attention of the nation, were a special affront to the American middle-class ethic and drew a resolution of condemnation that nearly passed the Senate. Roosevelt's attempt to wash his hands of the issue by declaring "a plague o' both your houses" satisfied almost no one.[19]

**The Failed Purge of 1938.** Never mind that Roosevelt had every right—constitutional, legal, and moral—to campaign against Democratic congressmen who had opposed him; never mind that as party leader he may even have had a duty to do so. In fact, he challenged the sense of localism that has always been a distinguishing feature of American political parties. Worse yet, he did it very badly, striking openly at opponents he could not topple. After the dust had cleared, he was a more diminished president than ever.

The pattern of American politics that emerged from these events was, at the most visible level, one in which a liberal president found himself checked by a loose, informal coalition of conservative Democrats (primarily from the South) and Republicans. Accompanying and facilitating this development was the reemergence, in somewhat different form, of the ideological and cultural differences that had split the party before the New Deal.

The argument, to be sure, was no longer about prohibition, immigration restriction, the alleged menace of a Catholic president, or the depredations of the Ku Klux Klan. Now it was about anti-lynching legislation, labor unions, and, in broad terms, the New Deal's threat to the conservative interpretation of Jeffersonianism as small, frugal, locally centered government. Yet the sides to the debate were much the same as in the 1920s, and the reciprocal sense of cultural hostility was rarely suppressed.

## WORLD WAR II

While the argument over the New Deal and a complex of domestic issues created the political coalitions of the 1930s, foreign policy and World War II also affected them. World War I had been a disaster for the Democrats, wrecking the nascent "Wilson Coalition" of 1916, breaking the health of their charismatic President, and leaving them bitterly divided. The party emerged from World War II intact and in a very real sense the war legitimized the Democratic party as the vehicle of national leadership in foreign policy.

Yet in 1945, it was weaker than in 1940. No political vehicle could escape all the corrosive effects of a total war. Moreover, the prosperity that the war made possible after 1945 created a society less amenable to the messages of class division and social reform that had served the Democrats so well in the 1930s.

However halting and inconsistent Roosevelt's pre-1939 foreign policy leadership may seem, it was in fact prescient and at times risky. Privately convinced that America could not remain isolated from the rest of the world, he did about as much as possible to prepare the country—intellectually, morally, and militarily—for the gathering storms he correctly discerned in Europe and Asia. True enough, he acquiesced in the Neutrality Acts of 1935-37, backed away from the "quarantine the aggressor" speech of October 1937 after a strong backlash against it, and publicly praised the Munich agreement. These moves need to be understood, however, as Fabian tactics being practiced by a leader who wanted to take the offensive but sensed that the correlation of forces was against him. Most Republicans and independent progressives were militant isolationists; very few Democrats displayed much concern about Europe.

After the collapse of France in 1940, Roosevelt took enormous chances to prevent a Nazi victory—the Destroyer Deal, Lend-Lease, aid to the Soviet Union. At times, to be sure, he was disingenuous, even guilty of outright deception, as he attempted to cope with a self-deceptive public opinion unwilling to accept either the triumph of Nazism or full American participation in the war. To criticize such behavior as among the many abuses of the "imperial presidency" strikes one as far less meaningful than recognizing it as a defense of the national interest—and indeed of the ideals of liberalism and democracy. Pearl Harbor, a consequence of a policy toward Japan that got tougher as the Japanese allied themselves more closely to Nazi Germany and Fascist Italy, finally plunged the United States into a fight that Roosevelt correctly realized it could not avoid.[20]

Roosevelt's World War II foreign policy is open to fair criticism. He really was too optimistic about relations with the Soviet Union and, above all, too prone to conduct diplomacy as an ad hoc exercise in personal relationships. His view of the postwar world mistakenly assumed the continued viability of Britain as a great power and never worked out a realistic scenario for postwar East Asia. Worried about American public opinion, he never engaged in the sort of frank *Realpolitik* that alone might have established a satisfactory basis for dealing with Stalin and the USSR after the war. Despite his private understanding that balance and accord among the great powers would be the only basis for a postwar settlement, he found himself mortgaging American diplomacy to the establishment of a United Nations organization and the accompanying illusion that total war would bring in its wake total peace.

That said, however, the dual legacies of Theodore Roosevelt (realism) and Woodrow Wilson (idealism) served him well as he went about the task of defining American goals. He successfully mobilized the United States for total war, kept the Grand Alliance together (no small feat considering that America's most important ally, the USSR, once had been aligned with the other side and, for a time, threatened a separate peace), and protected American interests around the world. It was primarily because of its geographical isolation and economic power that the United States, alone among the major nations of World War II, emerged with enhanced strength; but Roosevelt did much to establish the conditions for that development. When he died with ultimate victory in sight, a majority of Americans perceived him as a heroic leader who had brought the country through unprecedented ordeals with its ideals and institutions intact.

Yet, however much Roosevelt had established the Democrats as the party of leadership in crisis, the war also eroded the party's strength in significant ways. The casualty lists, the massive population displacements, high taxes (withheld from paychecks for the first time), shortages of consumer goods—all affected almost every American. The use of New Deal-style federal agencies to develop and enforce bureaucratic price control and rationing procedures equally aroused considerable resentment among farmers and businessmen. Millions of ordinary Americans had episodic difficulty finding objects as mundane as razor blades, a new set of tires, or a decent cut of meat. Labor strikes, infrequent to be sure, aroused widespread popular outrage when they occurred, or even were threatened.

The congressional election of 1942 was a particularly grim experience for New Deal Democrats. The party barely maintained control of Congress. Roosevelt faced a hostile conservative majority on Capitol Hill and experienced a near-collapse of his personal leadership, even among many legislators who agreed with him on policy issues. In 1944, Alben Barkley dramatized the new situation by resigning as Senate Majority Leader in protest against FDR's veto of a tax bill. He was unanimously reelected by Democratic senators in a show of solidarity that amounted to a direct slap at the President, who could only respond with a conciliatory "Dear Alben" letter. Little wonder that later that year, Roosevelt would dump Vice President Henry A. Wallace, who had been a model of ineptness in his congressional relations, for Senator Harry S. Truman, an able legislator who enjoyed widespread popularity in both houses of Congress.

Nevertheless, the Roosevelt coalition, a bit tattered about the edges, held firm, despite FDR's own visibly worn health, the multitude of resentments he had accumulated over 12 years, and all the strains of the war. On election day, Roosevelt defeated Thomas Dewey, polling about 53.3 percent of the vote and once again finding his decisive majorities in the cities. The most notable development was the rising importance of labor in the form of the newly established CIO Political Action Committee, which provided resources and organization that may have made the difference in Michigan and some other large industrial states.

The Democrats gained 24 seats in the House but lost two in the Senate—the conservative coalition and the divergent congressional party remained intact. The 1940 elections had left the party with 66 senators and 268 representatives; the 1944 elections returned 56 Democratic senators and 242 representatives.

When Franklin Roosevelt died a few months later on April 12, 1945, he left behind not simply a record of victory in four presidential elections but also a transformed Democratic party. What remained uncertain, however, was whether that party had an independent viability or whether it was, at bottom, a personal creation that would fly apart in his absence. Even if it could be held together, could any successor effect an ideological unification that would bring the Democratic congressional party back into line with the Democratic presidential party? It would be up to Harry S. Truman to provide the answers.

## THE MAINTAINING PRESIDENCY OF HARRY S. TRUMAN

Truman's presidency may be taken as an example of the way in which a chief executive lacking the assets that had meant so much to Roosevelt—style, charm, media charisma—could make so much of his office.[21] Truman assuredly deserves credit for the virtues that made him one of the most important twentieth century American presidents—hard work, determination, shrewd political judgment, and a gutsy approach to decision making. For all his differences in style and personality from FDR, he also showed that individuals make a difference. Consider what likely would have happened to the Democratic party under President Henry A. Wallace.

The Truman presidency demonstrated that the Roosevelt coalition, and the fact of a presumptive Democratic majority, possessed a social and political basis that extended beyond Roosevelt—and that it could be rallied by a Midwesterner with a considerably different cultural identity. Truman also showed that the party required a strong man in the White House in order to hold it together, shape its identity, and give it the leadership necessary to win national elections. Finally, the Truman years confirmed that the Democratic presidential-congressional split was an enduring fact of national life.

If Truman demonstrated that there was life after Roosevelt for the Democrats, the roller coaster ups and downs of his seven and three-fourths years in the White House equally displayed the fragility of the coalition. By the end of 1946, most political observers thought it was stone-cold dead. Truman, pulled between one Democratic faction and another, seemingly ineffective in his management of the economy, looked like a failure as President. The Republicans had swept to victory in the mid-term elections, winning control of Congress for the first time since 1928. Once in power, they quickly realized their major objective, passing the anti-labor Taft-Hartley Act and overriding Truman's veto of it. Any pundit or editorial writer with a functioning brain concluded that the Democratic era was over.

Remarkably, it was not. The Truman years, by and large, constituted a maintaining period rather than a transforming one, and for that reason it is not necessary to discuss them at the same length as the Roosevelt epoch. It is important, however, to arrive at some sense of just how Truman managed to hold together a party that seemed to be on the verge of flying apart. The following considerations suggest themselves:

**Centrist liberalism.** Truman picked up the heritage of the New Deal and added to it a series of his own programs (the Fair Deal) that seemed logical extensions. The broad public was not ready for most of them (national health insurance, federal aid to education, comprehensive civil rights legislation, repeal of the Taft-Hartley Act, the Brannan Plan for agriculture). The one item that did get through Congress, large-scale public housing, in 1949, is widely adjudged a failure.

Actually, Truman had done much to define an agenda for the next generation of liberal activism. His Fair Deal appealed to a substantial majority of non-southern Democrats who engaged themselves with policy issues; it maintained the allegiance of such critical constituencies as organized labor, African-Americans, and the liberal intelligentsia. What made it distinctive and gave it enduring significance was the way in which it adjusted Democratic liberalism to the new and apparently permanent prosperity that had emerged from World War II.

Truman's most momentous addition to the liberal agenda was civil rights.[22] His ideas about race—he thought in terms of "equal opportunity" rather than "social equality"—may seem primitive today, but in the world of the mid-twentieth century they were rather enlightened. Like Roosevelt before him, he doubtless preferred to dodge racial issues, but the end of the Depression made it impossible to satisfy African-Americans with distributional politics. As fairness and constitutional rights became the primary objectives of blacks and their white liberal allies, Truman had no fundamental inhibitions about taking up their cause. He deserves more credit than he usually gets for his civil rights stand. Inevitably, however, it added considerably to the centrifugal forces within the Democratic coalition.

The first President to offer a comprehensive civil rights program, he was never able to get legislation past a southern filibuster in the Senate, but he took major steps in other ways. His Justice Department submitted a series of path-breaking amicus curiae briefs to the Supreme Court, placing the executive branch squarely in favor of reversing *Plessy* v. *Ferguson* and thus setting the stage for the *Brown* decision of 1954. Despite determined opposition from the military bureaucracy, Truman desegregated the armed forces, thereby creating an integrated world that touched the lives of millions of Americans before desegregation became a norm in the 1960s.

After his election victory in 1948, Truman adjusted Democratic liberalism to postwar prosperity in another critical way. Under the leadership of Leon Keyserling, the second chairman of the Council of Economic Advisers, the administration abandoned Depression-era assumptions about an economy of scarcity and redistributionism.[23] Instead, it began to promote economic growth as a more fundamental objective of liberalism.

During the Truman era, which was characterized by a full employment economy in every year save 1949, this change was more in the realm of rhetoric than of policy. Keyserling, an eclectic thinker who lacked the credential of a Ph.D. in economics, never developed an elegant theoretical formula in the mode of the "New Economists" of the 1960s, although his policy directions paralleled theirs in many respects. His argument essentially boiled down to the assertion that the federal government should employ all the tools at its disposal to concentrate single-mindedly on enlarging the economy.

Understanding full well that redistributionism had limited political appeal, formulating his program at a time when stratospheric World War II marginal tax brackets remained in effect, Truman believed that only economic growth could accommodate the major objective of Democratic liberalism—the steady development of a social-democratic state with bigger and better social programs.

The "stagflation" of the Eisenhower Presidency, although not all that bad in the perspective of more recent economic trends, gave a special relevance to Keyserling's message and kept it at the top of the Democratic agenda. Walter Heller and other academic economists in the meantime developed a theoretical neo-Keynesian rationale for growth economics.[24] Presidents John F. Kennedy and Lyndon Johnson would adopt their proposals in the 1960s and pursue what appeared a promising growth program, built around the tax cut of 1964, before Vietnam overheated the economy.

Thereafter, partly because of mounting concern over the environmental consequences and partly because of the party's difficulties in controlling inflation, rapid growth would lose its salience on the Democratic economic agenda. Amazingly, in the 1980s, the issue was captured by the Republicans under Ronald Reagan, who talked about Kennedy-style tax cuts but were devoted to private investment and consumption rather than social democracy.

**Anti-Communism.** Leaving aside the merits, which were substantial, Truman's Cold War policies had the tactical advantage of disconnecting the party from what had become an embarrassing alliance with the Soviet Union and American Communists. The Truman Doctrine and the Marshall Plan protected American interests in Europe and the Middle East while sustaining liberal democracy in such countries as France and Italy. The President's diplomacy also provided a focus for a debate in the left wing of the party which led to the expulsion of Communists and pro-Communist "Popular Fronters" from the organized liberal movement and from leading labor unions. One suspects that Henry Wallace and the 1948 Progressives did more good for Truman by running against him than by remaining a conspicuous pro-Soviet faction within the Democratic party.

Truman's anti-Communist policies were, to be sure, not perfect. His diplomacy was well-crafted, thanks in no small part to a highly professional Department of State. The domestic extensions of these policies, however, included an ill-conceived loyalty program for the entire federal civil service and, worse still, the decision to prosecute the leaders of the American Communist party under the Smith Act. Truman himself came to realize that the loyalty program was a mistake, courageously (although unsuccessfully) vetoed the McCarran Internal Security Act of 1950, and emerged as a defender of civil liberties against the assaults of Wisconsin Senator Joseph McCarthy and others on the right (who were mostly Republicans but included a few Democrats).

In his diplomacy, as in his domestic reform program, Truman aligned himself with what Arthur Schlesinger, Jr. would characterize as "vital center" liberalism. Rejecting the totalitarianism of both the left and right, advocating civil liberties and democratic politics at home and abroad, renouncing full-scale socialism in favor of enhanced social welfarism, vital center liberalism reached a wide audience within the Democratic party, not least among them large ethno-religious minorities who were bitterly anti-Soviet.

**Truman's Leadership.** In the end, it was Truman himself who defined what the Democratic party meant in the immediate postwar years and then sold that definition to the American people in 1948. His foreign policy surely helped him. During his first term, by mutual understanding with the Republicans, his foreign policy was bipartisan and not a matter of debate between the two major parties. Nonetheless, the names of a Democratic President and his Secretary of State were on the two major instruments being used to contain Soviet power. During the campaign of 1948, the U.S. military transports were in the air around the clock, breaking the Soviet-imposed blockade of Berlin. Wallace, meanwhile, thundered away on the left, thus making it all the more impossible to accuse the President of being soft on Communism.

Another foreign policy issue had important political ramifications. The Arab-Jewish conflict in Palestine might seem to have been a bit of a sideshow when contrasted to the U.S.-Soviet confrontation in Europe, but the electoral stakes were large. Here also there was no real difference between the two parties; leaders of both generally sympathized with the concept of some sort of Jewish political entity in Palestine. But with the Jewish population overwhelmingly committed to the Democratic party, and Jewish leaders wielding substantial influence within it, Truman faced the toughest pressures.

As President, he struggled desperately with the issue of Palestine throughout his first term, striving to make decisions that would reconcile the national interest with his political interests. In May 1948, over the protests of the State Department, Truman ordered recognition of the newly proclaimed state of Israel. For the rest of the year, he would acquiesce in the department's resistance to further concessions, but what he had done was enough to hold the bulk of the Jewish vote. During his second term, the U.S.-Israeli relationship became closer, establishing a pattern of support for the Jewish state that has been a sine qua non of Democratic foreign policy ever since.

Thus the campaign of 1948 was largely about competing visions of domestic policy, which meant it was about liberalism. This in itself did not necessarily bode well for the Democrats. Truman was smart enough to realize that a campaign based on his Fair Deal initiatives was unlikely to get anywhere. A Congress controlled by Democrats in 1945-46 had been about as unwilling to do anything with these initiatives as the Republican Congress of 1947-48 had been. The Taft-Hartley Act, which placed significant restrictions on organized labor, had been supported by a majority of the Democratic delegation in the House. The civil rights program Truman had sent up to Congress in early 1948 attracted little public enthusiasm in the North and was fearsomely unpopular in the South. It in fact led to the establishment of a States Rights party, which nominated Governor J. Strom Thurmond of South Carolina for president. The "Dixiecrats," had only one raison d'etre—to deny the South, and the presidency, to Truman.

The President never repudiated anything in his own agenda, although he would have soft-pedaled civil rights in the Democratic platform; as it was, a convention floor revolt led by Hubert Humphrey, then the dynamic young mayor of Minneapolis, obtained a full-scale commitment to every point in the civil rights program. With that move, Humphrey and the liberals nailed the banner of civil rights to the Democratic party for once and for all. Truman, realizing that conciliation of the South was impossible anyway, thereupon issued his executive order desegregating the armed forces. During the campaign he became the first president ever to speak in Harlem. African-American leaders, who understood they were in a contest with the white South to determine who held the balance of power in a presidential election, took note. But the election was not primarily about civil rights nor any of the new items Truman had proposed.

Truman turned the election into a referendum on Roosevelt's New Deal. Criss-crossing the country, making hundreds of speeches, he repeatedly accused the Republicans of wanting to repeal the New Deal and turn the clock back to the 1920s. He turned the Democratic defeat in the elections of 1946 into a stroke of good fortune. No one, after all, could expect him to lead a Republican Congress—even if he had done so brilliantly on foreign policy issues—and the Republicans, especially those in the House, had managed to appear inflexibly negative. Truman's opponent, Thomas E. Dewey—Governor of New York, cool personification of the organization man, and perceived as a sure winner—never bothered to stoop to answer the President's charges.

It is oversimplifying, of course, to describe any presidential election as merely an ideological plebiscite. Truman's intensive campaigning no doubt heated up the blood of a lot of Democratic partisans whose loyalty to the party had little to do with programs and platforms. His fighting, ordinary-little-man-as-underdog role surely appealed to a lot of individuals who made their decisions on the basis of personal characteristics. Still, in the end, all explanations came back to Truman's defense of the New Deal and the conclusion that Roosevelt's achievements were established beyond recall.

Truman polled 49.5 percent of the popular vote, Dewey 45 percent. Thurmond and Wallace received about 2.4 percent each. Thurmond carried Alabama, Louisiana, Mississippi, and South Carolina for 39 electoral votes; Wallace pulled enough votes away from the Democrats to throw Maryland, Michigan, and New York to Dewey. Truman, with considerable justification, took the victory as a personal vindication. He was especially proud that it had been won without a solid South and without New York and some other large eastern industrial states. The count was close enough that numerous groups could claim some credit for the victory: African-Americans motivated by civil rights, farmers who resented cuts in the agricultural program, labor unions that supported Truman's fight against Taft-Hartley. The important question, however, was just what sort of a mandate Truman had been given.

The answer, to put it simply, was "not much of one." The public had voted *against* a largely fanciful threat to established New Deal programs they had come to cherish, not *for* a lot of new legislation. The Democrats had regained control of Congress, but by margins in the House that were almost the same as those of 1938, the election that had given birth to the conservative coalition; in the Senate, Democrats had only a 54-42 edge.

Congress would give Truman some significant enlargements of Social Security and other federal programs from the 1930s. However, aside from the Housing Act of 1949, the Fair Deal would run into a brick wall. What the President had done in 1948 was to arrest the disintegration of the party and just barely preserve the Roosevelt coalition, right down to maintaining its internal gridlock.

Perhaps most critically, the South emerged with more potential power within the party than it had shown in a generation, despite the apparent failure of the Thurmond candidacy. The region had been irrelevant to Roosevelt's four victories; Truman had won the election only because he had held on to most of it. If in addition to the four states he carried, Thurmond had carried Texas and any other two southern states, Truman would have failed to carry a majority in the electoral college, which would have left the contest to be decided by the House of Representatives.

If the Republicans could have laid claim to all those electoral votes, Dewey would have been elected. There already were plenty of stirrings of independence in Texas, where Governor Coke Stevenson had been friendly to the Dixiecrats and Houston publisher Jesse H. Jones, a leader of conservative Democrats in the Roosevelt years, had endorsed Dewey. The vision of the South, anti-civil rights and conservative in its broader outlook, voting Republican in presidential elections was by no means outlandish. It was probably the mathematics of his victory as much as anything that impelled Truman to avoid retaliation against the Dixiecrats and reject efforts to reduce southern influence in Congress after 1948.

Numerous developments cemented the pattern—the fall of China, the Soviet A-bomb, the Hiss case, the Rosenberg case, the Korean War. By the end of 1950, McCarthyism had become a dominating force in American politics and the Democrats had given back some of their gains in Congress. Truman was circling the wagons to defend his foreign policy, but to do so required uniting the party behind a holding action in Korea, the MacArthur dismissal, and a sharp military expansion to insure the defense of Europe. It was not a popular program. Revelations of small-bore corruption in the administration added to the damage. In 1952, a Republican strategist would describe the formula for his party's campaign as K-1, C-2: Korea, Communism, corruption.

Truman was by then a spent force politically, although feistier and more vehement than ever in his campaigning. The Republican presidential candidate, war hero General Dwight D. Eisenhower, eclipsed Dewey in charisma and political savvy; significantly, he went out of his way to reassure the voters explicitly that he would pose no threat to the achievements of the Roosevelt era. This pledge, given with at least a small degree of reluctance, underscored one of Truman's important accomplishments in Democratic party history. If he had been unable to achieve his Fair Deal program, he at least had shown clearly that a broad national consensus supported the New Deal. Republicans from Eisenhower on would demonstrate that they understood the lesson. Even the "Reagan Revolution" would be largely a reaction against the Great Society and the 1960s.

Truman also had committed the Democratic party to a foreign policy that both Republicans and Democrats would follow for a generation—active involvement in the world with the objective of establishing a liberal international order while containing expansionist totalitarianism in the form of the Soviet empire. Pursued with varying degrees of activism and passivity, skill and ineptness by his successors, frequently denounced by utopians of both the liberal left and the conservative right, containment nonetheless remained the guiding principle of American foreign policy until the collapse of the Soviet Union.

## THE DEMOCRATS IN THE IKE AGE

The "Eisenhower era" would amount to little more than an interregnum in the political pattern that Roosevelt had established. Except for 1953-54, the Democratic party controlled Congress throughout the old hero's years in the White House. Eisenhower himself, moreover, posed no serious challenge to the main outlines of foreign and domestic policy established under Truman.[25] His administration, for example, talked about liberation but practiced containment and made periodic attempts at conciliation with the Soviet Union in the post-Stalin era. At home, it trimmed some New Deal programs a bit but enlarged others. By and large, Eisenhower achieved a good working relationship with Democratic congressional leaders Lyndon Johnson and Sam Rayburn, both of them Texas moderates who were impressed by Ike's strength and popularity in their own state as well as throughout the country. It is with ample reason that the 1950s are usually remembered as years of consensus.

The new Democratic leader, Adlai Stevenson, who had lost to Eisenhower in the '52 election, seemed to add considerable substance to the impression of a period of moderation. Whatever the precise degree of liberalism one might find in a detail-by-detail examination of his pronouncements, Stevenson unquestionably looked moderate in contrast to Roosevelt or Truman. He possessed neither man's visceral appeal to the blue-collar classes, was widely perceived as to the right of Truman on civil rights, and was perfectly willing to declare moderation "the spirit of the times."[26]

The qualities that gave Stevenson his unassailable leadership of the presidential party were his wit, eloquence, and thoughtfulness. These were aspects of his character that transcended a hypothetical Americans for Democratic Action issues score, and in fact they made him especially attractive to that liberal constituency. Stevenson's rise coincided with, and may be partially explained by, the rapid growth of the "liberal intelligentsia"—well-educated, non-entrepreneurial professionals drawn by idealism (and at times by self-interest) to the concept of government as the ultimate solver of social problems.

By the end of the fifties, these types were spearheading a Democratic "reform movement" in New York that was on the verge of toppling what remained of the old regular Democratic Tammany machine. In a number of metropolitan areas across the country, they were highly visible in "citizen activist" movements that constituted a challenge to old, decaying Democratic machines. Not yet radicalized, as so many of them would become in the 1960s, they saw in Stevenson a political ideal. It is next to impossible to quantify their influence, but it seems safe to say that by the end of the fifties, they had become a force within the party nearly as significant as the labor movement.

Still, by 1960, it might have seemed that in many ways not much had changed since the end of the thirties. The congressional party, under Johnson and Rayburn, was distinctly more moderate than a presidential party still dominated by organized labor, minorities, and the liberals. Far from feeling irrelevant in the general prosperity of the Ike Age, the liberals promoted not simply the unfinished agenda of the Truman era but new programs designed to address the *quality* of American life (according to John Kenneth Galbraith) or to press ahead against the remnants of poverty (according to Leon Keyserling). The Democratic Advisory Council, created in 1957 primarily as a vehicle for liberal policy development, cranked out one new proposal after another.[27]

The South, on the other hand, seemed increasingly out of step with the party mainstream. It still sent Democrats to Congress but showed disturbing signs of independence in presidential elections. In 1952, Eisenhower took 57 of its 128 electoral votes; in 1956, he won 67, a majority. In both elections, he carried Texas, Virginia, Tennessee, and Florida.

The trend was all the more ominous because the civil rights movement was beginning to move out of the courts and into the streets in the form of direct action and demands for total integration, not just tokenism. "Massive resistance" by white southerners was the other element of what was beginning to appear to be an irrepressible conflict. The reaction of most leaders seriously concerned with political power was to treat this development as if it were a deadly virus, insulate it, and hope the party, continuing along the gradualist path that had met its institutional needs in the past, could regain the South in the post-Eisenhower era.

## JFK, LBJ, AND THE GREAT SOCIETY

The presidential candidacy of young Massachusetts Senator John F. Kennedy in 1960 rekindled all the party's cultural conflicts and ideological divisions.[28] His victory over Senate Majority Leader Lyndon Johnson for the Democratic nomination demonstrated that the northern urban liberals maintained an easy dominance of the presidential party. Moreover, Kennedy, unlike Johnson, was not an "insider" with close ties to the congressional establishment, and, unlike Johnson, he had sought the nomination by waging an exhausting national primary campaign. Thus in a very real sense, the struggle between the two had exemplified the continuing divide between the presidential and congressional parties.

Kennedy possessed a magnetic personality that transcended such conventional defining factors as section, religion, and ethnicity, but he could not escape his identity as a northeastern Irish Catholic. For that reason, his decision to make Johnson his vice presidential candidate was probably the most important of the fall campaign. It surely won him some southern states that would otherwise have voted for Republican nominee Richard Nixon. Kennedy carried Texas and cut the southern losses to 47 electoral votes, a showing comparable to Truman's in 1948.

Democratic optimists rejoicing in his razor-thin victory hoped that in tandem with Johnson he could overcome the forces of disunity and give the party exciting new leadership. By virtue of background, style, and education the new President seemed capable of uniting the party's traditional ethno-religious following with the newly important liberal intelligentsia. Perhaps Johnson could bring the South along.

Yet Kennedy's election was best interpreted as portending a return to 1949 in terms of the structure of the party and therefore of presidential-congressional relations. He won 49.9 percent of the total vote, little more than Truman in 1948; his 303 electoral votes were exactly the same as Truman's.[29] The Democratic delegation in the House was also almost numerically identical and would be barely altered by the 1962 midterm election. With just over 50 percent of the electorate having voted for someone else in what was essentially a two-party contest, the new President's electoral mandate was even vaguer than Truman's.

It is hardly surprising then that the achievements of Kennedy's presidency were more in the realm of symbolic leadership and policy formulation than legislation. He managed to obtain some bits and pieces from Congress—an area redevelopment plan that poured substantial federal assistance into Appalachia; the food stamp program (which passed primarily because it was an indirect subsidy to farmers); an ambitious agenda of aid to Latin America (the Alliance for Progress); and the Peace Corps. Other major programs, actually carryovers from Truman's Fair Deal, such as aid to education and national medical insurance for the elderly, went nowhere.

Kennedy's biggest legislative success was the Trade Expansion Act of 1962, a historic step that continued the postwar movement toward free trade and an integrated international economy. Primarily the work of the foreign policy establishment, it was the last great expression of what had been a hallowed Democratic principle. A good many multinational corporations, not exactly a Democratic core constituency, were enthusiastic about it. Industrial labor unions, at that time still the heart of the party, were brought behind the legislation only through the inclusion of substantial safeguards. Thereafter, as foreign competition weighed heavily on unionized segments of the economy, they moved toward protectionism, and elements of the party would move with them.

Kennedy had promised to "get the country moving again" economically and had been a strong critic of the slow growth of the Eisenhower years. Under the tutelage of economist Walter Heller, he made a decision to stimulate an economy already recovering from the recession of 1960-61 and to accept a big federal budget deficit in the process. What set him apart in some respects from the mainstream of Democratic thinking was his decision to use tools that assisted business (the investment tax credit of 1962) and to favor private consumption over public spending.

In 1963, Kennedy proposed a major tax cut, stunning some Democrats who thought that enhanced social programs, financed by deficit spending, could both stimulate the economy and serve important public purposes. (Leon Keyserling called the Kennedy proposal the moral equivalent of throwing $20 billion into the streets.) The major opposition, however, came from fiscal conservatives, Democratic and Republican, who believed that an economic recovery was a time for slashing deficits, not enlarging them. By November 1963, the political odds seemed only marginally in favor of the bill making it to Kennedy's desk intact.

With much less fanfare, the administration also started to give attention to an issue that had surfaced, or perhaps resurfaced, at the beginning of the 1960s—the persistence of poverty in an affluent society. Mainstream liberal Democratic thinking in the 1950s assumed that the "quantitative problems" of American society had been largely solved. Poverty, John Kenneth Galbraith proclaimed in his highly influential *The Affluent Society*, had become an afterthought. The major task of liberalism was to address the "qualitative problems" of America as manifested in inadequate public services and amenities—schools, parks, libraries, publicly-funded arts, and the like.[30]

All that was changed by the publication of Michael Harrington's *The Other America* in 1962.[31] A card-carrying member of the Socialist party, Harrington had every interest in exaggerating the extent of poverty and deprivation in America, but he worked from official, generally accepted statistics, and convinced all but the most skeptical of his readers that the condition he described was considerably vaster than they had imagined.[32]

Kennedy himself had been surprised and rather shocked at the visible poverty he had seen while campaigning in West Virginia. His administration at first nibbled around the edges of the problem with Appalachian aid, food stamps, and urban youth programs. By late 1963, however, his advisers were formulating a comprehensive war on poverty with the expectation that it would be a major part of his second term and perhaps of his campaign for reelection. No one can state with certainty how far he might have pursued it, but the issue assuredly had grabbed his attention. More fundamentally, Harrington had brought it to the consciousness of Democratic activists across the country.

Much more salient during the last year of the Kennedy presidency was the eruption of the long-festering problem of civil rights. In what was becoming the tradition of party leaders, Kennedy had tried in a variety of ways to mobilize northern blacks as part of the Democratic coalition without alienating the South. Martin Luther King's mass demonstrations in Birmingham during the Easter season of 1963, marked by the televised brutalization of demonstrators by police, forced the issues in ways Kennedy would have preferred to avoid. Once confronted with the need for choice, however, he seized the moral high ground and sent a comprehensive civil rights bill to Congress.

The bill's impact on the Democratic party was deeply divisive. Kennedy must have known that if it passed, the Deep South would be lost to the party for the foreseeable future, and he surely realized that there was little sympathy for it among the urban ethno-religious groups that had turned out so heavily for him in 1960. On the other hand, for the liberals, who had made themselves the conscience of the party, for northern blacks, and for many labor leaders, strong legislation had become a moral imperative. Kennedy, of course, had done the right thing; he also seems to have realized that the issue's time had come. To declare his own position, however, was one thing; to get a law through Congress was another. As with the tax cut bill, the odds in November 1963 slightly favored some sort of legislation, but with just what provisions remained uncertain.

Foreign policy allowed Kennedy more scope for independent leadership and accomplishment. Here he continued in the large framework of Cold War anti-Communism, but with a flexibility that had emerged among both Democrats and Republicans after the death of Stalin in 1953. While Kennedy continued to practice containment, he chose his causes carefully, refusing to intervene in Laos or to commit American forces to the overthrow of the Castro government in Cuba. In Vietnam, he attempted to follow a middle course of containing a Communist insurgency while building an indigenous regime that could muster popular support; an admirable purpose, it would end disastrously in a double assassination and a series of military dictatorships.

Conversely, he adamantly resisted Soviet pressures in Berlin, making it clear that the United States could be expelled from the city only at the risk of nuclear war. Most notably, in the fall of 1962, he forced withdrawal of Soviet missiles from Cuba, an act of leadership that made him the hero of the anti-Communist world. Having thus established his credentials, he entered into a period of *detente* with the USSR, symbolized by the Test Ban Treaty of 1963.

Kennedy's record on foreign policy, much more than his domestic record, made him an impressive leader to much of the public. By and large, this record has resisted the onslaughts of historical revisionists. Yet the very flexibility that made it commendable would present a difficult and ambiguous legacy to a successor who had never possessed Kennedy's interest in diplomacy.

If Lyndon Johnson lacked the mythic qualities Kennedy achieved in death, if he possessed a private and public personality almost dysfunctional in its unattractiveness, he nonetheless came to the presidency with valuable attributes that would for a time serve him well.[33] Above all, he knew Congress from the inside as had no other twentieth century president. A master of the legislative process, deeply respected by the congressional barons, he shrewdly capitalized on the sense of national tragedy and crisis that followed Kennedy's death, built strong public support for passage of the civil rights and tax cut bills, and made the deals necessary to get them passed.

The Civil Rights Act of 1964, similar in many respects to the bills offered by Truman in 1948 and 1949, opened a broad government offensive against discrimination and segregation in most areas of American life. In both its symbolic impact and its practical implementation, it was little short of revolutionary. The Tax Act was, in its way, a comparable departure in economic policy, emphasizing economic growth above standard definitions of federal fiscal responsibility. For a year or two, it seemed to work grandly—until the costs of the escalating Vietnam war overheated the economy.

Passage of these two statutes alone would have been enough to establish Johnson as a major President. He also adopted Kennedy's concept of a war on poverty and guided its beginnings through Congress in the form of the Economic Opportunity Act of 1964, which brought together a number of different antipoverty programs, all of them of modest scale but clearly slated for enhanced funding. In speeches, he proclaimed the goal of a "Great Society" for America.

Johnson had not undergone a sudden conversion. Although the realities of statewide Texas politics had forced him to position himself on the right for a time, he had started his career as a fervent New Dealer representing a hill-country district in the House of Representatives. Now, as President, he was able once again to express his sympathies for the poor and for minorities without reservation. He was, to be sure, vain, prone to see his legislative achievements as personal monuments, and perhaps more ambitious than realistic in his hopes of accomplishment for the social programs he backed. None of that detracts from what appear to have been honest feelings for the disadvantaged.

Riding a crest of legislative achievement and public sympathy, Johnson was all but handed the 1964 presidential election when the Republicans nominated Arizona Senator Barry Goldwater. Fondly remembered by a later generation as a blunt, plain-speaking old codger who expressed his admiration for Harry Truman, Goldwater in 1964 was a shrill, militant advocate of the far right. He was no doubt unfairly caricatured by the Johnson campaign as a warmonger and a mad bomber, but it is equally true that his public persona made the depiction credible. That November, Goldwater carried only Arizona and the five most race-conscious states of the Deep South.

The vast landslide that elected Johnson was a personal triumph and an opportunity for a surge of social legislation that would make the achievements of 1964 seem puny by comparison. The electorate had handed Johnson a House of Representatives dominated by 295 Democrats, the largest number since the heyday of the New Deal. Did these results mean the public wanted more and more of the Great Society? Johnson described his mandate as rather like the Rio Grande—broad but not deep. He was determined to use it for all it was worth.

Over the next two years, the possibilities seemed almost unlimited as Johnson and the Democratic Congress erected a Great Society far more grandiose than could ever have been imagined at the beginning of the decade: Medicare, Medicaid, large-scale aid to education, expanded Social Security benefits, big enlargements of the anti-poverty programs, aid to cities, a major housing act, immigration reform. Of all the items from Truman's old Fair Deal agenda, only repeal of Taft-Hartley remained stalled, a development that reflected not simply the determined opposition of the Republicans but also the already declining clout of the traditional labor unions inside the Democratic party.

Moreover, spurred by another set of civil rights demonstrations—this time in Selma, Alabama—Johnson managed to get through Congress the Voting Rights Act of 1965, an epochal achievement that, a century after emancipation, delivered meaningful guarantees of the right to vote to southern African-Americans. Over the next generation, the Act would transform the Democratic parties of one southern state after another from defenders of states' rights and segregation to racially integrated, socially liberal organizations. Remarkably, these parties would remain competitive in statewide politics, if usually not in presidential elections.

In retrospect, there were warning signs aplenty on the horizon by the end of 1965. Johnson had undertaken a major escalation of the U.S. military commitment in Vietnam with potentially serious consequences, and the first signs of opposition were appearing on college campuses. A growing counterculture was beginning to make itself felt as a force throughout American life, even here and there within the Democratic party. Early manifestations of black militance and separatism were beginning to show up in the predominantly integrationist and amalgamationist civil rights movement. It remained to be seen how easily the problem of poverty would yield to the soldiers of reform fighting the war against it. Inflation was beginning to rise beyond the nuisance level.

As Lyndon Johnson ended his first year as President in his own right, however, the country was richer than ever and devoting an unprecedented amount more of its wealth than ever to addressing long-festering social problems. America seemed on the way to becoming a fairer, more genuinely democratic society than ever, and likely to reach the mark without requiring real sacrifices from any group of its citizens.

The Democratic moment in American history had reached its high point. The party, it seemed, had achieved its rendezvous with destiny.

# NOTES

1. To attempt to divine the "true" meaning of the term "Jeffersonian" would be to embark on an endless tangent. Suffice to say that all the meanings in the text had acquired some currency by the early twentieth century. Those who would like to delve farther into the problem should consult Merrill Peterson, *The Jefferson Image in the American Mind* (New York: Oxford University Press, 1960); Merrill Peterson, *Thomas Jefferson and the New Nation* (New York: Oxford University Press, 1986); and Noble E. Cunningham, Jr., *In Pursuit of Reason: The Life of Thomas Jefferson* (Baton Rouge: Louisiana State University Press, 1987).

2. David Burner, *The Politics of Provincialism: The Democratic Party in Transition, 1918-1932* (New York: Knopf, 1967). See also Alan Lichtman, *Prejudice and the Old Politics: The Presidential Election of 1928* (Chapel Hill: University of North Carolina Press, 1979). Two classic works on American politics and society in the 1920s are William E. Leuchtenburg, *The Perils of Prosperity, 1914-1932* (Chicago: University of Chicago Press, 1958); and John D. Hicks, *Republican Ascendancy* (New York: Harper & Row, 1960).

3. Two classic works on the causes and character of the Great Depression are Charles Kindleberger, *The World in Depression, 1929-1939* (Berkeley: University of California Press, 1986); and John A. Garraty, *The Great Depression* (New York: Harcourt Brace Jovanovich, 1986).

4. *Historical Statistics of the United States* (Washington: U.S. Government Printing Office, 1975), 1:135, 224, 483; 2:1038.

5. See David Sarasohn, *The Party of Reform: Democrats in the Progressive Era* (Oxford: University of Mississippi Press, 1989); Robert Cherney, *Righteous Cause: The Life of William Jennings Bryan* (Boston: Little, Brown, 1985); Le Roy Ashby, *William Jennings Bryan: Champion of Democracy* (Boston: Twayne, 1987); Paolo E. Coletta, *William Jennings Bryan*, 3 vols. (Lincoln: University of Nebraska Press, 1964-69); Arthur S. Link, *Woodrow Wilson and the Progressive Era, 1910-1917* (New York: Harper & Row, 1954); Arthur S. Link, *Wilson: The New Freedom* (Princeton: Princeton University Press, 1956); Arthur S. Link, *Wilson: Campaigns for Progressivism and Peace* (Princeton: Princeton University Press,

1965); and John Milton Cooper, *The Warrior and the Priest* (Cambridge: Harvard University Press, 1983).

6. The scholarly literature on Roosevelt and the New Deal is vast. Among the significant single-volume works are William E. Leuchtenburg, *Franklin D. Roosevelt and the New Deal, 1932-1940* (New York: Harper & Row, 1963), a classic interpretation; and the more recent Anthony Badger, *The New Deal: The Depression Years* (New York: Hill & Wang, 1989); James MacGregor Burns, *Roosevelt: The Lion and the Fox* (New York: Harcourt, Brace & World, 1956), a thoughtful and provocative liberal critique; Frank Freidel, *Franklin D. Roosevelt: A Rendezvous with Destiny* (Boston: Little, Brown, 1990); and Patrick Maney, *F.D.R.: The Roosevelt Presence* (New York: Twayne, 1992). Paul K. Conkin, *The New Deal*, 3d ed. (Arlington Heights, Ill.: Harlan Davidson, 1992) is a brief critique from the left in the pragmatic, social democratic tradition of John Dewey. Arthur M. Schlesinger, Jr., *The Age of Roosevelt*, 3 vols. (Boston: Houghton Mifflin, 1957-60) is a celebratory, scholarly, and near-definitive blending of history and biography covering the years 1929-36. *The New Deal: The National Level*, John Braeman, et al., eds.(Columbus: Ohio State University Press, 1975) is an important collection of original essays.

7. Among the many works on New Deal policy toward various sectors of the economy, the following are possibly the most useful: Ellis W. Hawley, *The New Deal and the Problem of Monopoly* (Princeton: Princeton University Press, 1966); Irving Bernstein, *Turbulent Years: The American Worker, 1929-1939* (Boston: Houghton Mifflin, 1969); and Theodore Saloutos, *The American Farmer and the New Deal* (Ames: Iowa State University Press, 1982).

8. Leuchtenburg, *Franklin D. Roosevelt and the New Deal*, 68.

9. *Historical Statistics*, 1:135.

10. Garraty, *The Great Depression*, 197.

11. Keynes to Roosevelt, February 1, 1938, Franklin D. Roosevelt Papers, Franklin D. Roosevelt Library, reproduced in *New Deal Thought*, ed. Howard Zinn (Indianapolis: Bobbs-Merrill, 1966), 403-409.

12. *Historical Statistics* 2:1105

13. On tax policy, the most comprehensive treatment is Mark Leff, *The Limits of Symbolic Reform: The New Deal and Taxation, 1933-1939* (New York: Cambridge University Press, 1984), a work that is written, however, from a democratic socialist, redistributionist frame of reference quite different from that of the author of this essay.

14. Leuchtenburg, *Franklin D. Roosevelt and the New Deal*, 183-184.

15. Keynes to Roosevelt, February 1, 1938, in *New Deal Thought*, 403-409.

16. Leuchtenburg, *Franklin D. Roosevelt and the New Deal*, 154.

17. WPA workers often demonstrated and engaged in letter-writing campaigns in favor of continued appropriations for either their specific projects or for the agency in general. Occasionally they attempted to form labor unions. Sometimes they actually called strikes for better wages or working conditions, but invariably these were put down with a decisiveness akin to that with which Ronald Reagan smashed the air controllers' walkout.

18. *Historical Statistics*, 1:457.

19. Leuchtenburg, *Franklin D. Roosevelt and the New Deal*, 243.

20. My own response to the controversy that invariably swirls around this event is quite simple. I do not believe that Roosevelt had the slightest inkling of the Japanese plans. If he had known of them in advance, he in all likelihood would have welcomed them—and deployed American air and naval power to strike a surprise counterblow against the Japanese fleet. Such a stroke would have given him the war he *may* have wanted and would have started it with a U.S. victory.

21. The authoritative history of the Truman presidency is Robert Donovan's two-volume survey, *Conflict and Crisis* and *Tumultuous Years* (New York: Norton, 1977, 1982). Donald R. McCoy, *The Presidency of Harry S. Truman* (Lawrence: University Press of Kansas, 1984) is a more selective account by a distinguished historian. Alonzo L. Hamby, *Beyond the New Deal: Harry S. Truman and American Liberalism* (New York: Columbia University Press, 1973) pursues themes that may be of special interest to the readers of this work.

22. Among the many works on civil rights and the Truman administration, the fullest and most balanced is Donald R. McCoy and Richard T. Ruetten, *Quest and Response* (Lawrence: University Press of Kansas, 1973).

23. Hamby, *Beyond the New Deal*, 297-303.

24. Walter Heller, *New Dimensions of Political Economy* (Cambridge: Harvard University Press, 1966) is an accessible introduction to the New Economics.

25. The major scholarly works on the Eisenhower presidency are Herbert Parmet, *Eisenhower and the American Crusades* (New York: Macmillan, 1972); Charles Alexander, *Holding the Line* (Bloomington: Indiana University Press, 1975); Chester Pach and Elmo Richardson, *The Presidency of Dwight D. Eisenhower*, 2d ed., rev. (Lawrence: University Press of Kansas, 1991); Fred Greenstein, *The Hidden Hand Presidency: Eisenhower as Leader* (New York: Basic Books, 1982); and Stephen Ambrose, *Eisenhower: The President* (New York: Simon & Schuster, 1984).

26. Quoted in Eric F. Goldman, *The Crucial Decade—and After: America, 1945-1960* (New York: Vintage, 1961), 290. On Stevenson, see John Bartlow Martin's magisterial two volumes, *Adlai Stevenson of Illinois* and *Adlai Stevenson and the World* (Garden City: Doubleday, 1976, 1977); and Porter McKeever, *Adlai Stevenson: His Life and Legacy* (New York: Morrow, 1989).

27. On this development, see especially James Sundquist, *Politics and Policy: The Eisenhower, Kennedy, and Johnson Years* (Washington: Brookings, 1968).

28. Of the many works on Kennedy and his presidency, see especially the two works by Arthur M. Schlesinger, Jr., *A Thousand Days* (Boston: Houghton Mifflin, 1965), and *Robert F. Kennedy and His Times* (Boston: Houghton Mifflin, 1978); Herbert Parmet, *Jack: The Struggles of John F. Kennedy* and *J.F.K.: The Presidency of John F. Kennedy* (New York: Dial Press, 1980, 1983); Jim F. Heath, *Decade of Disillusionment* (Bloomington: Indiana University Press, 1976), a brief survey that also covers Lyndon Johnson's presidency; and Garry Wills, *The Kennedy Imprisonment* (Boston: Little, Brown, 1982), a volume that demonstrates Wills's bipartisan determination to reveal the inadequacies of contemporary political leadership. Perhaps the single best scholarly study of the 1960s, which deals intelligently with both the Kennedy and Johnson presidencies, is Allen J. Matusow, *The Unravelling of America* (New York: Harper & Row, 1984). More recent works are Irving Bernstein, *Promises to Keep: John F. Kennedy's New Frontier*

(New York: Oxford University Press, 1991), a laudatory work; Thomas C. Reeves, *A Question of Character: A Life of John F. Kennedy* (New York: Free Press, 1991), which emphasizes personal "character" issues over public policy; James N. Giglio, *The Presidency of John F. Kennedy* (Lawrence: University Press of Kansas, 1991), a solid, competent synthesis; and Michael Beschloss, *The Crisis Years: Kennedy and Khrushchev*, 1960-63 (New York: Harper Collins, 1991), a big, readable survey of foreign relations.

29. Kennedy, however, carried only 12 of the 28 states that had voted for Truman, a divergence perhaps best explained by their different ethno-religious identities and regional bases and by the regional identification of their opponents.

30. John Kenneth Galbraith, *The Affluent Society*, 1st ed. (Boston: Houghton Mifflin, 1958).

31. Michael Harrington, *The Other America* (New York: Macmillan, 1962).

32. The impact of Harrington's book demonstrated a fascinating subtheme of post-World War II American politics. The Socialist party of America became with the retirement of Norman Thomas an educational organization and social-democratic policy development caucus on the left wing of the Democratic party.

33. Johnson's administration has not yet attracted the outpouring of scholarship that Kennedy's has generated. Perhaps the best single book yet written on LBJ is Robert Dallek, *Lone Star Rising* (New York: Oxford University Press, 1991), the first volume of a two-volume biography. Robert Caro's two-volumes with the general title *The Years of Lyndon Johnson* (New York: Knopf, 1982, 1990) are detailed, readable, and remarkably hostile. Rowland Evans and Robert Novak, *Lyndon B. Johnson: The Exercise of Power* (New York: New American Library, 1966) is first-rate journalism that goes up into the first year of the Johnson presidency. Doris Kearns, *Lyndon Johnson and the American Dream* (New York: Harper & Row, 1976) is an arresting character study based on the author's close relationship with her subject. Eric F. Goldman, *The Tragedy of Lyndon Johnson* (New York: Knopf, 1969), although written by a distinguished historian, is more memoir than history. Good narratives may be found in Heath, *Decade of Disillusionment*, and Matusow, *Unravelling of America*.

## Chapter 12

# The Travail of the Democrats: Search for a New Majority

*Steven M. Gillon*

A cold morning rain fell on the picturesque streets of Lake Waverly, Minnesota, on election day in 1968. The grey sky and frigid air added to the gloom of the Democratic officials who had accompanied Hubert Humphrey to his Minnesota home. Even the usually buoyant Humphrey appeared downcast as he stepped out of the tiny, white frame Marysville Township Hall where he had cast his ballot. Worn from the strains of a long and bitter campaign, he glanced briefly at the army of photographers and reporters. "We've done the best job we could," he said. "The American jury is out now." The following day, after all the votes had been counted, Humphrey heard the verdict: Richard Nixon would be the next President of the United States.

Though tantalizingly narrow, the Democrats' defeat in 1968 represented an important turning point for the party. The election marked the end of the Roosevelt era and the beginning of a new conservative period in American politics. At no other time in this century has a major party suffered the electoral landslides experienced by Democratic presidential candidates in the years after 1968. In 1984, Republican Ronald Reagan carried as many states, forty-nine, as all the Democratic nominees for president combined won in the five elections after 1968. In losing four of these presidential contests, Democrats won less than 45 percent of the popular vote and less than 200 electoral votes. Since 1968, twenty-three states with a total of 202 electoral votes supported the Republican presidential nominee in every election. Only the District of Columbia voted Democratic in each election.[1]

After 1968, a combination of historical forces fragmented the Democratic presidential coalition, eroded support for liberal programs, and bolstered the Republican party. The emergence of divisive social issues, especially race, overwhelmed traditional Democratic appeals to economic self-interest and provided Republicans with a potent new populist message. At the same time, generational conflict, only temporarily obscured by Watergate, divided the Democratic party and blurred its message. These internal divisions paralyzed the Carter administration and confirmed public doubts about the party's ability to govern. During the 1980s, Ronald Reagan's value-laden rhetoric and masterful use of the media highlighted the Democrats' weakness. Nearly 25 years after Humphrey's defeat in the 1968 election, Democrats were still searching for a new message to win back disaffected voters.

In 1969, few issues frustrated Americans more than Vietnam. After years of bloody fighting, mounting casualty figures, and soaring costs, the war appeared stalemated. Many Democrats, even those who had supported Lyndon Johnson's 1965 decision to commit ground troops, were calling for an end to the hostility. But polls showed a nation ambivalent about the war. Though increasingly impatient with the military situation, most Americans were reluctant to accept defeat or to embrace antiwar protestors. Democrats who hoped to bring the war to a quick end had to walk a difficult path. They needed to provide a convincing rationale for extrication from the conflict without appearing to surrender to communism, weaken America's global position, or sound unpatriotic. Unfortunately, Vietnam defied that strategy, making Democrats easy prey for flag-waving Republicans.

Initially, Nixon had disarmed critics by promising troop withdrawals while talking of "peace with honor." His position satisfied the public's contradictory demands for an end to the war without an admission of defeat. But the President awakened the peace movement from its slumber in April, 1970, when he sent American forces into neutral Cambodia. A few days later, four students at Kent State University were shot to death by Ohio National Guardsmen as they protested against the war. Colleges across the nation exploded in fury. The killings produced what one college president called "the most disastrous May in the history of American higher education." Yet for all of its fury, the campus revolt did little to alter public attitudes. A poll found overwhelming support for the Guardsmen and a strong plurality in favor of the Cambodian invasion.

Responding to the mood on major college campuses, liberal Democrats denounced the invasion as unconstitutional and became more strident in their calls for an American withdrawal. An angry George McGovern took to the Senate floor to urge support for his resolution calling for an end to the war. "This chamber reeks of blood," he told his stunned colleagues. But Democrats underestimated the complexity of anti-war feeling. Though the public shared the peace movement's opposition to the war, they did not embrace its leaders or their tactics. The antiwar movement's abuse of revered national symbols, its often unfair association with violence and disorder, and its sometimes strident rhetoric of social revolution, frightened potential allies. More important, class differences separated antiwar protestors from the white working-class they hoped to attract. The popular journalist Jimmy Breslin ridiculed the "arrogance" that antiwar leaders displayed toward "people who work with their hands for a living." For white, working-class America, Richard Nixon was an anti-establishment figure, battling against a movement that ridiculed the symbols and values of patriotic Americans. "It was the abiding irony of the antiwar opposition that its most assertive advocates were held in such contempt not only by a population that increasingly termed the war a mistake," observed the historian Charles DeBenedetti, "but also by many of those who supported their policies."[2]

While fighting to bring a swift end to the Vietnam War, many Democrats also struggled to keep alive the fight for civil rights. During the 1960s, despite opposition from the southern wing of its party, Democrats passed legislation that barred discrimination in public facilities, guaranteed blacks the right to vote, and outlawed discrimination in the sale of housing. After 1970, many liberals hoped to continue the struggle through court-enforced busing to end segregation in public schools. This new phase of the civil rights movement produced an unanticipated consequence, however—massive white resistance. In cities across the country, angry whites expressed outrage at a political and judicial system that appeared insensitive to their rights. Opponents of busing viewed themselves as victims of a misguided social experiment conducted by affluent liberals who sent their own children to comfortable private or suburban schools. Like Alice McGoff, an Irish working-class mother depicted in J. Anthony Lukas's epic study of desegregation in Boston, many whites felt bitter and scornful "at the power, wealth, and privilege which seemed to be arrayed against" them.[3]

Republicans successfully defined the debate over busing, and other social issues, as a clash between the insurgent values of a liberal elite and the traditional values of middle-class Americans. This new conservative populism replaced contempt for greedy businessmen with a disdain for lenient judges, unresponsive bureaucrats, and arrogant minorities. Nixon, always the shrewd politician, capitalized on this discontent by pledging his fidelity to law and order and traditional values. "The time has come," he declared, "to draw the line . . . for the Great Silent Majority . . . to stand up and be counted against the appeasement of the rock-throwers and the obscenity shouters in America." As part of the populist strategy, Vice President Spiro Agnew attacked the news media and intellectuals as "vicars of vacillation," "nattering nabobs of negativism," and "an effete corps of impudent snobs" who encouraged a "spirit of national masochism."

The nomination of George McGovern by the Democrats in 1972 played directly into Republican hands. McGovern, a soft-spoken preacher's son whom Robert Kennedy once called "the most decent man in the Senate," took advantage of new party rules to outmaneuver Senator Edmund Muskie, his chief rival for the nomination. At the party's convention, McGovern supporters used rule changes calling for proportional representation to exclude prominent Democrats, powerful machine politicians, and representatives of various ethnic groups that had been the backbone of the party. Iowa's delegation, for example, did not include a single farmer. New York, the nation's most unionized state, had only three members of organized labor but nine members of gay liberation organizations. Mayor Daley's powerful Chicago delegation was replaced by unelected delegates led by black activist Jesse Jackson. "There is too much hair and not enough cigars at this convention," grumbled one labor leader.[4]

The Democrats' stands on controversial issues, such as abortion, the Equal Rights Amendment, and marijuana, and their willingness to forgive draft evaders—what one GOP strategist called "ass, grass, and amnesty"—marked McGovern as a defender of promiscuity, hippies, and traitors. Gleeful Republicans pounced on the opportunity. At their convention, Governor Ronald Reagan declared that McGovern's nomination "disenfranchised millions of Democrats." The Republican platform declared that the Democratic party "has been seized by a radical clique which scorns our nation's past and would blight our future." The GOP put on display movie stars who embodied their vision of a simpler America—John Wayne, Jimmy Stewart, Glenn Ford, and Pat Boone. They adopted a platform that praised women for their "great contribution . . . as homemakers and mothers." As one historian concluded: "Forced to choose," the American people, "preferred Julie Eisenhower to Jane Fonda."[5]

The Republicans dominated the debate throughout the fall campaign. With their pleas for limited government and equal opportunity, the Republicans embraced Jefferson's faith in the common man. Ironically, the incumbent president, Richard Nixon, successfully identified himself as an "outsider" fighting against the liberal establishment represented by his Democratic challenger. Outmaneuvered by his Republican opponent, McGovern suffered a decisive defeat in the general election. Nixon won over 60 percent of the popular vote and his 521 electoral votes came within two votes of matching FDR's record. Almost ten million Democrats, nearly one-third of all registered Democrats, voted for Nixon. McGovern carried only Massachusetts and the District of Columbia.

The 1972 presidential campaign marked an important turning point in the debate between the two parties. The journalist Samuel Lubell had argued that the glue of the New Deal coalition had been a sense of class-consciousness that transcended "not only regional distinctions but equally strong cultural differences." After 1965, the emergence of controversial social issues—such as school prayer, abortion, crime, and homosexual rights—eroded support for traditional Democratic appeals to economic self-interest and heightened concerns regarding cultural issues. A working class suffering from rising inflation and declining wages had little sympathy for Democratic efforts to extend recognition to disenfranchised groups. As one scholar noted, the Republicans "persuaded millions of voters in the great middle—including many well below the income median—to look not to the top but to the bottom for their class enemy."[6]

Race was the prism through which many of the social issues were filtered. As the national Democratic party became identified with civil rights struggles, the white South as well as many urban ethnics in the Northeast and Midwest moved comfortably into Republican hands. The reason, in the words of former Johnson advisor Harry McPherson, lay "in the white man's view that the Democrats had cast their lot with black Americans, to the ultimate disadvantage of the whites." Over the next 20 years, the racial issue eroded Democratic strength in every section of the country. After 1968, Democrats lost regions of the South that had voted Democratic since Reconstruction. Before 1964, nearly 55 percent of all southern counties voted consistently Democratic in presidential elections. By 1980, that percentage had dropped to only 14 percent. The population shift from the Rust Belt to the Sun Belt compounded the problem by increasing the South's electoral power. In 1932, the Northeast and the Midwest accounted for 54 percent of the nation's electoral votes. By 1980, that percentage had reversed. Over the past several decades, even in traditionally liberal strongholds such as New York, Massachusetts, and Michigan, white flight has divided the races and eroded support for Democratic candidates. In most major metropolitan areas a clear racial pattern has emerged: the booming suburbs white and Republican; the shrinking inner cities increasingly black and Democratic.[7]

Nixon may have discovered the formula for unraveling the Democratic coalition, but personal insecurity and paranoia prevented him from creating a permanent Republican majority. White House involvement in a clumsy attempt to break into the Democratic national headquarters in the Watergate complex in Washington precipitated a major constitutional crisis and led to the President's eventual downfall. Although Nixon declared that he had conducted a careful investigation that revealed "no one in the White House staff, no one in this Administration presently employed, was engaged in this very bizarre incident," investigators discovered a trail of illegal activity and cover-ups that led directly to the President. Under court order, Nixon released tapes of White House conversations that contained talk of extortion, blackmail, cover-ups, and hush money. The journalist Eric Sevareid claimed that the tapes constituted "a moral indictment without known precedent in the history of American government." On August 8, faced with impeachment, Nixon resigned in disgrace. His resignation left the presidency in the hands of an inexperienced Gerald Ford, who, one month after assuming office, issued a "full, free, and absolute" pardon of Nixon for "all offenses against the United States."

In the short-run, the Watergate crisis provided the Democrats with a political windfall. The steady stream of embarrassing revelations from the Nixon White House left the Republican party demoralized and disorganized. An angry public appeared eager to reap revenge for Nixon's transgressions and Ford's pardon. In Nixon, the Democrats found a common enemy and a new sense of unity. Taking advantage of the situation, Democrats made major gains in the 1974 congressional elections, winning 46 seats and increasing their control of the House to 290-145. Sixty percent of the voters who went to the polls chose Democratic congressional candidates.

Yet Watergate also carried many long-term risks for Democrats. The abuse of presidential authority during the Johnson and Nixon years contributed to an erosion of public trust in government. The pollster Daniel Yankelovich noted in 1977 that the percentage of the populace that trusted government declined from 80 percent in the late 1950s to about 33 percent in 1976. More than 80 percent of Americans expressed distrust in political leaders, 61 percent believed something was morally wrong with the country, and nearly 75 percent felt that they had no impact on the decisions of government. Over time, this cynicism would erode public support for activist government, limit the range of debate within the Democratic party, and boost conservative Republicans.[8]

Second, the Watergate affair exacerbated tensions between Congress and the executive branch and precipitated a stalemate between the institutions of government. Since the days of Andrew Jackson, Democrats had looked to the presidency to protect the public welfare against the provincial interests of Congress. But Vietnam and Watergate forced Democrats to reconsider their support of a strong presidency. During the 1970s, congressional Democrats moved to limit presidential power and to expand the power of Congress. In 1973, Congress passed the War Powers Act which required the president to notify Congress within 48 hours of American troop deployment to combat areas, and forced him to withdraw the soldiers after 60 days unless Congress specifically authorized them to stay. In 1974, Nixon's illegal impoundment of funds inspired passage of the Congressional Budget and Impoundment Act which, among other things, provided Congress with better economic management. In an effort to break dependence on the executive for information, Democrats expanded the resources of the Congressional Research Service and the General Accounting Office, and created the Office of Technology Assessment. When Senators Frank Church and Walter Mondale uncovered a history of FBI and CIA abuses of individual rights, Democrats passed legislation that provided greater congressional oversight of the intelligence community. Yet, while Congress successfully redressed specific wrongs, it proved incapable of providing the nation with direction and leadership. By the end of the decade, even leaders of the congressional resurgence, such as Senator J. William Fulbright, called for "a revival of presidential leadership."[9]

Finally, by helping to elect many non-traditional Democrats who represented suburban, middle-class communities, Nixon's downfall precipitated a major struggle for control of the party. A large percentage of those who voted Democratic in 1974 were educated business and professional people with high incomes who lived in small cities. "Can anyone seriously describe a contest in which Democrats secured the support of two-thirds of young college-trained, professional and managerial white voters as a 'New Deal type' election?" asked the political scientist Everett Carll Ladd. Many Democratic gains in the 1974 congressional elections came from previously Republican suburban areas with little taste for new social programs. These new members of Congress promised to make government more efficient and responsive, not to address economic grievances or class interests. Gary Hart won a Colorado Senate seat campaigning against the "bankruptcy" of New Deal liberalism. "We are not a bunch of little Hubert Humphreys," Hart declared after the election. Like other Democrats who won election that year, Hart ran a decidedly nonideological campaign, promising a balanced federal budget and better fiscal management.[10]

The victory of the "class of '74" intensified the generational conflict within the party. On one side stood those whose historical memory was rooted in the economic emergency of the Depression and the tragedy of Munich. Older Democrats drew strength from organized labor, city machines, and civil rights groups, all of which represented the interests of working-class citizens. Like other Democrats who traced their roots to the New Deal, they viewed politics as a clash between competing economic interests and found inspiration in the populist rhetoric of Franklin Roosevelt and Harry Truman. Though liberal on many social welfare issues, older Democrats were culturally conservative and stridently anticommunist. On the other side of the divide stood younger Democrats whose perceptions were shaped by postwar affluence and the "lessons of Vietnam." These white-collar Democrats tended to oppose higher taxes and expanded social programs but were more liberal on controversial social issues. Younger Democrats, based primarily in the suburbs, built their coalition around the educated, white middle class. They were anti-establishment and pragmatic political entrepreneurs who hoped to exorcise passion and social division from political debate and replace it with reasoned agreement among consenting groups. "We were the children of Vietnam, not children of World War II," declared Colorado Senator Tim Wirth in defining his differences with many older Democrats. "We were products of television, not of print. We were products of computer politics, not courthouse politics. And we were reflections of JFK as president, not FDR." Polls showed gaping differences between these groups on issues such as welfare, union rights, extramarital sex, homosexuality, abortion, divorce, and discrimination in the sale of housing.[11]

While the younger Democrats gained power, the traditional wing of the party watched its base of support erode. A decline in the percentage of workers who were unionized robbed it of a once reliable source of money and organization. In the 1950s, a third of the labor force was unionized; by 1980, one-fifth of it was—and in the sun belt, only one-tenth. Not only had the percentage of the work-force that was unionized declined, its membership had become more middle class. After 1965, service workers and public employees made up a much larger share of membership. The manufacturing share of union membership plummeted from 51 percent in 1956 to 34 percent in 1980, with half of this decline occurring between 1974 and 1978. In short, the changing demographics of union membership exposed a serious gap between the views of many union leaders and the concerns of their members. "Labor unions talk about class struggles and oppression to people who can't tell Phil Murray from Arthur," observed one commentator.[12]

As the journalists Thomas Edsall and Robert Kuttner have shown, a series of social and institutional changes in the 1970s reinforced the party's tilt away from the concerns of the working and lower-middle classes and toward the middle and upper-middle class. Campaign financing reform, which strengthened the power of political action committees, had narrowed the class divisions between the Democratic and Republican parties. Like Republican candidates, Democrats had to rely upon big business—real estate magnates, insurance agents, investment bankers—to fund their campaigns. A dramatic decrease in voting among the poor and working classes forced Democrats to compete with Republicans for economically conservative voters. From 1960 to the mid-1970s, voter participation declined by more than 20 percent, with nearly half of this decline occurring in the nation's three largest urban areas. In New York City, for one, voter participation dropped from 63 percent in 1960 to 42 percent in 1976.[13]

In the past, traditional Democrats and their constituencies exercised considerable influence within the national party. But by the mid-1970s, the party had become an ineffective tool for mediating differences between and among competing factions. Rule changes opened up participation; new financing methods provided candidates with checks from the federal treasury, not from the party; the proliferation of presidential primaries meant that party leaders could no longer control the awarding of the presidential nomination; and television bypassed the traditional party structure as broker of political information. A new atomized politics emerged in which special interest groups filled the role previously played by party leaders. These interest groups did not work for a common goal under a party umbrella; they were concerned with gaining specific benefits for their membership, regardless of party affiliation. These structural changes forced politicians to alter the way they campaigned and passed legislation. "Rather than build coalitions," commented Nelson Polsby, "they must mobilize factions."[14]

The election of Jimmy Carter in 1976 revealed the tenuous nature of the new Democratic coalition. The New Deal had built its electoral support on the white South, Catholics, blacks, Jews, urban ethnics, low-income voters, and union members. In 1976, Carter did not score well with either white southerners or Catholics. He won the loyalty of three traditional groups: blacks, Jews, and union members. While he retained support from part of the old coalition, it was nontraditional groups that made the margin of difference—white Protestants, educated white-collar workers, and rural voters. In a perceptive post-election analysis, Patrick Caddell argued that the Democratic party "can no longer depend on a coalition of economic division" to guarantee victory. The challenge of the new administration, he argued, was to retain the allegiance of those parts of the old coalition concerned with economic self-interest, while also attracting new voters who were conservative on economic issues but fairly liberal on social issues.[15]

The early months of the new administration exposed the tensions within the Democratic coalition. After eight years of Republican rule, the constituency groups argued that undernourished social programs were starved for social spending. In addition to seeking cabinet appointments, blacks demanded a massive attack on unemployment, increased aid to urban areas, welfare reform, and national health insurance. "Black people have a claim on Jimmy Carter—a strong one," wrote Vernon Jordan, executive director of the National Urban League. Labor concurred with these demands and added a few of its own, such as a raise in the minimum wage and quotas on foreign imports. But a large budget deficit, creeping inflation, and Carter's instinctive conservativism frustrated many of these plans. In keeping his campaign promise to attack unemployment and end the recession, the President proposed a two-year, $30-billion economic stimulus bill, which included a modest $8 billion for public works and $11 billion in tax rebates. The bill provided far more than the Ford administration had proposed, but it totalled only half of what labor leaders and liberals had requested. A few months later, Carter increased farm price supports, but far less than the farm belt had demanded and he disappointed labor by denying its requested increase in the minimum wage. He also canceled his promised tax rebate, claiming that changed economic conditions made the proposal inflationary. "In reviewing economic policy this spring," George McGovern said in the spring of 1977, "It sometimes seems difficult to remember who won last fall."[16]

Within the Carter White House, Vice President Walter Mondale played the role of liaison between the administration and the liberal community. Mondale had hoped to use his position in the White House to guarantee that the old constituency groups were properly represented and to use his prestige within the party to convince liberals of the President's noble intentions. Mondale felt the administration could win the battle against inflation without clumsily cutting politically explosive social programs. He hoped to bring the two sides together by increasing Carter's political awareness and lowering liberal expectations. "I had to carry the debate and I didn't have any ammunition," he recalled. Carter, insensitive to Congress and liberals, insisted on making politically costly cuts in cherished social programs. Liberals, for their part, refused to recognize the political threat created by inflation and persisted in their unrealistic calls for increased government spending. By 1979, Mondale's frustration with both sides nearly boiled over when, for a few weeks in May, he considered resigning as Vice President.[17]

Senator Edward Kennedy's decision to challenge Carter in an unsuccessful bid for the party's nomination underscored the intense ideological divisions within the party. The keeper of the flickering liberal flame, Kennedy tugged at the conscience of American liberals by admonishing the party faithful "to sail against the wind" of public opinion and support rationing gasoline and freezing wages and profits. "The party that tore itself apart over Vietnam in the 1960s cannot afford to tear itself apart today over budget cuts in basic social programs," he admonished the Democrats at their 1978 midterm conference. Then in a stirring address at the party's 1980 convention he asked delegates not to allow "the great purposes of the Democratic Party" to "become the bygone passages of history."

Aside from the domestic conflicts, memories of Vietnam haunted the Carter administration's attempts to construct a new framework for American foreign policy. With the party still divided over basic questions concerning America's role in the world, the proper use of force, and the nature of the superpower competition, Carter found it impossible to forge a consensus around a post-containment strategy. The passionate debates within the administration over the Panama Canal Treaties, the passage of SALT II, the proper response to Soviet aggression in Africa and Cuba, and the question of normalization of relations with China revealed the deep division with the party. The different perspectives were represented within the administration by the contrasting views of Secretary of State Cyrus Vance and National Security Advisor Zbigniew Brzezinski. Vance, a self-effacing corporate lawyer, believed Vietnam proved the fallacy of imposing a bipolar framework on local events. Rather than seeing the Soviets as a menace to global American interests, Vance observed a crumbling empire facing serious internal and external challenges. The image-conscious Brzezinski, on the other hand, saw the Russians exploiting postwar American malaise by testing America's will around the globe, probing for weak spots and moving actively to take strategic advantage. Despite Carter's numerous foreign policy accomplishments, the public viewed his administration's approach to the world through the prism of this internal debate. "Incoherence," observed Stanley Hoffmann, has "its roots deep in the Carter Administration's style of policymaking."[18]

In 1980, a rejuvenated Republican party reassured a public troubled by the complexities of stagflation and a hostage crisis. Calling for a "new beginning" that included large reductions in personal taxes, cuts in social spending, and massive increases in defense spending, Republican nominee Ronald Reagan promised to "renew the American spirit and sense of purpose." Recalling images of America's mythical past, Reagan promised to slay the federal monster. "Government," he said, "has grown too large, too bureaucratic, too wasteful, too unresponsive, too uncaring to people and their problems." Commentators pointed out obvious problems with Reagan's simplistic vision, but his value-laden rhetoric touched a chord deep within the American people. The journalist Garry Wills wrote that Reagan became a "symbol of America," an "angel of our better natures." His popularity, Wills concluded, stemmed from his "shared history" with the American public—his "shared innocence about the responsibilities of great power, about what he deplores as 'govment' in keeping the accounts of a great nation and a world power."[19]

On election day, Carter suffered an embarrassing defeat, winning only 41 percent of the popular vote and 49 electoral votes. The Republicans gained thirty-three House seats and twelve Senate seats, thereby winning a majority in the Senate—their first since 1952 and their largest since 1928. For many conservatives, the 1980 election represented the inevitable triumph of Richard Nixon's conservative majority. "Like a great soaking wet shaggy dog, the Silent Majority—banished from the house during the Watergate storms—romped back into the nation's parlor this week and shook itself vigorously," observed William Safire.[20]

In the aftermath of Reagan's victory, Democrats struggled to redefine the party's mission. Neoliberals, who sought an accommodation with Reaganism, appealed to independent, economically conservative voters who felt little kinship with the party's past. "The Democratic Party must govern well," declared Colorado Senator Gary Hart, "but it must not be the party of government." Many southern Democrats, through the creation of the Democratic Leadership Conference, continued to push the party in a more conservative direction. "There is a perception our party has moved away from mainstream America in the 1970s," declared founding member Senator Sam Nunn. Senator Edward Kennedy, New York Governor Mario Cuomo, and civil rights leader Jesse Jackson joined the chorus of eloquent defenders of the party's commitment to protect society's less fortunate. "My constituency is the desperate, the damned, the disinherited, the disrespected and the despised," Jackson declared in a moving address at the party's 1984 convention.

While Democrats debated their future, President Reagan initiated a spirited assault on the Democratic party's basic principles. In May 1981, the former California governor harnessed the emotional groundswell of sympathy generated by a failed assassination attempt into a significant legislative victory by forcing through Congress a budget resolution that called for deep cuts in social programs and increased spending for the military. In August, Congress passed Reagan's tax plan, which included a 25 percent reduction in tax rates over three years. Despite the opposition of the Democratic party leadership, Reagan convinced many southern and conservative Democrats to support his radical program. "I expected him to cut me off at the knee," said frustrated House Speaker Thomas P. "Tip" O'Neill, Jr., "but he cut me off at the hip."

Reagan's success demonstrated the growing importance of television in modern politics. One scholar observed that "no previous administration had devoted so many resources to managing the news or approached the task with so much calculation." The President's advisors, whom James Reston described as "the best public relations team ever to enter the White House," carefully orchestrated the media coverage. By controlling access to Reagan, the staff minimized the President's penchant for verbal slips, prevented the press from asking tough questions, and guaranteed that the public saw him in brief visuals that served to enhance his stature. These images, designed around a daily message, allowed the White House to focus public attention on Reagan's accomplishments, while ignoring his numerous failures. "So far, he's proving Lincoln was right," observed a veteran reporter. "You can fool all of the people some of the time."[21]

Reagan's masterful use of television and his stark ideological language exposed the limits of the Democrats' style of interest group politics.

Since the time of Roosevelt, Democratic candidates learned to arouse their coalition by traveling the country promising tangible benefits to specific groups—labor, farmers, teachers, Jews, minorities. The speeches, designed for local consumption and print coverage, were tailored to specific audiences. Party loyalty and effective organization were the glue that held the old system together. Since 1960, however, a new political universe had emerged, with media markets replacing union halls and thirty-second "visuals" on the evening news substituting for substantive discussions in the evening paper. The decline of partisanship and the rise of "the candidate-centered campaign" destroyed the old system. Mass media allowed modern candidates to bypass traditional power structures and appeal directly to the anti-establishment sentiments of most voters. "The image transmitted by TV and the other media is of a person, not of the abstraction known as a political party," observed one scholar.[22]

Democrats scorned ideology at a time when television increased the importance of ideological appeals in American politics. The 1960s left deep emotional scars on the conscience of American liberals. Many believed that their blind acceptance of Cold War assumptions had prevented them from foreseeing the tragic consequences of Vietnam, and that their unquestioning faith that social progress at home could be achieved through gradual, piecemeal reform had left them unprepared for the rise of black militancy and the resulting white backlash. They emerged from the decade uncomfortable with simplistic and painless suggestions that a growing economy could solve social problems, that removing legal barriers could end racial discrimination, or that fighting communism would secure America's position in the world. Convinced that problems of poverty and racial justice were far too complex and the patience of most Americans far too brief to allow for significant change, liberals began to pursue a more circumscribed agenda. "Afraid to run on ideology, the Democrats ran as technicians," Robert Kuttner wrote, "and they were beaten by better technicians who were clearer about their own ideology and thus better able to manipulate powerful symbols."[23]

The party's rejection of its populist heritage stands as the most striking example of its abandonment of ideology. In the years after 1932, Democrats translated public resentment against the wealthy and powerful into a political coalition that favored enlarged government services. The party united its diverse coalition by championing the cause of the "common man" and identifying Republicans as the defenders of special privilege. But over time, many of the programs and policies that owed their existence to populist sentiment had developed their own entrenched interest groups and indifferent bureaucracies. Just as important, years of service in the Washington establishment, and a strong sense of loyalty to the programs and institutions it had created, had made many Democrats uncomfortable with the populist message. Severed from their ideological roots, Democrats campaigned not as reformers promising to change the system, but as technocrats determined to make it function more efficiently. Liberals had always used government to challenge the status quo and assault the special interests. In their successful reverse approach, Republicans identified government with the status quo, and defined their antigovernment cause as an attack on special privilege. In response, Democrats failed to present a larger vision of government that defended prerogatives in universal language and served all groups.

These contrasting styles were clearly evident in the 1984 presidential campaign. Reagan's challenger, former Vice President Walter Mondale, had little appreciation for media campaigns and little understanding of how they had transformed the style of campaigning in America. A product of the Minnesota Farmer-Labor Party, and a protégé of Hubert Humphrey, Mondale practiced an older style of interest group-oriented politics. "Mr. Mondale is one of the few major figures on the American scene," observed a journalist, "whose political style and vocabulary fit comfortably in a world of Al Smith, Franklin Roosevelt and Harry Truman." In Reagan's campaigns, discussing issues was secondary, taking a back seat to invoking themes, creating visual images, and communicating shared values. In Mondale's campaign, programs and issues predominated. Reagan appealed to people's hearts; Mondale to their minds. Reagan understood that politics in a television age was performing art, not political science. "Reaganism is politics-as-evangelism, calling forth a majority with a hymn to general values," George Will wrote. "Mondalism is politics-as-masonry, building a majority brick by brick."[24]

The results on election day left no doubt as to the beleaguered state of the Democratic party. Reagan carried forty-nine states—all but Mondale's home state of Minnesota and the District of Columbia. He won 98 percent of the electoral votes (525 to Mondale's 13) and 59 percent of the popular vote. Mondale drew consistently strong support from only two areas: Frostbelt cities and black majority counties of the South. Race played a critical role in the voting. Nationally, more than a quarter of the votes for the Democratic ticket came from blacks, while in the South blacks constituted almost half of Democratic voters. In many northern cities, the coalition was splintered between minorities who voted for the Democratic ticket and white ethnics who voted Republican.

A similar pattern emerged in the 1988 presidential campaign. The Democrats selected Michael Dukakis, a successful governor of Massachusetts, to lead the campaign against Vice President George Bush. Dukakis, who survived a prolonged and bruising primary battle against Jesse Jackson, hoped to make "competence, not ideology" the central message of his campaign. But Bush had a much different idea. While calling for a "kinder, gentler America," Bush launched one of the most vicious campaigns in recent memory. Planning his campaign around quick one-liners aimed at the daily sound-bite on the evening news, Bush concentrated on ideological themes, hammering away at Dukakis for opposing organized prayer and compulsory recitation of the Pledge of Allegiance in the public schools. "The Pledge and the flag are little hammer taps directed just below the knee of the electorate," wrote columnist Richard Cohen. "They are designed to elicit a reflexive reaction, to obscure rather than explain, to camouflage a lust for office with a drop cloth made of red, white and blue." On election day, Bush won 426 electoral votes and continued the Republican dominance of presidential elections begun in 1968.[25]

The contrast between the 1948 and 1988 presidential campaigns revealed how much the political debate had changed over the postwar period. In 1948, Truman campaigned as a fire-breathing economic populist who denounced the "gluttons of privilege" dominating the Republican party. In 1988, Bush campaigned as a cultural populist who told cheering audiences about the "wide chasm" on "the question of values between me and the liberal Governor." Truman, playing to fears of economic uncertainty, embraced the New Deal banner and reminded voters that the Republicans were "the party of Hoover boom and Hoover depression." Bush, tapping into concern that Democrats were soft on defense and out-of-touch with mainstream voters, wrapped himself in the American flag to imply that his opponent was unpatriotic. In 1948, Truman traveled the country by whistlestop, carrying his powerful populist message directly to the people. In 1988, Bush campaigned by soundbites, seeking Nielson ratings, not crowds along the tracks. To make the role reversals complete, Dukakis was cast in the role of Dewey, the arrogant and aloof GOP candidate of 1948, who promised efficient administration and passionless government.

Though Democrats failed to secure the White House, they maintained their dominance in congressional and state elections. "If someone were to write a musical about the Democratic Party of the last generation," Massachusetts congressman Barney Frank observed, "it could be called *How to Win Everything in Politics Except the Presidency.*" The Democrats have controlled the House since 1954, and for all but four years since 1931. As of 1990, they occupied 29 governorships compared to 21 for the Republicans. In many cases, local Democrats won races while the national ticket suffered embarrassing losses. In 1984, for example, Reagan carried 109 of the 116 southern congressional districts, while Democratic congressional candidates carried 73 of those same 116 districts, and Democrats captured 78 percent of all state legislative seats in the South.[26]

As journalist Alan Ehrenhalt has argued, the Democratic Party produced better candidates than the Republicans on the local level. "Over the past two decades," he wrote, "Democrats have generated the best supply of talent, energy, and sheer political ambition." In addition, incumbent Democrats have made effective use of franking privileges and generous political action committee contributions to intimidate potential challengers and almost ensure reelection. In 1990, for example, all but one of the 32 Senate incumbents and 96 percent of House incumbents were reelected. This marked the fourth consecutive election in which 95 percent or more of House incumbents were reelected to office. Finally, polls taken at the time revealed that the public viewed the Democratic party favorably on constituent service and social welfare—issues which frequently shape local and congressional elections. "We do better the closer we get to people's garbage," said one Democratic consultant.[27]

Democrats face numerous obstacles in their attempt to recapture the White House. As a congressional party increasingly dependent on contributions from monied interests and concerned with local issues and constituent service, Democrats for many years failed to articulate a compelling national message that defined their differences with Republicans and established a clear agenda for the future. "They don't think in themes," observed a critic, "they think in amendments." After surveying voters in 1990, David Broder concluded that the "American people have only a vague and muddled impression of the Democratic message." The opposition of leading Democrats to the popular Gulf War revived bitter memories of Vietnam and exposed the party's weakness on issues of national security. The party also remains vulnerable to racial appeals. Support for affirmative action and quotas serves as a powerful metaphor conveying the discontent of white voters who see the party serving the poor and minorities at their expense.[28]

Perhaps most serious of all, public indifference, which corrodes the foundation of America's political institutions, may prevent either party from achieving a mandate to govern effectively. At a time when fledgling democracies around the world are looking to the United States for inspiration, Americans have seemed apathetic about their political institutions. "I get so embarrassed when I see elections in Central America where you can get shot by either the left or the right for voting, and yet they vote at twice the rate we do in this country," observed one congressman. Opinion surveys have revealed deep pessimism about the economy, uncertainty about the future, and unprecedented cynicism about political leaders. In 1990, a private study of the American democratic process cited voter apathy and ignorance as evidence of a disaffection that had "broad, perhaps dangerous implications for democracy in this country." Other analyses have suggested that Americans feel overwhelmed and impotent when confronted by the remoteness of government institutions, the magnitude of their activity, and the complexity of the public debate.

As it celebrates the beginning of its third century, the Democratic party finds itself in transition. Changing social and economic conditions have weakened the old Roosevelt coalition, rendering it incapable of winning national elections. But Democrats remain uncertain about what new coalition should replace it. Can the party articulate a philosophy of activist government that inspires a public grown cynical about government? Can it develop social programs that assist the needy but do not alienate the middle class? And, perhaps most important, can it address the plight of African Americans without antagonizing angry whites? How the party answers these questions will determine whether it will continue to serve as a vehicle for change and innovation in the next century.

## NOTES

1. William Schneider, "An Insider's View of the Election," *Atlantic* (July 1988), 31; William Galston, "The Future of the Democratic Party," *The Brookings Review* (Winter, 1985), 20; Peter Goldman and Tom Mathews, *The Quest for the Presidency* (New York: Simon & Schuster, 1989), 44-45.

2. Charles DeBenedetti, *An American Ordeal* (Syracuse, New York: Syracuse University Press, 1990), 282-291, 387-408. On the antiwar movement see also David W. Levy, *The Debate Over Vietnam* (Baltimore: The Johns Hopkins University Press, 1991); and Nancy Zaroulis and Gerald Sullivan, *Who Spoke Up?* (New York: Doubleday, 1984).

3. J. Anthony Lukas, *Common Ground: A Turbulent Decade in the Lives of Three American Families* (New York: Knopf, 1985); Jonathan Rieder, *Canarsie: The Jews and Italians of Brooklyn Against Liberalism* (Cambridge: Harvard University Press, 1985); Ronald P. Formisano, *Boston Against Busing: Race, Class, and Ethnicity in the 1960s and 1970s* (Chapel Hill: University of North Carolina Press, 1991).

4. Thomas Edsall, *The New Politics of Inequality* (New York: Norton, 1984), 55; Richard Wade, "The Democratic Party, 1960-1972" in Arthur M. Schlesinger, Jr., *History of U.S. Political Parties* (New York: Chelsa House, 1973), 2827-2868.

5. Brendan Sexton, "Middle Class Workers and the New Politics," *Dissent* (May-June 1969), 231-238; Kevin Phillips, *The Emerging Republican Majority* (New Rochelle, N.Y.: Arlington Heights, 1969); Richard Schier, "Can the Democrats Learn from Defeat?" *Intellect* (July-August, 1975), 13-16; John Stewart, *One Last Chance: The Democratic Party, 1974-76* (New York: Praeger, 1974), 3-36; Richard Scammon and Ben Wattenberg, *The Real Majority* (New York: Coward McCann, 1970), 21; Theodore White, *The Making of the President, 1972* (New York: Atheneum, 1973), 149; and William Leuchtenburg, *The Unfinished Century* (Boston: Little, Brown, 1973), 933.

6. Ronald Brownstein, "The Political Stakes," *National Journal* (January 12, 1985), 102-106.

7. Earl Black and Merle Black, *Politics and Society in the South* (Cambridge: Harvard University Press, 1987), 232-258; V.O. Key Jr., *Southern Politics in State and Nation* (Knoxville: University of Tennessee Press, 1984); John Hammond,

"Race and Electoral Mobilization: White Southerners, 1952-1968," *Politics Quarterly* 41 (1977): 13-27; Thomas Edsall, "Rings of White Anger," *Washington Post* November 3, 1988; Mike Mallowe, "Coming Apart," *Philadelphia Magazine* (September 1989), 97; Mike Mallowe, "A Campaign in Black and White," *Philadelphia Magazine* (May 1987), 88; Dianne M. Pinderhughes, *Race and Ethnicity in Chicago Politics* (Urbana: University of Illinois Press, 1987); and Paul Kleppner, *Chicago Divided: The Making of a Black Mayor* (Dekalb, Ill.: Northern Illinois University Press, 1985).

8. Steven M. Gillon, *Politics and Vision: The ADA and American Liberalism* (New York: Oxford University Press), 232.

9. James L. Sundquist, *The Decline and Resurgence of Congress* (Washington, D.C.: Brookings, 1981), 461.

10. William Schneider, "JFK's Children: The Class of '74," *Atlantic* (March 1989), 35-58; Edsall, *Politics of Inequality*, 23-66; Burdett Loomis, *The New American Politician* (New York: Basic Books, 1988); Everett Carll Ladd, "Liberalism Upside Down: The Inversion of the New Deal Order," *Political Science Quarterly* 91 (Winter 1976-77): 577-601; Ladd, "The Democrats Have Their Own Two-Party System," *Fortune* (October 1977), 212-223; and Sidney Blumenthal, "Hart's Big Chill," *New Republic* (January 23, 1984), 17-22.

11. Schneider, "JFK's Children: The Class of '74," 35-48; and Loomis, *The New American Politician.*

12. "Labor's Changing Profile," *Nation's Business* (April 1979), 31-35; Peter Pestillo, "Can Unions Meet the Needs of a 'New' Work Force?" *Monthly Labor Review* (February 24, 1979), 33-34; Sidney Lens, "Disorganized Labor," *Nation* (February 24, 1979), 206-209; *New York Times*, September 5, 1982; Sidney Lens, "The American Labor Movement: Out of Joint with the Times," *In These Times* (February 18-24, 1981), 12-13; and *San Francisco Chronicle* (September 18, 1981), 8.

13. Paul Kleppner, *Who Voted?* (New York: Praeger, 1982), 162; see also Edsall, *The New Politics of Inequality*; and Robert Kuttner, *The Life of the Party* (New York: Viking, 1987).

14. David Broder, *The Party's Over: The Failure of Politics in America* (New York: Harper and Row, 1972); See also Anthony King, "The American Polity in the late 1970s: Building Coalitions in Sand," and Austin Ranney, "The Political Parties: Reform and Decline," in Anthony King, *The New American Political System* (Washington, D.C.: American Enterprise Institute, 1979), 371-396, 213-248.

15. Walter Dean Burnham, *The Current Crisis in American Politics* (New York: Oxford University Press, 1982), 229-250; Norman Nie, et al., *The Changing American Voter* (Cambridge: Harvard, 1979), 357-388; "Carter Comes Through," *National Journal* (November 6, 1976), 1582-1606; Rhodes Cook, "Final Returns," *Congressional Quarterly* (December 18, 1976), 3332-3336; and Caddell to Carter, Powell Papers, December 21, 1976, Carter Library.

16. George McGovern, "Memo to the White House," *Harpers* (October 1977), 33-35; *Washington Post*, May 8, 1977; "Promises, Promises: Home to Roost in the White House," *Nation* (March 12, 1977), 295-298; and "Liberals and Carter," *Progressive* (July 1977), 5-6.

17. Mondale interview with the author. See also Steven M. Gillon, *The Dem-*

*ocrats Dilemma: Walter F. Mondale and the Liberal Legacy* (New York: Columbia, 1992).

18. Gaddis Smith, *Morality, Reason and Power* (New York: Hill and Wang, 1986); Stanley Hoffman, "View from Home: the Perils of Incoherence," *Foreign Affairs* (February 1979), 463-91; Thomas L. Hughes, "Carter and the Management of Contradiction," *Foreign Policy* (Summer 1978); John Lewis Gaddis, *Strategies of Containment* (New York: Oxford University Press, 1982); and George Moffett, *The Limits of Victory* (Ithaca: Cornell University Press, 1985). Also of value are the memoirs of administration members, especially Zbigniew Brzezinski, *Power and Principle* (New York: Farrar, Straus & Giroux, 1983); Jimmy Carter, *Keeping Faith* (New York: Bantam, 1982); and Cyrus Vance, *Hard Choices* (New York: Simon & Schuster, 1983).

19. John Kenneth White, *The New Politics of Old Values* (Hanover: University Press of New England), 37-55; and Garry Wills, "What Happened?" *Time* (March 1987), 40. See also Wills, *Reagan's America: Innocents at Home* (New York: Doubleday, 1987).

20. *New York Times*, November 6, 1980.

21. Sidney Blumenthal, "Reagan the Unassailable," *New Republic* (September 12, 1983), 12; Mark Hertsgaard, *On Bended Knee: The Press and The Reagan Presidency* (New York: Farrar, Straus & Giroux, 1988), 1-31; and Jane Mayer and Doyle McManus, *Landslide: The Unmaking of the President, 1984-88* (Boston: Houghton Mifflin, 1988): 7.

22. Frank J. Sorauf, *Party Politics in America* (Boston: Little, Brown, 1980), 255; Robert Agranoff, *The Management of Electoral Campaigns* (Boston: Holbrook Press, 1976); and Martin Wattenberg, *The Decline of American Political Parties, 1952-1988* (Cambridge: Harvard University Press, 1990).

23. Robert Kuttner, "Ron Brown's Party Line," *New York Times Magazine* (December 3, 1989), 126.

24. *Wall Street Journal*, November 5, 1984. George Will, *The New Season: A Spectators Guide to the 1988 Election* (New York: Simon and Schuster, 1987), 101; and Sidney Blumenthal, "Marketing the President," *New York Times Magazine* (September 13, 1981), 43.

25. *Washington Post*, October 13, 1988; and *New York Times*, November 18, 1988.

26. Michael Barone and Grant Ujifusa, *The Almanac of American Politics, 1992* (Washington, D.C.: National Journal, 1992), xxxviii-xxxix; *Washington Post*, June 25, 1989.

27. Alan Ehrenhalt, *The United States of Ambition* (New York: Times Books, 1991), 23; and Thomas Edsall, "Willie Horton's Message," *New York Review of Books* (February 13, 1992), 7-11.

28. *Washington Post*, January 29, 1990; November 11, 1990; January 28, 1990.

PART FIVE

# Bicentennial Appraisals

## Chapter 13

# The Irony of Democratic History

*E.J. Dionne, Jr.*

Arguments over the history of the Democratic party are often as contentious as the arguments within the party that the historians record. This is not just because most contemporary historians are either active or disheartened Democrats. It is in the very nature of the Democratic party to be controversial, because over the course of its history, it has put itself to the service of so many diverse causes and interests. Most famously, the New Deal coalition united a militant working class with the most reactionary Bourbons of the South. The Jacksonian era was made up of a curious coalition involving quasi-socialist mechanics and a newly emergent capitalist class. Grover Cleveland and William Jennings Bryan were part of the same party in the 1890s, though neither liked that fact very much.

Philosophically, the party has been just as torn. The Democrats' Jeffersonian forebears were deeply opposed to the designs of Alexander Hamilton for a strong central government with an activist approach to the economy. Franklin D. Roosevelt quoted Jefferson on behalf of what at least some have seen as the ultimate triumph of Hamiltonian energy in the federal executive. The Democrats have gathered to themselves radical free market advocates and socialists, globalists and anti-imperialists, inflationists and the paladins of sound money, machine politicians and earnest reformers, slave owners and free soilers. One is tempted to take Will Rogers' famous line about the Democrats not being an "organized political party" and argue that this applies to the party's philosophy no less than to its campaign apparatus.

But this, as Richard Nixon might say, would be wrong. If there is a unifying thread through this complex history, it is the concept of "irony." The best definition of irony in the sense that it applies to Democrats was offered by the late Reinhold Niebuhr in *The Irony of American History*, published, as it happens, in 1952, the year that the New Deal era finally came to the end of its electoral road. Niebuhr is careful to distinguish between the ironic situation on the one hand and pathos, tragedy and comedy on the other. These last three have all applied to the Democrats at one point or another, but irony works best. Niebuhr wrote:

> The ironic situation is distinguished from a pathetic one by the fact that the person involved in it bears some responsibility for it. It is differentiated from tragedy by the fact that the responsibility is related to an unconscious weakness rather than to a conscious resolution. While a pathetic or tragic situation is not dissolved when a person becomes conscious of his involvement in it, an ironic situation must dissolve, if men or nations are made aware of their complicity in it. Such awareness involves some realization of the hidden vanity or pretension by which comedy is turned into irony.[1]

In a sense, the history of the Democratic party can be seen as the effort of those who gravitated to it to understand and work out the ironies of their particular historical situations. Viewing the Democratic party in this light helps us understand why different generations of historians have viewed the party and its major actors so differently. The essence of irony is odd juxtapositions, and no party has been more specialized in odd juxtapositions than the Democrats.

The recent histories of the Jacksonian Era are revealing. The heroic account, *The Age of Jackson*, written by Arthur Schlesinger Jr. in 1945 under the influence of the New Deal's triumph, presents Jacksonianism as the first large step in the ultimate triumph of democratic values—with a small "d" as well as a big one.[2] Jacksonians are seen as the backwoods enemies of urban privilege, aligned eventually with their comrades in the urban working class. The view of Andrew Jackson as a forerunner to FDR came under challenge in the 1950s from a group of historians, notably Richard Hofstadter, who, in Harry Watson's words, saw the Jacksonians as "entrepreneurs or 'expectant capitalists' who fought monopoly to advance their own fortunes."[3] Writers influenced by the New Left cast an even more jaundiced eye on the Jacksonians—and especially on Jackson himself—by throwing light on Old Hickory's Indian policies, which by current standards (and even among Jackson's contemporaries such as John Quincy Adams) must be seen as racist.

The current view, championed notably by Watson, is far more complex and captures the full irony of the Democrats' situation.[4] Watson notes that for the Jacksonian Democrats, certain basic ideas of equality went hand-in-hand with deeply reactionary commitments to particular inequalities. Jacksonians were deeply committed to the view that all *white* men were equal. In this, they differed from the Federalist and Whiggish views that society was divided into orders and classes—and more healthy for being arranged that way. The egalitarian side of Whiggery held that all men, whether Native American or (for the northern Whigs, at least), black, fit somewhere into their continuum. Whigs were thus more resistant to certain racial notions popular among Democrats. As a result, New Jersey's anti-Jacksonian Senator Theodore Frelinghuysen could attack Jackson's Indian removal policy in language that still reads well in the context of today's attitudes. "Do the obligations of justice change with the color of the skin?" Frelinguysen asked. "Is it one of the prerogatives of the white man that he may disregard the dictates of moral principles, when an Indian shall be concerned?" [5] This view, not Jackson's, is the one that would receive the loudest applause at a present-day Democratic convention.

The irony of Jackson's Indian policy lay in the fact that it was a radically *inegalitarian* approach rooted in certain radically *egalitarian* ideals. As Jackson saw it, he was clearing Indians from the land in the interests of poor, white men who saw in that land an opportunity for their own self-improvement. Poor whites were clamoring for land, and Jackson meant to satisfy them.

A similar irony can be seen in the politics of Stephen A. Douglas, Lincoln's famous foe, who was deeply racist, yet also outspoken in defending the rights of immigrants, especially Catholics, who came under assault from the Know-Nothings in the 1850s. As Robert Kelley notes in one of his essays in this volume, Douglas argued that Democrats "make no distinctions among our fellow citizens." By contrast, Douglas said, the Democrats' political foes had waged "a bloody and revengeful way against Irishmen, Germans and Welshmen." [6]

The ironies of Douglas' politics went further still. Having cast blacks as essentially sub-human, Douglas could offer his notion of "popular sovereignty" as the essence of radical democracy. For Douglas, what could have been more democratic than to propose that the voters in the new states decide for themselves whether to permit slavery or not? George C. Wallace's famous slogan from his Democratic primary campaigns, "Trust the People," was the essence of Douglasism. In the case of both men, one senses that the people they had in mind to trust were white.

Thus, the first great irony of Democratic Party history: The party of Jacksonian equality would essentially be untrue to its own creed until it worked through the implications of its racial policies. Until African Americans were regarded as equal partners—citizens—in the democratic experiment, their rights could be denied, even as Democrats did so using a political language that was, in theory, far more inclusive than the language of its foes.

The second great irony of Democratic history lies in the party's theoretical solicitude for the rights of the average man and its opposition to the "money power," even as it endorsed laissez-faire economic policies that allowed for no state relief to embattled wage earners. This was not lost on all working-class voters. As Sean Wilentz showed in his fine study of the rise of the New York City working class, *Chants Democratic*, the first Working Men's Party rose up in opposition to the Jacksonians of Tammany Hall.[7]

Yet the radicalism of Jacksonian rhetoric was unmistakable. Jackson saw his war against the Bank of the United States as a class war, a battle against the use of government power on behalf of those who were already economically mighty. "It is to be regretted that the rich and powerful too often bend the acts of government to their selfish purposes," Jackson declared in his veto message against the Bank. He went on:

> In the full enjoyment of the fruits of superior industry, economy and virtue, every man is equally entitled to protection by law; but when the laws undertake to add to these natural and just advantages artificial distinctions, to grant titles, gratuities and exclusive privileges, to make the rich richer and the potent more powerful, the humble members of society—the farmers, mechanics and laborers—who have neither the time nor the means of procuring like favors to themselves, have a right to complain of the injustice of their government.[8]

The class character of Jackson's rhetoric was echoed throughout the party, especially in the big cities, and especially in New York. This was true even in the 1850s, when the party came to see itself as the great conservative force in American life. Faced with a difficult re-election battle from a coalition of reformers that included conservative Democrats like Samuel J. Tilden, New York City Mayor Fernando Wood resorted to radical class rhetoric aimed at pitting the New York working class against the aristocrats who wanted the city to be rid of him. Amidst prosperity, Wood said, workers struggled "for a mere subsistence, whilst other classes accumulate wealth, and in the days of general depression, they are the first to feel the change, without the means to avoid or endure reserves. Truly may it be said that in New York those who produce everything get nothing, and those who produce nothing get everything. They labor without income whilst surrounded by thousands living in affluence and splendor who have income without labor."[9] It is no wonder that the *New York Times* described Wood's message as "fiery communism."[10]

Wood's was a more extreme example of rhetoric that came to Democrats naturally, especially when they needed to rally the downtrodden. Even the conservative Tilden had resorted to such talk, especially in his younger days. As Kelley notes, it was Tilden who, in 1838, spoke of the wealthy as "an organized class which acts in phalanx . . . concentrating property in monopolies and perpetuities, and binding it to political power." This class, Tilden said, "has established an aristocracy more potent and more oppressive than any other which has ever existed."[11]

The key for Jacksonians—beyond a lively political opportunism—was the notion that state power could, in the end, only ally with the existing economic powers. In the purest strains of Jacksonianism, to check the power of the state was to check the power of the wealthy. It thus fell to the Whigs, and later the Republicans, to discover the creative uses of federal power in promoting internal improvements, economic development and a stable currency through a national bank. To the Jacksonians, such projects could only enrich the rich—which did not much bother the Whigs.

The transformation of the laissez-faire, states' rights Democrats into the party of the New Deal just 100 years after the Jacksonian era is described well at various points in this volume. A central figure in this transformation, as John Milton Cooper Jr. argues in his essay, was William Jennings Bryan. It was Bryan who first saw the potential of applying the rhetoric of Jefferson and Jackson in new ways that would transform the Democrats, slowly, into a party of economic reform.

The opening for the Democrats was created by the collapse of the radical cause inside the Republican party in the 1870s. The end of Reconstruction in 1877 under Rutherford B. Hayes can be seen as the Republican party's decision to abandon the great reform causes preached by the abolitionists and free soilers and to remake the party into a worthy, conservative, pro-business successor to the Whigs.[12] Reformist elements would stay alive in the G.O.P. and have their day again under Theodore Roosevelt. But the identification of the Republicans with the cause of industrial capitalism alienated small farmers and, eventually, industrial workers.

Bryan, as Cooper shows, has been too often seen as a force of reaction, the champion of a dying rural, fundamentalist America. The truth is more complicated. Bryan not only upheld the cause of rural America—and later, during the Scopes trial, creationism. He also championed reform. His causes included women's suffrage, the popular election of senators, the federal income tax, a tougher stand on railroad regulation, a Department of Labor, the reporting of campaign contributions, opposition to capital punishment. The philosopher John Dewey, who can hardly be seen as soft on fundamentalism, saw Bryan as "the backbone of philanthropic social interest, of social reform through political action, of pacifism, of popular education."[13] Irony was probably a concept alien to Bryan, yet his whole career was dedicated to helping Democrats work through the ironies of being devoted to Jacksonian populism on the one hand and laissez faire economics on the other. Bryan and his followers represented the first mass revolt against laissez faire inside the Democratic Party.

Cooper rightly sees Woodrow Wilson as the inheritor of many aspects of the Bryan legacy.[14] Although thoroughly southern and conservative in his attitudes toward race, Wilson was the first Democratic president to express sympathy for the cause of organized labor through legislation. In the past, Democrats had largely appealed to urban immigrant groups on cultural grounds; the Democrats were the party of inclusion and openness to outsiders (so long as they were white). Wilson linked this cultural affinity to an economic program which, however cautious, further pushed the Jacksonian legacy in new directions.

The limits of the Wilson breakthrough, however, should be noted. Wilson's attitude toward monopoly remained, in many respects, Jacksonian in spirit. The goal of the Wilsonians was to break up monopolies in the interests of freer market competition. Wilson's "New Freedom" contrasted not only with Eugene V. Debs's socialist approach to the problems of industrialism—an approach which enjoyed significant support in the progressive era—but also with Theodore Roosevelt's "New Nationalism." Roosevelt's doctrine, developed by the social thinker Herbert Croly, saw monopoly in some spheres as inevitable and preferred state regulation, direction, or outright control to trust busting. If regulated corporations "survived for some generations and increased in efficiency and strength," Croly wrote, "a policy must be adopted of converting them into express economic agents of the whole community and of gradually appropriating for the benefit of the community the substantial economic advantages which these corporations had succeeded in acquiring."[15] The Croly/Roosevelt doctrine was thus more "advanced" than Wilson's, being closer to the spirit of social democracy, yet also in the tradition of the Hamiltonian and Whiggish approach that sought to mobilize federal power in the interests of prosperity—and in cooperation with business. In this debate, Wilson was still on the side of his Jacksonian forebears.

Franklin Roosevelt saw himself as an heir to Wilson, and the New Deal—for all its incoherence—was in many ways the completion of Wilson's project. But pushed by the exigencies of the Depression, Roosevelt also drew into his orbit many of the ideas and individuals who had rallied to his cousin in the progressive era. Franklin Roosevelt largely completed the task, begun by Wilson, of coopting the Republican party's progressive wing for the Democrats. Roosevelt rallied Republicans and former Republicans such as George Norris and Fiorello LaGuardia—to name just two of many figures—to New Dealism. The New Deal thus represented an historic realignment, not only in electoral terms, but also in philosophical terms. In an analysis forever popular among historians, Roosevelt married Hamiltonian and Whiggish means to Jacksonian ends.

And it is important to see Roosevelt's more radical rhetoric not only as a response to left-wing challenges to the New Deal in the mid-1930s, but also as thoroughly in the tradition of Jackson's bank veto message. FDR's 1936 attack on "economic royalists," on "the forces of organized selfishness and lust for power," and on advocates of "a new industrial dictatorship," cited in Alonzo Hamby's essay, help explain why Arthur Schlesinger, Jr. could trace such a direct link from Old Hickory to Roosevelt.[16]

Still, the New Deal left many ironies unresolved. Roosevelt, despite the view of his conservative critics, was no radical. There was a good deal of incoherent stop-and-go in his program, as Hamby makes clear. He was capable of using class rhetoric, as conservative Jacksonians were, in order to mobilize majorities behind a wide assortment of policies. In light of Roosevelt's success in saving capitalism and maintaining support for the two-party system, his achievement can be captured accurately in the subtitle of New Left historian Barton J. Bernstein's important essay on the New Deal, "The Conservative Achievements of Liberal Reform."[17]

There was the additional irony of the continued presence of southern conservatives and segregationists inside the New Deal coalition—and Roosevelt's failure to do much to advance the civil rights agenda. In fact, Roosevelt may have done far more to help resolve the Democratic dilemma over race than he commonly is credited for.

As Hamby points out, one consistency about the Democratic party from the days of Jefferson forward was that it has been, in one form or another, an alliance "between southern agrarians and northern city politicians."[18] The crucial change, as Hamby notes, took place in the 1920s when the balance of power within this alliance shifted decisively toward the northern cities, culminating in Al Smith's nomination in 1928. The political power of the northern and urban wing of the party was augmented by the rise of organized labor, which gave the Democrats what Richard Hofstadter has called their "social democratic tinge." Southern conservatives already saw the direction of events in the 1930s. While they remained nominally aligned with the Democrats, they formed a powerful conservative coalition with congressional Republicans and, after 1938, foiled many of the New Deal's more progressive designs.

If southern conservatives saw the shape of the future clearly, so did African Americans, who decisively switched their allegiances in 1936 from the party of Lincoln to the party of FDR. The more social democratic aspects of the New Deal were of disproportionate benefit to the poor, and thus to blacks. With African Americans finally included in the party of Jackson, the Democrats' populist and egalitarian rhetoric took on a much more inclusive meaning. It would no doubt surprise Stephen Douglas to know that "popular sovereignty," as embodied in the Voting Rights Act of 1965, helped elect the first black governor of Virginia, a Democrat, and helped make African Americans one of the most important forces inside the Democratic party, especially in the states of the Old Confederacy.

Once blacks were included in the Democratic coalition, the exodus of southern conservatives was inevitable. What is important to remember is that capturing southern conservatives had been the dream of one wing of the Republican party since the Civil War. No less a Republican than Abraham Lincoln, ever the "practical Whig," as the historian Kenneth Stampp called him, had hoped that the party could be refashioned along conservative, Whiggish lines. It took a century, but that is what finally happened. Senator Strom Thurmond, Republican of South Carolina, can thus be seen as a logical successor to Lincoln's friend, the one-time Whig politician and Confederate Vice President, Alexander Stephens.[19] In working out their own ironies, the Democrats helped the Republicans work out some of theirs.

The danger of seeing Democratic history as a working out of ironies is not only that such a perspective might present too heroic a picture of a party that has traveled crooked paths; it also risks offering a mechanistic view that implies that a long series of events were somehow inevitable. It risks being parodied with Sydney E. Ahlstrom's wonderful tongue-in-cheek aphorism: "History had to happen the way it happened or it wouldn't have happened that way."[20]

In fact, events often pushed Democrats in certain directions despite themselves. Had the panic of 1893 not happened, the conservative forces represented by Grover Cleveland might have overwhelmed Bryan. Had Theodore Roosevelt triumphed over William Howard Taft in the Republican party battles of 1912, the forces of progressivism might not have moved toward the Democratic party and toward the realignment created by TR's cousin. Without the organizing efforts of the left and labor in the 1930s, Roosevelt might have given the nation a far more conservative version of the New Deal. Without similar organizing by African Americans, the civil rights triumphs might have come later. There was nothing inevitable about John F. Kennedy's solicitude for Martin Luther King after his arrest in 1960 or Lyndon Johnson's boldness in pushing for civil rights and voting rights legislation in 1964 and 1965. These events fundamentally changed the character of the Democratic party—and by extension, the Republican party, too.

But as Ahlstrom might tell us, things *did* happen that way, and for a variety of good reasons.

Still, the fact remains that many of the ironies that have influenced the Democrats through history are still very much with the party. The struggle over race is by no means over. When the Democrats embraced civil rights, they not only drove conservatives out of the party, their approach also endangered the loyalty of what had once been the Democratic heartland, the white working and lower-middle class. Democrats are still searching for an inclusive approach and language that could speak honestly to both constituencies simultaneously. This may be the ultimate irony of Democratic history: The party that so freely used racism to win votes 100 years ago must now diminish racism and calm racial feelings if it is to win presidential elections in the 1990s and beyond.[21]

There are two other ironies of Democratic history that seem especially relevant—and still unresolved. The first is a clash between two approaches to foreign policy, both rooted in a certain idealism that is easily attacked (or parodied) as moralism. It is the same clash that ultimately split Bryan, the great anti-imperialist who opposed both the Spanish-American War and World War I, from Wilson, the great internationalist who promised to keep us out of war and then fought "the war to end all wars." When sentiment against the Vietnam War arose in the Democratic party in the 1960s, it was common for the war's supporters to attack their foes as "isolationists" entirely outside the internationalist tradition of Wilson, Roosevelt, and Harry Truman. Yet opponents of the Vietnam War were entirely within the tradition represented by Bryan—and some of them, following the ideas of Hans Morgenthau and Niebuhr, also saw themselves as part of a "realist" tradition that could be traced to Roosevelt and Truman. The tension between engagement and disengagement, between a principled internationalism and an equally principled opposition to globalism, runs right through the American soul—and right through the Democratic party.

The Democrats also face the tensions between their deeply rooted populist economic rhetoric and the need to manage growth in a global market economy where capital is increasingly free to move. A party which in Jackson's day could manage to bash the rich and simultaneously run a radically laissez-faire economic policy is no doubt nimble enough to find new language for the 1990s. Finding policies will be harder. Like all reformist and social democratic parties in this era, the Democrats need to convince wary voters—ultimately through action—that government intervention in the marketplace can also produce growth and equity. If growth and a modicum of greater economic equality are incompatible, or are seen as such by voters, then the Democratic project may once again be engulfed by the ironies that are the plague and the glory of the oldest political party in the world.

The greatest challenge to the Democrats is the same as it has always been. If there is a consistency through the party's tortured history, it is that Democrats have sought to be the voice for an America of diversity and at the same time be the party best able to speak for the nation as a whole. Here, the ironies of Democratic history fully reflect the ironies of American history in which a nation struggled to find a unifying national vision and set of commitments even as it sought to accommodate visions brought to our shores from around the globe.

Roosevelt may have been the Democrat most gifted in accomplishing this task. He succeeded by speaking a language of an inclusive common citizenship. The New Deal won acceptance, said Mark Lilla, a neoconservative writer, "in no small part because Franklin Roosevelt spoke *to* citizens, *about* citizens."[22] The New Deal was no doubt a complex collection of interest groups. Yet as Schlesinger has argued, the New Deal worked because it was seen as representing "a concert of interests," not a collection of "sectarian veto groups."[23]

The party's historic purpose of giving voice to minorities and dissenters—from Catholics and Jews in an earlier age to feminists and cultural rebels in the 1960s and 1970s to gays and lesbians today—has often created dissonance with many of its traditional supporters. Democrats have succeeded best at this task when they have managed to integrate their commitment to minority rights with a vision for the nation as a whole. As Michael Barone points out in his essay, the New Deal was undergirded by a democratic popular culture that was accessible to all wings of the party, and thus to all Americans. Charges of being "alien" or "elitist" simply bounced off a coalition that, in fact, included millions of immigrants and their children, as well as a large share of the country's intellectuals.[24] The New Deal, in Lilla's words, "succeeded in capturing the American imagination because it promised to be a great act of civic inclusion."[25]

It is a neat trick to uphold the rights of minorities *and* to offer a national vision; to speak of the possibilities of the federal government *and* to celebrate the virtues of localism—including, in Ronald Reagan's famous phrase, the values of "family, work and neighborhood"; to be the party that heralds individual rights *and* greater equality. It is, indeed, ironic that one party has tried to do all these things. It often has failed to keep these goals in balance, and then it has lost to a Republican party that is often more coherent and more sure of its goals. But when the Democrats have succeeded, they have been the force that kept the First New Nation young, forward-looking and optimistic.[26] It is the Democrats often thankless task to manage its own ironies, and thus America's.

## NOTES

1. Reinhold Niebuhr, *The Irony of American History* (New York: Scribners, 1952), 8.
2. Arthur M. Schlesinger, Jr., *The Age of Jackson* (Boston: Little, Brown, 1945).
3. Harry L. Watson, *Liberty and Power: The Politics of Jacksonian America* (New York: The Noonday Press/Farrar, Straus and Giroux, 1990), 256. Richard

Hoftstadter's chapter on Jackson in *The American Political Tradition and the Men Who Made It* (New York: Vintage Books, 1974) is central to understanding the revisionist view. For a New Left view, see Michael A. Lebowitz, "The Jacksonians: Paradox Lost?" in *Towards a New Past: Dissenting Essays in American History*, Barton J. Bernstein, ed. (New York: Vintage Books, 1969), 65-89.

4. See Watson's *Liberty and Power*, and also his essay in this volume.

5. Frelinghuysen quoted in Watson, *Liberty and Power*, 109. For a fine treatment of John Quincy Adams' courage on the Indian and slavery questions, see Leonard L. Richards, *The Life and Times of Congressman John Quincy Adams* (New York: Oxford University Press, 1986), esp. 95-112, 148-154.

6. Robert Kelley, "A Portrait of Democratic American in the Mid-Nineteenth Century" in chap. 4 in this volume.

7. Sean Wilentz, *Chants Democratic: New York City and the Rise of the American Working Class* (New York: Oxford University Press, 1984), esp. 172-216.

8. Jackson's veto message quoted in Watson, 146.

9. Wood quoted in Kenneth M. Stampp, *America in 1857: A Nation on the Brink* (New York: Oxford University Press, 1990), 228.

10. *New York Times*, quoted in Stampp, 228.

11. Kelley, "A Portrait of Democratic America in the Mid-Nineteenth Century."

12. See Kenneth M. Stampp, *The Era of Reconstruction, 1865-1877* (New York: Vintage Books, 1965), esp. 186-215. See also Eric Foner, *Reconstruction: America's Unfinished Revolution, 1863-1877* (New York: Harper & Row, 1988), esp. 564-612.

13. The list of Bryan's reform commitments appears in Garry Wills, *Under God: Religion and American Politics* (New York: Simon & Schuster, 1990), 99. Wills offers a fine treatment of Bryan on 97-107. The quote from Dewey appears in Richard John Neuhaus, *The Naked Public Square: Religion and Democracy in America* (Grand Rapids: Eerdmans, 1984), 178.

14. John Milton Cooper, "Wilsonian Democracy," in chap. 9 in this volume. The Croly quote is drawn from John Judis, *Grand Illusion: Critics and Champions of the American Century* (New York: Farrar, Strauss & Giroux, 1992),

15. Judis's fine essay on Croly appears on 23-45.

16. Alonzo Hamby, "The Democratic Moment: FDR to JFK," in chap. 11 in this volume.

17. Bernstein, "The New Deal: The Conservative Achievements of Liberal Reform," in *Toward a New Past*, 263-288.

18. Hamby, "The Democratic Moment."

19. Stampp on Lincoln and Stephens, *The Era of Reconstruction*, 46.

20. Ahlstrom is quoted in Leo P. Ribuffo, *Right, Center, Left: Essays in American History* (New Brunswick: Rutgers University Press, 1992), 15.

21. My own treatment of the race issue here is necessarily cursory. For whatever they are worth, my own views on the subject can be found in E.J. Dionne Jr., *Why Americans Hate Politics* (New York: Touchstone/Simon & Schuster, 1992), 77-97, 335-338, 366-367.

22. Mark Lilla, "What is the Civic Interest?" *The Public Interest* 81 (Fall

1985): 76.

23. Arthur M. Schlesinger, Jr., "The Liberal Opportunity," *The American Prospect* 1 (Spring 1990): 10-18.

24. Michael Barone, "A National Party in a Diverse Nation," in chap. 14 in this volume.

25. Lilla, "What is the Civic Interest," 76.

26. The phrase "The First New Nation" is Seymour Martin Lipset's, see Lipset, *The First New Nation* (Garden City: Anchor Books, 1963).

Chapter 14

# Reform and Hope: The Democratic Party's Mission

*Gary Hart*

The great question—to go forward or to remain still—has always found itself near the center of the debate over the nature of human governments. Jefferson and Emerson, among many others, found it convenient to argue that virtually all democratic societies arrange themselves around two political parties, one of the status quo and one of change. Parties of change, in Emerson's terms "parties of hope," are also parties brought into existence by the need for reform—to achieve a greater degree of social equity, to replace archaic political structures, to adjust to the advent of eras of technological or economic upheaval, or to respond to dramatic events in world affairs.

The notion of reform does not suggest change for change's sake. Nor can it be confined, despite attempts to do so by defenders of the status quo, to cranky, intemperate meddling by discontented perfectionists. Rather, political reform is the response to, or anticipation of, changes in economic, social and political conditions in order to increase opportunity, equality, justice, and other human values through improvement of institutions and policies.

As the principal political instrument of cultural and ethnic assimilation, social innovation, political experimentation, institutional restructuring, and correction of maldistribution of wealth, the Democratic party can lay fair claim to having been, on most occasions, the legitimate party of reform in America.

The qualifier is important for these reasons: First, the early twentieth century tide of reform, usually called the Progressive era, was led, in part, by Theodore Roosevelt, who established himself in his leadership of his own party as a reformer; second, the Democratic party's sacrificial leadership on the question of racial justice throughout most of the nineteenth century; and third, the Democratic party's periodic tendency to conserve its own position in negotiated power-sharing arrangements, rather than challenge the status quo. Obviously, the complex two-century institutional odyssey so thoroughly rehearsed in this book shows the Democratic party to be an evolving phenomenon, an organic, dynamic political structure regularly undergoing self-examination and self-definition, to respond to a constantly changing world. In spite of periodic lapses into conservation of power, this very search maintains the party's quality as a fundamental instrument of reform.

This point is crucial, for when the Democratic party has become conservative, has resisted reform and hidden from change, has sought more to protect its existing power base than to innovate and challenge status quo authority, it has withered and failed. American voters sense intuitively and powerfully when the Democratic party betrays its beliefs, its historic role and mission, and its soul, and they turn it out of power and keep it out.

In this respect the Democratic party shares a burden with America itself. Both are held to very high standards, to historic missions not shared by their competitors. Therefore, they are both judged harshly when those standards are not upheld. People demonstrate frustration with the Democratic party by denying it power when it betrays its true nature.

The reform impulse springs from an ironic but cosmic gamble: to preserve is to risk; to conserve one must change; for society to save its most treasured values, it must confront and constantly challenge a world which refuses to stay static. To put it in pithy and direct American terms—adapt or die. Indeed, Professor Hamby and other contributors to this history underscore this crucial historic dichotomy in the concrete arena of the New Deal, establishing yet again the role of Franklin Roosevelt in saving the American capitalistic system from the folly of capitalism's own most ardent advocates, as much as from rampant depression.

This truth is central to the American experience and thus the American character. It is the reason why America will sacrifice both leadership and uniqueness when it decides to stop, to stay, to refuse to embrace change. This is why, again, it is intuitively obvious that Americans want a Democratic party that is true to a Jeffersonian and Jacksonian heritage and thus committed to resisting the forces of concentrated wealth and established interest.

Throughout most of the twentieth century, Americans have been more than comfortable with a situation in which a majority party, the Democratic party, is available to lead boldly when acceleration or change of direction is required by a changing, turbulent world, and in which a minority party, the Republican party (the "party of memory," according to Emerson) is available to consolidate and moderate, following bursts of creative energy.

But Americans are profoundly uncomfortable with a Democratic party either too cautious or too confused to lead when leadership is needed. A

Democratic party which is not a reform party—which is a toothless lion—is a contemptuous thing to Americans. Americans do not need a neo-protectionist party desperate to preserve outdated, uncompetitive industries. They do not respect a party more concerned with protecting the indexing of entitlement programs than with providing affordable health protection for all. They will not embrace a putative reform party that is more concerned with preservation of intra-party power sharing arrangements than with championing a reform agenda that threatens entrenched power.

Bodies at rest tend to stay at rest, and the Democratic party of the late twentieth century has been perceived by too many citizens to be too much at rest. Lack of insight and imagination, want of courage, the institutionalization of congressional power, and tacit understandings with the presidential party in power all have been seen by too many voters (and non-voters) as contributors to the absence of vigorous and bold alternative policies. It is very hard for any political institution to champion reforms that threaten important figures and institutions within it. The Democratic party undertook to do so after a bitter, divisive, undemocratic convention in 1968, and Washington pundits ever since have blamed the nominee of that more open party for every ill it has encountered. Elements of the party continue to overreact to this criticism, as if more concerned about the good opinion of the pundits than the good opinion of the people.

This is the epicenter of the late twentieth century reform dilemma. Those who share in power, those who by traditional position, negotiation or election mandate participate in the governing process—and this includes opposition parties, established constituency groups, the press and media, and sources of political finance (including lobbyists who double as "advisors")—all define the boundaries of acceptable behavior and debate. Rules, both explicit and implicit, govern the terms of acceptable participation. To participate, one must negotiate or win entrance into the established arena through one of these means or institutions. Among themselves these institutions and leaders constantly negotiate and renegotiate power-sharing arrangements. Manifestly, average people and so-called ordinary citizens have only limited access to these arrangements. Their best chance to make their views known is through their elected representatives, and even this small claim is usually handled by organizations to which they must first belong.

This classic republicanism—delegation of the powers of governance to elected representatives—works more or less satisfactorily in times of progress, expansion and growth. An electorate whose standard of living is expanding complains only marginally and often cares little for involvement in political controversy or debate over partisan policy or philosophy. "All men," said Disraeli, "are conservative after a good meal." Indeed, the state of current politics will instantly be recognized by every student of elementary civics as classic republican theory, a theory which large elements of the late twentieth century Democratic party have preferred over the radically more inclusive idea embodied in Jefferson's notion of "democratic republicanism."

But classic (i.e., non-democratic) republicanism is a beautiful theory murdered by a gang of brutal facts. This gang emerges under circumstances of social stress and civil unrest, urban riots, racial strife, and rising unemployment, and most of all when net family incomes are stagnant or falling—all conditions prevalent today. One fact predominates: Americans are increasingly angry at traditional power structures, and their arrangements for sharing power, that now compose "the people's" government. They believe, with a great degree of accuracy, that their government is "out of touch" with them. The link of legitimacy perpetually being granted by the people to the governing power structure is seriously disintegrating.

The late twentieth century Democratic party has been seeking primary leadership *within* the established power structure. But Americans do not particularly like the established political power arrangement and resent their historic reform party being co-opted by it. How can the Democratic party change "things," they ask, when it is already so much part of "things"?

Sadly, the Democratic party became part of "things" largely during the radical anti-reform years of the 1980s. It did so because it did not have a Big Idea of its own, a new central organizing principle with which to govern in a rapidly changing world, and because the person who was President was believed to have a "mandate," but a mandate never granted to be used as he used it. To a degree, one finds some historic resonance in the 1950s, when the Democratic congressional leadership, represented by Lyndon Johnson and Sam Rayburn, worked in close partnership with the then popular Eisenhower White House. But in striking ideological contrast to the more substantive thrust of the Eisenhower years, the Reagan program was profoundly anti-reform, anti-progressive, and anti-democratic. It is now widely perceived to have been so. In the beginning, however, many Democratic elected officials went along or kept silent, intimidated into quiescence by the "Great Communicator" (a myth) even as he ridiculed every traditional belief the Democrats and their party professed to have. The banner of reform, and the rhetoric attendant to it, were claimed in the name of anti-reform, while Democrats permitted themselves to be herded into a pen called "liberalism" and cowed into silence.

In congressional Democratic caucuses in the crucial years of the early 1980s, the prevailing mood was to acknowledge President Reagan's popularity, quietly profess belief that his policies were potentially disastrously wrong, but operate on the premise that he should be given sufficient rope to hang himself and his party. Many congressional Democrats voted for unfair, budget-shattering tax cuts as well as cuts in critically needed, workable human resource programs in 1981 and '82. There is much about cynicism and want of courage on the part of party "leaders" to be considered here. Hindsight now shows, however, that Reagan took the rope of debt which Democrats helped provide him and used it to hang the American economy.

In addition, President Reagan used "anti-big government" rhetoric to turn the middle class against the Democratic party. But the Democratic party was created by the Jeffersons and Jacksons in opposition to a big government designed to promote and protect the interests of monopolistic business. Behind the smokescreen of concern for the middle class, Reagan simply dismantled Democratically-enacted regulations on giant corporations and, Hamilton-like, used the power of government to promote the interests and concerns of concentrated wealth. The 1980s were simply a repeat of McKinleyesque corporate socialism so opposed by William Jennings Bryan. One's attitude toward "big government," it turns out, is heavily influenced by which way its guns are pointing. In the 1980s, they were turned against the middle class without its members realizing it.

During this dark period, when America's future was being mortgaged, the middle class saw wealth evaporate, and young people were seduced by chimeras created of nothing more than debt and deficit, borrowing and buy-out, Democrats might have had recourse to the thoughts of their founder Thomas Jefferson. Jefferson had two crucial messages for us. First, that he and his colleagues created a *democratic* republic; and second, that laws and institutions must go hand in hand with the progress of the human mind.

As to the first, the Jeffersonian party of the late twentieth century could use a stern reminder that it represents "ordinary people" in more than just rhetorical ways. For this party has preferred in important ways to share its opposition power among its constituency groups rather than engage, in any meaningful and consistent way, real people in the administration of their own affairs.

It was Jefferson not Hamilton, after all, who advocated self-government through "ward-republics," like New England townships. These ward-republics had as their purpose the prevention of centralization of power and the institutionalization of civic duty. Most important, however, is the sense of participation: "a government is republican in proportion as every member composing it has his equal voice in the direction of its concerns." "Every day," Jefferson argued, one must be a "participator in the government of affairs." This must be read as an instruction not only to the participator but also the government which must assure participation.

If a republican form of government is not also democratic, that is, if it is not also structured in a way that invites the active participation of all its citizens, it will falter and crack under the mounting economic, social, and political pressures of a complex society. Given its Jeffersonian and Jacksonian commitment to the ideal of civic virtue, that is active citizen involvement in self-government, the Democratic party should undertake dramatic measures to open its doors more widely if it is to avoid both becoming purely a "republican" party and the possibility of the formation of a third "citizens'" party in the late twentieth century.

Ahead of his time in this as in other things, Jefferson had given this considerable thought and had the notion of "ward-republics" well thought out:

> Divide the counties into wards of such size as that every citizen can attend, when called on, and act in person. Ascribe to them the government of their wards in all things relating to themselves exclusively . . . and by making every citizen an acting member of the government, and in the offices nearest and most interesting to him, will attach him by his strongest feelings to the independence of his country, and its republican constitution . . . These wards, called townships in New England, are the vital principle of their governments, and have proved themselves the wisest invention ever devised by the wit of man for the perfect exercise of self-government, and for its preservation.[1]

It is much too easy today to dismiss democratic republicanism as some kind of anachronistic Jeffersonian sentimentality. Whatever other faults Jefferson may have had, sentimentality was not one of them. Indeed, Jefferson saw clearly and intuitively that, regardless of party or faction, the Hamiltonian formulation which necessarily drove power upward and toward centralized concentration would prevail—unless so-called ordinary people had real opportunity to participate in decisions affecting their lives and their progeny's future.

Even more important, however, was Jefferson's belief that only the "common sense of the American people" could guarantee the adaptability of the country to change. The enemy of reform—conservatism—is the natural by-product of concentrated wealth. In three successive elections in the 1980s, a profoundly conservative Republican party convinced middle-income Americans that economic security rested in protecting and conserving what Democratic programs had helped them achieve, rather than in undertaking new experimental economic policies designed to increase the ranks and living standards of the middle class by taking advantage of global evolutionary changes. The Democratic party permitted itself to be portrayed as an instrument of radical redistribution, rather than as an engine of growth, because it failed to put forward comprehensive new economic ideas and policies.

For Jefferson, the idea of progress was associated with the "improvability" of the human mind, his assurance of which was central to his understanding of human nature. But the progress of the human mind required constant reformation of human, political institutions to keep pace with a changing world, a notion anathema to the conservative forces of centralized power.

Looking back, in an 1813 letter to John Adams, he said it this way:

> One of the questions . . . on which our parties took different sides, was on the improvability of the human mind, in science, in ethics, in government, etc. Those who advocated reformation of institutions, pari passu, with the progress of science, maintained that no definite limits could be assigned to that progress. The enemies of reform, on the other hand, denied improvement, and advocated steady adherence to the principles, practices and institutions of our fathers, which they represented to us as the consummation of wisdom, and akme [sic] of excellence, beyond which the human mind could never advance.[2]

Not only do certain individuals and classes separate on the issue of progress and reform versus conservatism and resistance to change, political parties and the philosophies they represent divide along these lines as well. Using Emerson's famous description, there will always be "parties of memory" and "parties of hope."

So, to believe that knowledge expands and improves the human mind one must believe that the human mind is capable of expanding and improving with it. And to encourage, even to permit, the improvability of the human mind, human institutions and laws must be reformed to keep pace with the progress of knowledge. To Jefferson's regret, this even required a political party to champion the cause of reform against the conservative forces of concentrated power and wealth. Such a cause was not and is not "liberalism," as it was calculatedly misdefined by 1980s Republican ideologues; it is the cause of progressive reform.

No more singular and powerful argument can be made for the necessity of reform than this. Indeed, if such reform would ensure that many post-war young people would belong to the Democratic party, not because their forefathers did, but because it still offered the promise of becoming what Jefferson wished it to be: the party which truly distributes power, rather than keeping it in the salons of Washington, and the party of participation, progress, and reform, the party of hope.

In the main, the Democratic party of the late twentieth century has not been a true reform party. Indeed, there is no such party at present. That fact accounts more than any other for the multitude of angry non-voters. Too many of those who speak for the Democratic party are spokespersons perceived to be pandering for votes with protectionism. Too few have the courage to advocate progressive reforms in the economy, our military institutions, or our foreign policy. An army of "ordinary Americans" genuinely have come to believe they have no more voice in the Democratic party than in the Republican party. Everyone knows the country must change, but Democratic leaders have been reluctant to step forward to say *how* this will be done.

The hope for the Democratic party, and for America, rests in our ability and willingness to exchange encrusted power-sharing arrangements, which are cordial and comfortable for those involved, for genuine democratic republicanism and truly broad-based citizen involvement, and to select leaders committed to the Jeffersonian and Jacksonian notions of reform: reform of party structures, political rules and power arrangements, reform of political and governmental institutions, and reform of fundamental policies that guide our nation.

Fate—in the form of the collapse of communism and the end of the Cold War—has given the Democratic party and America an historic opportunity to restructure our priorities and change directions on the eve of the twenty-first century. The twentieth century has experienced three decisive years, three hinges in time, which fundamentally altered the course of western history. Nineteen ninety-two is one of those turning points, and if the other two departure points offer any instruction, we can choose (or have chosen for us) one of two dramatically different directions. The end of World War I, in 1918, signaled the dawn of a period of American isolation, escalating protectionism, stagnation leading to depression, bitter European nationalism, and finally another world war. The end of World War II, in 1945, opened onto an American economic boom, expanding employment, opportunity and prosperity, internationalism and world leadership.

Now, at the end of another war, the Cold War, the choices of 1918 and 1945 are before us. The American people intuitively understand that basic decisions affecting their national life and purpose must be taken. The hinge of history represented by the end of the Cold War offers the Democratic party the greatest opportunity in a half-century to regain its role as the reform party and to recapture national leadership with it. Untapped economic opportunities, a new wave of social justice and equity, recreation of democratic-republican politics, and world leadership based upon the democratic ideal, all offer vivid alternatives to Republican party values and the basis for a renewed and revitalized Democratic party in the late twentieth century. Central to a new departure from the 1992 hinge of history, and central to the creation of reformed economic structures designed to maximize opportunity, is a new definition for the role of the national government in the twenty-first century. The fault line along which the philosophical divisions between the two major parties have occurred, at least since the age of Roosevelt, has been the role of the national government. Therefore, to redefine America's destiny for the next century, the reform party should begin with a redefinition of the role of government.

The post-Cold War American government should create the conditions for growth and competitiveness; it should reward productivity measures originating in the private sector; it should arbitrate a worldwide open market regime; it should assist private enterprises in anticipating new market opportunities; it should modernize the public infrastructure; and it should insure domestic tranquility by providing a bridge to job markets for those who can work and at least basic subsistence for those who cannot.

First, to create conditions for growth and competitiveness the national government should require high school graduation or its equivalent for all young Americans, and certification of completion of this requirement should be based on achievement of a reasonable national standard. This standard should include at least the ability to speak and write English, some familiarity with one foreign language, basic scientific and technical skills, and basic knowledge in other fields such as history and geography. For those beyond school age, business-government programs for computer training, skill enhancement, sabbaticals, and higher education must be created. Government has the responsibility to produce a well-trained work force. Business has an equal responsibility to maintain training and skill levels.

National research budgets must be redirected from super-sophisticated weapons programs to new technologies and new production techniques. Non-partisan, business-government scientific panels can decide where national competitive advantages exist and where the most promising new fields lie. The same laboratories and scientists that develop stealth technology and silent submarines can manufacture new consumer products that the private sector can produce and take to markets. For example, business-government scientific panels can explore future markets in biotechnologies without the dreaded government interference in corporate policy.

Second, a system of rewards or incentives should be created for enterprises which increase productivity, job opportunities, and exports. Each of these standards is readily measurable. And it would be equally easy to create a tax system that reduces corporate taxes, provides credits, or otherwise rewards a company that meets any of these three goals. The key is in rewarding results, not hopes. Unlike "supply-side" economics, which assumed certain behavior from tax cuts, only companies that actually achieve concrete results should get tax, or "incentive," benefits.

Under such a "results first" approach, enterprises will make their own decisions about whether to invest in worker training, new equipment, ground-breaking research, or foreign market development to achieve the desired goals of new jobs, new markets, or greater productivity. Unlike the 1980s, buyouts, mergers, executive greed, and paper manipulation would receive no rewards from the national government under this "result oriented" incentive system.

Third, only a national government, not single corporations or industries, can negotiate open international markets. Part of the reason the U.S. government has been so ineffective in negotiating fewer trade barriers is that we, too, are a protectionist nation. Political and moral leverage is gained in direct proportion to our own willingness to risk competition. Part of our government's job is to convince American industries and producers to forego our own trade barriers. Consumers in America are paying $70 to $80 billion annually to protect American producers. Needless to say, this fact alone limits our credibility in bashing Japan, Europe, or anyone else.

Fourth, using as an example Russia and the Commonwealth of Independent States, our national government should help private enterprises learn about and anticipate new global markets. Too many American businesses, perhaps still bearing the propaganda burden of the Cold War, are reluctant to explore vast new markets in the former Soviet Union. Once in two or three centuries do such staggeringly large new markets open up, and we are in danger of losing out to our Western competitors. Presidential encouragement, government sponsored investment insurance policies and trade delegations, trade credits and a host of other incentives would stimulate American corporate interest.

This is not some kind of Japanese heresy. We have done it for more than three decades with military weapons. Democratic leadership must remind American business that our principal competitors are performing very well with much closer business-government relations than we have.

Fifth, a public infrastructure rebuilding program is crucial to economic growth in the twenty-first century. A substantial element of the American military-industrial complex must find new work to do. With some adjustments, it can put its talents and energies into the design and construction of mass transit systems, bridges, and the rebuilding of dams and other public works. At present, there is no national program to phase defense industries made redundant by the end of the Cold War into domestic production.

A new, reform-minded Democratic party can demonstrate that public dollars invested in needed public works return public investment threefold: they decrease public assistance rolls; they provide jobs for and make taxpayers out of unemployed people; and they increase national productivity. No one disputes that our overall productivity today is decreased by fractured national transportation systems and creaking urban public facilities.

The hinge of history in the twenty-first century also provides the occasion for a new consensus around the need for universal health care and the notion that those who cannot work will have the basic necessities and those who can work will have jobs. Personal bankruptcy from illness, or even the threat of such catastrophe, must be eliminated by the adoption, finally, of an equitable national health care system. Outdated arguments about socialism emanating from the health care industry must be set aside in the national interest. An unhealthy work force is not a productive one. Robbing the elderly of human dignity is beneath a great nation. A wealthy country, led by a Democratic party committed to social equity and justice, can and must address this issue and resolve it in the 1990s. Additionally, no political debate in recent years has featured more demagoguery or been more debilitating than the debate over "welfare." The vast majority of those on public assistance are too old, too young, or too disabled to work. The nation should face this fact and agree that everyone in these categories will receive the basic necessities of life with the minimum of bureaucracy and hassle. The able-bodied but chronically unemployed minority should be given training, transportation, and child care assistance, and be required to accept employment—in public works if no private sector employment is available.

The Democratic party has both the opportunity and responsibility to rethink, redefine, and reform both its security and foreign policies in the wake of the collapse of communism. Uniquely, as it heals its own divisions created by the Vietnam war, it can also reawaken the notion of democratic idealism or American "exceptionalism" which characterized both Democratic and American foreign policy at its best before our lapse into "realpolitik" in the 1970s and 80s.

There has also been no better time in recent history in which to reform our military systems. America can become the first power in modern times to transform its military establishment without a serious military defeat. Communism, our unifying foe in the second half of the twentieth century, is gone, and unless we abandon both our duty and our self-interest in building democracy in the new Commonwealth of Independent States, it will not return. Therefore, now is the time, not simply to reduce their size, but also to reshape and remold our military forces.

For a decade and a half, military reformers have argued for reforms in the way our military leaders think: in the structure of the forces they command, and finally in the kind of weapons they possess. We know little of the threat of the future. But we do know that it cannot be addressed with the force structures, doctrines and tactics of the mid-twentieth century.

Likewise, as a crucial part of a new policy of "fixing the roof while the sun is shining," the United States should enact a tax on imported oil. Such a tax would simultaneously reduce wasteful consumption, reinvigorate our domestic energy industry, make cleaner, alternative energy supplies more competitive, reduce our reliance on foreign supplies, reduce the risk of fighting a war for someone else's oil, and provide a new source of revenue for education, health, and deficit reduction. Very few single, simple policies can achieve so many worthy results. Unnecessary and unreasonable dependence on foreign oil supplies weakens our national security. An energy independence policy, with an import fee as the centerpiece, is also central to a new national security policy.

But even if we make ourselves independent of foreign oil supplies for economic and security reasons, and even if the Cold War is over, we will live in an increasingly interdependent world in the twenty-first century. A new Democratic foreign policy for a new millennium requires more than simply the avoidance of protectionism and America-firstism. We must structure a future reformed foreign policy around the democratic ideal and remain consistent with the principles and standards we hold out for ourselves. America's role in the world of the twenty-first century must be four-fold: to prevent a North-South polarization between haves and have-nots; to help create a bridge for the former Eastern Bloc between communism and democratic stability; to lead the arbitration for an open international trade regime; and to create a new system of global environmental controls.

Having successfully survived a frequently harrowing half-century of East-West confrontation, the West (presumably including the former Soviet Union and Eastern Bloc) must now take care not to become the "North" in a looming confrontation between industrialized nations with reasonably high standards of living and the considerably poorer Latin American, African and Asian countries. The fault line to watch as the next century nears is Central America and the Mediterranean. As ideology is replaced by economic resentment, friction will increase. This friction will intensify as darker illegal immigrants from Latin nations and North Africa face often underemployed or unemployed lighter skinned workers in North America and Southern Europe. Most Americans are at least vaguely aware of the enormous cultural changes underway in Southern California and South Florida. The politics of Italy, France, and Spain are also being substantially affected by the same phenomenon.

North America and Europe, and possibly to a lesser degree Asia, must prepare for a century in which economic disparity replaces ideology as the dominant force. We are beyond the historic point where the United States can assist everyone or heal every wound. There are certain natural divisions of labor. The United States, together with Canada, can accept the burden of gradually lifting the standard of living in Central and South

America through creation of low-wage production, encouragement of political and land reforms in exchange for debt reduction and forgiveness, insistence on a dramatic reduction in corruption, long-term exchanges of raw materials for consumer products, and development of modern public infrastructures in communications and transportation. Europe can assume the same responsibilities in Africa, as wealthy Asia can for her poorer neighbors.

A "Northern" policy of narrowing the income deficit in the Southern world will require both technical and financial resources. It will also require great commitment on the part of southern hemisphere nations, their leaders and their people. But all this is required to prevent economic despair from giving way in the twenty-first century to another round of self-imposed dictatorships.

American leadership is required immediately to construct a pan-Western bridge for the former Eastern Bloc from totalitarianism to democracy. Current efforts are tentative, dispersed, and uncoordinated. The Western alliance must create a transition loan and credit fund which will last for perhaps five years and be repayable over the next 20 or 25 years. The fund's resources should be available for basic necessities such as food, fuel, and medicine.

Further, the political leadership in the West, especially in America, must provide greater encouragement to major private enterprises to invest in coproduction facilities to generate hard currency accounts. Much greater efforts must be made in converting military production facilities to non-military, consumer production. Rather than wargaming around the potential for a "resurgent expansionist Russia," it would be monumentally less expensive and dangerous to help the Russians and others replace the manufacturing capacity presently committed to weapons production with tractor, truck, and bus factories.

Even as we tax oil imported from the unstable Middle East, we should consider long-term oil purchase contracts from the Russians at a stable price level. This violates the proposed policy of reduced dependence on foreign imports, but for a justifiable reason. If other economic assistance measures are taken, Russia will prove to be a much more stable source of oil supply. Further, predictable and dependable sources of hard currency can help the Russians stabilize the ruble as well as balance their trade accounts.

The third pillar of a new foreign policy must be the arbitration of a new international trade regime. Three trading blocs are emerging at the close of the twentieth century: the North American trading alliance, the European community, and a de facto Asian trading bloc led by the Japanese. Ideally, these blocs will smooth the elimination of trade barriers within each bloc; and, even more ideally, each bloc will assume responsibility for the prevention of trade friction between and among the three blocs.

But here statesmanship is absolutely crucial. The real leaders of the future will be those of sufficient dimension to tell narrow interest groups within their own borders to forego trade protection in the interest both of consumers as well as the competitive position of other producers in the society. The Democratic party, historically the free trade party, must produce such leaders if we are also to structure an open trading system in the world of the next century. Having defeated fascism and communism in one century, we cannot now succumb to a wrenching, devastating trade war in the next.

The fourth pillar of an enlightened Democratic foreign policy for the future must be international environmental leadership. In the past several years, environmental issues went swiftly from local to regional to national to international in scope—depleted ozone layers, ocean pollution, Chernobyl catastrophes, chemical and nuclear dumping, destruction of forestries and fisheries, endangered and eliminated species. All of these and more have brought an over-saturated natural environment to the international community's political doorstep. The industrialized nations, especially the United States, are expected to provide remedial solutions. Presently, these problems are shuffled to the bottom of our foreign policy priority lists.

A reform Democratic party must insist on the primacy of global environmental concerns in the next century. Stricter national and international standards, regulations and sanctions must be adopted. Greater international cooperation must be adopted in identifying and penalizing harmful interests. Special international funds must be created from fines and penalties to aid multinational victims of harmful conduct. International standards and enforcement agencies must be strengthened to cope with cross-border polluters and to monitor hazardous dumps of chemicals and nuclear wastes. In virtually every respect environmental concerns must be forced to the top of the international agenda.

But reform of policies and ideas requires reform of political institutions. For those who have had recent experience in American politics, it is doubtful that true reform of the Democratic party and the Democratic party's reform of America's domestic and international policies can occur under present political rules. The power of interest groups inside the party, as well as the external pressures they bring to bear—especially in the form of campaign and party financing—make self-generating reforms practically impossible.

The most complex challenge facing the Democratic party on the doorstep of the twenty-first century is that of liberating itself from its present over-reliance on constituent and financial interests. The Democratic party as a presidential party has been seen to be too much a creature of its own constituency groups, rather than a free-standing, independent political force with a powerful agenda based not upon a collection of special interest agendas but upon the national interest, the commonwealth, and the common good.

The Democratic party must champion radical reforms in campaign financing, replacing special interest political action committee (PAC) contributions with public financing. It must insist on reasonable access for qualified parties and candidates to the public media. It must continue its efforts toward simplification of registration and voting requirements. It must constantly seek new ways to involve "ordinary citizens" in the governance of their own lives.

Nothing in this regard could be more dramatic than an effort by the Democratic party to revitalize the Jeffersonian notion of ward-republics as the centerpiece of twenty-first century democratic-republicanism. Required to respond, too many American people today would undoubtedly subscribe to Rousseau's characterization of the English: "The English people think that it is free, but is greatly mistaken, for it is only during the election of members of Parliament; as soon as they are elected, it is enslaved and counts for nothing." No one has more clearly understood both the radical and vital nature of the Jeffersonian ideal than Hannah Arendt:

> [Jefferson] knew, however dimly, that the Revolution, while it had given freedom to the people, had failed to provide a space where this freedom could be exercised. Only the representatives of the people, not the people themselves, had an opportunity to engage in those activities of "expressing, discussing, and deciding" which in a positive sense are the activities of freedom. . . . On the American scene, no one has perceived this seemingly inevitable flaw in the structure of the republic with greater clarity and more passionate preoccupation than Jefferson. His occasional, and sometimes violent, antagonism against the Constitution . . . was motivated by a feeling of outrage about the injustice that only his generation should have it in their power "to begin the world over again."[3]

One or two times in the past, the Democratic Party has found itself at such a crossroads. Now, it can either choose to be a minority party which protects the interests of its constituent groups through power brokering in the closed corridors of Washington, or it can once again become the principal instrument by which the people of America control, change, and reform their own public agenda through bold, experimental and equitable policies. The historic window represented by the end of the Cold War will remain open only for a brief period. To be worthy of its Jeffersonian, Jacksonian, and Rooseveltian heritage, the Democratic party of the future must once again shed the shackles of conformity and convention, of comfort and compromise, and lead the American people to a new era of reform, great progress, and justice for all.

## NOTES

1. Thomas Jefferson to Samuel Kercheval (July 12, 1816), *Works of Thomas Jefferson* (New York: G. P. Putnam's Sons, 1904-5), chap. 12, 8-9.
2. Thomas Jefferson to John Adams (June 15, 1813), Lester J. Cappon, ed., *Adams-Jefferson Letters* (New York: Simon & Schuster, 1971), 332.
3. Rousseau, *Social Contract* (Baltimore: Penguin Books, 1968).
4. Hannah Arendt, *On Revolution* (Westport, Conn.: Greenwood Press), 238, 235.

Chapter 15

# The Democrats and African Americans: The American Idea

*Hanes Walton, Jr.*

The Greek philosopher, Heraclitus, believed that change is the only enduring feature of human existence, permeating all of life. It was, he said, the inevitability of change that makes one moment different from the next, that distinguishes beginnings and makes possible the concept of time, of past, present and future.

If change is central to life itself, it also is an inescapable reality for those organizations—such as political parties—that serve and assist humankind in a democratic society. It is therefore essential for parties, in carrying out their functional roles in a democratic process, to adapt and adjust to societal, economic, and political change. Those that do will remain viable and competitive; those that don't will die out.

As described in various preceding chapters, the history of the Democratic party is clearly a history of how this party, over its two hundred years of existence, has transformed itself in different eras to meet the challenges brought by societal change. It is also the history of how, whenever the Democratic party has failed to meet these challenges, the party suffered political losses. Thus, there has been a direct correlation between party empowerment and the adequacy of party response to change. As the contributions to this volume make clear, these engines of change have driven this relentless party renewal.

The first of these is leadership, as exhibited in the personal qualities and influence of such figures as Jefferson, Jackson, Bryan, Wilson and Roosevelt. The second is external events. Powerful external factors, including economic crisis and war, have produced the complex circumstances that have made change inevitable.

Also critical, however, have been internal forces—that is, those related to or inherent in the party organization itself. These have included occasional disturbances, such as those caused by the scandals and the corruption of elected and appointed leaders; but, equally important as an internal force for party transformation, has been the continuing dynamic of political coalitions within the parties. The parties have had not only competing wings, but also dominant and subordinate ones, as Lawrence Grossman illustrates in his chapter on racial politics in the Gilded Age. In his discussion of the power and influence of the southern wing of the Democratic party, Grossman quotes a newspaper editorial of the time as stating that the "Southern tail" had begun to wag the "Northern head" of the Democratic party in the post Reconstruction era.[1]

V. O. Key, in a famous 1940s study, described the strength of the southern political coalition as resting not only in its congressional leaders, but also in the solidity of its electoral base.[2] With these two elements of support, the southern coalition has been able over the years to affect the party's goals and objectives. More recently, Democratic defeats in the 1980s and a shift in the voting patterns of the southern electorate toward Republicanism at the presidential level have caused pundits, commentators, consultants, and some party leaders to demand more influence for the old southern coalition in party politics.

The impact of other transforming forces has been to change the Democratic party from an organization that championed white, protestant culture, states' rights and limited government—its initial Jeffersonian heritage—to one that now favors genuine pluralism, broad cultural diversity, and government intervention in society to remove barriers to individual and group achievements. In other words, it has been transformed, in contemporary terms, from a "conservative" to a "liberal" institution.

In the Democrats' ongoing attempts to transform their party to meet the challenges and needs of the future, the forces resisting change have not yet permitted them to totally resolve and eliminate one continuing national legacy, the old equation of racial injustice. Indeed, in the past, the transformation process has found the Democratic party more frequently on the negative side of the social justice issue with regard to race, placing it in direct conflict with one of the most fundamental of American ideas—equality.

## EQUALITY AND THE AMERICAN IDEA

While both liberty and equality permeated the thought and writings of the founders of the American nation, including the Declaration of Independence and other early documents, the concept of liberty was enshrined in the original Constitution, but the idea of equality among individuals was not officially preserved until the adoption of the Fourteenth Amendment.[3] Perhaps more importantly, the founders, who later went on to run the new government and play leading roles in the initiation of the Democratic party, were ambiguous not only about the implementation of the concept itself, but also about its application both to a slave population and to free African Americans. Of this ambiguity John Hope Franklin has written, ". . . in both of the Continental Congresses and in the Declaration of Independence the founding fathers failed to take an unequivocal, categorical stand against slavery. Obviously, human bondage and human dignity were not as important to them as their own political and economic independence."[4]

John R. Roche, in explaining the context for this now-astonishing omission, said, "The point must be reemphasized; they *made* history and did it within the limits of consensus . . . what they did was to hammer out a pragmatic compromise which would both bolster the 'national interest' and be acceptable to the people."[5] In short, the founders were deeply aware of the political and social milieu of their time and sought practical solutions within the context of public acceptance. Roche continues, "The morality of slavery was by design not an issue, but in its other concrete aspects, slavery colored the arguments over taxation, commerce and representation."[6]

Because the concept of equality initially was not incorporated into the Constitution, it remained a potentially divisive political issue in the new Republic. As Jefferson and his political decendents transformed the party over the next two centuries, they carried with them this burden of ambiguity, i.e., that equality for all men should be treated as a political rather than a moral issue—as one delegate to the Constitutional Convention put it.[7] Of Thomas Jefferson's political use of the slavery issue, Franklin writes:

> For although Jefferson insisted he was strongly anti-slavery, his antipathy toward the institution never took him to the point of freeing his own slaves or of using his enormous prestige to oppose slavery unequivocally in word or deed.[8]

The authors in this volume examine major Democratic party transformers and leaders who perpetuated the practice of addressing inequality as a political instead of a moral question. The story of the party's evolution from the Jeffersonian era through the mid-twentieth century occurred within the context of a limited version of the American idea, with Democratic leaders mortgaging the party's future to its past, and with it part of the nation's ideals. By the 1960s, party transformation and acceptance of the ideal of equality had been achieved, but this acceptance also coincided shortly with a period of electoral defeat at the presidential level. Numerous observers blamed these setbacks on those who led the transformation. Despite the Democrats' loss of the presidency, the party was winning vast majorities at the congressional, state, and local levels—and this fact fostered the view that retaking the White House would require denying the hard-won notion that full equality should be a part of the "American idea."[9]

But the Democratic party of the 1990s cannot return to the days when it supported a limited notion of equality. For today, the primary force that transformed the party over 100 years, the African American community, is an indispensable part of the national Democratic coalition.

## THE PRELUDE: AFRICAN AMERICAN PARTICIPATION

If neither the leadership of Jefferson, Jackson, Bryan, or Wilson, nor economic crisis, nor even civil war could induce the Democratic party to begin to embrace a comprehensive view of racial equality, how then did the party accomplish it? Lawrence Grossman in his chapter in this volume demonstrates that, despite the overwhelming allegiance of nineteenth-century African American voters to the Republican party, some northern Democratic leaders began courting the African American vote in the aftermath of the Civil War. But in the end, it was up to African Americans to assume the point position in this matter and, with the help of their party allies, to build a broad coalition that would lead the party to adopt a new and eventually strong position on equality for all, instead of the old equality for whites only.

The seeds of the African American coalition in the Democratic party were originally planted at about the same time that the party's southern wing was attempting to forge regional unity and fashion a regional outlook around an abbreviated version of equality known as "White Supremacy"—first for the regional party organization and later for the national party organization and the governing party.

Both efforts began during Reconstruction, and particularly during the era called "Black Reconstruction," when many local governments in the South had, for the first time, a visible number of African American elected officials. At no time did these minority officeholders begin to approach a governing majority in any of the states of the old Confederacy, but their sheer presence fostered the myth that "Negro Domination" was underway, and started the move to "recapture" southern governments by and for whites. It is a bitter irony of American history, and a painful memory for Democrats that in order to do so, and to institutionalize an exclusionary concept of equality—a narrow, circumscribed version of the American idea—white Democrats successfully drafted African American voters and later African

American elected officials into a "redemption" crusade, in a two-stage process.[10]

**Stage One.** This phase occurred primarily in the South, first in statewide then in countywide and citywide elections, especially in places like South Carolina, where the African American and white populations—and most importantly the number of registered voters within those populations—were roughly equal. White South Carolina Democrats—including even rabid racists, demagogues and later segregationists like Ben "Pitchfork" Tillman, Wade "Red Shirt" Hampton, and "Cotton" Ed Smith—would appeal to "Negro voters" for support, so as to shift the electoral balance of power in their favor.[11] Their pleas for help in establishing themselves and their ideas of equality fell upon reluctant, but receptive, ears.

"As early as the Spring of 1868 white Democrats had succeeded in several areas of the State in organizing Black Democratic Clubs. . . . In 1870 the Democrats had two Blacks . . . speaking for the party throughout the state."[12] Although these attempts at first proved marginal, the Democrats, with their local leader Wade Hampton, would redouble their efforts in the 1876 gubernatorial contest. Hampton himself reached out to the African American community by organizing "Hampton Day" celebrations with "Negro Democratic Clubs" permitted to march in the parades. His election promised African American political appointments, support for African Americans for minor offices on the Democratic ticket and, shortly thereafter, the election of African American Democrats to the state legislature.

Evidence of the success of these practices can be seen by examining the percentage of African American Democrats elected to both houses of the South Carolina State legislature from 1877 through 1891. There were eight legislatures elected during this period; in all but two, Democratic African Americans were seated. In the legislative term of 1879-80, Democrats actually composed one-half of all African Americans elected. As late as 1888-89, Democrats were 40 percent of all African American state legislators. The data clearly reveal a pattern of African Americans being persuaded to offer their candidacies on the Democratic ticket in return for their communities' support for the entire slate.

**Stage Two.** African American inclusion in the Democratic party on the national level can be traced back to the elections of Democrat Grover Cleveland to the White House. In his first term, "Cleveland followed the Republican practice of appointing colored men to the 'Negro Jobs,' of Minister to Haiti and Liberia, and recorder of deeds of the District of Columbia."[13] He also invited Frederick Douglass and his white wife to dinner at the White House—a symbolic act which set off a storm of protest.

These minor efforts on the national level led to attempts by Democratic African Americans to organize nationally. In fact, "African American Cleveland Democrats continued to be active during the Harrison administration. The platform of the New York State Cleveland League . . . added a new note, that the Democratic party was the 'poor man's party' . . . the exponent of Labor, which is our lot."[14]

By the time of the 1892 election, "a handful" of African American Republicans in Missouri, led by Dr. William J. Thompkins, "deserted the party" to "cast their lot with the Democrats" and organize the "National Colored Democratic Association" (NCDA). Each presidential election year, they would meet three days before the Democratic National Convention to develop and present a lengthy platform for consideration and possible adoption. Their platform would contain specific plans to establish the American idea of equality for all.[15]

Elsewhere, "a Negro National Democratic League (NNDL), with C. H. J. Taylor as president, and H. C. Astwood, Peter Clark, J. E. Thompson, J. C. Matthews, and James M. Turner among its leaders, campaigned for Cleveland in 1892."[16] By the end of Cleveland's second term, due to Republican party indifference, the number of African American Democrats had started to expand.[17] Adding to the impact of these highly visible and articulate spokesmen were African American newspapers like the *Indianapolis World*, the *New York Freeman* and the occasional *Washington Bee*.[18]

These early efforts to mobilize the community on behalf of the Democratic party were followed by campaigns of support for William Jennings Bryan in 1896 and 1900. George E. Taylor, president of the Negro National Democratic League, wrote an editorial endorsing Bryan in 1896, and other letters appeared in the African American press in the 1900 presidential contest.[19] A significant minority of the African American community threw its support to Bryan once again in 1908.

In the election of 1912, ". . . the Wilson managers made an open bid for Negro support that has hitherto gone unnoted by historians."[20] It was ". . . the apparent closeness of the three-cornered campaign among Wilson, Taft, and Roosevelt [that] drove the Democratic managers to the unprecedented step of seeking the Negro vote in the North."[21]

The first step was taken in September of that year when the Democrats approved the formation of a national Negro Wilson League to provide Negro orators for the northern campaign. "The league issued an address to the Negro voters of the United States, calling on the Negroes of the South to cooperate with their southern white neighbors and appealing to the Negro voters of the North to break their traditional allegiance to the Republican Party."[22]

Next, "Wilson . . . personally recognized the National Independent Political League of Washington, a Negro Democratic organization, as one of his representatives and the publications of the League had the approval of the National Committee." Eventually the national campaign would spend over $50,000 on attracting Negro voters.[23]

In addition to these organizational efforts, the party also was making appeals to the African American community such as that in the form of a political ad in a major African American journal, the NAACP's *Crisis*. The copy read, "The Democratic party, standing on the Jeffersonian principle of [equal rights to all; special privileges to none] is opposed to the practice of placing in its party platforms declarations making of any class or race its special pledges. . . ." The ad offered an earlier example of Democratic friendship toward the African American voter:

> An earlier instance of this disposition of the Democratic party to extend the olive branch to the black man was afforded shortly after the Congressional campaign of 1910, when colored voters in unprecedented numbers assisted in the election of the first Democratic Congress since 1894. Speaker Champ Clark addressed a delegation of colored men in the Speaker's Room at the Capitol, and in a speech remarkable for its profound sincerity assured the colored people that inasmuch as colored men were finally beginning to identify themselves with the Democratic party, the Democratic members of the House would see to it that no legislation inimical to Negroes should be given serious consideration as long as he was Speaker. And this promise was religiously observed to the closing day of the Sixty-second Congress.[24]

In addition to these examples of the party's commitment to African American voters, the ad listed reasons for opposing the Republican and Progressive parties and went on to note the social courtesies that the Democrats had extended African Americans by inviting the members of the National Colored Democratic League and their wives to be seated in the convention.[25]

One of the most significant African American efforts of the time was organized by Bishop Alexander Walters of the African Zion Church, who had joined the Democratic party in 1909 and who by 1912 was president of the National Colored Democratic League.[26] Bishop Walters arranged for Wilson to write a letter to be read aloud at a meeting of the League in New York City. Walters put this letter and the message that it contained to good use in further mobilizing the community. "Apparently this unequivocal promise of fair dealing, although stated in vague and general terms, had the effect of swinging [W. E. B.] DuBois and many other leaders of militant opinion in the North to the Wilson ranks."[27]

The letter also had the effect of offsetting an earlier statement by Wilson in *Crisis* magazine which Wilson had tried to disavow. The article in *Crisis*, an account of a meeting with African American leaders, indicated that Wilson "needed and sought African American support" and that upon becoming president would deal with them "fairly."[28] Wilson had asked the editor to provide him with a more moderate statement. Obliging, the editor asked W. E. B. DuBois to draft such a statement and sent it to Wilson. But when the statement arrived Wilson refused to sign it.

"The conclusion is inevitable that the DuBois statement, although it was exceedingly moderate in tone, went entirely further than Wilson was willing to go; obviously, he was not willing to assure the Negroes, as DuBois had suggested, that the Democratic party sought and would welcome their support as American citizens, and that the Democrats were opposed to disenfranchisement on the account of race."[29] The American idea of equality, it seemed, was still limited. But the letter sent to Bishop Walters nullified the earlier Wilson statement, and DuBois wrote an editorial in *Crisis* endorsing the Democrat for president. He said:

> We have, therefore, conviction that Mr. Wilson will treat black men and their interest with farsighted fairness. He will not be our friend, but he will not belong to the gang of which Tillman, Vardaman, Hoke Smith and Blease are the brilliant exhibitors. He will not advance the cause of oligarchy in the South, he will not seek further means of 'Jim Crow' insult, he will not dismiss black men wholesale from office, and he will remember that the Negro in the United States has a right to be heard and considered . . .[30]

Following DuBois' efforts to rally African American voters for the Democratic presidential candidate, Bishop Walters, working through the National Colored Democratic League, took out his own ad in *Crisis*, asserting: "It is clear then that the Democratic party, which dominates the Southern States, is the one party which has the power to restore to the Negro the right of suffrage." Then, of the Democratic Congress, Bishop Walters said: "But, the act for which this Congress will be forever remembered is the formation by its Congressional Campaign Committee of the National Colored Democratic League, the first bon-a-fide [sic] national political organization of colored men ever formed in this country. This fact sets at rest for all those the argument that the Democratic party does not want the Negro. It has met us half way."[31]

These efforts to mobilize the African American community on behalf of the Democratic ticket paid off. Wilson fared extremely well in at least five northern urban areas. A study of African American districts in five northern cities (Boston, Chicago, New York City, Philadelphia, and Pittsburgh) revealed that Wilson polled more votes than Republican President

William Taft in all but one city. In two of the five cities Wilson even outpolled Progressive party candidate Theodore Roosevelt.[32] The 1912 national effort had proven fruitful.

Over a period of 20 years, African American leaders had created a national base for the party within the African American community, composed of both rank and file voters and the political elite. Yet President Wilson failed to support this constituency. Once in office Wilson attempted to segregate the civil service and under his administration a rigid form of segregation was introduced in the nation's capitol.[33] Moreover, during the same 20-year time frame, the Democratic party throughout the South led a successful effort to disenfranchise African American voters.[34] The few remaining African American Democrats went along, for the most part, with this cleansing political wind.

The loss of southern African American voters was accompanied by the rise of a growing northern bloc of voters. During the Reconstruction era, African Americans on an individual basis had begun to vote for and identify with the Democratic party in the North.[35] Unlike the southern coalition, the northern wing of the party was not burdened with the institutionalization of white supremacy. Many northern Democratic politicians proved more sympathetic to African American aspirations than their Republican contemporaries."[36]

In their competition with the old Republican organizations, the local Democratic machines in the large urban centers of the North actively recruited African Americans into the party organization, albeit on a segregated basis. In New York City, the Democratic Tammany Hall organization formed an African American Democratic Club known as the United Colored Democracy. In Chicago, the Cook County Colored Democratic Club came into existence, along with similar organizations in Boston, Detroit, Philadelphia, Kansas City, Pittsburgh, and Columbus, Ohio.[37]

At the turn of the century, these urban political machines included only a few African Americans. But as African Americans moved into the big urban centers looking for an improved way of life and better opportunities, the machines, through their African American operatives, made sure that they were registered to vote. By the mid-twenties, northern cities had African American Democratic elected officials on the state and local levels. The new African American voting bloc grew with each succeeding year. By 1928, Chicago would send an African American Republican to Congress, and in 1934, it would send a Democrat, African American Arthur Mitchell—the first in a long line of African American Democrats to be elected—to the U.S. Congress.[38]

## TRANSFORMATION: ACCEPTING TRUE EQUALITY

Political expediency forced post-Civil War Democrats in the North, in the South, and at the national level, to adopt and implement a "policy of attraction" toward the African American community. Likewise, political disaffections, political abandonment, and political ambition drove African Americans toward a party that persisted in rejecting a holistic and coherent concept of the American idea of equality for all individuals.

In point of fact, political deals were offered in lieu of a firm position on equality. Vagueness, ambiguity, empty promises, and general platitudes were the tools of attraction. Later, minor offices and patronage policies lured the politically motivated to the Democrat banner. Economic rewards, offered by the political machines of the North, helped to supplement these approaches. With this growing base came access to the party elite, including party managers and the candidates themselves; and, as different groups and organizations were granted access, promises had to give way to concessions, no matter how minor.

Among those concessions were demands for a more dynamic and inclusive stand on the American idea of equality. Figure 1 reveals the key African American forces affecting the Democratic party over time—creating an ever widening sphere of political access. In the formative years of the African American movement, political alliances within the Democratic party took the form of individual leadership and officeholding—in both North and South. But this limited access did not force the party or its leaders to restructure the Democratic position on equality and racism.

By the early 1890s, however, the formation of African American national Democratic organizations like the National Colored Democratic Association and the Negro National Democratic League brought demands for equitable treatment and opportunity as conditions for political support; and to these requests, vague promises were made. Failure to keep even these vague promises led to even stronger demands, and as more people joined the party, the African American voting bloc became increasingly powerful.

All this would enter a new phase with the New Deal era, which brought the first African American Democratic congressman, a wave of African American advisors dubbed the "Black Cabinet,"[39] and ultimately, the realignment of the African American voter with the Democratic party. In addition, the New Deal Era saw the first attendance ever by African American delegates at a national Democratic convention.[40] (African Americans had attended Republican Conventions since 1868.) Despite their late arrival on the political scene, these Democratic delegates became another factor working to change the party.

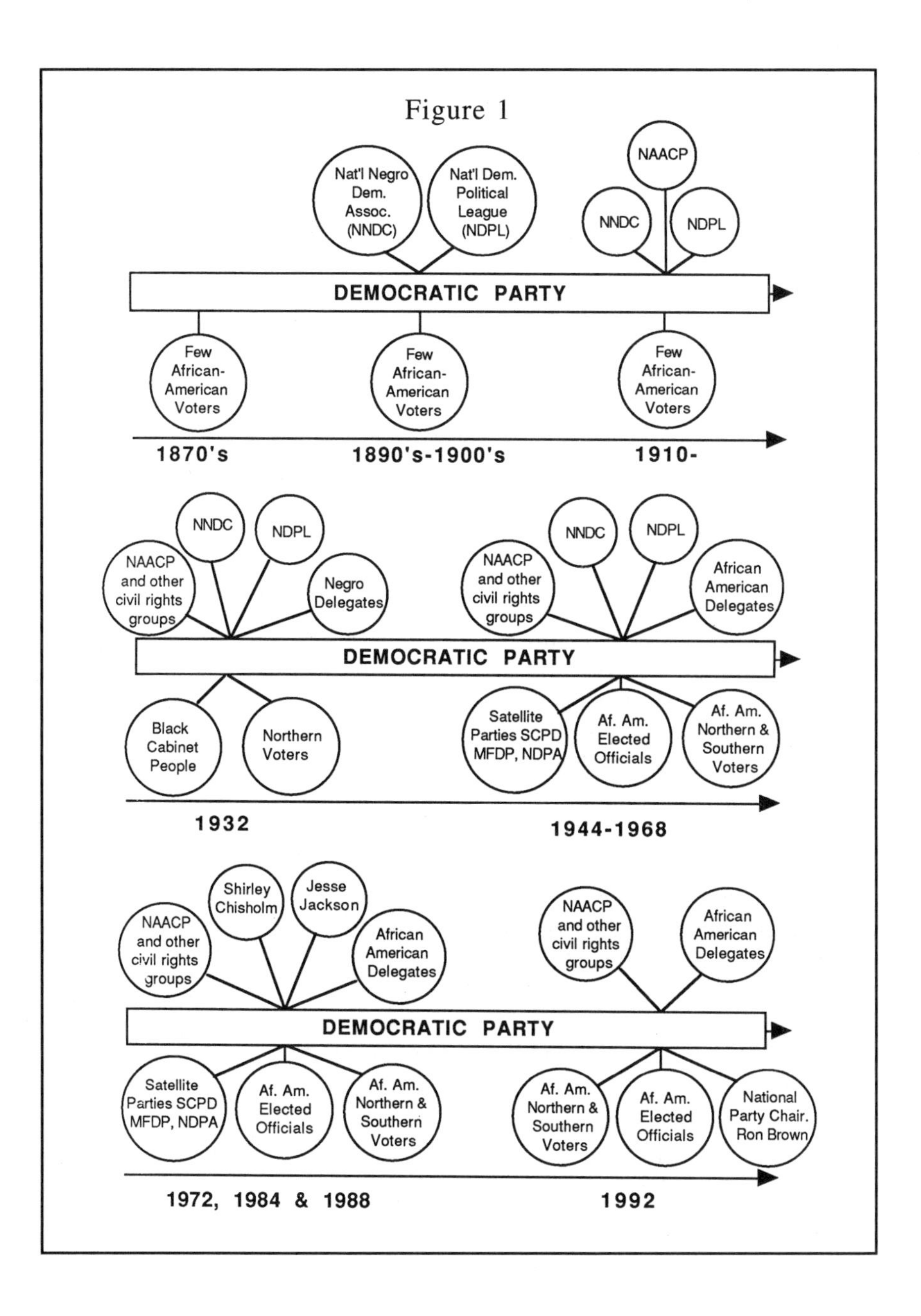
Figure 1
Nat'l Negro Dem. Assoc. (NNDC)
Nat'l Dem. Political League (NDPL)
NAACP
NNDC
NDPL
DEMOCRATIC PARTY
Few African-American Voters
Few African-American Voters
Few African-American Voters
1870's
1890's-1900's
1910-
NNDC
NDPL
NAACP and other civil rights groups
Negro Delegates
NNDC
NDPL
NAACP and other civil rights groups
African American Delegates
DEMOCRATIC PARTY
Black Cabinet People
Northern Voters
Satellite Parties SCPD MFDP, NDPA
Af. Am. Elected Officials
Af. Am. Northern & Southern Voters
1932
1944-1968
Shirley Chisholm
Jesse Jackson
NAACP and other civil rights groups
African American Delegates
NAACP and other civil rights groups
African American Delegates
DEMOCRATIC PARTY
Satellite Parties SCPD MFDP, NDPA
Af. Am. Elected Officials
Af. Am. Northern & Southern Voters
Af. Am. Northern & Southern Voters
Af. Am. Elected Officials
National Party Chair. Ron Brown
1972, 1984 & 1988
1992

Democratic presidential candidates began to respond. Roosevelt, with his appointment of the Black Cabinet, elevated political recognition to a higher level. The old practice of appointing African Americans to low-level positions, or to positions outside the country, was no longer sufficient. The establishment of the Fair Employment Practice Committee (FEPC) and passage of commemorative legislation for African Americans—like George Washington Carver Day and National Freedom Day—were further signals that the party was moving toward a more comprehensive version of the American ideal of equality.[41] President Truman's actions—his platform plank on civil rights, his civil rights commission, and his desegregation of the armed services—was a further signal of the rising African American influence on the party.

Moreover, the revolt of the Dixiecrats and their departure from the 1948 convention in protest of the civil rights plank demonstrated that the southern wing's hold on the party from 1868 until 1948 was beginning to wane.[42]

Another pressure point on the Democratic party was the rise of satellite African American state parties in a number of southern states. In 1944 the South Carolina Progressive Democratic party (SCPD) attended the national convention to protest the lily-white state delegation.[43] In 1964 the Mississippi Freedom Democratic party tried to unseat the regular Democrats. In 1968 the National Democratic party of Alabama actually was seated at the convention and broke open the previously segregated Alabama party.

In the 1970s and 1980s the extensive African American influence on the party has been demonstrated in a number of ways. In 1972 Congresswoman Shirley Chisolm made history with her presidential candidacy, and laid the groundwork for the Jesse Jackson candidacy in 1984 and 1988. The election of Ron Brown as the first African American to serve as chairman of a major political party is only the culmination of a one-hundred-year-old process.

## BIPARTISANSHIP AND RACE

Over most of the party's 200-year history, until very recently, the American idea of equality has been only a selectively applied concept. And, while the party ultimately has succeeded in coping with profound and rapid changes, it frequently has been less than forceful in responding to these changes by institutionalizing the American idea of equality in a comprehensive way. Instead, it usually bought time, leaving the problem to future generations, opting instead for practical and immediate solutions. Whenever, as in the 1960s and 1980s, the party has tried to address the issue forthrightly, it has lost ground at the presidential ballot box. Some have suggested, albeit in an indirect fashion, that the party would be better off abandoning its new approach to racial equality and reverting to a more limited, exclusive, and circumscribed position. This, they believe, will guarantee election to the White House. Not only is this position morally questionable, it ignores what historically has been one of the party's greatest strengths, an ability to meet even the greatest challenges of the future by transforming itself.

This advice also ignores the important political fact that African Americans have themselves been the cause of transforming the party and moving it in a new direction, reflecting another traditional Democratic strength, the party's ability to respond to the creative energy within it, whether from its immigrant, or southern wings or later from its African American bloc.

At the end of the twentieth century, Democratic leaders at all levels must do something they have rarely done in the past: reach out to the leaders of the Republican party and establish a rapprochement on the issue of equality. Constitutional equality for all Americans should not be a political bargaining chip to be used by one party to generate racial fears. When the Republicans embraced equality as an inclusive concept during Reconstruction, they lost political ground, and an entire region of the country. When the Democrats adopted a similar approach in recent years, they too have paid at the polls.

Unless the leaders of both parties reach a consensus on this central aspect of the American idea, the cycle will continue into the tricentennial of the country and the Democratic party. Bipartisanship has been achieved in the past, particularly in foreign policy, and occasionally on domestic issues. In this bicentennial of its existence, the Democratic party can take the next steps toward transforming the country by finally putting the race question to rest and establishing firmly and permanently the American idea of equality.

## NOTES

1. Lawrence Grossman, "Democrats and Blacks in the Gilded Age," chap. 6 of this volume.
2. V. O. Key, Jr., *Southern Politics: In State and Nation* (New York: Vintage Books, 1949), Part Two, in chaps. 15-17, 315-384. Analyzes the national influence of the southern coalition wing.
3. Donald C. Nieman, *Promises to Keep: African-Americans and the Constitutional Order: 1776 to the Present* (New York: Oxford University Press, 1991), 64-70.
4. John Hope Franklin, "The Moral Legacy of the Founding Fathers" in his

*Race and History: Selected Essays, 1938-1988* (Baton Rouge: Louisiana State University Press, 1989), 156.

5. John P. Roche, "The Founding Fathers: A Reform Caucus in Action," *American Political Science Review* 60 (December, 1961): 799.

6. Ibid., 811.

7. Ibid. Roche notes that [Rufus] "King seems to have expressed the sense of the Convention when he said, the subject should be considered in a political light only.

8. John Hope Franklin, *Racial Equality in America* (Chicago: University of Chicago Press, 1976), 15.

9. *The Social and Political Implications of the 1984 Jesse Jackson Presidential Campaign*, ed. Lorenzo Morris (New York: Praeger, 1990).

10. Rayford, Logan, *The Negro in the United States: A Brief History* (New Jersey: D. Van Nostrand, 1957), 33-34.

11. Thomas Holt, *Black Over White: Negro Political Leadership in South Carolina During Reconstruction* (Urbana: University of Illinois Press, 1977).

12. Hanes Walton, Jr., *Black Republicans: The Politics of the Black and Tans* (New Jersey: Scarecrow Press, 1975), 107, 110.

13. Logan, *The Negro in the United States*, 60.

14. August Meier, "The Negro and the Democratic Party, 1875-1915," *Phylon* 28 (2d Quarter, 1956): 181.

15. "National Colored Democratic Association," ed. Florence Murry, in *The Negro Handbook* (New York: Wendell Maliet, 1942), 171.

16. Meier, "The Negro and the Democratic Party," 181.

17. Ibid., 179.

18. Ibid., 177, 179.

19. "A Pro-Bryan Editorial, 1896" and "A Pro-Democratic Letter, 1990," in *A Documentary History of the Negro People in the United States*, ed. Herman Aptheker (New York: Citadel Press, 1969), 818-820.

20. Arthur S. Link, "The Negro as a Factor in the Campaign of 1912," *Journal of Negro History* 32 (January, 1947): 85.

21. Ibid., 84.

22. Ibid., 85.

23. "Quo Vadis," *The Crisis* 5 (November, 1912): 45.

24. Ibid.

25. Ibid., 44-45.

26. Link, "The Negro as a Factor," 92.

27. Ibid., 93.

28. "Along the Color Line: Political," *The Crisis* 4 (September, 1912): 216-217.

29. Link, "The Negro as a Factor," 91.

30. "Editorial: Politics," *The Crisis* 4 (August, 1912): 181.

31. Alexander Walters, "Subject: Make Friends of Thine Enemies," *The Crisis* 4 (October, 1912): 307.

32. Douglas C. Strange, "The Making of a President 1912: The Northern Negroes' View," *Negro History Bulletin* 31 (November, 1968), 21. Votes from

Boston's Ward 18, New York City's Assembly Districts 13 and 21, Chicago's Wards 2 and 3, Philadelphia's Ward 7 and 30, and Pittsburgh's Ward 5.

33. Hanes Walton, Jr., *Black Politics* (Philadelphia: Lippincott, 1972), 114-115. See also K. L. Walgemonth, "Woodrow Wilson's Appointment Policy and the Negro," *Journal of Southern History* 24 (November, 1958): 457-471, and her "Wilson and Federal Segregation," *Journal of Negro History* 46 (April, 1959): 158-173.

34. Meier, "The Negro and the Democratic Party," 174.

35. Walton, *Black Politics*, 104. See also Lawrence Grossman, *The Democratic Party and the Negro: Northern and National Politics* (Urbana: University of Illinois Press, 1976).

36. Meier, "The Negro and the Democratic Party," 183.

37. Harold Gosnell, *Negro Politicians: The Rise of Negro Politics in Chicago* (Chicago: University of Chicago Press, 1967).

38. Ibid.

39. Kirby, *Black Americans in the Roosevelt Era,* 112, 147; and Harvard Sitoff, *The Struggle for Black Equality: 1954-1980* (New York: Hill and Wang, 1981), 10-11.

40. Hanes Walton, Jr. and C. Vernon Gray, "Black Politics at National Republican and Democratic Conventions: 1868-1972," *Phylon* (September, 1975), 269-278.

41. Hanes Walton, Jr., et al., "R. R. Wright Congress, President Truman and the First National Public African-American Holiday: National Freedom Day," *PS: Political Science and Politics* (December, 1991), 685-688. See also U. S. Congress, Senate, Hearing Before the Subcommittee of the Committee on the Judiciary: "S.J. Res. 37 National Freedom Day," May 13, 1947.

42. Ralph Goldman, *The Democratic Party in American Politics* (New York: Macmillan, 1966), 102-104.

43. Hanes Walton, Jr., *Black Political Parties: An Historical and Political Analysis* (New York: Free Press, 1972), chaps. 3, 4.

## Chapter 16

# A National Party for a Diverse Nation

*Michael Barone*

The Democratic party has not walked through history in single file. It has marched boisterously, it has gone off on circuitous detours and excursions. Its phalanxes have seldom lined up in any orderly way and on occasion have found themselves arrayed against each other. This is the oldest and largest and quite possibly the most diverse political party in the world: the party that invented the political convention and the balanced ticket, produced the torchlight parade and the fireside chat, and, more than any other, invented electoral democracy as it is practiced around the globe today. The Democratic party has governed much of America for most, and most of America for much, of the last 200 years. Yet there remains a whiff of the rebel about it, a sense that there is something a bit raffish about being a Democrat. Indeed there always has been "a slight flavour of rowdyism," as Lord Bryce put it more than a century ago.[1] It takes nothing away from the Republican party or from the great political parties of other long-lasting democracies to say that the Democratic party is richer in complexity, more densely textured, more elaborately convoluted, than any other democratic party that has ever existed.

The history of the Democratic party can be seen, as Lord Macaulay saw the history of Britain's Whigs, as a story of progress, interrupted occasionally to be sure, but reasonably steady and certain over the long run of years. But it does better justice to the party's rich complexity to see its history as a series of struggles to resolve persistent tensions caused by contradictory impulses:

On economics, Democrats have been tugged between competing yearnings for growth and for equity.

On cultural issues—always so important in American politics—Democrats have oscillated from a celebration of the ordinary to a toleration of diversity and critical detachment from everyday American life.

On foreign policy, Democrats alternatively have expressed impulses toward expansion and contraction of the American reach.

Most important, the Democratic party, in its general attitude, oscillates from being an adversary of America to being the embodiment of America. For this is a party that has usually been made up disproportionately of those considered in some sense outsiders in our country—of southerners and city-dwellers, Baptists and Catholics, blacks and union members. Yet it is also the party that, at its best, has more persuasively articulated the American purpose and come closer to embodying the American people than any of its rivals. Throughout its history the Democratic party has sought to rally the out-people without turning off too many of the in-people.

This oscillation between contradictory impulses is, at best, a harmonic vibration of the diversity of American life, and, at worst, the betrayal of an unsteadiness of heart and a frivolity of purpose. But it is not in either case accidental; for this is a country of immense variety, and we are a people, like all people, imperfect in character. Let us examine how the Democratic party, over the years, has tried to resolve the competing tensions that have persisted through the history of the Republic. Let us see how on widely spaced occasions it has produced governing formulas capable of winning electoral majorities, and how each of those majorities has been shattered as an issue has arisen that split the majority apart.

## ECONOMICS

American political history has often been portrayed as a battle between the people and the interests, with the people represented primarily by the Democratic party (and occasionally by Populists and Progressives) and the interests by the Federalists, Whigs, and Republicans. Yet it cannot have been as simple as that, and it hasn't been; for if it were, the interests would have been outnumbered by the people every time in a country where the idea of property qualifications for the franchise quickly died out and the people have enjoyed a standard of living so affluent by world standards that historian David Potter could aptly entitle a book on Americans *"People of Plenty."*

Anyway, what is in the interests of the people—equity or growth? A case can be made for either, and has been, by Democrats in different eras. Andrew Jackson called for an end to the Bank of the United States and vetoed federal funding of roads and canals, arguing that leaving banking and internal improvements to states, localities, and individuals would open the field equally to every ordinary American hoping to earn his way to wealth. But the practical effect of Jackson's policies, felt later on during the administration of his political manager and heir, Martin Van Buren, was the Panic of 1837, which left the nation and a great many ordinary Americans poorer.

Later in the nineteenth century, under leaders like prosperous New Yorkers Samuel Tilden and Grover Cleveland, the Democracy stood for a program very much like William Gladstone's in Britain: free markets, free trade, hard money, low taxes, balanced budgets, and little government interference in the economy. This governing formula was more capable of winning governing majorities than the roll call of Republican presidents suggests; Democrats won a plurality of presidential votes between 1876 and 1892 and controlled the House of Representatives for 16 of the 20 years between 1874 and 1894. But the sharp depression of the 1890s, plus the Populist rebellion of the great prairies and the move for free silver, shattered the Tilden-Cleveland consensus. In 1896, William Jennings Bryan, at the age of 36, seized the party's nomination, but he did not have Cleveland's support and failed to carry the big cities or the settled farmlands of the Great Lakes states, thus losing the presidency three times. By the 1910s, after nearly 20 years of growth, the next Democratic President, Woodrow Wilson, followed the cues of Populists and Progressives by seeking equity through government action, pushing through Congress the income tax, the Federal Trade Commission, the Clayton Antitrust Act, and the Federal Reserve. Wilson's New Freedom, and the government's mobilization of the economy in World War I, provided much of the inspiration for Franklin Roosevelt's New Deal and the Democratic programs that followed.

But New Deal Democracy should not be seen as a pursuit of equity to the exclusion of growth; instead, this electorally very successful form of Democratic politics sought both goals. The major programs of the First New Deal—the National Recovery Administration (NRA) and the Agricultural Adjustment Administration (AAA)—were designed to stabilize prices and wages and to stop the dizzying downward spiral of the Hoover years, in which the gross national product fell nearly 50 percent. That goal was achieved by early 1935, but by then it also was becoming apparent that the NRA was unwieldy and seemingly incapable of producing either growth or equity, and when the program was ruled unconstitutional by the Supreme Court in May 1935, it was already politically dead. At that point, Franklin Roosevelt adopted the agenda developed over the years by New York Senator Robert Wagner and a few other liberals who favored more equity-minded policies—steeply progressive taxation, the encouragement of labor unions, and Social Security. But the Democrats' command of majority support was problematical: Roosevelt won in 1936 mainly as a reward for stopping the downward spiral; New Deal supporters did poorly in congressional elections from 1938 to 1946; and, Roosevelt was reelected in 1940 and 1944 because of his strength as a war leader and despite the unpopularity of his domestic policies.

Then, as the economy grew vastly in the war years, Democrats adopted an agenda of economic growth, manifested in Roosevelt's social democratic agenda unveiled in his 1944 State of the Union, in the full employment act passed by the last Roosevelt Congress in 1946, and in the policies of Harry Truman's economic adviser (and former Wagner aide) Leon Keyserling. In addition, the postwar strength of the Democratic party owed much to its association with policies that encouraged, subsidized, and honored upwardly mobile behaviors—the G.I. Bill of Rights, FHA home mortgage guarantees, and the children's allowance for families created by the combination of steeply progressive tax rates and generous public assistance spending. These were policies that produced growth and equity to a degree never before seen in American history; and for 25 years the Democratic party was rewarded electorally, except when it plunged the country into wars from which it could not get out.

Since the middle 1960s, the Democrats have shifted away from emphasizing growth and toward emphasizing equity, to their electoral detriment. The rediscovery of poverty in the 1960s—such discoveries, as Gertrude Himmelfarb tells us, come when a society gets prosperous and confident enough to think it can abolish poverty that has been there, unnoticed, all along—moved Democrats to apply to every policy question the test of equity. They opposed oil price decontrols, on the theory gas would be too expensive for the poor—though decontrol quickly lowered the price for everyone. They favored cumbersome bureaucratic mechanisms to deliver services and educate children, on the theory they served all equally—even as it became apparent that, in some cases, they were botching the job. They opposed 1980s tax cuts, on the theory the rich would benefit—though the rich ended up paying more and the economy entered eight years of low-inflation economic growth. They crunched numbers and squeezed statistics to prove that just about everyone in the country was becoming worse off, on the theory that the voters would throw the Republicans out—and then watched as Democrats lost one election after another.

Democrats, who entered the 1980s unable even to promise low-inflation growth, tried later to pretend that such growth hadn't occurred, instead of learning intelligent lessons from it.

The stagnant economy of the Bush years, in vivid contrast to the vibrant growth of the Reagan years, presented Democrats with their best chance in years to offer their own growth agenda. They will do better if, unlike the Democrats of the 1980s or the Republicans of the 1940s, they stop denying that growth didn't happen and start imagining how they could produce growth with equity themselves. Democrats should remember that their party's greatest success came when it combined—an intellectual might say muddled—these two great objectives and came up with policies that enabled ordinary American people to move up and grow richer.

## CULTURAL ISSUES

From its progenitor Thomas Jefferson the Democratic party inherits a tension on cultural issues: for this highly extraordinary intellectual was a celebrator of the ordinary American farmer; this founder of our longest string of party presidents insisted on the rights of dissent and toleration of the heterodox. The Democratic party was the enemy of the establishment of religion in states (which lasted into the nineteenth century) and early on earned the devotions of Baptists and Catholics, Mormons and Jews. The party's aim was to embrace all Americans, or at least all white males. "The Democracy," wrote John L. O'Sullivan, Van Buren's public relations man, "is national; it is America, it embraces the continent."[2] Americans—that is, adult white males—were treated as equals, without gradation, though those outside the circle—Indians, blacks, women—could be treated as enemies or as incompetents. (The Whigs, in contrast, respected hierarchy and gradation, but also had sympathy for Indians, blacks, and women.) And in the 1830s and 1840s, the Democrats were indeed the party of national expansion, taking over Indian lands in the Southeast and Old Northwest, bluffing Britain out of the Oregon Territory, annexing Texas, and fighting Mexico to gain what would become the Southwest and California.

This national expansionism formed an important part of the Jacksonian Democrats' governing formula. But their majority coalition came apart in the 1850s when they had to decide what to do with the new lands. The issue was extension of slavery, which Stephen Douglas, a Democratic expansionist, thought a troublesome detail of the Kansas-Nebraska Act. But his solution of popular sovereignty—a classic Jacksonian plebiscitarian device—destroyed the Democracy in the North and opened the way for the creation of the Republican party and the outbreak of the Civil War. It also initiated a long period during which being a Democrat was equated by many with being not entirely American. During and after the Civil War, the Democracy fell into a critical stance toward the powerful nation-state created by its archenemy Abraham Lincoln, and criticized his violations of civil liberties. Mainstream culture—northern, Protestant, urban—seemed solidly Republican well into the twentieth century and the New Deal years; while pre-Civil War authors, like Hawthorne and Melville, were Democrats, post-Civil War authors, from Mark Twain to Henry James, were clearly Republicans.

Against this backdrop, the New Dealers tried to create an Americanism of their own, and to a considerable extent succeeded. They developed visual arts with kinship to socialist realism but a definite American—and Democratic—accent: the Works Projects Administration (WPA) and Post Office murals of the Depression, and the paintings of Thomas Hart Benton (namesake of a great Democratic politician) and Norman Rockwell (a liberal Democrat all his life). This style echoed the cheery optimism of 1940s movies, an expression of popular culture as fine and enduring as any since Dickens, whose tone was echoed in the persona of Franklin D. Roosevelt and, years later, by one of its most competent practitioners, Ronald Reagan. The friendly egalitarianism of 1940s America was noticed by such diverse observers as the anthropologist Margaret Mead, in her book *The American Character*, and General George Marshall in his molding of the U.S. Army in World War II.

This was still a racially segregated America, an America that sharply restricted immigration, an America in which women were assumed to be subservient, an America that would in the 1990s be seen as intolerant; and yet the thrust of the popular culture was friendly, cheerful, inclusionary—and democratic with both a small and large "D." The majority popular culture certainly included many Republicans, but its tone was clearly much more Democratic, while its most articulate critics—tradition-obsessed intellectuals, stuffed-shirt plutocrats—were clearly Republicans.

The 1940s popular culture was a universal one: almost everyone went to the movies every week, and for most Americans for many years it was inconceivable that the president would be anyone but Franklin Roosevelt. Inevitably, over the next four decades, the culture segmented—as movies were replaced by television, which in time fragmented as radio had, as universal institutions like the military draft and the comprehensive high school vanished, and as affluence enabled Americans to choose neighborhoods and lifestyles according to their cultural preferences. It could hardly be expected that the Democrats' 1940s majority-boosting cultural style could exist forever. But Democratic politicians moved the party away from it faster and more vigorously than they need have done. The irony and detachment of Adlai Stevenson, which grew greater after he lost to Dwight Eisenhower in 1952 and 1956, made the Democratic party more attractive to intellectuals, who adopted a critical attitude toward American society, but less attractive to a majority of voters. The small ranks of university professors who were New Dealers, heavily outnumbered on their own campuses, were joined by hundreds of thousands of well-educated, articulate, reform-minded liberals in the newly prosperous America of the post-World War II years. In the late 1960s, the angry attitude of the antiwar protestors and those who claimed to speak in the name of the urban rioters came to be identified with the Democratic party, first as these groups stormed (peacefully and not) the convention in Chicago in 1968, then as they seemed to take over the party when George McGovern was nominated in 1972.

While Democrats in the 1970s and 1980s were arguing, not terribly convincingly, that they had become economic populists, they were in too many cases seen as precisely the opposite of cultural populists—sneering at the religious beliefs cherished by most voters, deriding the sexual moral codes of most voters, and careless of the need for physical safety and freedom from crime in the neighborhoods of most voters. This reputation was not always fair. But there was a large enough kernel of truth in it to make it a political liability for the Democratic party. At the state and local level, many Democrats were able to convince voters that they shared their basic values, and indeed some of those values have been moving some distance toward those of the 1960s protestors. But at the national level, Democrats have seemed too often set apart from the mainstream, rather than serving as the personification of it, as they were half a century ago, when they regularly won rather than lost national elections.

## FOREIGN POLICY

The Democracy of the first half of the nineteenth century was a nationalistic, expansionist party. While Alexander Hamilton and the Federalists modeled their national policies—the Bank of the United States, the national debt, encouragement of maritime commerce—on Great Britain's, the followers of Jefferson and Jackson saw themselves as champions of a singular republic in a world of monarchies, an island of liberty in a vast sea of tyranny, an example to be held up while America was weak in the hopes that someday it would be followed around the world when America became strong.

Thomas Jefferson, reluctantly and against constitutional scruple, doubled the area of the United States for $15 million with the Louisiana Purchase of 1803. Andrew Jackson, the victor of New Orleans, was unambiguous in his urge for expansion, as were many of his followers. Within four years of the election of James K. Polk in 1844, the United States grew west from the Louisiana Purchase to the Pacific, taking in lands where some 67 million Americans live today. Other Democrats in these years yearned to go farther, urging an advance into Canada and the annexation of Cuba and Nicaragua. This expansionism, as noted, led proximately to the secession of the South over the issue of slavery in the territories.

After the Civil War, the Democrats retained their sense of American exceptionalism—that this was a special country, with a special place in the world—but it took on forms of both expansionism and isolationism. William Jennings Bryan in his anti-imperialist campaign of 1900 protested our annexation of former Spanish colonies and our fighting in the Philippines. This country, he seemed to be saying, is above the sordid business of having colonies. Woodrow Wilson in 1918 and 1919 crusaded for a League of Nations, which could involve the United States in military efforts around the world to preserve an order of nations Wilson himself had been instrumental in shaping. This was a country, he seemed to be saying, which could serve not only as a model but also as an active ruler of the whole world. Democrats, like Americans generally, seemed to sink back into isolationism in the aftermath of the League controversy; and, the early Roosevelt administration, with the President's breakup of the London economic conference and his signing of Neutrality Acts, represented a high-water mark of isolationism.

Then, the Democrats, with their hawkish southern congressional ranks and their Anglophile leader, became the interventionist party, as Republicans provided most of the articulate leadership against Franklin Roosevelt's attempts to help Britain resist the Hitler-Stalin alliance in 1939, 1940, and 1941. After Pearl Harbor, isolationism lost its moral sanction, and there began a period of bipartisan expansionist foreign policy. But the motive for the expansion clearly came from Roosevelt, who contemplated and designed the United Nations to insure a continued American military presence around the globe. Roosevelt and Truman, and the Republicans who helped make their war and Cold War policies bipartisan, planned ahead with a steely realism, but spoke in the language of American idealism and exceptionalism. They were explicitly concerned about making this, as Henry Luce had urged in 1941, an American century, a world in which American ideals of political democracy, individual rights, and market capitalism tempered by welfare state protections, would prevail. Opposition came almost exclusively from Republicans who opposed the Truman Doctrine and the NATO treaty in the late 1940s, even as they were criticizing the Democrats for not pursuing a more assertive policy in China and Korea. Republicans bitterly charged that Democrats lost China and prevented General MacArthur from winning a military victory in Korea. But the bitterness dissipated after Dwight Eisenhower became President, ended the Korean war and made it clear we were not about to liberate China. A post-World War II consensus on foreign policy, stressing American idealism and featuring American expansionism, prevailed.

Then came Vietnam. This was a war characteristic of Democratic expansionism of the post-World War II period. It was begun in the confidence that the United States would prevail. Yet the military effort was carefully limited, as it had been in Korea, for fear the Communists would respond with nuclear arms. As in Korea after December 1950, in Vietnam after April 1965, the American military effort was aimed not at achieving total military victory, as in World War II, but at persuading the other side to negotiate. As in Korea, in Vietnam this strategy was criticized by some Republicans on the grounds that we should either "win or get out," a criticism that was regarded by Democrats at the time as naive but in retrospect seems wise.

Where Vietnam differed from Korea was in the reaction of many in or near the Democratic elites. To Korea the response of Democrats was that Americans must keep fighting for a tie; when Adlai Stevenson said "Let's talk sense to the American people" in 1952, that is what he was talking about. And, in retrospect, what Lyndon Johnson believed was plainly true, that the Vietnamese would have been better off if the side backed by the United States had prevailed. To Vietnam, the response of Democrats—first on prestigious campuses where students had carefully been exempted from the draft, then in various seats in the Congress, notably on William Fulbright's Senate Foreign Relations Committee, then among influential and essentially pro-Democratic voices in the press, from David Halberstam to Walter Cronkite, and finally, within the administration itself, notably in Robert McNamara's and Clark Clifford's Pentagon—was that we must abandon the Vietnam War as soon as possible, but with little or no regard for the safety of our Vietnamese allies. Yet, every one of these sources (except perhaps the youths on campus) had urged limited military action only a few years before.

The war suddenly seemed unworthy of this exceptional nation. It was a classic example of an elite turning its face away from the results of a policy for which it was wholly responsible and, in this case, opposing it vigorously as soon as Richard Nixon was in office, in the hope that others would forget they had ever supported it with just the same vigor.

Recoil from Vietnam—and an insistence on repeating its mistake—has characterized large parts of the Democratic party ever since. When the United States has been caught up in foreign struggles, Democrats' instincts have been to avoid military involvement or—as in the Iran hostage crisis—to use military power in a limited way with the explicit aim of seeking negotiations with an adversary. Thus, Jimmy Carter sent Ramsey Clark to negotiate with the Ayatollah Khomeini. Thus Democrats, always ready to charge the CIA with terrorism and harshly critical of right wing regimes' human rights records, dismissed as absurd the charge that the KGB was behind the attempted assassination of the Pope and berated Ronald Reagan for voicing the obvious truth that the Soviet Union was an "evil empire." As Jeane Kirkpatrick told the Republicans after attending several Democratic national conventions, "They always blame America first." Thus, large majorities of Democrats in Congress voted to negotiate with Saddam Hussein rather than use the military force which plainly was the only thing that would make him yield. In speech after speech, Democrats made it clear where the emotional force behind their opposition to the Gulf War resolution came from: when they were voting against American military action in the Persian Gulf, they were really voting, 27 years later, against American military action in the Tonkin Gulf. To be sure, the Democrats were not unanimous in these views; but overall, the Democratic party in the 1970s and 1980s was more isolationist than at any other time in its history.

As we examine the varying ways in which Democrats have resolved tensions in economic, cultural, and foreign policy over the years, a pattern emerges. The party has had its greatest strength, as in the Jacksonian years, in the late nineteenth century, and in the decades during and after Franklin Roosevelt's presidency—when it has resolved these competing tensions by emphasizing growth at least as much as equity; when it has combined identification with ordinary Americans with a friendly and inclusive attitude toward those regarded as outsiders; and, when it has harnessed and directed the expansionary and nationalistic impulses of the American people. It has not done as well when it has emphasized equity to the exclusion of growth, when it has taken an adversarial stance toward mainstream American culture, and when it has tended more toward isolationism than nationalism.

The Democratic governing formulas associated with Andrew Jackson, Grover Cleveland, and Franklin Roosevelt—formulas concocted by less famous politicians like Martin Van Buren, Samuel Tilden, and Robert F. Wagner, Sr.—endured for at least a generation, producing not automatic victories but, with fair regularity, absolute majorities, until they were torn apart by responses of different Democratic groups to divisive issues—slavery in the territories, free silver and populism, the Vietnam war.

At its best, these Democratic parties have done what few political parties have done in any free democracy—win an absolute majority of votes in national elections, in years as far apart as 1832, 1888, 1936, and 1976. Those national majorities have helped to bind together and strengthen a geographically vast, culturally disparate, economically vibrant nation. That is a considerable achievement, and it is entirely possible that the Democratic party, if it can learn the right lessons from its successes and failures of the past, may do it again.

## NOTES

1. *The American Commonwealth* 2:32.
2. *Democratic Review*, 9 (October 1841): 354; Broadside Collection (Library of Congress, 1860).

# Afterword

*Arthur Schlesinger, Jr.*

The questions before us are why the Democratic party has lasted so long—long enough to be the oldest political party in the world—and whether it deserves to last any longer.

It is ironic that the second question should be on our agenda. For this presumably should be a time for joyous renewal of the democratic faith. After all, liberal democracy has just emerged triumphant from the great ideological wars of the twentieth century—the hot war against fascism, the cold war against communism. Free society has won both wars, fascism perishing with a bang, communism with a whimper. Totalitarianism is for the moment an extinct alternative, and democracy stands unchallenged as the worlds's political ideal—so much so that pundits even write about the 'end of history.'

Alas, history does not end that easily. At the start of the twentieth century democracy appeared as it does at the end—that is, as the creed destined to spread across the globe. Yet within a few years into this century of ours, the Great War showed that the democratic way could not assure peace. Within a few more years, the Great Depression showed that the democratic way could not assure abundance. The failures of democracy handed the initiative to the totalitarian creeds with the result that, forty years into the twentieth century, democracy found itself desperately on the defensive, its back against the wall, fighting for its life. By 1942, half a century ago, there were only twelve democracies left on the planet.

So let not temporary success go to our heads. We are not home free. If liberal democracy fails again, as it failed before, to construct a humane, prosperous, and peaceful world, we invite the rise of alternative creeds very likely to be based, like fascism and communism, on the rejection of freedom. What we have today is no more than a second chance for liberal democracy to show its stuff.

This is a particular challenge to our party, for we have been the particular party of liberal democracy. The reason the Democratic party has lasted so long is because, as the party of the people, it has eloquently articulated the American purpose of a free, self-governing, just and civilized society—and because, as the party of innovation and experiment, it has been in its better hours prepared to adapt the means to this end as required by changing problems and circumstances. It has survived because of its relative success in meeting a succession of crucial challenges—and, I might add, when the Democratic party failed, as it did in the 1850s, to understand and confront national challenges, it narrowly avoided self-destruction.

Of course our party has always been a coalition of jostling and sometimes quarrelsome groups—southern planters and northern artisans, ex-slaveowners and ex-slaves, big city and small town, trade unionists and intellectuals, fundamentalists and Catholics, immigrants and old-stock Americans. We should not, however, overlook what it was that bound these disparate elements together. The thing they had in common was that they all felt themselves to be outsiders, excluded from the citadels of economic power in American life.

In a capitalist democracy power naturally gravitates to the business community, but when those who wield the economic power of the country wield the political power too, you have a concentration of power that threatens the liberties of the people. "Commerce," as that stout Jacksonian James Fenimore Cooper put it, "is entitled to a complete and efficient protection in all its legal rights, but the moment it presumes to control a country . . . it should be frowned on, and rebuked."[1]

The abiding theme of the Democratic party has been to unite the outsiders against what Andrew Jackson called "the money power" and FDR called the "economic royalists." Our party has never disdained men of business; it has always included public-spirited and socially responsible merchants and bankers and entrepreneurs. Nor has it ever denied the vital importance of private property. Individual freedom cannot be sustained unless people have resources of their own independent of the state. But the tradition of our party is to oppose the ethos of greed and the sacrifice of people to profits. The domination of government by business, Democrats have argued from Jefferson on, is bad for the people—and bad for business itself.

And there is more than opposition to business domination of government to unite Democrats. The great Democratic presidents have not just mobilized a straggle of outsider interests; they have offered a large conception of the public interest in which group interests find their appropriate places. Recall Franklin Roosevelt's warning against going "from group to group in the country, promising temporary and often inexpedient things." Let us return to FDR's emphasis on a "concert of interests," each unit thinking of itself "as part of a greater whole; one piece in a large design"—a concert of interests dedicated to wider and richer opportunities for the ordinary American.[2]

The idea behind the Democratic party is that people matter. As the party of outsiders, we Democrats have been historically committed to policies of inclusion and growth. Ours has been the party that has provided shelter and hope to dissenters, workers, immigrants, women, and blacks, and that has striven to enlarge their chances for self-fulfillment. Ours has been the party that has strengthened American cohesion by promoting assimilation and integration and that has fortified American freedom by affirming and defending the Bill of Rights.

For the Jeffersonians, limited government seemed the best way to contain the money power and to enlarge popular opportunities. The Jeffersonians objected to giving power to the state because, as the radical editor William Leggett wrote, power acquired by the state was "always" exercised "for the exclusive benefit of wealth. It was never wielded on behalf of the community."[3]

Suppose, however, power acquired by the state could be used on behalf of the community? With the end of property qualifications for voting, it seemed increasingly possible to enlist government in the cause of the general welfare. Moreover, while negative government served popular interests in a predominantly agricultural society, the rise of industry and the corporation was creating a new role for government as a protector of the people.

Thus followers of Andrew Jackson, while remaining anti-statist in principle, in practice carried forward a quite aggressive program of government intervention and regulation. "A good deal of positive government," as the editor of the *Democratic Review* put it, "may be yet wanted to undo the manifold mischiefs of past misgovernment."[4] Laissez-faire, wrote George Bancroft, the Jacksonian historian, might be a good rule for international trade, but "its abandonment of labor to the unmitigated effects of personal competition can never be accepted as the rule for the dealings of man to man."[5]

In a changed economic order, Jeffersonian means now seemed inadequate to attain Jeffersonian ends. Government, once rejected as the instrument of those whom Jackson called "the rich and powerful," appeared increasingly the source of hope for those whom he called "the humble members of society—the farmers, mechanics, and laborers."[6] As the Populists put it in their 1892 platform, "We believe that the powers of government—in other words, of the people—should be expanded to the end that oppression, injustice and poverty shall eventually cease in the land."[7]

The new industrial economy, in short, demanded Hamiltonian means in order to achieve Jeffersonian ends. Local government was more and more the government of the locally powerful. The way the locally powerless found to vindicate their human and constitutional rights was through appeal to the national authority. As James Madison had predicted to George Washington, national authority was essential to counter the aggression of local majorities on the rights of minorities and individuals. And, as Woodrow Wilson put it in 1912, "I feel confident that if Jefferson were living in our day he would see what we see. . . . Without the watchful interference, the resolute interference, of the government, there can be no fair play between individuals and such powerful institutions as the trusts."[8]

Nineteen-twelve marked the year when our two parties acquired their modern identities. In 1912, Wilson, carrying forward William Jennings Bryan's purposes, made the Democrats the party that used affirmative government to create new opportunities for the outsiders in American society. And in 1912 the Republicans, by expelling Theodore Roosevelt, made theirs the compliant party of big business. That year defined the character of American politics ever since.

Or almost ever since. In recent times, one feels, some Democrats have lost that clarity of identity that our party inherited from Jefferson and Jackson, that Wilson renewed and Franklin Roosevelt vindicated and Harry Truman, John Kennedy, and Lyndon Johnson carried forward. The Reagan episode seems to have administered a shock to Democratic confidence in the party's own tradition.

Too many Democrats, convinced that they could no longer lick the economic royalists, evidently decided to join them and developed compromising ties with the corporate lobbyists, the developers, the hustlers and confidence men of the Reagan era. Too many Democrats stood aside and held their peace while the most business-dominated government for half a century redistributed wealth from the middle class and the poor to the rich, promoted a casino economy of unparalleled financial irresponsibility, encouraged graft and greed in the savings and loan industry and elsewhere by a senseless assault against regulation in the public interest, abandoned the quest for racial justice, reduced environmental protection, cut aid to the cities and so on.

The predictable results of Reaganism?—jobless families, homeless people, bankrupt business, closed factories, broken-down schools, fallen-down bridges, spiralling national debt, unprecedented peacetime deficits, 37 million Americans without health insurance, acid rain, a depleted ozone layer; one can go on and on enumerating areas vital to civilized living in which the Reagan and Bush administrations could have taken action—and, disdaining to do so, left the republic a financial, social, and moral wreck.

Instead of reacting to such policies as FDR, Truman, Kennedy, and Johnson would have reacted, too many Democrats preferred to make the party of Jefferson and Jackson a junior partner in Reagan's great barbecue. And too many other Democrats, forgetting the public-interest frame that sustained the New Deal, allowed the party to break up into a bundle of clamorous single-issue groups insisting on their own particular concerns at the expense of the greater whole.

As the Democratic party lost identity, it lost support. Voters looking at Democrats of the right no longer saw much difference between the parties, and wondered increasingly whether voting is worth the bother. Looking at Democrats of the left, voters feared the perversion of affirmative government to benefit one or another insistent minority.

Frustration became the keynote of American politics. One result of course was Ross Perot. If the Democrats had provided a strong alternative to Reaganism, the Perot movement would never have arisen. Whatever else the Ross Perot phenomenon was, it was proof of the rising popular demand for change.

Polls in 1992 reported that an extraordinary 80 percent of the people felt that the country was on the wrong track. The revulsion against the values and policies of the Reagan years, against the gospel of greed, against the orgy of a nation living beyond its means, has been manifest on every side. How many of us who were never great admirers of Jimmy Carter rejoice every time a new poll shows him to be more popular than Ronald Reagan?

Anyone who spends time on college campuses can testify to the radical transformation of mood among the young since the 1980s. The mood today is reminiscent of that thirty years ago, when young people began to ask not what their country could do for them but what they could do for their country.

The tide is plainly turning. Every candidate in the election year of 1992 represented himself as an apostle of change—even, incredibly, the candidate totally identified with the failed policies of the last dozen years. President Bush tried to preempt the cycle by calling for a kinder, gentler America and by describing himself as the education president, the environment president, etc., but his failure to live up to his labels made it hard to persuade voters that he could lead the country out of the wilderness he and his predecessor had created.

All this is evidence that we are moving once again from the conservative to the liberal phase of the political cycle. For our politics display an alternation between times when private action, private interest, and private enterprise seem the best way to meet our problems and times when we think that public action and public interest can do the best job.

From this perspective, the Reaganite private-interest 1980s were a replay of the Eisenhower 1950s, as the 1950s were a replay of the Harding-Coolidge-Hoover 1920s. As each conservative phase runs its course, the republic turns at roughly 30-year intervals to public action—Theodore Roosevelt ushering in the Progressive era in 1901, Franklin Roosevelt the New Deal in 1933, John Kennedy the New Frontier in 1961.

There is no mystery about the 30-year cycle. Thirty years is the span of a generation. People tend to be formed politically by the ideals dominant in the years when they first arrive at political consciousness. Young people who grew up when TR and Wilson were setting the nation's sights—Franklin Roosevelt, Eleanor Roosevelt, Harry Truman—carried forward the progressive ideals of their youth thirty years later in the New Deal and the Fair Deal. Young people who grew when FDR was inspiring the country—John Kennedy, Lyndon Johnson, Hubert Humphrey, Robert Kennedy, George McGovern—brought the New Deal up to date thirty years later in the New Frontier and the Great Society. In the same manner John Kennedy touched and formed a political generation in the 1960s. Governor Clinton and Senator Gore are indeed JFK's children, as the Kennedys and Johnson were FDR's children. If the rhythm holds, the Kennedy generation's time will arrive in the 1990s.

It is essential to emphasize that these cycles are cycles of opportunity, not cycles of necessity. The cycles do not dictate the future. The Democratic party will not reach home by a base on balls. As the national mood swings back and forth, new leaders arise and confront new possibilities. What the leaders do with these possibilities depends on their own ideas, capacities, skills, and visions. A passive Coolidge will make one thing of a conservative area; an accommodating Eisenhower another; and an ideological Reagan something different. The coming phase of the cycle offers no more than an opportunity for new departures. What we will do with this opportunity is up to us.

James Bryce formulated the problem a century ago in *The American Commonwealth*. "In a country so full of change and movement as America," Bryce wrote, "new questions are always coming up, and must be answered. New troubles surround a government, and a way must be found to escape from them; new diseases attack the nation, and have to be cured. The duty of a great party is . . . to find answers and remedies."[9]

That is what the Democratic party must do today if the oldest party in the world deserves to live much longer. And it must do so in a time when parties no longer command the political terrain as they did when Bryce wrote a century ago—when indeed government and politics are objects of vociferous distrust and disgust.

This anti-political mood springs from a sense that the political system isn't working. Deficits pile up, the national debt grows, the infrastructure deteriorates, cities decay, schools are in a mess, medical care costs too much and covers too few, pollution, homelessness, drugs, crime abound, government no longer does its job—and the political class seems impotent before the gathering troubles.

The alienation of the voters from the world of professional politics has rarely been so acute. Voters take out their frustrations on a generalized and diabolized "Washington," a term that includes both political parties and both the executive and legislative branches of government. The popular mood today is that foreseen by Paddy Chayefsky in *Network*, where people, goaded beyond endurance, began to cry: "I'm mad as hell, and I'm not going to take this any more."

"Gridlock" is one of the terms employed, as if the problem the republic faces is chiefly one of the structure of government. Insofar as gridlock is a structural problem, the best way to overcome it would be to elect a president and Congress of the same party—and, given the present and future composition of Congress, the only way that can be done is to elect a Democratic president. Nor, when we consider structural problems, should we forget Justice Blackmun's heartfelt plea in the recent abortion decision. The only way to stop the Supreme Court from becoming a bar to progress as effective as the Nine Old Men were in blocking the New Deal is to put a Democrat in the White House.

But we must not overdo structuralism. Remember Bryce's warning: "The student of institutions, as well as the lawyer, is apt to overrate the effect of mechanical contrivances in politics."[10] The problem today is not at all that our leaders know what to do and are stopped from doing it by structural gridlock in the system. The problem is that they know not what to do. Structure can easily become an alibi for policy failure. Let us not be beguiled by structural reform from the real tasks of statecraft.

The duty of a great party is to find answers and remedies—and providing answers and remedies is the best way not only to revive the Democratic party but also to defend the party system against personalist movements like that of Ross Perot. In the end, politics is the high and hard art of solving substantive problems.

Our dilemma is not structural. It is analytical. The Democratic party has to address problems, propose solutions, and persuade the electorate that Democratic solutions make sense. It must do so in this era marked by distrust of government, disgust at politicians, and dislike of taxes. It can do this convincingly and effectively only if the answers and remedies emerge from the party's great traditions—the traditions that separate the party of concern from the party of greed.

How is this to be done?

It will not be done by rejecting the Democratic past, disparaging the New Deal and the Great Society and mimicking the Republicans. If the voters want four more years of conservative government, they will take the real thing every time, not a Democratic imitation.

Nor will it be done by pandering to various interests that participate in the Democratic coalition. Their legitimate claims must be incorporated in a larger definition of the national interest; but going from group to group making promises only turns the voters off.

It can be done by reaffirming the Democratic commitment to reform, by renewing the readiness shown by Wilson and FDR, by Harry Truman and John Kennedy and Lyndon Johnson, to attack the private interests that seek to turn government and the parties, including our own party, to their own selfish purposes and by reviving the great Democratic crusades to reduce disparities of income, opportunity and power in our stricken society—FDR's crusade on behalf of one-third of a nation ill-housed, ill-clad, ill-nourished; John Kennedy's and Lyndon Johnson's war on poverty; Robert Kennedy's crusade for the humiliated and dispossessed.

I know the objections to this course. John Kenneth Galbraith in his brilliant new book makes the bleak point that reform requires the discontented to be a voting majority but that today, in great part because of past reforms, we live in a culture of contentment.[11] Yet polls—and the Perot phenomenon—suggest that a lot of voters are no longer so very content with the way things are going.

Some sages claim that success requires candidates who position themselves in the center of the road. This would be a revelation to Wilson, FDR, Truman, Kennedy, Johnson, not to mention Ronald Reagan—all pretty successful candidates who won not by trimming their convictions but by expressing them with eloquence and force.

Then there are those who say that the Big Government tag will be the kiss of death and that Democrats should run away from their own past. But have deregulation and betting everything on private enterprise been such a wild success? Look at the problems that assail the republic today: how many of them will be solved by private action? Private action will not repair our infrastructure or rescue our cities or improve our public schools or provide adequate medical care or protect the environment or fight drugs and crime. The very nature of such problems leaves no alternative but a resort to affirmative government.

Others tell us that excessive preoccupation with the ill-housed and ill-nourished will repel the middle class. Of course the middle class is and must be a major concern and target. However, we middle classers are not so hard-hearted or short-sighted as not to understand that a safe and healthy society must be built on fair employment and equal opportunity all the way down.

A more substantial objection is the argument that reforms cost money, that we already have a ferocious deficit and that advocacy of a tax increase to pay for reforms is political suicide. Reagan's double success was first to reduce taxes for the rich, thereby contriving a deficit so large as to block further social spending, and then to persuade voters of the wickedness of meeting the deficit by raising taxes.

We are in fact the most lightly taxed capitalist democracy in the world; we also have the least progressive tax structure. Yet polls do confirm a broad and deep resistance to the idea of a general tax increase. After all, why pay higher taxes when so much of it goes to Pentagon contractors or to pay interest on the swollen national debt?

Still, when voters are asked whether they would pay higher taxes for specified purposes—-to improve schools, to repair dams and bridges, to protect the environment, to combat homelessness, to extend medical care, to fight drugs and crime—they answer yes, often by large majorities.

This may constitute an argument for dedicated taxes. Carried too far, the earmarking of taxes reduces flexibility in government. Administered in the wrong way, targeted taxes may only replace general funds diverted to other purposes. Still, in the present mood of cynicism about government, dedicated taxes may provide a means by which government can begin to regain popular confidence.

In any case, we know by now that tax reduction is not the key to economic growth. The Reaganite illusion that tax cuts would pay for themselves produced the greatest peacetime deficits in American history. We had a much higher rate of economic growth in the 1950s and 1960s when the top marginal tax rates were more than twice as high as they are today. The Bush administration has the most miserable record of economic growth of any administration since the Great Depression.

The key to growth is not lower taxes but increased productivity, and the key to increased productivity is increased investment in education, in research, in job training, in infrastructure. In setting forth a program of public investment and national renovation, the Democratic party is putting itself back in touch with its historic mission.

Growth, moreover, will help relieve the racial tensions that harass and demoralize our society. Jobs will not abolish the racism that lurks in human hearts, but they will reduce the bitterness engendered by economic competition when jobs are scarce. Increasingly we must meet urgent minority needs by universal policies—programs that benefit people of all colors and creeds. Government itself should become the employer of last resort, providing jobs for all those willing and able to work. Heaven knows there is enough to be done in the great adventure of rebuilding America. The Democrats must recapture the large vision of FDR, the "concert of interests"—and we are on our way to doing it.

We could do worse than to look to FDR's Economic Bill of Rights, set forth in his state of the union message of 11 January 1944. He called it "a second Bill of Rights. . . . under which a new basis of security and prosperity can be established for all—regardless of station, race, or creed."[12]

FDR's rights included the right to a job; the right to earn enough to provide adequate food and clothing and recreation; the right of every family to a decent home; the right to adequate medical care; the right to a good eduction; the right to protection from the economic fears of old age, sickness, accident and unemployment; the right of farmers to stable income and the right of businessmen to trade without fear of monopolies and unfair competition.

Conditions have changed since FDR's day, and new problems require new remedies, but FDR's agenda of half a century ago is still unfulfilled—and the 1992 Democratic program of putting people first and rebuilding America translates the spirit of the party into the challenges of the twenty-first century.

When we invoke the heritage of the Democratic party, we must not forget foreign policy. No one should confuse our concern for our domestic future with a return to isolationism. The Democratic tradition of internationalism is as robust as ever. Indeed, one compelling reason for the project of national renovation is to provide our foreign policy with a solid domestic base. A chaotic and crumbling nation, no matter how bristling in planes and missiles, will not long retain international leadership. A superpower that cannot even pay for its own wars will not last in the superpower business very long.

Our internationalist tradition—the vision of Wilson, reinvigorated by FDR, of collective action to safeguard the peace, to promote economic abundance, to advance the Four Freedoms—has never been more important than it is today. This vision contrasts sharply with the Republican foreign policy thesis, which is oldtime isolationism now reborn in the shape of unilateral action: the republic as a law unto itself in the world. Democrats believe that a world of law is in the interest of the United States; and, while the United Nations cannot solve all the problems of the world, the more foreign policy that can be conducted through international institutions, the safer the world is likely to be.

In short, it does not appear, whether you look abroad or look homeward, that the tradition of the Democratic party is spent and irrelevant. Rather the need today is for our party to regain its historic identity and apply the spirit of the past to the problems of the future. The spirit that has kept the Democratic party going for two centuries—the spirit of concern, innovation, and experimentation based on the conviction that greed is not enough and that people matter—has not lost its function or its bite in 1992. If we renew that spirit in all its defiance and all its hope, our party may continue to be around for another century or so.

## NOTES:

1. James Fenimore Cooper, *The American Democrat* (London: Penguin, 1969), 217.

2. The FDR quotes are from his radio address to the Business and Professsional Men's League, October 6, 1932. Franklin D. Roosevelt, *Public Papers and Addresses, 1928-1932* (New York: Random House, 1938), 781-784.

3. William Leggett, "True Functions of Government," *New York Evening Post,* November 21, 1938, in *Social Theories of Jacksonian Democracy,* ed. Joseph L. Blau (New York: Hafner, 1947), 77.

4. John L. O'Sullivan, "Note," *Democratic Review* (May 1843).

5. George Bancroft, "The Necessity, the Reality, and the Promise of the Progress of the Human Race," in Bancroft, *Literary and Historical Miscellanies* (New York: Harper & Brothers, 1855), 514.

6. Jackson's Bank Veto message, July 10, 1932. Arthur M. Schlesinger, Jr. *The Age of Jackson* (Boston: Little, Brown, 1945), 90-91.

7. Edward Stanwood, *A History of the Presidency* (Boston: Houghton Mifflin, 1898), 510.

8. Woodrow Wilson, *The New Freedom* (Englewood Cliffs, N.J.: Prentice Hall, 1961), 164.

9. James Bryce, *The American Commonwealth* (New York: Macmillan, 1888), 1:660).

10. Bryce, *American Commonwealth,* 1:349.

11. John Kenneth Galbraith, *The Culture of Contentment* (Boston: Houghton Mifflin, 1992).

12. Franklin D. Roosevelt, *Public Papers and Addresses, 1944-1945,* (New York: Macmillan, 1950), 41.

# ELECTORAL MAP APPENDIX

## Electoral Votes for Jefferson

(Dem.-Rep.) vs. Adams (Fed.)

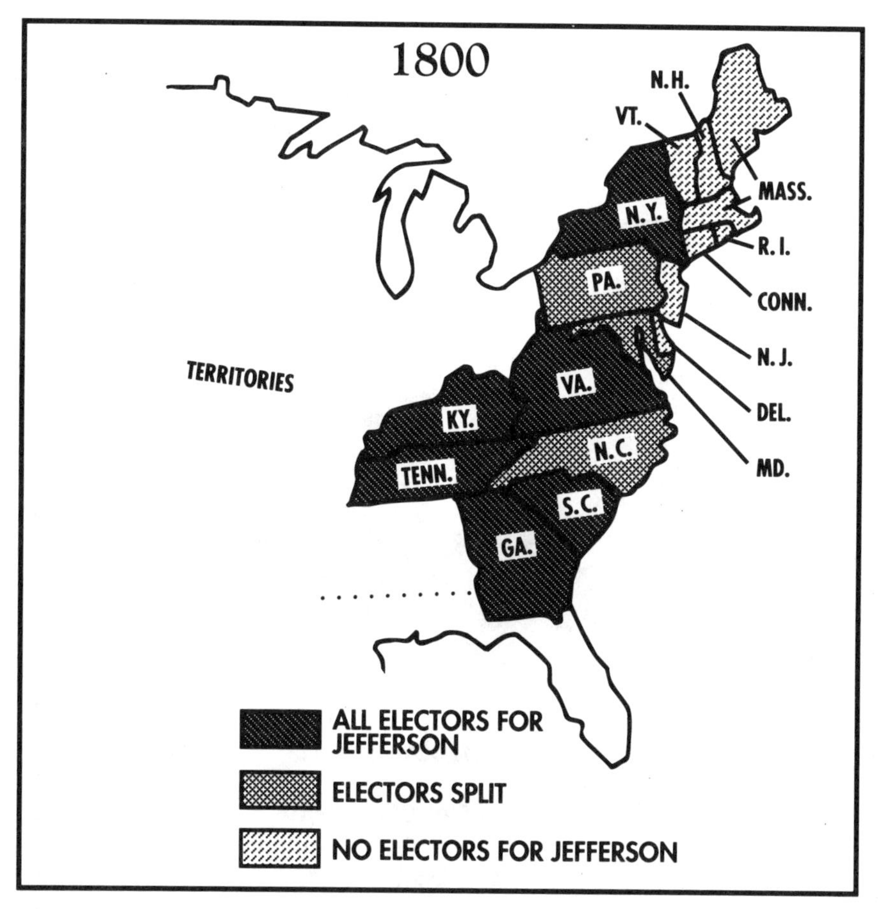


**Note of Explanation for Map Appendix**

All maps except 1800 electoral vote map are coded to show which states were strongly Democratic (greater than 55% of the total presidential vote), competitive (45%–55%) or weak Democratic (less than 45%).

# Democratic Percentage of the Total Vote for President

Pierce (D) vs. Scott (Whig)

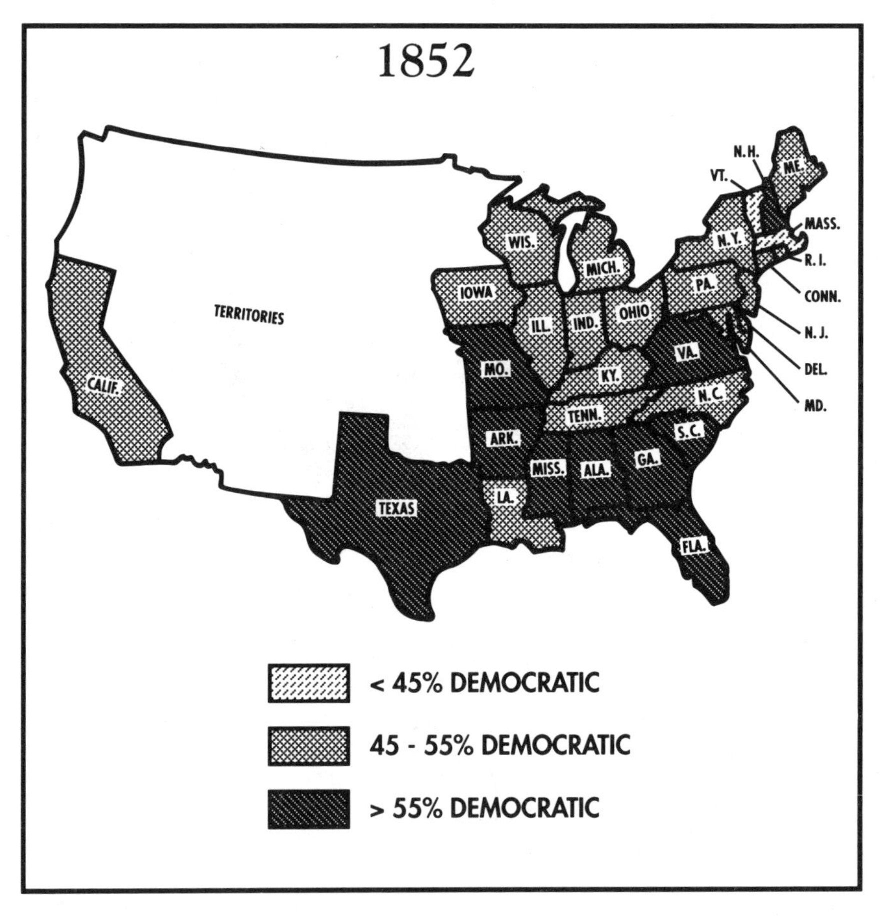


*Significant minor party candidate: John P. Hale (Free Soil)

# Democratic Percentage of the Total Vote for President

Cleveland (D) vs. Harrison (R)

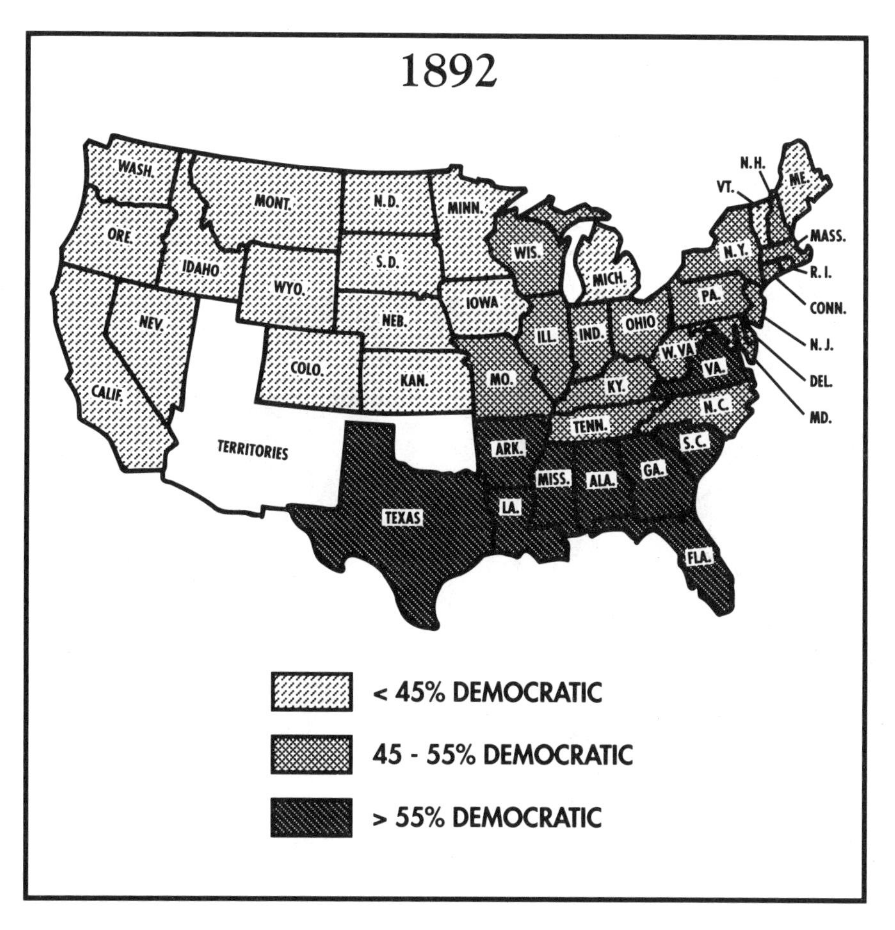


*Significant minor party candidate: James Weaver (Populist) carried Colorado, Idaho, Kansas, Nevada, and North Dakota

# Democratic Percentage of the Total Vote for President

Bryan (D) vs. McKinley (R)

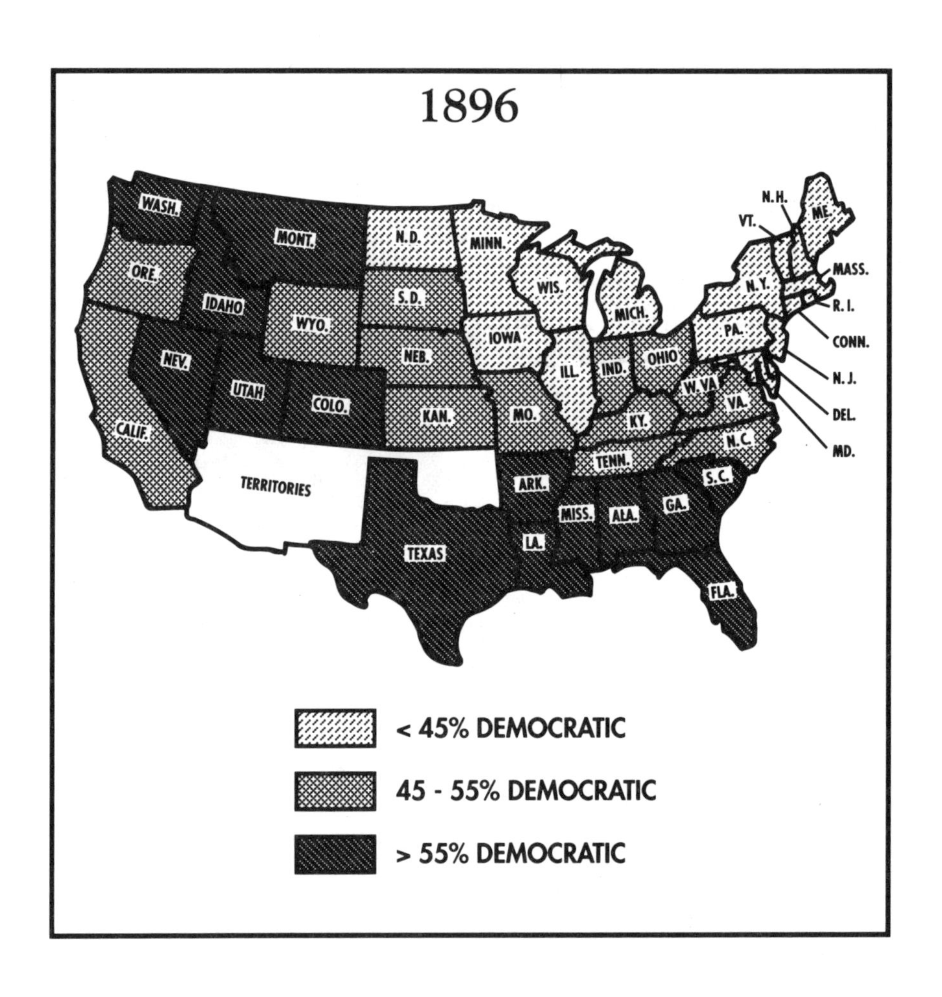

# Democratic Percentage of the Total Vote for President

Wilson (D) vs. Hughes (R)

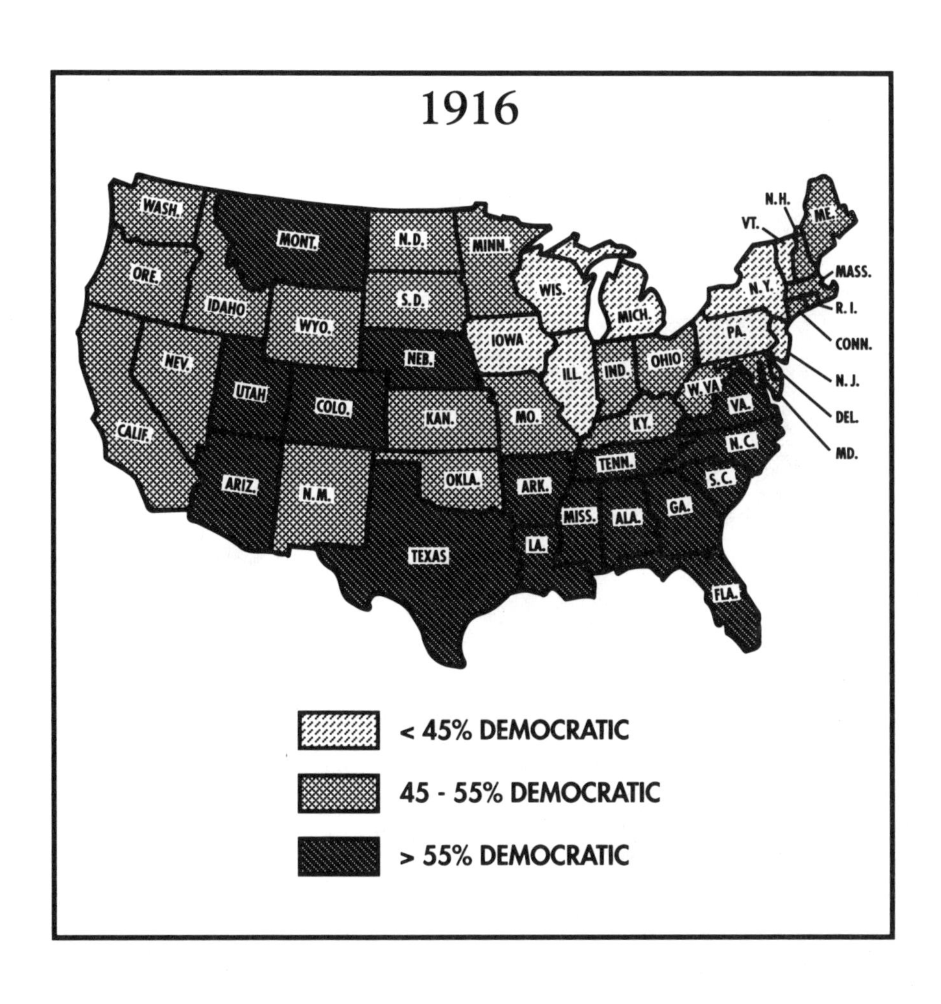

# Democratic Percentage of the Total Vote for President

Truman (D) vs. Dewey (R)

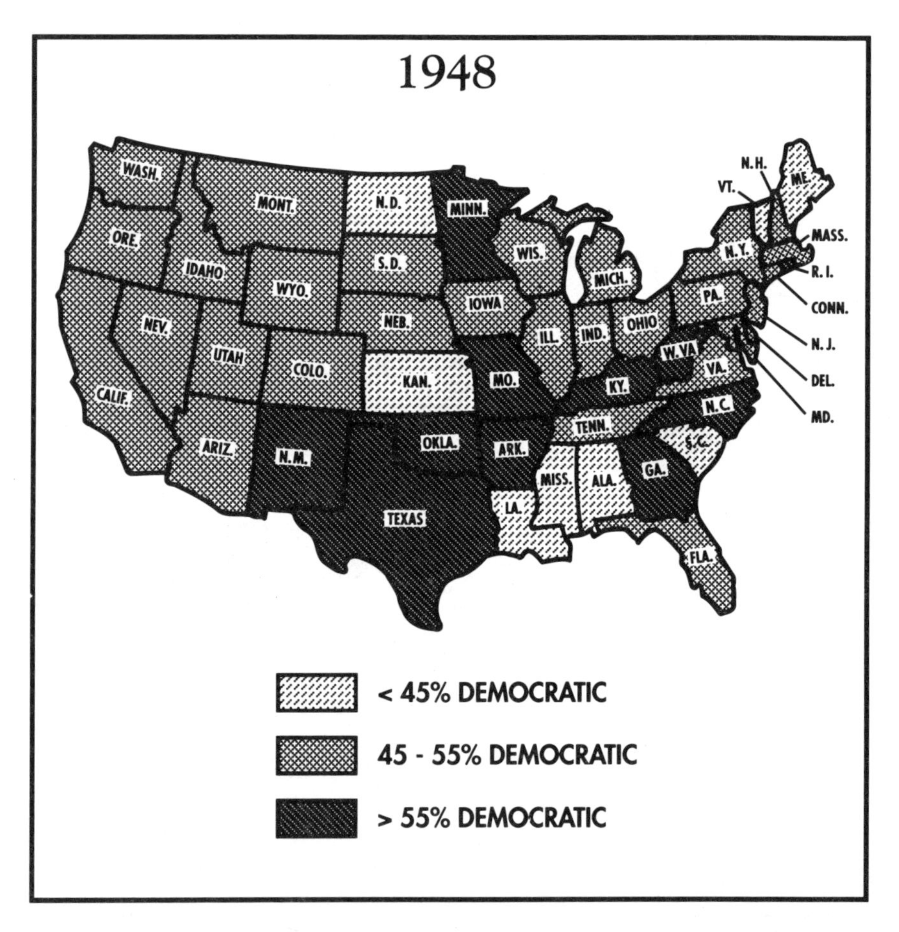


*Significant minor party candidates: (1) Strom Thurmond (States Rights) carried South Carolina, Alabama, Mississippi and Louisiana (2) Henry Wallace (Progressive)

# Index

# About the Authors

Jean Baker is professor of history at Goucher College. She received her M.A. and Ph.D. from The Johns Hopkins University. Baker is the author of several books and articles on American political history, including *Affairs of Party: The Political Culture of Mid-Century Democrats*. She currently is working on a biography of the Adlai Stevenson family of Illinois.

Lance Banning is professor of history at the University of Kentucky, where he has taught since 1973. He has held fellowships from the National Endowment for the Humanities, the John Simon Guggenheim Foundation, and the National Humanities Center. He is editor of *After the Constitution: Party Conflict in the New Republic* and co-editor of the University Press of Kansas series "American Political Thought." His publications include *The Jeffersonian Persuasion* and many articles on the founding of the United States and the first party struggle. He currently is completing a book on James Madison and the constitutional era.

Michael Barone is a senior writer at *U.S. News and World Report*. He was formerly an editorial page staff member at *The Washington Post* and a vice president of the polling firm, Peter D. Hart Research Associates. He is author of *Our Country: The Shaping of America From Roosevelt to Reagan* and co-author of *The Almanac of American Politics*.

Robert Cherny is professor of history at San Francisco State University. He received his M.A. and Ph.D. from Columbia University. His books include *A Righteous Cause: The Life of William Jennings Bryan* and *Populism, Progressivism, and the Transformation of Nebraska Politics, 1885-1915*. Professor Cherny will hold a National Endowment for the Humanities Fellowship in the 1992-1993 academic year.

JOHN MILTON COOPER, JR. is William Francis Allen professor of history at the University of Wisconsin. He has held the Fulbright Professorship in United States History at Moscow State University and the John Simon Guggenheim Foundation Fellowship. He has written numerous articles and books, including *American Isolationism and the First World War, 1914-1917* and *The Warrior and the Priest: Woodrow Wilson and Theodore Roosevelt.*

E.J. DIONNE, JR. covers politics for *The Washington Post.* He attended Oxford University as a Rhodes Scholar, where he received a doctorate in sociology. Before joining the *Post* in 1990, he worked for *The New York Times.* He is author of *Why Americans Hate Politics*, which earned a National Book Award nomination and won the L.A. Book Prize.

IRA N. FORMAN is a Fellow in American Politics & The Economy at the Center for National Policy. He received his A.B. from Harvard University and his M.B.A. from Stanford University. He has served in senior level positions in a number of political campaigns at the local, state, and national level.

STEVEN M. GILLON is associate professor of American history at Yale University. He received his A.M. and Ph.D. from Brown University. He is author of *Politics and Vision: The ADA and American Liberalism, 1947-1985* and, most recently, *The Democrat's Dilemma: Walter F. Mondale and the Liberal Legacy.* He currently is working on an analysis of the impact of suburbanization on American politics since 1965, entitled *The Revolt of the Suburbs.*

LAWRENCE GROSSMAN is director of publications at the American Jewish Committee. He received his Ph.D. in American History from the Graduate Center of the City University of New York. He has been associate professor of history at Yeshiva University, Herbert H. Lehman College, Queens College, and New York University. He has authored several reviews and essays, and a book, *The Democratic Party and the Negro: Northern and National Politics, 1868-1892.*

ALONZO L. HAMBY is professor of history at Ohio University. He received his B.A. from Southeast Missouri State College, his M.A. from Columbia University, and his Ph.D. from the University of Missouri. Among his research grants and awards are fellowships from the National Endowment for the Humanities, the Harry S. Truman Library Institute, and the Woodrow Wilson International Center for Scholars. He is the author of numerous books and articles, including *Beyond the New Deal: Harry S. Truman and American Liberalism*, *The Imperial Years: The United States Since 1939*, and *Liberalism and Its Challengers: F.D.R. to Bush*.

GARY HART is an author and international business advisor, currently president of Hart International Ltd., a strategic advisory group. A Democrat, Hart served as U.S. Senator from Colorado from 1975 to 1987 and was a candidate for his party's nomination for President. While in the Senate, he was actively involved in refocusing public debate in the areas of military reform, economic revitalization, nuclear arms control, and environmental protection. His latest book is entitled *Russia Shakes the World*. He is a graduate of Yale Law School, Yale Divinity School, and Southern Nazarene University.

ROBERT KELLEY is professor of history at the University of California-Santa Barbara. He received his Ph.D. from Stanford University. Professor Kelley has been a Senior Fulbright Lecturer at Moscow University and a fellow of the John Simon Guggenheim Foundation, the Woodrow Wilson International Center for Scholars, and the National Endowment for the Humanities. Professor Kelley's books include *The Cultural Pattern in American Politics: The First Century* and *The Transatlantic Persuasion: The Liberal-Democratic Mind in the Age of Gladstone*.

PETER KOVLER has served in government and has written articles and produced documentaries about U.S. policies and U.S. history. He was on the staffs of Senator Hubert H. Humphrey, Congressman Sidney Yates, and Carter Administration Secretary of Commerce, Philip Klutznick. In 1981-1982 he was Chairman of the Franklin D. Roosevelt National Centennial Committee and in 1989 co-produced the Academy Award winning documentary *Hotel Terminus: The Life and Times of Klaus Barbie*. He has written for numerous publications, including *The New York Times*, *Time*, and *Commonweal*.

ALLAN J. LICHTMAN is professor of history at The American University. He received his Ph.D. from Harvard University. Professor Lichtman has been honored as Scholar of the Year at The American University and was Sherman Fairchild Distinguished Visiting Scholar at the California Institute of Technology. Among his many publications are *Prejudice and the Old Politics: The Presidential Election of 1928*, *The Thirteen Keys to the Presidency*, and *Historians and the Living Past*.

ROBERT V. REMINI is professor emeritus of history and research professor of Humanities at the University of Illinois-Chicago. He received his M. A. and Ph.D. from Columbia University. He is the author of seventeen books, including *Andrew Jackson and the Course of American Democracy, 1833-1845*, for which he received the National Book Award for Non-Fiction.

ARTHUR SCHLESINGER, JR. holds The Schweitzer Chair in The Humanities at the City University of New York. Among his books are *The Age of Jackson, The Age of Roosevelt, A Thousand Days, The Imperial Presidency, Robert Kennedy and His Times*, and *The Cycles of American History.* Schlesinger has received Pulitzer Prizes for History and for Biography as well as the Gold Medal for History of the American Academy of Arts and Letters. In 1961-1963 he served as Special Assistant to President John F. Kennedy.

HANES WALTON, JR. is Fuller E. Callaway Professor of political science at Savannah State College, where he has taught since 1967. He has held fellowships from the John Simon Guggenheim Foundation, the Ford and Rockefeller Foundations, and the National Endowment For The Humanities. He is author of several books, the most recent of which is *The Native Son Presidential Candidate: The Carter Vote in Georgia.*

HARRY L. WATSON is professor of history at the University of North Carolina at Chapel Hill. He received his A.B. from Brown University and his Ph.D. from Northwestern University. He is a co-recipient of the American Historical Association's James Harvey Robinson Prize for the series, *The Way We Lived in North Carolina, 1770-1820*, and he has been a Fellow of the Woodrow Wilson International Center for Scholars. He has authored two books on the politics of Jacksonian America, *Liberty and Power: The Politics of Jacksonian America* and *Jacksonian Politics and Community Conflict: The Emergence of the Second American Party System in Cumberland County, North Carolina.*